DATE DUE

Mexicans at Arms

Mexicans

Puro Federalists and the

at Arms

Politics of War, 1845-1848

Pedro Santoni

Texas Christian University Press
Fort Worth

Copyright © 1996, Pedro Santoni

Library of Congress Cataloging -in-Publication
Santoni, Pedro.
    Mexicans at arms : puro federalists and the politics of war, 1845-1848 / Pedro Santoni.
        p.   cm.
    Includes bibliographical references (p.).
    ISBN 0-87565-158-5
    1. Mexican War, 1846-1848 —Causes. 2. Mexico—Politics and government—1821-1861. I. Title
E407.S26 1996
973.6'21—dc20

95-52183
CIP

Cover and Text Design by Barbara Whitehead

CONTENTS

For

Nettie Lee Benson

Acknowledgments

Research for *Mexicans at Arms* would not have been possible without the generous assistance of the staffs at Mexico's Archivo General de la Nación, Archivo del Ayuntamiento de la Ciudad de México, Centro de Estudios Mexicanos (Condumex), El Colegio de México, Hemeroteca Nacional, Lafragua Collection of the Biblioteca Nacional, Benson Latin American Collection at the University of Texas at Austin, Bancroft Library at the University of California at Berkeley, Library of Congress at Washington, D. C., and the Inter-Library Loan Department at California State University, San Bernardino. Dan Haworth donated his time and energy to track down the illustration that serves as the cover. The Organization of American States helped fund my doctoral studies in Mexico City and the initial stages of research, while California State University, San Bernardino, provided me with release time and a research grant in 1989.

I accumulated many other debts in the course of writing this book. Manuel Alvarado Morales of the University of Puerto Rico kindled my interest in Mexico and my parents encouraged me to pursue a Ph.D. in 1982. From that time on, several talented scholars shared their insights on Mexican history throughout the book's manifold phases. My dissertation advisers at El Colegio de México—Josefina Zoraida Vázquez, Anne Staples, Dorothy Tanck de Estrada, and Miguel Soto—helped me shape the text and always provided valuable advice. Other colleagues helped me turn the dissertation into a book. Don Stevens sent me his candid comments on an early version of the book's opening chapters. Margaret Chowning graciously accepted my plea to read an unpolished draft of the manuscript. She encouraged me not to shy away from interpreting events in favor of the safer but duller route of simple narrative. I hope to have done justice to Margaret's counsel. William Beezley read and reread the manuscript. Not only did his abundant suggestions improve both the mechanical and scholarly aspects of the work, but "Beez" also gave me moral support when I needed it most. Ralph Salmi of the political science department at California State University, San Bernardino, provided keen editorial advice. Just as importantly, his jocular remarks kept me plugging away when the light at the end of the tunnel seemed to be far away.

Two scholars read the manuscript that I originally submitted to TCU Press. I am delighted to acknowledge their help. Paul Vanderwood insisted on further contextualization of the events discussed in these pages. His insights forced me to be more open with my analysis. I hope to have succeeded. I had the good fortune of meeting Richard Warren at an academic conference in November 1994. Many of his judicious suggestions have been incorporated into the book. I am also particularly grateful to one of TCU Press' anonymous readers for his detailed remarks and critical reading of the manuscript. Tracy Row, my editor at TCU Press, helped to get the manuscript in its final form.

In the end, however, it is only appropriate to dedicate this volume to the memory of Dr. Nettie Lee Benson, the late dean of United States' nineteenth-century Mexicanists. I moved to Austin, Texas, from Mexico City in May 1985 to finish researching and writing my dissertation. Although I was not enrolled at the University of Texas, for the next two and a half years Dr. Benson treated me as one of her doctoral students. She took time from her busy routine to read and comment on the dissertation's progress. Furthermore, her recommendations proved instrumental in helping me launch my academic career. I hope that this analysis of nineteenth-century Mexican politics will serve as a belated payment of my scholarly debt to her.

Some of the material in Chapters II and III first appeared in my article "A Fear of the People: The Civic Militia of Mexico in 1845," *Hispanic American Historical Review*, 68:2 (May 1988), 269-288. Reprinted with permission.

Translations of foreign-language passages are my own.

"Crisis to Crisis": A Preface

After a violent and destructive eleven-year war to free itself of Spanish colonial control, Mexico began a long struggle in 1821 to achieve social, economic, and political stability. But several factors soon dampened the aspirations ushered in by independence. Regionalism, fiscal insolvency, acerbic political discord, incessant military rebellions, and class apprehensions destroyed the hopes of stable government. The new republic became submerged in a "system of institutionalized disorder" that propelled it "from crisis to crisis."[1] Consequently, the process of state-building in nineteenth-century Mexico remained incomplete when the United States confronted the young republic with war in 1846.

The tumultuous state of affairs has obscured a full understanding of Mexico's history during the early nineteenth century. Scholars have been challenged recently to rethink the historical epoch spanning from the end of independence to the *Reforma* of the 1850s—a period labeled as "the black hole of Mexican historiography." The chaotic events that afflicted the nascent republic were not "a giant exercise in futility that left all the great questions to be settled all over in the twentieth century." Rather, the first half of the nineteenth century formed part of the process, "imperfect as always, of defining, creating, [and] building nationhood."[2]

Mexicans at Arms examines the determined efforts of Valentín Gómez Farías and his political confederates—the radical federalists, who took the name of *puros* in 1846—to build a sense of national identity and rally public support when Mexico came face to face with aggressive United States expansionism between 1845 and 1848.[3] At the same time that Gómez Farías and the *puros* sought to prepare Mexico to resist a foreign invasion, they also tried to solve several questions critical to the route that the new nation should follow. These issues had fostered acrimonious debate between three major rival factions that composed the political spectrum in early republican Mexico. They included the relationship between the state, the Church, and the military, methods of social control, what form of government Mexico should adopt and, after 1836, how Mexico should deal with an independent Texas republic. But the answers that the *puros* proposed only heightened political strife, which made fighting United States troops all the more difficult.

The *puros* tried to eradicate all vestiges of traditionalism. They wished to limit the Catholic Church's economic and political privileges. The *puros* also hoped to establish a volunteer civic militia to break the regular army's control over politics. In addition, the *puros* wanted to mobilize the urban masses and use them to install their agenda. The *puros* favored a republican form of government, which in 1845 entailed a return to federalism under the auspices of the Constitution of 1824. They also pursued a belligerent policy against Texas and the United States. The *puros* believed that these two last issues were intimately connected. Restoration of the federal system would bestow numerous benefits upon Mexico, not the least of which would be to facilitate the reconquest of Texas.4

The two other principal parties—moderates (*moderados*) and conservatives—disagreed with the *puros* over the means of accomplishing these goals, as well as others critical to building a nation. Like the *puros*, the *moderados* believed that it was necessary to restrain the political role of the regular army and to restrict the Catholic Church's privileges. But the *moderados* did not demand immediate reforms to limit Church power. Moreover, the *moderados* feared the lower classes and referred to the urban poor with denigrating terms such as *léperos* or *leperada, populacho, sansculottes, canalla,* and *chusma*. Their apprehension toward the *leperada* is illustrated most vividly by their belief that enrollment in civic militias should be limited to property-owning citizens. The *moderados* also identified a republic with mob rule and the 1793-1794 French Reign of Terror. They may have preferred, like conservatives, a constitutional monarchy, but in 1845 the *moderados* supported efforts to reform the *Bases Orgánicas*, a term frequently used to denote the 1843 centralist constitution. As far as foreign affairs were concerned, the *moderados* hoped to reach an amicable accord with the United States over the Texas question.5

In general, conservatives sought to salvage those elements of the Spanish colonial state that had benefited them. They wanted a strong centralized government. Conservatives hoped to create such a state by allying the Catholic Church with the regular army and by using the two institutions as a means to consolidate political power in their own hands. Like most *moderados*, conservatives feared the participation of the lower classes in politics. They dreaded the possibility of a class war in which the urban masses would overturn the existing socioeconomic order. Conservatives, therefore, sought to restrict social mobility by denying full citizenship to the populace. By late 1845, two failed experiments in constitution

3

making led conservatives to advocate establishment of a monarchy. At that time, prominent conservative statesmen such as Lucas Alamán also found it impossible not to be influenced by the pro-war atmosphere that prevailed in Mexico. They had little choice but to take up a jingoistic banner and publicly advocate war against the United States.[6]

Yet one cannot adequately explain the disagreements between the *puros* and their political enemies without considering the way personal enmities exacerbated hatreds between the various factions. Organization of cohesive resistance to the United States army would have required a "fusion" of Mexico's most prominent men and the parties they represented. Harmony proved to be a mirage because "the scars of past battles ran too deep" and prevented the emergence of a national consciousness.[7] In a similar vein, the nineteenth-century Mexican thinker José María Luis Mora commented that politically conscious Mexicans "were not yet over the antipathies caused between them by the mutual attacks on each other which earlier revolts had brought about."[8]

Indeed, on several occasions during the war with the United States, the foremost *moderado* statesman, Manuel Gómez Pedraza, refused the overtures of *puro* leader Gómez Farías to reach a compromise. Gómez Pedraza's antagonism toward Gómez Farías can be traced to the political skirmishes of the 1830s. Something happened to estrange the men in 1828 (the nature of the argument remains unknown), and all ensuing peace overtures collapsed. Upon becoming president in 1832, Gómez Pedraza asked Gómez Farías to serve in the administration, but the *puro* leader refused. Gómez Farías apparently sought to displace Gómez Pedraza as the principal leader of the combined *puro* and *moderado* political blocs, and Gómez Pedraza responded by spreading the belief that Gómez Farías' 1833-1834 administration would lead to social anarchy.[9] Their mutual dislike did not abate. In June 1838, for instance, Gómez Farías did not endorse Gómez Pedraza's

4

-the priest Jose Maria Morelos y Pavon, who had been recruited by Hidalgo,

Calleja Vicerry — provincial governor who represents the sovereign (supreme ruler)

- 1615 executed

-1816 the fighting was so sporadic that Spain felt safe enough to replace Calleja.

1819 offer amnesty to the insurgent

proposal to restore federalism. A meeting of reconciliation held two months later proved to be a total failure. Gómez Farías told Gómez Pedraza that he concurred with a pamphlet that labeled the latter a traitor and an impostor, and Gómez Pedraza stormed out of the encounter, vociferously threatening his rival. The incident surely remained vivid in the *moderado* leader's memory, and the unmerciful tirades that *puro* newspapers directed against him in 1845 no doubt influenced Gómez Pedraza's decision to reject Gómez Farías' subsequent offers of reconciliation.[10]

The turbulent party battles that ensued from such personal, ideological, and socioeconomic differences have discouraged historians from undertaking scholarly analysis of political strife in Mexico during the war with the United States. These divisions gave birth to an internal panorama so complex that even one astute contemporary observer, Guillermo Prieto, hesitated to delineate the precise make-up and goals of the *puros* and their rivals between 1845 and 1848. Prieto commented that it was "extremely difficult to classify political parties and to determine the exact cause of each social movement."[11] *Mexicans at Arms* attempts to correct this deficiency by examining the hopes, motivations, strengths, and weaknesses of the *puro* political bloc during the Mexican War. It helps fill what diplomatic historian David Pletcher referred to in 1977 as "the widest gap" in the historiography of the Mexican War—that of Mexican domestic affairs during the conflict.[12]

The volume also fits into a growing body of literature concerning the roots of political instability and the lives of the statesmen who dominated public affairs in Mexico during the early nineteenth century. It complements two recent studies of a Spanish intrigue to restore monarchy in Mexico during the mid-1840s.[13] *Mexicans at Arms* also augments the profile of the *puros* drawn by two other recent accounts of Mexico's domestic politics during the early 1800s. One of these monographs puts forth a comprehensive portrayal of the politicians who dominated public affairs in early republican Mexico, a group commonly known as men of property *(hombres de bien)*, while the other developed a classification of the areas that distinguished political factions in the decades that followed independence.[14]

As a member of the upper middle class, the archetypal *hombre de bien* desired economic growth, political stability, and social harmony. To implement these goals, the *hombres de bien* helped dismantle the federal republic established in 1824 and moved to consolidate power in their own hands through the centralist project of 1835-1836. Yet the inclusion of *puro* leader Gómez Farías among the *hombres de bien* is somewhat perplexing, if not unwarranted. While Gómez Farías may have sought at times to restrict the participation of the masses in civic affairs, on those occasions pragmatic political considerations motivated him, not an overwhelming sense of solidarity with the *hombres de bien*.[15] The *puro* statesman demonstrated a propensity for populist politics throughout his career. Moreover, if conservative *hombres de bien* orchestrated the transition to centralism in 1835 and 1836 to depose Vice-President Gómez Farías, where does the *puro* leader fit?[16] After all, his alliance with General Antonio López de Santa Anna in the summer of 1846 held that Mexico needed to oust the *hombres de bien* who had betrayed and deceived them a decade earlier.

In addition, no scheme to categorize political factions in nineteenth-century Mexico should be indiscriminately applied between 1821 and 1867. Exceptions to general patterns must be allowed for, particularly for the years 1845 to 1848. *Mexicans at Arms* illustrates this point by highlighting Gómez Farías' efforts to forge an alliance with senior army officers during the Mexican War, a strategy that ran contrary to the *puros'* desire to restrain the political role of the regular army. Moreover, Gómez Farías and his closest allies pursued the tactic as they tried to develop a powerful civic militia—which would have threatened the regular army's prominence—to assert their authority and lead armed resistance against the United States.

Historians who have evaluated the *puros'* wartime objectives between 1845 and 1848 have generally overlooked the social, political, and economic hurdles that confronted Gómez Farías and his political associates. Consequently, writers such as the late Jesuit priest Mariano Cuevas characterized the *puros* as a corrupt faction that sold out Mexico to the Americans.[17] Some have cast doubts concerning Gómez Farías' organizational talents and asserted that he "never [was] an effective practical leader."[18] Still others have emphasized the flaws in his personality in an attempt to lessen Gómez Farías' political skills and abilities. Guillermo Prieto regarded him as "inflexible,"[19] while one modern historian described the *puro* politician as an ideologue who desired to put his ideas into practice "even at the most inopportune moment."[20]

These criticisms must be weighed against the historical evidence. The gamut of Gómez Farías' activities between 1845 and 1848 included political agitator, cabinet member, and acting president. While his uncompromising character stood out on several occasions during the Mexican War, one eyewitness remarked that he would always attribute to Gómez Farías a "pure [and] unselfish patriotism."[21] At times, such as during the uprising that broke out on June 7, 1845, Gómez Farías seemed willing to compromise his ideology for the sake of political power. On those occasions, however, he was merely searching for an avenue to consolidate the *puros* as the dominant force in Mexican politics. Mexico would be able to fight back against the United States only if the *puros* led the way.

Mexican nationhood remained elusive in the mid-1840s, however, and no political group managed to forge unified resistance against the American armies. The conflict brought the "tensions, strains, and conflicts within Mexican society to the breaking point," and ushered in the *Reforma* of the 1850s.[22] Mexico still faced another round of political strife, civil war, and foreign intervention before it set its house in order—albeit temporarily—in 1867. Rather than judge Gómez Farías and the *puros* a failure because they did not reach their goals in the mid-1840s, the *puro* political bloc should be measured against the manifold obstacles that it encountered at a time of foreign war and domestic chaos. As one contemporary observer wrote, the prevalence of "disorder, asperity, and anarchy" made it difficult to "uphold the defense and salvation" of the Mexican people in the war with the United States.[23]

The Seeds of Dissension

Several unresolved questions hovered over the Mexican political landscape in 1845. Perhaps the two most important were what form of government best suited the young nation and how to deal with the United States over Texas. Valentín Gómez Farías and the *puros* advocated reestablishment of the Constitution of 1824 and the reconquest of Texas. Their position was not entirely illogical. Federalism had been "a real force during much of the nineteenth century,"[1] and the dismal failure of the centralist experiment made the 1824 charter an attractive alternative once again. Moreover, Mexican leaders could not relinquish national claims to Texas for a multitude of reasons that included their sense of honor, an idealistic streak, and the risk of being branded a traitor. The *puros'* agenda helped them regain political prominence, but whether their goals could be met remained to be seen.

The Double-Edged Sword of Federalism

Mexico's size as well as its peculiar geography contributed to the evolution of federalism. At the time of independence,

Mexico occupied 1,170,000 square miles; the nation was approximately fourteen times larger than Great Britain and nine times as large as Spain.[2] Great distances separated Mexico City and the country's regional centers of production, a fact that one historian characterized as "the principal axis of the federalist ideal."[3] Jagged mountain ranges, lowlands and gorges, as well as climatic extremes hampered development of effective communications. Many roads were no more than paths fit only for mules and burros, the main highways were rough and bumpy, and the few navigable waterways were located in the sparsely populated southeastern states of Veracruz and Tabasco. Forced by prohibitive transportation costs, many cities and their hinterlands became self-sufficient economic units, which enhanced feelings of regionalism throughout the country. Moreover, the growth of the great haciendas—particularly in northern Mexico, where landowners organized small, private armies that exercised almost complete control over political positions in the region—further weakened Mexico City's precarious control over the remote borderlands.[4]

The Spanish Bourbons' attempt to correct the administrative confusion created by the three territorial divisions that had been superimposed on each other since the mid-1500s within the Viceroyalty of New Spain also nurtured federalist sentiments. A decree of December 4, 1786, grouped into twelve intendancies the precincts within the Catholic Church's administrative structure, the smaller districts within the *audiencias'* jurisdiction, and New Spain's *provincias mayores*.[5] Intendants took over the duties of the former provincial officials and assumed full control over their district's administrative, financial, legal, and military affairs. As a result, each intendancy acquired a certain degree of autonomy. The territorial divisions established in 1786 remained virtually unchanged until independence and served as the model for parceling territory after 1821.[6]

The prosperity reached by the United States under a federal constitution also fostered a spirit of identification and association among Mexican politicians with its northern neighbor. Publications such as Vicente Rocafuerte's *Ideas necesarias a todo pueblo independiente que quiere ser libre* recommended the United States political system as a model for the newly born Latin American republics. Mexican journalists bestowed praise on the United States constitution. One newspaper editor called it "one of the most beautiful creations of the human spirit . . . [and] the basis for the most felicitous, liberal, and simple government in history." The United States and its federalist regime became symbols of progress and modernity, and many politically conscious Mexicans believed that their country could achieve similar benefits by copying its neighbor.7

The 1812 Spanish constitution further influenced Mexican federalism. It provided a representative monarchical government for Spain and its colonies and established the institution of the provincial deputation. These were locally elected administrative bodies controlled by two royal officials—a political chief (*jefe político*) and an intendant who would govern if the *jefe político* was absent. Because this constitution did not provide for a viceroy, each *jefe político* reported directly to the Spanish government and thus became constitutionally independent of the other provinces and of the central government in Mexico City. Initially Spain's 1812 constitution awarded only six provincial deputations to New Spain, but a May 1821 decree of the Spanish *cortes* ordered the creation of provincial deputations in those overseas intendancies which did not have them. Twenty-three provincial deputations had been installed in Mexico by December 1823, and their establishment served as the legal precedent for the renascent regionalism and subsequent federalism of 1822-1824.8

The deterioration of Mexico's war of independence into a series of local rebellions also strengthened the leaders of many peripheral regions. By 1816-1817, royalist armies had only superficially restored order to New Spain; insurgency did not decline thereafter but continued across the countryside. The consequent economic dislocation, as well as the burdensome militia taxes introduced by Spanish authorities to set up a counterinsurgency system, turned many provincial elites against the viceregal regime. Helped along by the 1812 Spanish constitution, regional elements began to formulate their opposition to the policies that emanated in Mexico City and to protect their own interests.9

The vigor of these emerging feelings of provincialism became evident during the empire created by a creole officer in the Spanish army, Colonel Agustín de Iturbide. He conspired to separate Mexico from Spain and authored the Plan of Iguala. Issued in February 1821, this proposal declared Mexico's independence, established a constitutional monarchy, and offered the crown to Ferdinand VII. In August 1821, the Treaties of Córdoba confirmed Iturbide's plan with the modification that if Ferdinand VII did not accept the crown, it would be offered to another Bourbon prince. But the Treaties of Córdoba did not specify that Mexico's future ruler had to come from a European dynasty. If the Bourbon candidates refused the throne, Mexico's Congress would choose the monarch, a loophole that Iturbide used to his advantage when Spain rejected the treaties in February 1822.10

By that time, several factors had helped to pave the way for Iturbide's coronation. One was the praise that contemporaries lavished upon Iturbide for achieving independence. His deification became a "juggernaut that no one could resist, not even Iturbide himself." In addition, several regional military chieftains impressed upon Iturbide during the fall of 1821 and spring of 1822 that the establishment of a constitutional monarchy would meet with public support. Thus, Iturbide pushed forward his own interests shortly after Spain refused to recognize Mexico's independence. On the evening of May 10, 1822, Iturbide's personal regiment and a large crowd pro-

claimed him emperor. The next day pro-Iturbide military officers influenced Congress to ratify his ascent to the Mexican
throne.[11]

Iturbide's monarchical experiment proved to be short-
lived. Newspaper editors and members of masonic lodges,
which included military officers, had discussed the possibility
of establishing a republic in Mexico for some time. Their
opposition to the monarchical postulates of the Plan of Iguala
and Iturbide's arbitrary conduct prompted them to take
action. General Antonio López de Santa Anna reacted first by
proclaiming a republic in Veracruz on December 2, 1822.
Four days later, the Plan of Veracruz was published to attract
followers to the uprising. The plan did not mention the
republic proposed by Santa Anna, but it left the door open for
its establishment. The document granted Congress the
capacity to decide what form of government Mexico would
adopt once it had examined the wishes of the provinces and
the opinions of the wise men of the country. Yet at that
moment it appeared that the rebels' hopes would be frustrated. Imperial troops had nearly crushed Santa Anna's uprising by late January 1823.[12]

The situation improved for Santa Anna almost immediately. Disheartened by their inability to defeat Santa Anna
and influenced by the masonic lodges, the generals besieging
him issued the Plan of Casa Mata on February 1, 1823. This
carefully written manifesto breathed new life into Santa
Anna's moribund revolt, as it contained every element necessary to insure establishment of a federal republic. Article 9 of
the Plan of Casa Mata stated that Veracruz' provincial deputation would take over its internal administration. Within six
weeks of its publication, the plan received the endorsement of
many provincial deputations that declared their independence from Iturbide's government. Mexico had been divided
into autonomous provinces or regions that neither emperor
nor Congress could control.[13]

Since the Plan of Casa Mata did not provide for the establishment of a central government, Mexico had to select the system of administration best suited for the nation after Iturbide's abdication on March 20, 1823. The national legislature, dissolved by Iturbide in October 1822 and then reconvened in early March 1823, regarded itself as the repository of the national sovereignty. On the other hand, the restitution of Congress did not fulfill the expectations of the provinces. Since the distribution of deputies had been based on the number of districts (*partidos*) in each province and not on the population, the national legislature failed to insure proportional representation among the provinces. In addition, provincial leaders wanted the opportunity to elect a new legislature whose deputies would uphold regional interests. Finally, the Plan of Casa Mata stipulated that a new assembly would be convened and the provinces insisted that this clause be fulfilled at the earliest possible moment.[14]

A May 21 congressional declaration inviting a new legislature to meet in early November 1823 momentarily solved the impasse. Nevertheless, several provincial delegations did not trust Congress and began to discuss restructuring the national government. Some even announced the creation of state governments during the late spring and early summer of 1823. Deputies in Mexico City faced one major crisis in July when the provinces of Jalisco and Zacatecas nearly went to war with the central government to protect their sovereign rights as states. Politically conscious Mexicans who believed in a strong central authority feared that the disintegration of the country was close at hand.[15]

In the end, the provinces seemed to have prevailed in this argument because the second constituent Congress had a federalist majority when it formally convened on November 7, 1823. Recent research suggests, however, that the victory of federalism was a "distinctly mixed achievement." Supporters of centralism undertook vigorous military and parliamentary efforts after July 1823 to moderate Mexican federalism. As a result, the 1824 constitution did not specifically include the main federalist argument—that the states had created the Mexican union.[16] This document also preserved certain features reminiscent of the Spanish colonial regime. It made Catholicism the official religion and guaranteed special privileges (*fueros*) for both the Church and the army.[17] Despite these provisions, Mexico's first elected president, General Guadalupe Victoria, believed that the federal charter would allow Mexico to "leave behind ignominy and slavery," and raise itself to the "noble rank of free, independent, and sovereign nations."[18]

Unfortunately, such euphoria proved ephemeral, and numerous obstacles strained the framework of Mexico's newborn republic. Mexico's economy was in shambles. In December 1804, the Spanish Crown, desperate for money to finance its war with Great Britain, issued the Royal Law of Consolidation. This decree expropriated the assets of the Catholic Church's charitable funds, and from this time on revenue constantly flowed out of New Spain. The ravages of the eleven-year struggle for independence not only severely damaged mining, agricultural, and industrial production, but also claimed the lives of as many as 600,000 people, an estimated ten percent of Mexico's population. The breakdown of the national credit system further complicated matters, as did the reluctance of Mexico's elite to pay more taxes to sustain post-independence governments.[19]

Mexico's stormy political atmosphere also proved to be destabilizing. The two masonic lodges that gave the young nation its early manifestations of a political system soon found themselves at odds with each other. Scottish Rite masonry was established in 1813 and its members dominated public affairs until 1825. Scottish Rite masons (*escoceses*) were sympathetic to the colonial experience. Most *escoceses* belonged to society's upper crust and favored establishment of a centralized republic that would not disturb the existing social and economic order. The York Rite lodge, founded in 1825 to offset growing Scottish influence in the government, aimed to defend Mexico against the Spanish threat, both domestic and foreign. York Rite masons (*yorkinos*) recruited for their lodges individuals from the less affluent classes. *Yorkinos* also advocated the creation of civic militias to protect regional autonomy against the centralizing tendencies of Mexico City. The clash of such diametrically opposed factions in the mid-1820s challenged the legitimacy of federalism as an alternative form of government.[20]

One episode in the struggle between the masonic lodges, the Parián riot, commonly known as the *motín de la Acordada*, would be critical to Mexico's political future. In 1826 and 1827 the *yorkinos* attempted to mobilize Mexico City's urban masses to increase their access to the ballot box, but these efforts were insufficient to guarantee the victory of *yorkino* candidate General Vicente Guerrero in the 1828 presidential elections. As a result, Guerrero's backers claimed fraud and instigated a revolt to put their nominee in the presidency. On December 4, 1828, a crowd of approximately 5,000 pillaged shops and stores in the Parián building in Mexico City's central square. This chaos dampened the democratic idealism of the early independent republic. Mexico's elite viewed the upheaval as "the inevitable culmination of the urban poor's political enfranchisement," and most *yorkinos* and *escoceses* came to fear that mass mobilization would lead to class warfare.[21]

But not all politically conscious Mexicans retreated from appealing to the populace. *Puro* leader Valentín Gómez Farías repeatedly tried to mobilize urban crowds throughout the 1830s and 1840s.[22] Indeed, Guillermo Prieto commented in his memoirs that "the masses instinctively acclaimed and followed [Valentín] Gómez Farías, who had at his command a veritable army of shirtless ones (*descamisados*)."[23] Carlos María Bustamante, who chronicled nineteenth-century Mexico's political chaos in numerous books, pamphlets, and journals, concurred with this assessment. He once noted that Mexico City's poor "blindly obeyed" Gómez Farías.[24]

Consequently, federalism became linked with the lower classes, an association that seriously hindered the *puros'* efforts to establish an alliance with *moderados*, conservatives, and senior army officers during the war with the United States.

Guerrero's presidency provided the enemies of federalism with sufficient ammunition to launch a response. *El Correo de la Federación Mexicana* exacerbated tensions when it suggested that the clerical and military *fueros* should be removed from the 1824 constitution. In addition, Guerrero's minister of finance, Lorenzo de Zavala, tried to raise revenue by selling Church property nationalized by colonial authorities, and by decreeing a progressive income tax. Zavala's well-known friendship with the first United States minister to Mexico, Joel R. Poinsett (who had helped organize *yorkino* masonic lodges), also made Guerrero's regime unpopular with conservatives and the hierarchy of the Church. Guerrero's refusal to relinquish the emergency wartime powers that Congress had granted him during the 1829 Spanish invasion provided General Anastasio Bustamante with a pretext to stage a coup. He seized power in December 1829.[25]

The new administration set out to eliminate federalism. The most influential member of General Bustamante's cabinet was conservative statesman Lucas Alamán, then minister of foreign relations. Alamán deposed federalist governors and legislatures in eleven states, closed down federalist newspapers, and ordered Poinsett out of the country. *El Sol*, one of Mexico City's leading centralist newspapers, published several articles in mid-February 1830 arguing that federalism, although an ideal system, had only brought poverty, divisiveness, and ruin to commerce and agriculture. *El Sol* also attacked the civic militia, already firmly established in Jalisco, Mexico, Oaxaca, Puebla, San Luis Potosí, Yucatán, and Zacatecas, criticizing the states for spending their meager finances on the militia and questioning whether the states had a right to maintain an armed contingent in peacetime.

Later on, Congress released *cívicos* from duty in the Federal District and in the territories. In addition, several states eliminated or reduced the number of their militia units, giving further impetus to Alamán's centralizing endeavors.[26]

Despite their efforts, General Bustamante and Alamán failed to consolidate the regime. Gómez Farías, liberal theorist José María Luis Mora, and Zacatecas' Governor Francisco García spearheaded federalist efforts to create a viable resistance movement. The well-organized civic militia in Zacatecas served as their main tool. Since this was merely a state force, federalists sought a partner in the regular army. They joined with Santa Anna in July 1832 in nothing more than a marriage of convenience. Neither side really trusted the other, yet both knew they needed mutual support to achieve their goals—the presidency for Santa Anna and sufficient political power to protect state sovereignty for the federalists. Rebellion spread throughout the country and General Bustamante admitted defeat in December 1832.[27]

The victory by Gómez Farías and Santa Anna started a period of reform to eradicate all colonial vestiges from Mexico. In January 1833 various Mexico City newspapers began publishing articles that urged reform of both the Church and the army to root out centralism. The propaganda campaign caused alarm among the Church hierarchy and officer corps. Under the circumstances, Santa Anna decided it would not be wise to claim the presidency to which he had been elected in March 1833. Vice-President Gómez Farías took charge of the government and, by late November, he and his allies in Congress had unleashed a powerful attack against the Church and the army. They drew up legislation that reduced the size of the army and put the maintenance of internal peace in the hands of the civic militia. Other new laws were intended to weaken the economic and political status of the Church. When opposition to Gómez Farías' reforms among military and clerical leaders intensified, Santa Anna decided that it would be politically expedient to break his alliance with Gómez Farías and the federalists. In April 1834 Santa Anna issued a manifesto condemning Gómez Farías' program. He forced the resignation or ouster of leading federalists (including Gómez Farías) and closed Congress, state legislatures, and other federalist bodies that threatened his dictatorial ambitions.[28]

The purge created a constitutional vacuum, which, coupled with Santa Anna's failure to declare his political agenda publicly, allowed the principal conservatives and *moderados* to abolish federalism. Newspaper articles and pamphlets argued that it was not a suitable form of government for a country in its infancy and that it had failed to fulfill the expectations it roused in 1824. Critics charged that the federal system had brought political and factional strife, higher taxes and administrative expenses, general lawlessness, and a decline in moral standards. Centralism would remedy these maladies, restore national unity, guarantee law, order, and public morality. To put their plans into effect, supporters of centralism had to crush the civic militia, primarily the powerful units still afoot in Zacatecas. On March 31, 1835, a Congress dominated by centralists passed a decree that restricted the size of the civic militia in the states to one militiaman for every 500 inhabitants. When Zacatecas Governor García refused to obey the law, Santa Anna marched north and crushed his forces in May 1835. With this obstacle out of the way, the legislature began remodeling Mexico into a centralist republic.[29]

The transformation was a gradual process. On May 2, 1835, Congress declared that it had the right to alter the constitution. Then, a series of popular demonstrations in favor of centralism convinced Santa Anna to forego any plans to replace federalism with a dictatorship. The centralist era in Mexico became operative in October 1835 after two new decrees converted states into departments without political or fiscal autonomy. Finally, the centralist constitution known as the *Siete Leyes* was ratified in December 1836. Hoping to provide stability, it stipulated that presidents were to serve for eight years. The *Siete Leyes* also sought to restrict popular participation in public life to prevent the social and economic upheaval that federalism seemed to nourish. Full citizenship, which carried with it the right to vote, was restricted to men with a yearly income of at least 100 pesos. Qualifications for election to the Chamber of Deputies included a minimum annual income of 1,500 pesos. The financial prerequisites to be a senator were even more stringent; to be eligible an individual needed a minimum annual income of 2,500 pesos.[30]

But federalism regained its appeal as a viable political alternative even before the *Siete Leyes* had been adopted as Mexico's constitution. By late June 1836 federalist newspapers blamed the separation of Texas on the adoption of centralism. Then, Mexico's failure to reconquer Texas and the deterioration of relations with France, highlighted by the 1838 "Pastry War," caused widespread disillusionment across all social classes. In addition, these two episodes gave rise to federalist revolts throughout the country that halted the flow of revenue to the national treasury. Mexico had to operate with enormous fiscal deficits; the national debt in 1840 reached nearly fourteen million pesos. Efficient fiscal management became an impossibility and General Bustamante, who had been chosen in April 1837 to serve a second term as president, could not fulfill his promises to restore law and order, provide political stability, create an honest administration, and bring about economic progress. The *Siete Leyes* came to be seen as incapable of maintaining a peaceful and tranquil atmosphere.[31]

The deficiencies of General Bustamante's regime insured that numerous petitioners from around the country clamored for the restoration of federalism. The Mexican president also fueled these hopes by refusing to curtail freedom of the press and allowing Valentín Gómez Farías to return to Mexico in 1838. But the Gómez Farías-led July 15, 1840, coup d'état, perhaps the most significant of the insurrections that sought to reinstate federalism while the *Siete Leyes* functioned as Mexico's constitution, dashed any expectations. This rebellion turned Mexico City into a caldron of violence, and thieves and other criminals committed numerous acts of vandalism. Government propaganda stressed that the *léperos* were the rebellion's sole source of support. *Hombres de bien* were appalled at the widespread destruction and did not support Gómez Farías.[32] Just as importantly, by the 1840s the elite's dread of the lower rungs of society remained strong. Gómez Farías' brand of federalism came to be considered a potential element of subversion, a challenge to the established order. These apprehensions remained throughout the Mexican War and hindered Gómez Farías' ability to muster public support at critical times during that conflict.

The next opportunity to restore federalism arose within two years. Following a military revolt that ousted General Bustamante in October 1841, a constituent Congress met in June 1842 to revise Mexico's political structure. But the legislature's proposal for a new charter that granted departments increased autonomy and attacked the clerical and military *fueros* threatened Santa Anna (who had been provisional president since late 1841) and other army officers, who argued that the constitutional project would "have led to the triumph of the cruel and intolerant demagogy of 1828 and 1833." In mid-December 1842 Santa Anna and his allies orchestrated a cycle of military rebellions that spread throughout the country. Santa Anna then dissolved the constituent Congress and called on an assembly of notables to draft a new constitution. The deliberations resulted in the code commonly known as the *Bases Orgánicas* of 1843.[33]

Under the powers of the *Bases Orgánicas*, Santa Anna established a dictatorship that widened the powers of the executive branch, restricted popular representation, and gave the national government almost total control over the departments. Moreover, the government's plan for a public contribution of ten million pesos, as well as steadily increased taxes and expansion of previous revenue-raising schemes, created intense public opposition. Encouraged by leaders in Querétaro and Jalisco, General Mariano Paredes y Arrillaga rebelled against Santa Anna in November 1844.[34] This uprising culminated in a coup led by national legislature known as the December 6 movement.

Santa Anna's actions of late November led Congress to step into the fray. Santa Anna took command of the army to crush Paredes' insurrection, and, on arriving in Querétaro, he imprisoned the members of that departmental assembly after learning that they supported Paredes' revolt. Congressional leaders in Mexico City had been ready to claim that Santa Anna had violated the *Bases Orgánicas* by putting himself at the head of the army, and news of his conduct at Querétaro added to the uproar. Attempting to restore public order, on November 29 General Valentín Canalizo—acting president ad interim in lieu of Santa Anna—issued a decree dissolving the national legislature. The legislation—first taken to Santa Anna for his approval—was not published until December 2. On that day Canalizo also ordered all civilian and military officials to take an oath supporting the Santa Anna administration.[35]

Spain's minister to Mexico remarked that "a revolution would be born out of this state of affairs," an observation that quickly came to pass.[36] On December 6, a coalition of military chiefs and legislators deposed Canalizo and named General José Joaquín Herrera chief executive. Despite having 12,000 soldiers at his disposal, Santa Anna tried but failed to defeat the troops supporting the new government. He was arrested in late January 1845.[37] The victory of the December 6 movement appeared to be long-lasting. Not only did it prove successful in the quest to end Santa Anna's arbitrary rule, but it also brought together the *puros* and *moderados*. The December 6 coup seemed to herald the beginning of an era of stability.

Unity, however, proved to be a mirage; the uprising

became a divisive element in Mexican politics. The national legislature's role in the December 6 revolt transformed it into the "one and only power" in Mexico by early 1845. *Moderados* like Manuel Gómez Pedraza, Francisco Elorriaga, Juan Bautista Morales, Juan José Espinosa de los Monteros, and General Pedro María Anaya controlled Congress, and their efforts to promote their group's political, diplomatic, and social views shattered the fragile alliance with the *puros*.[38] Both factions bickered constantly during the next three years, straining their relationship as the threat of war with the United States worsened and increasing Mexico's vulnerability to the expansionist aims of its northern neighbor.

Valentín Gómez Farías and the Lone Star Republic

Government anxiety for Mexico's territorial integrity can be traced to its days as a Spanish colony. One of the advisors to Spanish king Charles III predicted in 1783 that the United States, although it had been born a "pygmy," would some day become a "formidable colossus" with no other goal than territorial expansion.[39] Indeed, numerous American filibustering expeditions into Spanish possessions during the early 1800s clearly demonstrated the danger that Spain's American colonies faced. Fear of United States' pressure seemed to diminish with the signing of the 1819 Transcontinental or Adams-Onís Treaty, which set the boundary between Spain and the United States. The border ran from the Sabine River to the Pacific Ocean. Nonetheless, American attempts to modify the treaty in subsequent years showed that designs to encroach on Spanish possessions had abated little, if at all.[40]

The United States coveted Texas, which was no more than a desolate Spanish province with approximately 7,000 settlers in 1800. Spanish colonial authorities believed that populating and colonizing that territory would protect it from the westward advance of the United States. The commandant general in Monterrey granted permission for American families to settle in Texas, a policy that Mexico also adopted after winning its independence. But the colonists who followed Moses Austin and his son Stephen into Texas in the early 1820s did not abide by several provisions designed to foster peaceful integration into the Mexican community. They did not adhere to the requirement that they be Roman Catholics, for example, and few learned to speak Spanish. The Texans retained their ties to American culture, and this soon led to an uneasy relationship with Mexico.[41]

Other factors magnified the perils inherent in this potentially dangerous situation to Mexican territorial integrity. The Constitution of 1824 combined Texas and Coahuila as one state, which assumed responsibility for the colonization of Texas. Officials of Texas and Coahuila began to grant land concessions independently of the national government in Mexico, a practice that transformed the state capital at Saltillo into "a mecca for American colonists and Mexican land speculators."[42] As a result, American settlers made up a majority of the population in Texas by 1830. Tensions also increased because the problems that wracked the central government of Mexico after independence forced authorities to pay more attention to national, not regional, affairs. The Texans' complaints, such as their lack of adequate representation in the Coahuila state legislature, were largely ignored. In addition, the endeavors of Minister Joel R. Poinsett to purchase as much of Texas as possible amplified Mexican distrust of the United States.[43]

The Mexican government viewed these developments with apprehension and in 1827 commissioned General Manuel Mier y Terán to examine problems along the Texas border. He traveled across the province one year later and was alarmed by a growing population of foreigners who were abusing and disregarding Mexico's colonization policies. Mier y Terán's reports led Mexico to devise a strategy to regain control of Texas and halt the United States' efforts to acquire the province. President Vicente Guerrero abolished slavery throughout the republic in September 1829 to dissuade those settlers who owned slaves from remaining in Texas, but Mexican authorities in Texas did not enforce the decree because they feared it might provoke the Americans into rebelling. Mexico's national Congress then issued the Law of Colonization of April 6, 1830. The measure incorporated a number of suggestions drawn up by Lucas Alamán earlier that year. Among other things, it forbade all further immigration from the United States into Texas.44

The Law of Colonization did not produce the results Alamán had anticipated. It proved to be a "much weaker and more diplomatic law than the one recommended in Alamán's initiative."45 But even if this measure had been as Herculean as first envisioned, other circumstances would have sabotaged its effect. Not only was Mexico incapable of enforcing the major stipulations of the accord, but the decree also heightened resentment among American colonists in Texas. They requested repeal of the Law of Colonization and asked for statehood within the Mexican nation in the fall of 1832. Two years of negotiations between Alamán and Poinsett's replacement, Anthony Butler, made the situation worse. In fact, Butler was no closer than Poinsett in convincing the Mexicans to sell Texas and Mexico's distrust of the United States remained unabated.46

Recent scholarship suggests that the desire of Gómez Farías' 1833-1834 administration to discredit the centralist policies instituted by General Bustamante's government might have led it to give "serious thought" to the sale of Texas because they "unquestionably considered" that territory to be a "burden." The premise for this assertion is a January 1833 dispatch penned by Mexico's minister of foreign affairs that subsequently appeared in a widely read news magazine, the *Niles' Weekly Register*. The note was characterized as a "genuine overture of friendship to the United States" that provided the American government with an excellent opportunity to negotiate for Texas. The United States did not take advantage of the opportunity due to Butler's avowal that Mexico's stormy political situation precluded entering into serious negotiations.47 The contention that Gómez Farías would have considered selling Texas is debatable, however. The January 1833 dispatch merely informed the United States government that the rebellion against General Bustamante had ended and that Manuel Gómez Pedraza had taken on the presidential duties to which he had been elected in 1828. It further stated that Mexico's chief executive hoped that the "amicable relations" that had existed between the two countries would continue.48 Moreover, Gómez Farías had not come to power at the time the letter was written. Given Gómez Farías' belligerent attitude toward Texas, his administration would not have entertained any entreaties related to the sale of that territory in 1833 and 1834.

Any chance for a peaceful settlement disappeared when the Gómez Farías government collapsed in April 1834. Supporters of centralism prepared to reinstate the 1830 Law of Colonization and replace the 1824 constitution with the *Siete Leyes*. This turn of events horrified American settlers in Texas and a majority of them revolted by the fall of 1835. Santa Anna rushed north as he had to overpower the Zacatecas civic militia earlier that year. He defeated the Texas rebels in March 1836 at the battles of the Alamo and Goliad, but his victories proved costly. Although the Mexican Congress had decreed that foreigners who attacked the national territory were to be treated and punished as pirates (which meant the death penalty), the execution of the Alamo's defenders and Goliad's prisoners turned these encounters into symbols of barbaric cruelty. Opposition to Mexico in the United States increased, and supplies and men began to pour into Texas. This support provided the Texans with the confidence to make a stand, and they routed Santa Anna's forces at the Battle of San Jacinto on April 21, 1836. To avoid being lynched after the humiliating defeat, Santa Anna signed a treaty recognizing the independence of Texas.

Mexico's Congress later repudiated the agreement, but to no avail. For the next nine years endemic federalist unrest, economic crisis, and the 1838 French invasion obstructed efforts to bring Texas back into the Mexican union.49

Gómez Farías' refusal to accept this state of affairs transformed him into a stout Yankee-hater by 1845. In the early 1820s he actively participated in legislative efforts to maintain Mexico's territorial integrity, and as vice-president in 1833 he took steps to prevent the loss of Texas. Gómez Farías had instructed the military commander of the Eastern Interior Provinces to inform the inhabitants of Texas that they could attempt to modify their political status by relying on the mechanisms provided by the 1824 constitution; any effort to do otherwise would be met with force. Meanwhile, Stephen F. Austin had traveled to Mexico City to persuade the government to allow Texas to establish itself as an independent state within the Mexican federation. Austin met with Gómez Farías twice. The first interview turned out to be a courteous encounter, but Austin told Gómez Farías during the second conference that the Texans would take the law into their own hands if the Mexican government failed to meet their demands. Contemporary observers remarked that the threat rankled Gómez Farías. Following the interception of Austin's December 1833 letter to the Béxar (San Antonio) city council urging it to declare Texas a separate state, the Mexican vice-president issued an order for Austin's arrest and kept him in jail for nearly a year.50

After his fall from power in 1834, Gómez Farías went into exile in New Orleans and plotted to invade Mexico the following year. In an ironic twist, he and other banished Mexicans raised money and volunteers to aid the Texas rebels, believing that most of the Texans were federalists and not secessionists. The invasion called for the Texans to distract the Mexican army while General José Antonio Mejía captured Tampico. Several historians have relied on these activities to accuse Gómez Farías of betraying his country.

This charge seems unlikely given the *puro* leader's lifelong service to Mexico and the determination with which he clamored for war against the United States in the mid-1840s. In fact, the New Orleans federalists broke all connections with the Texans once it became evident that the rebels favored independence.[51]

The efforts made in the 1840s by the centralist governments to reconquer Texas disillusioned Gómez Farías. In August 1841 he questioned whether the funds intended to underwrite a Texas campaign would be used for that purpose. Much of that money financed the military operations designed to reincorporate the department of Yucatán (which seceded from Mexico in February 1840) into the Mexican union. Three months later Gómez Farías expressed his disappointment because the Mexican government did not match the zeal shown by the inhabitants of the department of New Mexico, who volunteered to defend Santa Fe and defeated an expedition dispatched by the Texas republic earlier that spring. The *puro* leader subsequently commented that Mexican troops should not abandon San Antonio after its occupation, as General Adrian Woll had done after holding that city for two days in March 1842.[52]

By late 1843 it was becoming increasingly apparent that Mexico could not reconquer Texas; the issue became whether it could prevent the annexation of its former province by the United States. Gómez Farías kept a close watch on the situation from his exile in New Orleans. American expansionist policies—which only amplified his Yankeephobia—gave him an abundance of reasons to be concerned. In May 1844 he wrote that the United States would surely annex an independent Texas. This would allow the United States to "colonize Texas calmly, promote smuggling, slowly take possession of our rich and fertile terrains, sell them, increase its income, and begin the invasion, deliberately planned many years ago, that would extend [their territory] as far as California."[53]

At the time Santa Anna was president of Mexico. His contradictory behavior during the 1820s and 1830s and his well-known duplicity in affairs of state added to Gómez Farías' worries. Early in 1843 Santa Anna became absorbed with the idea that Texas might accept reunification with Mexico if there was a bilateral arrangement to preserve its local autonomy (a similar agreement had been signed with Yucatán). The ensuing negotiations came to nothing and by the following spring Santa Anna's administration hoped to organize a large military expedition to reconquer Texas and bring the province back into the union.[54]

Having heard similar announcements before, Gómez Farías did not give credence to the government's proclamations. In April 1844 he informed a close associate that Santa Anna would solve the Texas question "with his accustomed perfidy." After displaying "a noble and energetic patriotism," and offering to die before consenting to the dismemberment of Mexican territory, Santa Anna would concoct a "covenant advantageous for that republic, profitable for himself, and ruinous for Mexico."[55] Gómez Farías also sent José María Luis Mora several pamphlets disclosing the possible annexation of Texas by the United States. He came to the conclusion that Santa Anna and his cabinet were collaborating with the Americans to consummate this "act of iniquity." Gómez Farías made it clear that he would never accept annexation, and neither would the Mexican people, whom he believed would rather die than submit to the domination of the United States.[56]

Gómez Farías, after consideration, decided that Mexico's prosperity could only be guaranteed by the reconquest of Texas. In his view such a task would not be difficult. According to Gómez Farías, Mexican troops could easily occupy San Antonio because its inhabitants were largely Mexicans who desired to rejoin the bosom of the mother country. The Mexican army could travel by land and by sea, via Havana and perhaps from New Orleans, and "build a line of fortifications that the Texans would fear attacking." Ten thousand men could guard these defenses and occupy the ports where smuggling had flourished.57

The *puro* leader believed that only a new government could undertake this war, for Santa Anna lacked the "talent to direct and to wage" a successful campaign. Gómez Farías proffered his evaluation of Santa Anna: the people detested him, his soldiers did not love him, and he could not generate sufficient enthusiasm to lighten "the fatigues, privations, and dangers" of a military expedition. The "hero" of San Jacinto would gamble away his soldiers' equipment and would not pay them their full salary. As Gómez Farías put it, Santa Anna's leadership would result in a shameful treaty that ridiculed Mexico or granted a foreign power the opportunity to intervene in the dispute.58

Gómez Farías' expectations of an easy military victory were naïve, if not ingenuous. One estimate states that the reconquest of Texas would have required not only a well-drilled army of 20,000 men, but also a navy capable of blockading three to four thousand miles of coast.59 Mexico had neither element available. The correspondence of General Mariano Paredes y Arrillaga, especially those letters he received from General Mariano Arista, commanding the Army of the North, vividly illustrates the wretchedness of Mexican soldiers along the frontier. In addition, Mexico's naval forces were hardly adequate to defend its Atlantic shore in peacetime, so it was foolhardy to believe that they could blockade Texas' seacoast.60

Some *puros*, however, had more practical military objectives in mind than the reconquest of Texas. Despite the weaknesses of the Mexican forces, the eminent politician José María Lafragua, who served as an intimate confederate of Gómez Farías in 1845, did not believe that the army was so "demoralized that it would prove incapable of waging [war]." Lafragua was confident that Mexico could find an honorable way out of this predicament. A military campaign with Texas would be a means to enhance Mexico's leverage in negotiations. Lafragua believed that if the army won one battle in Texas, the Mexican government could then sue for peace and establish Texas as an independent republic under the guardianship of Great Britain.[61]

It is impossible to determine if Gómez Farías would have listened to Lafragua's counsel on the matter. In any event, however, the annexation of Texas by the United States in February 1845 would have prevented the *puros* from implementing the strategy advocated by Lafragua. This development transformed the *puros'* prospects of reconquering Texas from improbable to chimerical, but it did not shake Gómez Farías' determination to pursue his agenda in 1845.

II

"Great Evils
Will Befall The Nation"

Mexico seemed ready for a bright and prosperous future early in 1845. The ouster of General Antonio López de Santa Anna led newspapers of different political ideals to remark that the country was headed toward an era free of turmoil and internal dissension. *La Voz del Pueblo*, which became the most outspoken *puro* journal in 1845, stated that the victory of the December 6 movement represented "the dawn of popular liberties" and proved that Mexicans were "determined to work for a promising future."[1] *El Siglo XIX*, widely regarded as the unofficial voice of General José Joaquín Herrera's government,[2] noted that even the most unswerving politicians had put aside their own beliefs to "prevent the gangrene of disorder and immorality, which had already taken giant steps, from invading and destroying the entire body politic."[3] British representative Charles Bankhead echoed these magnanimous sentiments, reporting that tranquillity prevailed and that the new cabinet was earning public confidence. Herrera's ministers were completely dedicated to the task of restoring the different branches of government to prosperity and vigor.[4]

33

Herrera's regime, however, could not take advantage of the circumstances. While military realities and political considerations help explain why Herrera and his advisers refused to accommodate the *puros* on constitutional reform and Texas, the personality of Mexico's chief executive also affected the way he approached the decision-making process. Herrera's contemporaries considered him to be upright and honest, but he was a poorly schooled man who "accepted docilely the counsel of others."[5] Herrera often listened to the advice rendered by Bankhead on the Texas question. The British representative did not want war.[6] In addition, many politically conscious Mexicans believed *puro* arch rival Manuel Gómez Pedraza to be the "soul of the cabinet."[7] One may presume that Valentín Gómez Farías' sworn enemy held considerable sway over Herrera and his ministers on affairs of state and that his recommendations sought, in part, to nullify the *puros'* influence.

In reply, the *puros* launched an extensive propaganda campaign condeming the policies of Herrera's administration. The publicity crusade weakened the *moderados'* political position. At the same time, the *puros* worked to mend fences with the regular army and to develop a powerful civic militia. This apparent contradiction was a pragmatic move to help Gómez Farías and his associates reach power. Reestablishment of the militia would allow the *puros* to restrain the ambitions of self-seeking generals and prepare the country for war.

"The Symbol of Ineptitude in Politics"

The leaders of the December 6 movement made their position on constitutional reform clear from the rebellion's outset.[8] The *moderados* did not intend to abolish the 1843 *Bases Orgánicas*. On December 6, 1844, the Chamber of Deputies unanimously decided that departmental assemblies should submit to Congress those changes which, in their opinion, would make the *Bases* a better law.[9] Upon being sworn in as interim president nine days later, Herrera affirmed that his government would scrupulously guard this code, for it was the "only point of departure" that would preserve Mexico's social order.[10]

Herrera reiterated this point of view when he addressed Congress three weeks later, saying that the *Bases Orgánicas* had been "fortunately saved from the scorn and destruction to which they had been condemned by the ill-fated decree of November 29 [1844]." This constitution was "the only solid foundation upon which the social edifice could be raised." If the *Bases* were to produce the great benefits expected from them, they needed "several prudent and gradual reforms . . . that experience and local necessities deem[ed] imperative."[11] Herrera could not have stated the guiding principle of his political ideology more clearly. In his opinion, the deliberate process of reforming the *Bases Orgánicas* through lawful means was the only option available to Mexico.

To garner public support for Herrera's policies, the *Diario del Gobierno de la República Mexicana* published several articles that enumerated the advantages of modifying the *Bases Orgánicas*. The first of the essays appeared on January 19. It pointed out that only the *Bases*, although far from being a perfect work of constitutional politics, could save the country. The *Bases* should be revised to perfection. Moreover, since the *Bases* did not contain any precept declaring them unchangeable, there was no need to deviate from the path they outlined.[12] One week later, the *Diario's* editors made their point even stronger; it was indispensable to reform the *Bases*, for the December 6 revolt had no other purpose.[13] Over the next three months, the departmental assemblies of Jalisco, Tamaulipas, Oaxaca, Nuevo León, Mexico, Durango, Sinaloa, Querétaro, Coahuila, Puebla, and Michoacán responded to the government's call and their reports were promptly brought to the legislature's attention.[14] The Chamber of Deputies' Special Commission on Constitutional Reform put the finishing touch on the campaign when it issued two reports on April 16 and May 26 detailing the changes that should be made to the *Bases*.[15] With this type of legislative, departmental, and journalistic support, Herrera hoped to enhance public appeal for the constitution.

Meanwhile, numerous newspaper articles and petitions had demanded the immediate reestablishment of the federal system. Yet Herrera's will remained unchanged. Early in July he pointed out that each passing day witnessed increased public support for modifying the *Bases*. After emerging victorious in the August presidential elections, Herrera remarked that constitutional reform was an "urgent and imperious" necessity. Lawful correction of the *Bases* would be an "efficient means to repress the revolutionary spirit that sometimes wore the clothes of improvement and perfection, and undertook detestable and pernicious enterprises with that pretext."[16]

Herrera had spent almost ten months in the presidency by that time, but these statements were the only concrete measures he adopted to solve Mexico's constitutional controversy. According to his biographer, the speed with which he proceeded was not a sign of indecisiveness or weakness; rather it showed good judgment and a desire to follow established legal procedures.[17] Another twentieth-century writer expressed a similar opinion. Herrera's administration hoped to "establish a constitution that shunned extremes, that would edify instead of destroy, and that, moving away from the fateful party spirit, would be founded on patriotism."[18] Unfortunately, such wishes would not prevail in Mexico in 1845. Many pundits associated the *Bases Orgánicas* with Santa Anna's abuses and believed that the charter should be abolished.

The Texas question proved to be another stumbling block that Herrera and the *moderados* could not overcome. Herrera's regime came to power under pressure to meet certain expectations raised by General Mariano Paredes y Arrillaga's November 1844 *pronunciamiento*, which blamed Santa Anna for Mexico's failure to subdue its former province. Santa Anna's inability to make reconquest a popular national crusade, however, may have impressed upon Herrera the necessity of negotiating a peaceful solution to this issue. In addition, by late February 1845 Herrera's government had received several reports from General Mariano Arista that emphasized the dismal state of readiness of the Army of the North. Herrera and his advisers no doubt realized the remote possibility of victory in a war with the United States. As a result, Herrera began negotiations to recognize the independence of Texas with the stipulation that the new republic not join any other power. Such an arrangement, Herrera hoped, would prevent the former province from passing into the hands of the United States.[19]

Minister of Foreign Relations Luis G. Cuevas began to pursue this course on March 11. At the time, however, Cuevas did not know that the United States Congress had approved annexation almost two weeks earlier. Once aware of this development, Cuevas notified United States' Minister Wilson Shannon that diplomatic relations between the nations would be terminated. War seemed imminent by late March, but diplomatic advances by Great Britain's chargé d'affairs in Texas gave Mexico another chance to settle the problem with honor. The British diplomat persuaded Texan authorities to discuss a settlement with Mexico that would accommodate Herrera's wishes.[20]

The Mexican government sought to build a network of support for the new policy during the next two months. Cuevas not only emphasized to departmental governors the importance of negotiating an amicable settlement to the Texas question, but he persuaded Congress to grant the government permission to consider the British proposal. The request was technically required by the *Bases Orgánicas*, which prohibited Mexico's executive from ceding territory to a foreign power. Finally, Herrera indicated to the national legislature on May 30 that the recent conduct of both the executive and the Congress was justified by the need for "a peaceful negotiation."[21]

But the July 15TH decision by Texas to annex itself to the United States dashed all hopes of a harmonious agreement. On the following day, "amidst the most profound silence," Cuevas informed Congress that negotiations had failed.[22] The clamor for war, which had diminished while there was still a chance of reaching an accord with Texas, revived with great intensity. "The tribune resonates every day with warlike declamations"—wrote Spanish Minister Salvador Bermúdez de Castro—"the press predicates war as it tries to raise the crestfallen public spirit, [and] official newspapers are full of pompous statements in which military men offer their swords to the nation."[23] War seemed inevitable.

Herrera and his advisers tried to avert an armed confrontation nonetheless. After being elected president in mid-August, Herrera appointed *moderado* attorney Manuel de la Peña y Peña as his new minister of foreign relations. Peña y Peña was known for his cautious, yet conciliatory attitude toward the United States. Herrera's wish to avoid war can also be seen in the speech he delivered to Congress on being sworn in as chief executive in mid-September. It would have been a propitious moment to castigate the United States if he intended to prosecute war vigorously. But Herrera, surprisingly, did not even mention the Texas problem. He said that he would strive to insure Mexico's external security, and to "conserve and foment" its "friendly relations" with foreign powers. In doing so, his regime would look to safeguard "the republic's sovereignty and independence, its decorum and dignity, and the observance and respectability of the national laws."[24] No one could have stated the Mexican government's peaceful intentions more clearly.

By this time, the reports of several American officials in Mexico motivated United States President James K. Polk and his cabinet to negotiate a solution to the Texas issue. Polk decided to send a minister to Mexico to arrange a boundary agreement. The delicate mission fell on John Slidell, a promising Louisiana politician fluent in Spanish and said to be prudent and well mannered. The resurgence of war cries in Mexico City convinced Polk to postpone Slidell's journey, but the mission's chances for success had improved by October 15. On that day Peña y Peña informed the United States consul in Mexico City that Mexico would entertain a commissioner invested with "full powers from his government to settle the present dispute in a peaceful, reasonable, and honorable manner."[25]

Having agreed to receive Slidell, Herrera's government again sought a consensus that would allow it to negotiate with the United States. Peña y Peña first solicited two cabinet members to evaluate Mexico's capacity to engage in an armed conflict with its northern neighbor. Their reports did not offer a favorable prognosis. Minister of Finance Pedro Fernández del Castillo stated that the government's fiscal resources were "almost completely exhausted." Minister of War General Pedro María Anaya's outlook was slightly more optimistic. He noted that a military campaign against the United States would be successful if the government could raise the money or assemble the men needed for war. Nonetheless, Fernández del Castillo's report strongly suggested that mustering an army was extremely doubtful.[26]

On December 9, Peña y Peña tried to broaden the public support that Herrera's conciliatory foreign policy required. He asked departmental authorities to voice their opinion on war or peace. Mexico's response should be "the fruit of a truly national opinion and the faithful expression of the republic's constituent parts." Although justice would undoubtedly be on Mexico's side in the event of a conflict, Peña y Peña reiterated the country's dismal financial situation and the army's weaknesses. He also indicated that Mexico should not expect any assistance from Great Britain and explained why it would not be convenient to fight for the recovery of Texas even if Mexico could make the necessary human and monetary sacrifices. He added that negotiations with the United States would not besmirch Mexico's honor.[27] In the end, Peña y Peña's appeal went unheeded, and other measures taken by Herrera's administration to solve the intricate problem did not bear fruit.

The quandary among Mexican officials extended to the motives behind Slidell's mission. Peña y Peña probably felt that Slidell—in his charge as a commissioner—was coming to Mexico to discuss the annexation of Texas. But did Polk's disdain for Mexico motivate him to send a minister plenipotentiary to solve pending questions, including the purchase of New Mexico and California? To admit Slidell in this capacity would have reopened diplomatic relations with the United States, thus weakening Mexico's position in the negotiations. As a result, the Mexican Council of State decided on December 16 that it would not receive Slidell, in part because he lacked appropriate credentials.[28]

Herrera's failure to articulate his foreign policy clearly also undermined his administration's credibility. His political enemies demanded that the government assert itself against Texas and the United States. Herrera's stance, however, lacked the warlike furor that characterized statements made by the *puros*. Once Herrera's intentions became clear, his strategy became less effective and fostered public perceptions of his regime as weak and indecisive, allowing his adversaries to intensify their attacks.

The Preachings of Opposition Newspapers

The Valentín Gómez Farías-led *puros* were the most vociferous of all the groups who disagreed with Herrera's foreign and domestic policies. Early in 1845 the *puros* had hoped to collaborate with Herrera, but they soon became disillusioned and began to defend the virtues of the Constitution of 1824 as well as the necessity of waging war, first with Texas and later with the United States. Three Mexico City newspapers served as the standard-bearers for the campaign: *La Voz del Pueblo, El Estandarte Nacional*, and *El Amigo del Pueblo*. The *puros'* journalistic crusade met with partial success. As these newspapers spread the *puros'* ideals among the politically active, many Mexicans came to believe that Herrera's administration was irresolute and withdrew their support. This contributed to the collapse of Herrera's government, but the *puros* could not capitalize in 1845. They would have to wait until August 1846 to carry out their political aspirations.

Of the three *puro*-subsidized journals, *La Voz del Pueblo* clamored most vehemently in favor of federalism. Its principal editor was Agustín Franco, a dissident from *El Siglo XIX* whom contemporaries characterized as possessing both a "fiery pen" and "the fanatical conscience" of a Roman tribune.[29] Franco and his collaborators first relied on historical precedent, territorial size, and regional differences to bolster federalism's popularity. In their opinion, the history of the republics of Sparta and San Marino confirmed that small countries were better ruled under a centralist government. Centralism, the journalists reasoned, was inadequate for a large country whose "population, scattered over many leagues of terrain, was not proportionally located." The *puro* writers maintained that local governments capable of satisfying local demands should be instituted in regions where the population had diverse needs, professions, and customs. At the same time, these societies would benefit from a presiding national government to stimulate their development.[30]

Application of these considerations to Mexico in 1845 confirmed to the editors of *La Voz del Pueblo* that centralism did not suit the country's best interests. Mexico's seven to eight million inhabitants were concentrated in Mexico City and some provincial capitals. Few people lived in the rest of the republic, and travelers between Chihuahua and New Mexico were hard-pressed to find a single town. In addition, Mexico's diverse provinces specialized in different trades, giving the inhabitants a profound local spirit. These peculiarities, the many grades of cultural development, and the varied customs of the residents indicated that it was "impossible to govern them with general laws." Outlying regions had the right to self-government, but only if they pledged allegiance to a common central polity.[31]

In the opinion of *La Voz del Pueblo*, circumstances were auspicious for a political renaissance. The revolt of December 6, 1844, had inaugurated an era of "complete regeneration." Consequently, "the deadly politics that gnawed away at our riches, weakened our public spirit, and exposed us to the jeers and derision of foreign nations during the fateful centralist regime" should be abandoned.[32] It would be only a matter of time before *La Voz del Pueblo* openly endorsed restoration of the 1824 federal charter, a step that Franco and his colleagues took when they published an article titled *"Pronunciamientos"* on February 12. After praising the December 6, 1844, revolt for placing Mexico in the position of being able to choose its leaders and determine the scope of their power, *La Voz del Pueblo* moved to demonstrate federalism's necessity. Its editors sketched the history of Mexico between independence and the proclamation of the *Bases Orgánicas* in 1843, concluding that the 1824 constitution remained operative because *"it had not been validly or legally revoked and reformed; but since the [governmental] system it guaranteed had been destroyed as a matter of fact,* THE NATION IS NOT CONSTITUTED."[33]

La Voz del Pueblo then sought to determine the reforms that the constitution needed, whether or not implementation of the changes required a completely different charter, and if the existing legislature could authorize the new pact.[34] Its editors reiterated the concept that federalism had been adopted in 1824 due to the country's geography and particular needs of its citizens. *La Voz del Pueblo* also claimed that the 1824 charter could provide Mexico with internal tranquillity and the respect of foreign powers, for the nation had been able to repel the 1829 Spanish invasion "thanks to the states' unanimous concurrence." But naïve declarations also crept into the pages of *La Voz del Pueblo*. The paper maintained that under the federal system every citizen actively participated in civic affairs and aspired to public office.[35]

These *puro* journalists espoused a line of reasoning that resembled the strategy adopted by the *hombres de bien* to criticize federalism in 1834 and 1835. They maintained that centralism had only extinguished enthusiasm and public spirit. The energy which had been evident during the conflict with Spain in 1829 was not present to repulse the French ten years later.[36] Consequently, the so-called "Pastry War" did not become a "golden page" in Mexican history. The national government took advantage of centralism to seize state revenues, but numerous complications emerged due to diverse systems of taxation, collection, and administration in each federal entity. Since states were slow in paying their taxes, the centralist regime imposed new duties that also went unpaid. Misery and desperation, according to the *puro* writers, prevailed among the people at a time when the central government could not meet the nation's needs.37

This state of affairs, coupled with the successful uprisings that won self rule for Yucatán and the need to exempt other departments from various prevailing taxes, led the editors of *La Voz del Pueblo* to conclude that it was *"impossible* to adopt a uniform legal system for all departments." In their opinion, the only suitable form of government for Mexico was the "REPRESENTATIVE POPULAR FEDERAL REPUBLIC." They also pointed out that the *Bases* were illegitimate, laid the foundations to create an aristocracy, and completely annulled civil liberties. The *Bases*, even if modified, would never make a good constitution. One could only infer from these facts that the existing Congress, which had been in session since early 1844, lacked the legitimacy to issue a new charter.38

In a subsequent essay, *La Voz del Pueblo* emphasized the deficiencies inherent in the *Bases Orgánicas*. An anonymous writer characterized the *Bases* as "an ensemble of powers stacked in favor of one man and disguised with the name of a constitution." Any reforms made to this code would only worsen the republic's situation, for the *Bases* were a "monster." In conclusion, the writer made evident the *puros'* increasing displeasure with the constitutional reform policies adopted by Herrera and his advisers. The correspondent questioned the present rulers' promises to act with integrity and promote the nation's welfare. Those pledges, he affirmed, were incompatible with the continued existence of the *Bases*.39

La Voz del Pueblo continued to criticize Herrera's administration for its silence on the issue of constitutional reform. According to a February 19 editorial, the government's reticence on the matter could only imply that the victory of the December 6 movement would be used to confirm the *Bases* as Mexico's constitution. This was a distinct possibility; both Herrera and the *Diario del Gobierno de la República Mexicana* had previously suggested that the *Bases*, duly reformed, could subsist in such a capacity. *La Voz del Pueblo* rejected this prospect. The December 6 movement had not "canonized the *Bases Orgánicas.* . . . *Not now nor ever* could the people be in favor of such an unfortunate code, and it would be a notorious contradiction to curse General Santa Anna and bless the charter he had conferred."[40]

A week later, *La Voz del Pueblo* tried to rouse the departments into openly declaring their allegiance to federalism. If they wished to correct their public finances, the federal system consigned that right. If they wanted to govern themselves under their own laws, that was the essence of federalism. If they yearned for progress, they only had to turn to the time when the federal constitution was in effect. Once Herrera's government witnessed this "explicit and general declaration," it would not vacillate in reestablishing the "regime of salvation" that guaranteed a prosperous future for Mexico.[41]

El Estandarte Nacional had joined *La Voz del Pueblo* in its crusade on behalf of the 1824 constitution and against the *Bases Orgánicas* by the early spring of 1845. Its April 12 editorial highlighted the advantages of federalism. Federalism was the only system that could check the "impudent ambitions of all parties" and prevent reestablishment of the "pernicious system of disorder and arbitrariness" from which Mexico had freed itself. Moreover, even if the *Bases* were "transformed into a perfect model for federalism," their implementation would turn Mexico into "a battlefield." Such an occurrence would insure that the country, in the long run, became "prey to the vile usurpers from the north."[42]

Puro writers also used the reconquest of Texas to emphasize the imperious necessity of reestablishing federalism. On March 26, shortly after Minister Cuevas informed Congress that the United States had approved the annexation of Texas, the editors of *La Voz del Pueblo* clamored for war. Only a united nation, they wrote, could hope for a triumphant campaign. They doubted, however, whether "the reunion of Mexicans without a pact that linked them, without any fixed laws or principles, in a constant state of *circumstances*, always in transition," could achieve that goal. Reestablishment of the 1824 constitution could provide Mexico with a legitimate system of administration. Once state governments were organized in accordance with the 1824 charter, enthusiastic backers of war and those that supported a strong army would increase.[43] *La Voz del Pueblo* wielded similar arguments in subsequent issues. One contributor wrote that federalism would "facilitate the means of making war, excite enthusiasm, and promote sympathies in favor of a government that would never have them if it obstinately persists in denying the popular will."[44]

La Voz del Pueblo continued its offensive in early May by concluding that none of the three alternatives available to Herrera's administration to solve the Texas problem would suffice. The first option, recognizing Texas' independence, was incompatible with the *Bases Orgánicas* and would place Mexico in a perpetual state of war. Mexico would have to confront the United States and Great Britain, which regarded the independence of Texas as an opportunity to expand their commercial interests into California as well. The second choice was to accept the annexation of Texas to the United States, which also violated the *Bases* and jeopardized the territorial integrity of Mexico and other Latin American republics. The third alternative was to admit Texas as one of Mexico's departments under special laws. This was impossible, for other departments could then claim a similar privilege that the government surely would not grant. In short, Mexico had to reestablish federalism.[45]

Besides examining the links between federalism and Texas, *puro*-subsidized newspapers acridly criticized Herrera's foreign policy and its architects. When Minister Cuevas suggested recognizing Texas' independence on March 11, *La Voz del Pueblo* noted that Cuevas proposed in 1838 the idea of "killing those Mexicans who had pronounced for federalism in Tampico [before] fighting the French who were attacking Veracruz." According to an anonymous journalist, Cuevas did not care if Mexico lost Texas or if the nation "came to an end." The minister only wanted to keep his post to "carry out his centralist ideas."[46] When Herrera's government later asked for congressional authorization to enter into negotiations with Texas, *El Estandarte Nacional* demanded that the cabinet resign immediately. The paper characterized the ministers as "miserable pygmies" who advocated legislation that would sink Mexico "into the mire of opprobrium and ignominy."[47]

The criticism of Herrera's appointees paled when compared to that which was published in *El Amigo del Pueblo*, a newspaper that appeared on the public scene in late June 1845. Edited by *santanista* advocate Francisco Lombardo, who aided Gómez Farías in his quest to overthrow Herrera, *El Amigo del Pueblo* began to castigate Herrera's cabinet within two weeks of its debut.[48] A July 7 editorial affirmed that Herrera's advisers had failed to prepare the nation for war. Instead, they had "deadened public spirit as much as possible . . . kindled civil war, and set on fire our domestic divisions." To that effect not only had Herrera's ministers overestimated both the United States' power and Mexico's weaknesses, but they had popularized the idea that war with Texas was "not worth the sacrifices it demanded." *El Amigo del Pueblo* believed that Herrera's cabinet depicted this conflict as a "mask that concealed [the *puros'*] revolutionary and anarchistic aims."[49] Such conduct was unpardonable, and in early August *El Amigo* demanded the resignation of Cuevas and his colleagues.[50]

The cabinet, in fact, did resign in mid-August after learning of Herrera's election as president. Minister of Justice Mariano Riva Palacio commented that the members of the cabinet relinquished their positions to provide the incoming ministers with time and freedom to develop their own policies. Herrera's government had begun to pursue the "very serious matters" of war with the United States and the means of obtaining the resources to wage it. Riva Palacio argued that "the worst of all evils" would befall Mexico if the cabinet could not come to a concensus of opinion.[51] Regardless of how Riva Palacio tried to rationalize about the state of affairs, the *puros'* acrimonious denunciations surely influenced the cabinet members' decision to quit.[52]

Yet any hopes that *El Amigo del Pueblo* may have had about the new cabinet's ability to correct the errors of its predecessor soon vanished. On August 20, departmental authorities in Nuevo León requested weapons and ammunition from the national government to repel attacks by Indian raiders. Minister of War Anaya responded that frontier departments required rifles, not muskets (*fusiles*), and the weapons would have to be ordered from Europe and forwarded as soon as they arrived.[53] Anaya's reply disgusted the editors of *El Amigo*. In their opinion, the current ministers worked with "the same apathy, the same stagnation, the *same gift for erring*" that guided their predecessors.[54]

For a brief moment, it seemed as if these bitter attacks on Herrera's administration would cease. On October 4, *La Voz del Pueblo* reported that the minister of justice had recently informed the national legislature that the government had no intention of making war against Texas, and that proceeds from a September 15 decree authorizing the government to secure a fifteen million peso loan exclusively earmarked to help defray war expenses would be used to offset other administrative responsibilities. Surprisingly, *La Voz* did not launch any invectives against Herrera's regime on the occasion. Instead, *La Voz* recognized having erred about "the justice and necessity of making war." Its editors exhorted the government to make clear whether there were any reasons that made it more prudent to arrange a "honorable peace with the United States." They argued that the nation should not bear the burden of additonal "taxes and sacrifices . . . if, in the end, [war] will not be carried out."[55]

The change in attitude was due in part to the persuasive reasoning of William S. Parrott, who had arrived in Mexico earlier that spring as a confidential agent of the United States.[56] Parrott doubted, however, that he could convince the editors of *El Amigo del Pueblo* to abandon their belligerent tone. He commented that his arguments were "too feeble" to prosper "among gentlemen who rode in coaches and kept boxes at the theater."[57] The respite from the opposition was brief indeed and recriminations against Herrera's regime resurfaced ten days later. *La Voz del Pueblo* argued that the government's urgent necessities were none other than to distribute money raised by the September 15 loan decree "whimsically," to "buy with gold filthy secrets from spies and informers, [and] keep themselves in posts they took by storm, thus vilely deceiving the republic."[58]

Puro-controlled newspapers were not the only ones that clamored for the reconquest of Texas and the reestablishment of federalism. Many public-spirited civilians and departmental assemblies also supported the *puros'* position. José María Lafragua penned the first of these petitions, which appeared in the inaugural edition of *El Estandarte Nacional*. After outlining the fateful consequences of centralism, comparing conditions in several states under that regime and federalism, and enumerating the attempts made to reestablish federalism since 1836, Lafragua made two main demands: the convocation of a special Congress to reform the Constitution of 1824 within six months and the inauguration of the Texas campaign, "solemnly declaring war on the United States."[59]

Similar pleas became a regular feature of public life during the spring and summer of 1845. Between late April and early August, the departmental assemblies of Guanajuato, Zacatecas, and Californias urged Congress to adopt the 1824 constitution. Petitions from residents of Puebla, Oaxaca, and Jalapa requesting the restoration of federalism reached the national legislature, while registries were opened in Ciudad Victoria and Tampico so citizens who wished to sign like petitions could do so. Four members of Chihuahua's departmental assembly, the authors of an anonymous plan published by *La Voz del Pueblo*, and *puro* sympathizer José María del Río, a Mexico City councilman, also worked to reestablish the federal constitution.[60]

Herrera and his *moderado* supporters stubbornly rebuffed these entreaties. In early April, one of the main leaders of the

December 6, 1844, movement, Guanajuato Governor Juan Bautista Morales, characterized the proposal made by his departmental assembly as "very untimely."[61] He explained why reestablishment of federalism was not sensible at the time. Seeing the propaganda value of this communication, government supporters had it published in *El Siglo XIX*.[62] The national legislature also refused to discuss the petitions that had been forwarded by residents of Mexico City and Puebla in favor of restoring the 1824 federal charter; congressmen did debate the request from Jalapa, but it was easily defeated.[63]

The government's attitude annoyed the *puros* beyond measure. An unnamed army officer refuted the arguments raised in Bautista Morales' letter,[64] and Mexico City's press fiercely attacked Congress' refusal to entertain the proposals. The most stinging rebuttal came from the pen of Lafragua in *El Estandarte Nacional*. He noted that Congress' decision regarding the appeals made by residents of Mexico City and Puebla could not be justified under any circumstances. The legislature should have examined the petitioners' ideas "to show the nation that principles and not arbitrary acts, reason and not whim, presided over the discussion of such an important affair." Moreover, the Chamber of Deputies was under no obligation to grant the requests, and its Committee on Constitutional Reforms could challenge the arguments and issue a judgment.[65] This reasoning led Lafragua to conclude that Congress' denial was based on a simple truth. If the national legislature "did not agree to what had been requested it would have had to take off its mask and contradict the general will, and thus Congress would commit suicide, for everyone had faith in its promises of federation." In conclusion, Lafragua noted that both Herrera's government and Congress could still acquire a "glorious name by putting themselves in front of the people who clamor for the Constitution of 1824." He also issued a warning that proved prophetic. Congress would bear full responsibility if it continued to postpone the nation's wishes and the people, as a last resort, turned "to other measures besides reason."[66]

In the end, *puro* newspapers did not limit their attacks on Herrera and his advisers about how they handled the Texas and constitutional reform issues. The way in which Herrera's government manipulated the concept and reality of Mexico's regular army and civic militia also fueled the *puros'* wrath.

Two Specters that Refused to Die

For almost 250 years after the conquest of Mexico, the Viceroyalty of New Spain possessed a minimal colonial military establishment. In 1762 England wrested the fortified city of Havana from Spain, and the Bourbon kings, fearful of further British encroachments upon their possessions, ordered a rapid expansion of their colonial militia. By 1800, the army in New Spain was firmly established as a corporate body, enjoying the full *fuero militar* of Spain. It numbered 6,150 regular army troops and 11,330 provincial militiamen—a significant increase from the estimated 3,000 regulars and an unknown number of provincial militias that bore the burden of defense in 1758. Rather than being defeated by the insurgents during Mexico's struggle for independence, the royalist army led the ultimate break with Spain and its Spanish-recruited creole professional hierarchy remained intact and powerful. As a result, the army retained a strong sense of purpose and, after independence, filled part of the vacuum left by the Spanish regime.[67]

Mexican statesmen like José María Luis Mora and Lorenzo de Zavala recognized that the army's role as arbiter in national politics was an evil that had to be tolerated until civilian power could be consolidated. Nevertheless, they hoped that development of a civic militia, to be composed of citizens in the states and the Federal District, would curb the army's strength. In 1822 lawmakers drew up a decree for the civic militia that would guide later organizational efforts. The law placed the civic militia under the control of local authorities, provided for elected officers, authorized it to preserve order and security, denied militiamen the *fuero*, and included all males (with some exceptions) between the ages of eighteen and fifty.[68]

These guidelines made the civic militia a bastion of federalism and civilian government during the first half of the nineteenth century, bringing it into conflict with high-ranking military officials, conservatives, and some *moderados*, who feared it would be used to destroy the national army and their privileged position in society. Since the sentiments threatened the *puros'* aspirations, their newspapers launched a two-pronged publicity campaign in 1845. First, they sought to diminish the mistrust that had characterized their relations with the regular army since the 1820s. Second, the *puros* wanted to dispel any notion that the civic militia intended to overturn the traditional social order.[69]

The military reforms that Herrera began to implement shortly after taking power allowed the *puros* to strengthen their links with the army. Herrera sought to improve the structure of the army, which was at the root of Mexico's chronic string of military revolts. A September 1823 decree had created twenty-four military commandancies, roughly one for each state and territory. Each unit was in the charge of a state commandant general, who was responsible to the minister of war and ultimately to the commander-in-chief of the Mexican armed forces. According to the 1824 constitution, the republic's chief executive held that post. In the 1830s, however, commandant generals (in the absence of supervision by national bureaucrats) had ample opportunity to abuse their responsibilities and became virtual provincial autocrats by combining authority over civil affairs with their military powers.[70]

To correct the abuses, Herrera's government gave civil magistrates authority over the prosecution of military felons. Herrera and his military advisers instituted a complete separation of powers so civil governors and military chiefs could keep to their respective commands. The government also redrew Mexico's military map, creating four military divisions (also known as cantonments) and five general commands in place of the twenty-two general commandancies then in existence.[71] The measures, however, abetted the *puros'* political goals. *Puro* newspapers criticized the way Herrera's administration handled the armed forces, and the periodicals lavished praise on the army to bolster ties with the *puros'* former enemy.

One of the first articles exemplifying this strategy appeared in the February 1 issue of *La Voz del Pueblo*. Its editors noted that the administration's recent decision to establish four military cantonments would leave frontier departments defenseless. How would the forces stationed in the Toluca cantonment, argued *La Voz*, benefit Durango's population? In addition, the *puro* journal contended that the cantonments would demoralize the armed forces. The army's presence in central Mexico would perpetuate the shameful practice of having military officers strutting and swaggering in departmental capitals, while soldiers stationed near the northern frontier lacked ammunition, weapons, clothing, and even food. The army had to be dispatched to stations where "its honor and duty" demanded. That would provide "discipline" and help the forces fulfill the mission of preserving Mexico's territorial integrity.[72]

El Estandarte Nacional also denounced the installation of the military cantonments. This action, including the appointment of General Paredes to head those forces located in Lagos, was one of the "most direct attacks" against the cause of liberty. The editors of *El Estandarte* argued that Herrera's administration should station as many troops as necessary to protect Mexico's borders. According to *El Estandarte*, not only did the cantonments threaten to deny prestige and glory to the military, but they were irrefutable proof that Herrera and his advisers had no intention of waging war with the United States.[73]

The accusations made by the editors of *La Voz del Pueblo* and *El Estandarte Nacional* no doubt had partisan purposes, but they also possessed a scintilla of truth. Several contemporary observers held that Herrera's administration set up the cantonments with ulterior motives in mind. A correspondent of *moderado* politician Mariano Otero noted that the redistricting indicated clearly that the government feared the *puros*. The opinion of British

Minister Bankhead was even more categorical. He thought that Herrera wanted enough troops to crush federalism and smother any departmental pretensions of autonomy.[74]

The editors of *La Voz del Pueblo* continued to publish articles that sought to bind the *puros* with the regular army over the next few months. On February 15, an essay titled "Army of the Republic" noted that the Mexican army had once been a "fecund spring of discord and disagreeable sensations." At present, however, the army only concerned itself with *"the interests of the people,"* for it was "completely dedicated . . . to the sacred cause of liberty."[75] One month later, *La Voz* called for the Texas campaign and published another conciliatory statement in an attempt at a rapprochement with the army. The gist of the article, which brimmed with optimism, argued that federalism:

> would be as useful to soldiers as it was to other classes; now only one government occupies itself in taking care of your wages and in promoting your progress; [by] adopting that system, each [state] governor, each legislature, each public official will be interested in your fortune. . . . A fatal preoccupation has sometimes separated you from the people; from it you have emerged, you are our brothers, the nation esteems you as its favorite sons and entrusts the defense of its most sacred rights to your valor and patriotism.
>
> The nation will reorganize under the [federal] system of government, the only one capable of making it felicitous and respectable, you will march to Texas to cover yourself with glory, and a legitimate government, assisted by that of the states, will take care that provisions are placed beforehand where it is convenient, and meanwhile . . . the citizen militia will replace you in the garrisons or march at your side to receive examples of valor and good citizenship.[76]

According to *La Voz*, the army should not look at the federation as its enemy. Instead, it should recognize federalism as a friend that would allow it to reconquer Texas with greater ease and efficiency. A Zacatecas newspaper echoed the argument in early April. An anonymous writer affirmed that reestablishing federalism would insure that the soldier who resisted "the Texas campaign until recently . . . would joyfully fight to be out in front, and, with him, the public and the spirited youth will carry the Mexican eagles triumphantly to the [banks of the] Sabine [River] and even to the *capitol* in Washington."[77]

The June 7, 1845, uprising in Mexico City aimed at unseating Herrera as chief executive also tried to lessen suspicions between the *puros* and the military. The introductory segment of the revolt's plan criticized Herrera's government for having squandered "an army of twelve to fifteen thousand well-equipped and well-disciplined troops, with good officers, valiant chiefs, and highly reputed generals." Article Four declared that the army would receive "such organization and splendor that will hereafter stimulate those who undertake the noble military career," while Article Eight promised the army would be duly attended so it could march to Texas.[78] The rebellion was unsuccessful, but it represented another attempt by Valentín Gómez Farías and his followers to establish a cordial relationship with the army, the institution that "maintained itself as the embodiment of the state, as the final repository of sovereignty."[79]

Approximately two months later, on August 9, General Vicente Filisola's troops staged a mutiny known as the Peñasco uprising. Filisola's soldiers had received orders to reinforce General Mariano Arista's Army of the North, but on reaching the hacienda of the Peñasco, near San Luis Potosí, they refused to continue their march on the grounds that they lacked basic necessities. The detachment, however, had been exposed to rumors that portrayed Filisola as a *puro* federalist and confirmed that the government merely pretended to reconquer Texas. Herrera's administration wished to keep the army far away from Mexico City to establish a federal republic.[80]

The Peñasco uprising had, in fact, been organized by General

Paredes, a decided enemy of federalism who was also plotting against Herrera's regime. He wanted to cultivate the army's allegiance and lay the foundation for his December 1845 *pronunciamento*.[81] Nonetheless, the *puros* capitalized on the incident to enhance their image as advocates of the army's welfare. *La Voz del Pueblo* blamed Herrera's regime for the army's reluctance to march to the border. Its editors noted that the Mexican soldier, whose "valor and endurance" were by now self-evident, finally realized that the government contemplated him with the utmost "negligence." If troops generally lacked "even the most miserable nourishment" while stationed in cities, soldiers could only conclude that the administration "would abandon them in the desert." Thus, the government's insistence that the army march north was even worse than imposing the death penalty; it was equivalent to asking the soldiers to commit suicide.[82]

El Amigo del Pueblo also tried to deny the Herrera government of the army's sympathies. On July 26, its editors accused Herrera's ministers of seeing "the enormous desertion of troops consummated since December [1844] to date with the most criminal apathy."[83] Subsequently, *El Amigo* denounced Herrera's administration for squandering the funds of the national treasury, depriving the soldiers of clothes and basic provisions.[84] Furthermore, *El Amigo del Pueblo* published an anonymous letter from San Luis Potosí which affirmed that the government sought to destroy the army with "the most positive determination," that it had never desired to wage war on Texas or the United States, and that army officers realized "an undeniable defeat" awaited them if they marched to Texas without resources. The unknown writer also emphasized the bravery and the combative nature of the Mexican army's officer corps. He noted that they only requested that the size of the army be increased to either 8,000 or 10,000 men, and that these soldiers receive in the desert, not their salaries, but a small ration of food.[85] *La Voz del Pueblo* took full advantage of the opportunity to condemn the government. After republishing the note, its editors demanded that Herrera's administration admit that it lacked the money to pay the troops and yield to a "more popular and prudent" regime.[86]

The mistrust and wariness that Herrera and his advisers exhibited toward the civic militia provided the *puros* with another weapon. Santa Anna had been at the head of an army of 12,000 men in Querétaro when the December 6, 1844, rebellion broke out, so it seemed that the uprising would only succeed if Santa Anna suffered a crushing military defeat. To prepare for the upcoming battle, Congress passed a law on December 9 reviving the civic militia under the name "Voluntarios Defensores de las Leyes." This decree allowed departmental assemblies to organize militia units, and authorized the national government to spend the funds necessary for the militia's maintenance until order was restored. According to nineteenth-century Spanish historian Niceto de Zamacois, as soon as the law was passed "every town wanted to show their alliance to the new order by taking up arms. In Mexico City, merchants, artisans, everybody enlisted to fight against Santa Anna's army." To try to take the capital—which was also defended by 8,000 soldiers led by Generals Paredes and Nicolás Bravo—was to court disaster, so Santa Anna besieged the city of Puebla between January 4 and 11, 1845. The civic militia, however, spearheaded the resistance and refused to surrender before Santa Anna's onslaught.[87] Consequently, many public-minded Mexicans expected the militia to be a pillar of Herrera's administration.

Mexico City's *ayuntamiento* was the first of many voices to plead on behalf of this military force. On January 14, three of its *regidores*—Lafragua, Francisco Modesto Olaguíbel, and Manuel Robredo—proposed asking the departmental government of Mexico for permission to organize the militia units recently raised in the capital. This suggestion led to a furious debate between two other *regidores*, *moderado* sympathizer Mariano Otero, who opposed the proposition, and *puro* supporter Francisco Carbajal, who favored it. Although the debate was inconclusive, Carbajal attempted to gain the upper hand by making two proposals. The first consisted of two parts: it called for an *ayuntamiento* committee to urge Mexico's departmental assembly to ask Congress to sanction the existence of the civic militia as a reform in the *Bases Orgánicas,* and demanded that the units of "Voluntarios Defensores de las Leyes" already standing not be dissolved until Congress reached a decision on the first part of the motion. Carbajal's second proposal called for a *cabildo extraordinario* to be held on the following day because rumors had begun to circulate that the government planned to disarm the civic militia and Carbajal wanted to prevent that. The *ayuntamiento* then adjourned and all suggestions were passed on to a committee formed by Carbajal, Olaguíbel, Robredo, Lafragua and Rafael de la Peña, who delivered their report three months later.[88]

Neither Carbajal's efforts nor the valiant deeds of Puebla's *cívicos* sufficed to prevent the government from carrying out its plans. The Ministry of War issued a circular letter on January 15 that stunned politically conscious Mexicans. The directive ordered the new militia units to disband. Herrera's administration ostensibly wanted militiamen to return to their homes and occupations.[89] This contention, in view of the gallantry displayed by the civic militia during the December 6, 1844, revolt, is dubious at best. Guillermo Prieto referred to the movement as "a paragon of the popular revolution," a judgment that one modern historian has echoed.[90] Given the plebeian nature of the December 6 uprising and considering that on January 13, 1845, an eyewitness reported that groups of *léperos* fired their weapons and shouted *"vivas y mueras"* against several of Santa Anna's ministers as they ran through the streets of Mexico City,[91] it is reasonable to assume that Herrera was convinced that chaos would follow if armed mobs continued to roam the capital. Herrera and his ministers also disarmed the militia because they feared that the force could bring about their downfall just as easily as it had helped topple Santa Anna. Social apprehensions and political expediency, then, were the real reasons behind the January 15 directive.

Discontent aroused by this measure did not take long to find expression. On January 23, *El Monitor Constitucional*, a newspaper generally supportive of Herrera's administration, indicated that the capacity to raise and disband the civic militia belonged to the departments. The December 9, 1844, law only authorized the national government to reduce or augment the units and to spend the funds necessary for organizing them. Consequently, the January 15 circular letter violated the *Bases Orgánicas*. According to the same newspaper, other reasons supported conservation of the "Voluntarios Defensores de las Leyes." Militiamen could preserve internal order and security, which had been badly neglected. It would be advantageous if Mexicans learned how to handle firearms, for a country built on military discipline inspired respect. Finally, relations between soldiers and *cívicos* had been congenial during the December 6, 1844, revolt and this harmony should be preserved, as many of Mexico's problems derived from the "sinister division that evil spirits had ingrained between soldiers and civilians."[92]

El Siglo XIX did not criticize the disbanding of the civic militia severely, but it did point out the militia's importance. On January 25, one of its correspondents wrote that the militia, whose performance in the December 1844 revolt showed it to be an "effective and absolutely necessary tool" to overthrow tyrants, was indispensable to prevent another despotic regime from ruling the country. Since a "feeling of conformity and union" now prevailed in Mexico, it would be "much easier to organize the true national militia without awakening any resentments or the ominous memories that were once associated with it, and without fearing that it would become the instrument of a particular political faction."[93] Three weeks later, an editorial of *El Siglo XIX* noted that both France's monarchical constitution and that of the United States contained clauses that provided for a civic militia. The *Bases Orgánicas*, on the other hand, did not even have "the seed of the institution." The only constitutional reference to militia units that were not part of the national army was to departmental police forces. These, however, had nothing in common with the civic militia. In the doubtful case that the *Bases* had intended those forces to serve as a militia, the president's omnipotent powers could easily neutralize their usefulness. Thus, Mexico's constitution should clearly spell out guidelines for a civic militia.94

At the same time, several legislators requested that Congress revive the *cívicos*. On January 30, *puro* Manuel Alas and four other deputies asked that all regular army corps, with the exception of those assigned to the Army of the North and those stationed in departments threatened by Indian raids, be relieved of active duty. The proposal did not refer specifically to the civic militia, but conservative politician Carlos María Bustamante, who probably erred in suggesting that the intent of Alas' bill was to destroy the army, correctly indicated that the legislation sought to elevate the militia to prominence. A week later, Deputy Antonio María Rivera argued that revival of the civic militia was necessary because many Mexico City militiamen refused to surrender the weapons received in December 1844. Congress did not approve either plan, but supporters of the civic militia were not discouraged. On February 28, Alas and nineteen other deputies asked the national legislature to reform Article 19 of the *Bases* so that Mexican citizens would have the right to belong to the militia. The Chamber of Deputies referred the matter to one of its committees on March 3 (it did not specify which one), but available documentation suggests that the issue was never resolved.95

Congress denied or did not act upon these requests because the *moderados* controlled the legislature. This group, while not openly bickering with the *puros* over the Texas question and that of constitutional reform in early March, had reason to fear that revival of the civic militia would enhance the political influence of their rivals. A subsequent dispatch written by United States agent William S. Parrott lends credence to this assertion. He apprised his superiors on June 10 that Herrera's regime would never arm civilians. The *moderados*' intolerance had been foreseen by *puro* Deputy Alas in early February. He attempted to undermine *moderado* power by demanding, although unsuccessfully, the complete reorganization of Congress.96

Thus, the hopes of those who championed the *cívicos* had been stalled but not for long. At the end of March, Mexico learned that the United States had annexed Texas. Resentment flared immediately; politicians made rash statements and Mexico City newspapers demanded war. At the same time, many correspondents emphasized the role that the civic militia would play in the struggle. According to *El Siglo XIX*, it would not be enough to revive public spirit, acknowledge the urgency of war, or announce that steps had been taken to prepare to fight against a foreign power. Those measures were necessary, but the most important one was to *"arm the nation."* The government had

> no need to fear the civic militia that brought it to power. As long as the cabinet remained the loyal and zealous defender of the rights of the people, it had no reason to mistrust them. The nation would not be fickle: it would only overthrow an administration to preserve its rights and its future, and in that case its downfall would be as just as General Santa Anna's.97

Herrera could no longer hesitate in arming the citizens, according to the editor, for to do so would be to "abandon the country's best interests." In order to carry out a successful campaign, Texas had to be invaded by a large army. The army, however, could not march forth if Mexico's interior remained defenseless, a problem that was "virtually impossible" to overcome with regular army troops. The entire military could only be used in the war without endangering national security by raising, once again, the civic militia.98

On April 1, five *regidores* of the Mexico City *ayuntamiento* asked for reestablishment of the militia. Three—Olaguíbel, Lafragua, and Robredo—had already argued in favor of the civilian force; the two who joined them were José María del Río and Rafael de la Peña. Their arguments now focused on the annexation of Texas. It was "a more horrendous crime than the one committed in 1521," and such a "scandalous offense" had to be punished. The war against Texas was necessary not only to recover the territory, but to prevent Mexico's ruin. American influences in Texas would drain Mexico's natural resources, and it would suffer a "prolonged and agonizing death." Since the most appropriate means of expediting the campaign entailed revival of the militia, the five *regidores* hoped the government would once again call on the *cívicos* to help preserve Mexico's political existence.99

The special committee formed on January 14 was to review this proposal, but *moderado* politicians tried to derail the process. First, Eulalio María Ortega unsuccessfully argued that a new special council had to be formed since three of its members— Lafragua, Robredo, and de la Peña—had subscribed to the April 1 plan. On April 22, the special committee decided to send the proposal to Congress. The entire *ayuntamiento* met three days later to discuss the matter. Four *regidores* voted against the committee's decision: Otero, Ortega, Manuel Reyes Veramendi, and Leopoldo Río de la Loza. Otero also argued that passing resolutions on political issues was not among the *ayuntamiento's* responsibilities. But the *moderados* did not prevail; fourteen *regidores* voted to forward the *ayuntamiento's* April 1, 1845, plan to Congress.100

The final version of the document was an exact replica of the one presented before the *ayuntamiento* on April 1 with one exception: a new concluding paragraph, arguing even more vehemently in favor of the civic militia, had been added. Since Herrera's administration boasted that it owed its existence to the popular will, it had to yield to the people's desires or the war against Texas would remain a distant fantasy. The government could either raise a new army or divide the one that already existed. Either choice, however, would prevent it from waging war. In the first case, a levy and new taxes would have to be imposed to recruit soldiers and cover their expenses, but such measures were "conspicuously hated and harmful." Should

Herrera exercise the second option, Mexico would lack sufficient manpower to fight a war and would probably suffer a
humiliating defeat. The solution to this vexing problem, according to the *ayuntamiento*, was reestablishment of the civic militia.[101]

By the time the *ayuntamiento's* decision reached Congress,
other voices had joined the call for revival of the militia. Several
departmental assemblies (Tamaulipas, Nuevo León, Guanajuato, Durango, Querétaro, and Coahuila) had proposed establishment of a militia when suggesting reforms to the *Bases
Orgánicas.* [102] The April 5 petition penned by Lafragua on behalf
of a group of Mexico City residents called for Congress to "arm
the nation" so the Texas war could be carried out, while *El
Monitor Constitucional Independiente* criticized the government
more than once for disbanding the "Voluntarios Defensores de
las Leyes" and urged recreation of the civic militia.[103] *El
Estandarte Nacional* made the same demands. On May 27, one
correspondent wrote:

> the immediate result of the disarmament of the people [in
> 1835] was the destruction of the federal system; to arm them
> now will bring about the return of federalism: let us not
> smother the popular vote, and a truly national government
> will be ours: because it is a shame that the people are feared
> every time they are armed for Mexico's defense, just as in
> 1838 and in recent times [1845].[104]

A week later, another *El Estandarte* editorial expressed the hope
that *cívicos* would form half of Mexico's army, doubling its size
and allowing professional soldiers to serve as role models for militiamen. Mexico would have to resist the territorial ambitions of
the United States sooner or later, and it had to be ready to fight
honorably to preserve its national integrity.[105]

The annexation of Texas forced Herrera's administration to
act. On April 7, the Chamber of Deputies' Committees on
Foreign Relations and Texas presented Congress with a bill that

authorized the government to arm the militia under the name "Voluntarios de la Independencia y de las Leyes." Although the proposal became law on June 4, supporters of the militia remained convinced that Herrera's regime had not moved fast enough or far enough. The Mexican president and his advisers then tried to make amends for their earlier refusal to revive the militia, but other problems surfaced and made organization of the force a more difficult task.[106]

Herrera's political rivals posed the first problem. They were already critical of his vacillating policies toward the Texas question and toward constitutional reform. Now the administration's failure to act promptly on the militia issue gave them another excuse to plot against Herrera. Prominent among the cabal was *puro* leader Valentín Gómez Farías. Article Eight of the plan he authored in support of the aborted June 7, 1845, coup d'état demanded the immediate reorganization of the civic militia.[107] Herrera's regime also came under criticism because the June 4 legislation that revived the militia included no governing bylaws. To remedy the situation, late in June Minister Cuevas ordered the Council of State to draft an ordinance that would regulate the *cívicos*; Congress made it law on July 7.[108]

The bylaws did not enjoy a warm reception. Although most Mexico City newspapers did not protest the ordinance, *El Amigo del Pueblo* filled the void by printing several articles from regional dailies that pointed out its drawbacks. One Zacatecas paper warned that citizens could only "scoff and jeer" at the bylaws, cautioning that their terms would hasten a popular revolt against the government.[109] A Puebla correspondent provided a more penetrating analysis of the problems inherent in the July 7 decree. The writer concluded that that none of the three classes that made up Mexican society would contribute to the establishment of the civic militia. He indicated that the rich viewed military service with disdain, most of the middle class worked in public administration, and a majority of the lower class consisted of artisans, many of whom did not earn the 200 pesos a year required by the constitution to be considered citizens.[110] The judgment of the Puebla writer was apparently accurate. American agent Parrott echoed his reasoning, noting:

> the class designated for enlistment in the general regulation is not to be found in this country; the rich have neither the patriotism nor the inclination to serve for nothing... the poor day laborer, excluded by the regulation, could not be expected to perform the duty required of him without compensation.

Parrott saw the object of the law as "defeated by the government and council, no doubt intentionally, to avoid the arming of the militia."[111]

Indeed, responsibility for the July 7 militia ordinance most likely rests with General Gabriel Valencia, whom Herrera designated president of the Council of State in early January 1845. The appointment was a reward to Valencia for his support in December 1844.[112] Valencia—who despised the militia—was an opportunist and had tried to seize power in 1841. It would not be unreasonable to suggest that Valencia—who plotted to overthrow Herrera in December 1845 and then also disbanded the militia units raised by the government—purposely drafted an unworkable statute to undermine Herrera's popular support and enhance his own opportunities of reaching the presidency.

Regardless of whether or not Valencia wrote the July 7 law, the results of the recruiting process proved discouraging. On July 16, the Ministry of Foreign Relations authorized departmental officials to take the necessary steps to fulfill the June 4 legislation, and one month later the ministry asked authorities to comment on the militia units raised, the obstacles encountered in organizing them, and the best way of overcoming problems.[113] The reports showed that the militia legislation was grossly inadequate and enrollment lagged far behind expectations. Only thirty-seven men registered in Morelia, twenty-seven in Zacatecas, less than twenty in Tampico, ten in all of Querétaro, three in Guadalajara, two in Aguascalientes, and one in Puebla.[114] No one enrolled in Ciudad Victoria, Guanajuato, or San Luis Potosí.[115] Enlistment in Mexico City, which began on August 20, totalled only eleven on the first day, but no more than thirty had registered after the first week.[116] Enemies of the civic militia, such as Carlos María Bustamante, were overjoyed. He wrote that results in the Mexican capital were not "a great evil, but a . . . *great benefit,* as these soldiers are the former *cívicos* famous for their wickedness and *offenders* of laws and Christian piety. This only proves the common sense of the nation, for it hates and abhors this rabble."[117]

What factors contributed to this dismal failure? *La Voz del Pueblo* attributed the fiasco to "Herrera's whimsical refusal to reestablish the 1824 constitution," but this was mere partisan propaganda.[118] Most departmental governors believed one of the main problems was Article One of the July 7 decree, which stated that enrollment in the civic militia was to be voluntary. Therefore, some governors advocated that service be made mandatory.[119] Other governors remarked that Article Two was particularly objectionable. The clause stipulated that enlistees had to meet five criteria: 1) they would have to be citizens with full rights; 2) not be employed in public administration; 3) not be a day laborer (*jornalero*); 4) not be clergymen; and 5) not be disabled, physically or morally, with any permanent handicaps or vices. Article Three of the ordinance, which prescribed that militia officers would be named by Mexico's president and prevented them from keeping their posts for more than one year, was also deemed detrimental. Departmental leaders urged that local governments be granted the power to name their own militia officers for terms longer than a year. Other governors believed that militiamen ought to be paid a salary for their services as well as being preferred, under equal circumstances, for public positions. Finally, some letters indicated that lack of arms was a problem.[120]

The national government quickly moved to remedy deficiencies. On October 14, then Minister of War General Pedro María Anaya asked the Chamber of Deputies to abolish the prohibition of importing firearms into Mexico. This measure, he argued, would ease establishment of a true civic militia.[121] Six days later, Manuel de la Peña y Peña, minister of foreign relations, addressed the chamber and pointed out the obstacles encountered by the government as it had tried to carry out the June 4 law. The number of men who had taken up arms in the entire republic was "truly ridiculous," and, whether this was due to Mexico's continuous revolts or to the sinister ideas spread by the government's enemies, the administration was indeed saddened to see Mexicans avoid "one of their primary duties." Taking into account many of the governors' suggestions, Peña y Peña unveiled an eight-point plan to serve as a new ordinance to regulate the *cívicos*. Service was to be compulsory for all citizens from the time they could exercise their rights until they were fifty years of age. *Cívicos* could name their own officers and leave their posts to settle personal affairs. Militia units were not to be removed from their districts or departments unless several authorities granted permission. Finally, under the terms of the foreign minister's proposal, only churchmen, public workers, and those who worked in educational or charitable institutions were exempt from service. As of November 24, however, the Chamber of Deputies had not acted upon Anaya's and Peña y Peña's suggestions.[122]

The legislature's delay, whether intentional or not, was but one factor that undermined the government's efforts to create a strong militia. Herrera's administration took other actions that further convinced the *puros* that the government's intention to revive the militia was misleading. In mid-September, General Ignacio Inclán offered to organize the same militia force that Puebla had raised to resist the Spanish invasion led by General Ignacio Barradas in 1829. It would consist of twenty-six infantry battalions, an artillery brigade, four cavalry regiments, and various small pickets. The minister of war tersely responded that the government could not accept this proposal, for Puebla's militiamen would then have to abandon their occupations.[123]

As expected, the press strongly voiced its opposition. One Puebla newspaper recorded that not even the "chief of the Texas bandits" would dare utter such a hypocritical response, for no one doubted that the civic militia should be organized in a way that would allow its members to be ready to protect their homes without having to leave their jobs.[124] In late October, Gómez Farías joined ranks with the press and openly criticized the government for not arming the civic militia. He believed Manuel Gómez Pedraza and Lucas Alamán encouraged the policy to facilitate the establishment of a monarchical regime in Mexico. If the people were armed,

> they would vigorously oppose those that want to give us a king and they would repulse anyone who tried to subdue them, and if the government did not provide them with weapons, they would find them; if that were the case, they would not lack the means to defend themselves during an invasion, and they would not be deceived with lies that arms had been ordered from Europe because there are none in our depots, which is false since there are 14 or 15,000 muskets in Perote, most of which are brand-new while the rest only need minor repairs.[125]

Gómez Farías erred in linking Gómez Pedraza to the monarchist plot, but his judgment underscores the fact that Herrera's policies towards the militia caused many to regard his administration with disdain as 1845 drew to an end. By that time Gómez Farías had already tried to save Mexico from an abysmal fate through an appeal to arms.

III

A Call to Arms

In the early 1840s politically active Mexicans regarded Valentín Gómez Farías as "one of the few civilian leaders who rejected violence as a means of achieving change and as a believer in observing wherever possible constitutional procedures."[1] This reputation was due in part to José María Luis Mora, who, after reflecting on Gómez Farías' 1833-1834 presidential term, concluded that the *puro* leader missed a propitious opportunity to carry out his reforms. Gómez Farías could have mustered the armed forces needed to crush Santa Anna and the supporters of centralism, but he did not because "the measure was unconstitutional, and so that no one would suppose in [him]...a desire to be in command he did not have."[2]

Gómez Farías, however, abandoned pacifism in the 1840s. The lessons of the 1833-1834 experience were not lost on the *puro* statesman, while the indigence that his political peregrinations forced upon his family probably nourished his rebellious streak as well. After Gómez Farías participated in the July 15, 1840, revolt, he told José María Jáuregui and his future son-in-law in 1841 that violent revolution was a necessity, and two years later he advocated rebellion to prevent General Antonio López de Santa Anna from using the *Bases Orgánicas* to gain permanent political power.3 Yet Gómez Farías' fanaticism was not extreme. He began to scheme to overthrow General José Joaquin Herrera's administration in 1845 only after it became clear that Herrera and his advisers did not intend to change their policies on constitutional reform and on the Texas question. In the end, Gómez Farías' machinations weakened Herrera's government and paved the way for its downfall. As the year came to a close, however, the *puros* did not have the support to capitalize on the circumstances and seize power.

The Making of a Rebel

In much the same manner as the *puro* newspaper *La Voz del Pueblo*, Gómez Farías first thought that Herrera's regime would provide an antidote for Mexico's problems. From his exile in New Orleans Gómez Farías wished Herrera well as chief executive, cautioning him not to make any false promises and warning him that conditions were dangerous and his task difficult. "I hope"—the *puro* leader wrote—that "a ray of light descends upon your head so that you may successfully fulfill your mission."4 Gómez Farías believed that Herrera needed to take advantage of the era inaugurated by the December 6 revolt to eliminate the "political deformities" and the "monstrous errors" of the *Bases Orgánicas*. Gómez Farías also advocated lowering taxes, fostering education, and taking care of all branches of public administration.5

The *puro* leader—perhaps because he expected to be called on by Herrera to assist with the implementation of these objectives—moved to secure the support of the army.6 He sought General Adrian Woll's backing and requested that Antonio Canales, an influential regional leader in northeastern Mexico,

solicit a rapprochement with General Mariano Arista, the officer commanding the Army of the North who held steadfast to
the idea that the *puros* threatened the army's best interests. The
time had come, pleaded Gómez Farías, to "set aside all complaints, all personal considerations," and "sacrifice private sentiments" on behalf of the nation.7 Whether Arista responded to
Gómez Farías' appeal remains a mystery; it is not far-fetched to
suppose, however, that Gómez Farías learned through one of
his informants that efforts to sway Arista failed. Arista's disposition toward the *puros* remained fixed through 1845: he was
determined to "crush any of the *sansculottes'* rash attempts to
seize power."8

Arista's attitude must have disappointed Gómez Farías, but it
was Herrera's vacillating foreign and domestic policies that led
the *puro* leader in April 1845 to solicit the views of others on the
questions of the return to federalism, the Texas matter, and war
with the United States. Gómez Farías' political stock had risen by
late 1844 as disenchantment with Santa Anna's dictatorship grew
(one acquaintance wrote that several of his former enemies in
1833 "had recognized their error" and regarded Gómez Farías as
"the only man who could save the situation"9), and the *puro*
statesman concluded that he had to act quickly to rescue Mexico
from imminent disaster. Luis Gago was among the first men
Gómez Farías contacted. The *puro* politician argued that the
opinions advocated in the inaugural issue of *El Estandarte
Nacional* were the only ones that would lead to a successful,
"just, and indispensable war" against the United States. Gómez
Farías encouraged Gago to spread such views quickly across
Veracruz to influence public opinion. If he delayed, Mexico
would suffer "the most fatal results."10

Two men from Camargo who participated in federalist uprisings during the late 1830s and early 1840s shared Gómez Farías'
anxiety. Antonio Canales was pleased with the *puro* leader's presence in the capital, since Gómez Farías' profound knowledge
about the Americans would halt the spread of anti-war attitudes.
Canales pointed out that the distance between the Sabine and

Bravo Rivers was less than that which separated Camargo from Querétaro, and if the Americans controlled navigation on the Bravo it would be "almost impossible . . . to contain their advance." He added that Mexico should not pass on misery and slavery to its children. It would be preferable to die than to allow such an insult.[11] José María Carvajal warned that the objectives stated in the decree annexing Texas to the United States were false. That legislation should be interpreted according to its spirit, for its real aim was to seize two times, maybe four times, the size of the annexed territory.[12]

Other correspondents of Gómez Farías were troubled by Herrera's hesitance to act. Tamaulipas resident José Núñez de Cáceres remarked that reintroduction of the federal system would be accompanied by "havoc and all the disturbances consequent to the use of force" if Herrera and his cabinet squandered the opportunity to institute a "natural and non-violent" change. Núñez de Cáceres doubted, however, that Mexico could weather yet another political revolt.[13] One of Durango's most distinguished intellectuals, José Fernando Ramírez, also counseled Gómez Farías to move with prudence. Ramírez believed that the critical circumstances that Mexico faced did not make the present moment the most appropriate time to discuss the restoration of federalism. Since the country's independence could be at risk, Mexicans should back any administration to face the difficulties inherent in a war for Texas.[14]

By late May 1845, however, Gómez Farías' confidants no longer shared Núñez de Cáceres' and Ramírez' conservative advice. Bernardo González Angulo, a former foreign secretary and minister of finance, lamented that since the Battle of San Jacinto in 1836 Mexico's governments had taken money away from the people but had left Texas—an "interesting and beautiful possession"—completely abandoned.[15] According to Pedro Zubieta, a *puro* sympathizer from Jalisco, only a return to the 1824 constitution and a new government could prevent Mexico from falling into an "abyss."[16] Zacatecas politician Manuel González Cosío condemned the December 6 movement for it had placed

Mexico in the hands of "a more terrible and infamous enemy than the damned cripple [Santa Anna]." The country was ruled by a "hypocritical, astute, beguiling, and scheming party" that had sold itself out to Great Britain and to European interests. Only a "strong and violent revolution" could restore federalism, but González Cosío felt that the elements that would guarantee success did not exist.[17] Francisco Vital Fernández expressed surprise at the government's decision to "perpetuate . . . the aristocratic tendencies" of the *Bases Orgánicas*. The possible loss of Mexico's northern departments, should Texas become independent or be annexed by the United States, also concerned Vital Fernández. In his opinion, Herrera's administration ignored this predicament because it feared the likely consequences of war. War would compel the government to arm the people, who then could demand restoration of the Constitution of 1824.[18]

Despite some differences of opinion about the possibility of rebellion, most of Gómez Farías' correspondents agreed that the *Bases Orgánicas* were flawed, that Herrera's regime did not intend to reestablish the 1824 charter, and that its policies toward the Texas question were dangerous. The *puros'* growing strength as of mid-April gave Gómez Farías confidence that Herrera could be ousted.[19] He began to mobilize his supporters and tried to pacify potential foes.

June 7, 1845

To insure success for the insurrection that would break out on June 7, *puro* loyalists moved to get the support of both the regular army and the *santanistas*. Although Santa Anna did not "build any enduring military constituency" during the central republic, high-ranking generals remained loyal to him in the spring of 1845. While many career military officers disliked the *puros*, their recent journalistic fanfare notwithstanding, a number had been relieved of command by Herrera because of their association with Santa Anna, which more closely allied them with the *puros* than the *moderados*. Herrera's efforts to reduce the size and status of the army played right into Gómez Farías' hands.[20]

Santa Anna's incarceration during the early spring of 1845 gave his followers another motive to resent Herrera's administration and to join forces with the *puros*. After a group of Indians captured Santa Anna in mid-January 1845 near the town of Xico, Veracruz, Congress indicted him for treason, transferred him to Perote's prison, and ordered him to stand trial. To occupy his time, Santa Anna wrote numerous letters protesting his treatment, one noting that his situation as a prisoner of war in Texas during the 1830s had been significantly better. While Santa Anna most likely exaggerated conditions in Perote, his backers no doubt blamed Herrera for their fallen leader's sufferings.[21]

As Santa Anna waited for the case against him to commence, his adherents embraced the banner of federalism. The editors of *El Monitor Constitucional* alerted the public to the dangers inherent in this irreverent association on March 11. The editors pointed out that the *santanistas* had been extoling the 1824 constitution to excite public opinion and foster a civil war—the one constant "element of life and power" for Santa Anna. A proclamation of federalism would "intoxicate the nation with enthusiasm, and make it forget the crimes and errors of the past provisional administration, whose examination they [the *santanistas*] would like to avoid at all costs."[22] *El Monitor's* warning was not empty. Proof of the *santanistas'* strength and resilience were their endeavors to spark two rebellions against Herrera during March. Government agents thwarted the rebels' plans, arresting fifty to sixty army officers on one occasion and later apprehending two men—General José Vicente Miñón and civilian Guadalupe Perdigón Garay—who assisted Gómez Farías' subsequent efforts to overthrow Herrera.[23]

It is important to note, however, that Gómez Farías did not sanction an alliance between *puros* and *santanistas* in March 1845. In late February, Francisco Modesto Olaguíbel warned Gómez Farías that his delay in coming to Mexico City from Veracruz gave his enemies time to plot against him. He did not refer to Santa Anna's followers by name, but Olaguíbel probably had the *santanistas* in mind. Gómez Farías' response, although equally vague, did not hint at any cooperation with his rivals. Moreover, Gómez Farías only began to correspond with federalist statesmen to gauge public opinion toward Herrera's administration in early April, suggesting that he was not ready to resort to arms at that time. Nevertheless, the March 1845 disturbances, and the ready access Santa Anna's followers had to the prisoner pointed to a collaboration between lesser *puro* supporters and *santanistas*.[24]

Various departmental governors provided more evidence that by early April *santanistas* and *puro* activists were working together against Herrera. A friend of Guanajuato Governor Juan Bautista Morales overheard General Manuel María Lombardini remark that the army, which was to march to Texas, would rebel and name Santa Anna its commanding general once the troops assembled. Santa Anna, according to the conversation, was the "only man in the republic capable of waging the campaign."[25] One month later, Bautista Morales remarked that the *puros* would use Santa Anna to proclaim federalism, after which they would depose him in favor of Gómez Farías.[26] Past episodes of *puro* popular agitation frightened Puebla's leading civil authority; he noticed "symptoms and indications of a *pronunciamiento* in favor of the federation of the years [18]29 and [18]33."[27] The Veracruz governor was alarmed because various civilians and disgruntled army officers had gathered at the departmental capital to plan a coup d'état to establish federalism under Santa Anna's name.[28]

The prospect of an alliance between *santanistas* and *puros* worried some of Gómez Farías' friends and supporters. In late April, General Juan Alvarez, head of the *tierra caliente* in southwestern Mexico, warned Olaguíbel of a scheme afoot in Mexico City with goals "so devious that they lack[ed] the slightest shred of liberty even if sweetened with federalism." In Alvarez' opinion, the "hidden hero" (Santa Anna) who pretended to care about the republic's welfare would not hesitate to "sacrifice you and other true liberals should he prevail."[29] Similar admonitions reached González Angulo in Puebla a few weeks later. He reminded Gómez Farías that Santa Anna, after gaining power with the federalists' help in 1832, gave "in to the entreaties and counsel of [Gómez Farías'] present enemies . . . and toppled the federation." Santa Anna's perfidy should not be forgotten; the federalists' triumph would be "transitory and ephemeral" if circumstances repeated themselves.[30] Several of Gómez Farías' most intimate advisers paid little attention to these warnings and their disregard proved fateful for the *puros'* plans.

Why did some of Gómez Farías' closest supporters collaborate with Santa Anna and his agents? One historian has suggested that the *puros'* "zealous desire for war no doubt helps explain their willingness to combine with their previous archenemies."[31] Nonetheless, the judgment of Gómez Farías' loyalists is perplexing in light of Santa Anna's notorious political opportunism and the fact that former *santanista* officers, as late as June 7, had been overheard in Mexico City boasting with the "greatest impudence" about the real objective of the coup that they would soon lead. Its sole purpose was "to destroy the actual government, abolish the federation, and bring about the return of . . . Santa Anna."[32] In the final analysis, it appears that a number of *puro* politicians, with the exception of Gómez Farías, decided to take a calculated gamble. They allied themselves with the *santanistas* to grab political power. Once firmly in control, as José María Lafragua explained in his retrospective account of the years 1845-1848, the *puros* hoped to foil Santa Anna's plans and restrain his and the army's influence by establishing a strong civic militia.[33]

Preparations for the revolt against Herrera were underway by early May 1845 when Gómez Farías obtained the support of General Miñón.[34] Later that month, Gómez Farías apprised Miñón that General Valentín Canalizo had joined the conspiracy, that he should be ready to "act without delay," and that he would soon receive a copy of the plan and manifesto. Goméz Farías also made it clear that the success of the coup d'état depended on notifying those involved that Santa Anna would not participate in it. Everything related to the upcoming struggle had to be "truly patriotic."35

Miñón responded five days later with news that surely delighted Gómez Farías. The plotters eagerly awaited his orders to "act as planned." He added that since the bishop of Puebla— Francisco Pablo de Vázquez—was an influential man "in the best disposition with regards to our cause," it would be convenient to dispel the idea that Gómez Farías was his personal enemy.36 The comment implied that the revolt would be supported by a high-ranking clergyman, a welcome development in light of Gómez Farías' anticlerical reputation and a remark attributed to the bishop. Pablo de Vázquez had said that he would rather support "one who likes cockfights [Santa Anna]" than a person "who amuses himself by persecuting religion and destroying everything to put it in a federal fashion [Gómez Farías]."37 Gómez Farías followed Miñón's advice and tried to secure the good will of Puebla's leading cleric, writing Pablo de Vázquez that "he was not a personal enemy of anybody, notwithstanding his opinions," especially of one "so commendable for his services, wisdom, and virtues."38 The bishop's response, if any, remains unknown.

The state of alarm that prevailed in Mexico City also fostered unbridled optimism among the plotters. On the evening of June 2, a rumor that General José Ignacio Basadre and Gómez Farías were conspiring to proclaim the federation startled city residents.39 Three days later, Gómez Farías pointed out that Herrera's government was "extremely apprehensive." Public opinion against the *moderado* administration was so widespread that it found support even in the army. Mexican soldiers, wrote the *puro* leader, were unwilling "to kill their compatriots" to sustain a regime that only "fooled and exploit[ed] them." The people of Mexico City and other departments "eagerly awaited" the opportunity to help "bring about a change."40

The developments worried Herrera and his advisers and they took steps to forestall a coup. Since the government knew it was too "weak and impotent to subdue" Gómez Farías, in early May it tried to quiet the *puro* chief by naming him to a vacancy in the Senate. But the plan, which apparently was devised by *moderado* statesman Manuel Gómez Pedraza, went astray after Gómez Farías lost the election. Gómez Farías was named senator a few weeks later after several departmental assemblies renominated him for the post, but he tried to avoid the office. On June 2 Gómez Farías asked Senator Ignacio Trigueros not to support his candidacy, arguing that he did not want to sit with Gómez Pedraza. In fact, Gómez Farías probably did not want to belong to a body that would be dissolved if the coup proved successful.[41]

On May 24, in another effort to prevent an armed insurrection, Congress issued a verdict in the case against Santa Anna. Instead of holding a court-martial for Santa Anna (he might have been executed if found guilty), Congress granted amnesty to all those who resisted the December 6 movement except Santa Anna and his ministers; the complaint against Santa Anna would be dropped if he left the country immediately and forever. Cognizant of the plot against Herrera, Santa Anna requested permission to delay his exile for two weeks. The government, however, denied his petition and he sailed for Venezuela on June 3.[42]

Although Santa Anna's exile rattled the plotters, they had adopted several meticulous measures that they hoped would lead to success. First, the conspirators had ample financial assistance. Francisco de Paula Mora, who helped sponsor *La Voz del Pueblo*, contributed 2,000 pesos, and General Canalizo added an undisclosed amount.[43] The money probably formed part of the 8,000 pesos later given to the troops who abetted the uprising. Second, General José María Tornel, whom contemporaries regarded as a Santa Anna lackey, tried to insure the backing of several unspecified departments and Querétaro's military cantonment.[44] Third, Olaguíbel and other *puros* visited Mexico City's precincts to incite the urban masses to join the uprising. The plotters also procured the assistance of the entire Mexico

City garrison and half the 4th Infantry Regiment, which was posted in the capital.45

The conspirators' hopes were also buoyed because two prominent military officers joined the conspiracy. Lafragua and Olaguíbel took advantage of their role as the attorneys representing Generals Canalizo and Basadre, on trial for their role as Santa Anna's ministers in 1844, to secure their services. Canalizo won Lafragua's and Olaguíbel's trust by assuring them that the sole objective of the November 29, 1844, decree had been to facilitate prosecution of the war with Texas. Available documentation does not reveal what pretext Basadre used, but he probably employed a similar one. Then, like Santa Anna, both Basadre and Canalizo tried to extend their stay in Mexico City as the day planned for the revolt drew closer. In early June they requested that the Supreme Court of Justice set them free on bail for at least one month to settle their personal and family affairs before leaving the country. Basadre also asked Gómez Pedraza to help him with his plea.46

Designed to gain the rebels widespread public backing, Gómez Farías' plan to justify the rebellion exemplified his political acumen. The document made no reference to Santa Anna and did not antagonize those institutions whose support was required to put the *puros* in power. Its introduction echoed the complaints leveled by *La Voz del Pueblo* and *El Estandarte Nacional* against Herrera's regime. While the army remained neglected in central Mexico, the government was accused of indifference about the problems in Texas. In addition, Congress had erred by rejecting those petitioners who called for the restoration of federalism and failing to organize the civic militia. The plan featured eight articles calling for, among other things, the immediate reestablishment of the 1824 constitution, the meeting of a special reform Congress within four months charged with revising that charter, and the organization of the civic militia. The plan also promised the preservation of Catholicism, clerical and military *fueros*, and the fulfillment of all of the army's needs.47

The plotters still had to overcome one final hurdle. With Canalizo and Basadre in prison and Miñón stationed in Puebla, Gómez Farías and his associates had to find a leader to command the revolt in Mexico City. Lafragua and Olaguíbel met with General Joaquín Rangel, whose past relationship with Santa Anna and the resentment he harbored toward Herrera's regime made him an ideal choice. Not only was Rangel the former artillery chief of Santa Anna's army, but since early 1845 he had been constantly harassed by Herrera's minister of war, General Pedro García Conde. Following his arrest on December 27, 1844, while guarding Santa Anna's ammunition train, Rangel was tried by a military court *(tribunal de artillería)* but set free on bail. The court's decision upset García Conde, who was jealous of Rangel because he had lost various military commissions and business deals (Rangel was a well-known building contractor) to the artilleryman. García Conde placed Rangel under house arrest, sent numerous insiders to spy on him, and deprived Rangel, who had been diagnosed as an apoplectic, of medical care. Finally, on March 27 García Conde ordered Rangel out of Mexico City; by mid-April Rangel was in Huichapan, a small town in the department of Hidalgo.[48]

The circumstances surrounding Rangel's return to Mexico City cannot be determined, but he accepted Olaguíbel's and Lafragua's invitation to lead the uprising and took a number of steps that boded well for the rebels. He surveyed the National Palace's botanical garden on the eve of the revolt to direct the artillery at the time of the attack. More importantly, Rangel chose both the day for the uprising and the unit to lead the rebellion with great care. Rangel picked the "Granaderos de la Guardia de los Supremos Poderes," a battalion quartered in the small patio of the National Palace, for his troops. June 7, which fell on a Saturday—a day marked for a full review of weapons and uniforms—was the chosen date. It was almost certain that the National Palace guard would not be alarmed when the Granaderos marched out in formation, assuring the rebels easy access to the palace.[49] The plotters only had to wait the clarion call to battle, which came in mid-afternoon on June 7.

At three o'clock, the bells of Mexico City's cathedral began to peal and gunshots rang out. The Granaderos, under the command of Captain Juan Othón, stormed the National Palace yelling "*Federación y Santa Anna.*" At first it seemed that the conspirators would prevail: they captured the minister of finance and came close to grabbing Herrera. The president, however, remained calm, even convincing the mutineers to remain loyal to the government. In a counter attack, Colonel José María Uraga arrived at the National Palace with the 4th Infantry Regiment and restored order following a brief skirmish in which the Granaderos were defeated and Captain Othón killed. Herrera, escorted only by the minister of war and Gómez Pedraza, mounted his horse and rode through the capital immediately after the attempted coup to put to rest rumors of his fate. Jubilant crowds cheered the president as he passed. It seemed that his administration had emerged unscathed from the day's events.[50]

Notwithstanding Herrera's bravery and despite the plotters' careful preparations, the conspirators made several mistakes that help explain why the revolt collapsed so rapidly. First, Captain Othón entered the National Palace half an hour ahead of schedule, and his eagerness disrupted the timing of the coup.[51] Gómez Farías' correspondence, though scanty on the details, indicates that this was a major blunder. The *puro* leader observed: "If two scatterbrained and conceited youngsters [the second man remains unknown] had not moved ahead of time, the Constitution of 1824 would have been reestablished in a few short hours; but their haste laid to waste all our efforts."[52] The bearing of the 4th Infantry Regiment commander also contributed to the failure. Colonel Uraga betrayed the conspirators at the last minute and chose to support the government. Francisco Mejía, who served as General Rangel's clerk at the time, explained in his memoirs that Rangel visited the Granaderos and the 4th Infantry Regiment on the morning of June 7. After giving 4,000 pesos to

Captain Othón, Rangel told Mejía to pay Uraga a similar amount and get a receipt. Uraga, however, took the money, informed Mejía that he would not give him a voucher, and advised him to leave at once unless he wanted to be arrested.53 Uraga made a tidy profit, emerged as one of the heroes of the day, and he avoided leaving any evidence that the government could use to implicate him with the rebels.

The coup's most serious flaw, however, was the use of Santa Anna's name during the initial attack. It gave the mutiny a different twist than Gómez Farías had in mind and deprived the uprising of popular support. According to *La Voz del Pueblo*, the people rejected the revolt because it did not defend the liberal principles or institutions they coveted. If Rangel had proclaimed the "holy cause" that the *puros* defended, the results of the uprising would have been different. *La Voz'* editors hoped that the "horrors of a fratricidal war" remained fresh in Herrera's memory so he would uphold "the will of the nation which favored the federal system."54 The journal later absolved the *puros* from participation in the revolt. Members of the federalist party acted "just as the people, who followed their instincts that afternoon: [they] appeared to join the rebels while [they] understood that they proclaimed the federation, and broke away from them once [they] heard they only cheered General Santa Anna." The sole wish of *La Voz del Pueblo* was "the federal system without ... Santa Anna."55

El Siglo XIX also exonerated supporters of federalism from any complicity. According to its editors, the federalist party responded to the rebels' call "with the most profound indignation. The entire capital saw that in the moments of danger the men who had worked on behalf of the federation with the most constancy did not hesitate to side with General Herrera, rejecting the federation offered by D[on] Joaquín Rangel."56 Responsibility for the revolt rested solely with the *santanistas*, whose existence many had denied until then. Other newspapers, such as *El Monitor Constitucional Independiente* and *El Amigo del Pueblo*, rationalized the rebellion's failure in a similar manner.57

The June 7 episode provided Herrera's administration with an excellent opportunity to consolidate its grip over Mexico's political scenario. In the words of *El Siglo XIX*, the peaceful conduct of the "naturally turbulent" urban masses during the mutiny proffered additional proof that the government still enjoyed ample popular support.[58] Members of Mexico City's elite echoed this sentiment. They were relieved because Herrera's victory over the "demagogues" prevented the looting and ransacking of the capital.[59] Another 1828 Parián riot had been averted. But Herrera failed to capitalize and carried on with his unpopular policies on Texas, the army, and constitutional reform. His inflexibility, coupled with the inability of his regime's judicial apparatus to punish the coup's perpetrators adequately, damaged his administration's credibility and paved the way for its downfall in December 1845.

Leading diplomatic and political figures made it known in the days following the rebellion that the government should deal firmly with the insurgents. British Minister Bankhead hoped that some rebels received a just punishment, for he doubted that Mexico City would remain tranquil if Herrera's regime did not "assume some energy and resolution."[60] Bustamante was more adamant and noted that Rangel should be "hanged from the balconies of the [National] Palace."[61] Three correspondents to the minister of justice held similar opinions. According to Atilano Sánchez, only the government would be harmed if the mutiny's chiefs were not executed. Another amnesty (such as the one granted to Santa Anna and his ministers in May) would be a sign of fear and weakness; the conspirators should end up in the San Juan Ulúa prison if they did not "hang in the gallows."[62] Francisco Facio, who feared the upcoming August presidential elections would provoke a crisis that might lead to more revolts, hoped that the events of June 7 spurred the government to "display a little energy and rigor."[63] General Mariano Paredes y Arrillaga also warned that it was imperative to make an example out of the conspirators. Otherwise they would continue plotting until they brought the government down.[64]

Aware of public opinion, Herrera relentlessly prosecuted those suspected of participating in the uprising. General Tornel received orders to report to the Army of the North on the morning of June 8.[65] Generals Pedro Lemus, José María Heredia, José Ignacio Gutiérrez, Luis Pinzón, and José Mariano Salas were scattered throughout the country, while Generals Canalizo and Basadre were transferred to the dungeon fortresses of Perote and San Juan Ulúa. Herrera's emissaries also arrested Colonels Manuel María Giménez, Tomás Santibañez and Benito Zanca, Captain Mariano Aguada, Lieutenant Ignacio Jáuregui, civilian Bernardino Alcalde, and several officers of the Granaderos battalion. But the regime's efforts to punish Olaguíbel, Lafragua, and Gómez Farías were less successful, further undermining Herrera's prestige among politically aware Mexicans.[66]

Both Olaguíbel and Lafragua managed to avoid the clutches of Herrera's agents. The government could not find sufficient evidence to indict Olaguíbel, who was strolling through the streets of Mexico City by June 21.[67] Lafragua's ties with the *moderados* prior to 1845 earned him leniency but such treatment accentuated the lack of determination that often characterized Herrera's administration. On June 12, Lafragua asked the government to allow him to go into exile; he hoped to set sail for France eight days later. Gómez Pedraza read Lafragua's request at a cabinet meeting and told Lafragua that the government would not object. In the end, Lafragua did not get past the city of Jalapa, Veracruz. He returned to Mexico City in late September and reoccupied his post in the *ayuntamiento*.[68]

Herrera's agents showed more energy pursuing Gómez Farías, but to no avail. Gómez Farías spent the evening of June 6 at the home of close friends near Mexico City. He learned of his election to the Senate on the following morning, but went into hiding after the coup. Since Gómez Farías proved elusive, Herrera's administration launched a psychological war against him, spreading rumors that his correspondence had been intercepted, that it had evidence of his complicity in the revolt, and that many of those arrested had denounced him as the rebellion's leader.

Minister of Foreign Relations Luis G. Cuevas accused Gómez Farías of being one of the plotters of the June 7 uprising before the Senate's Grand Jury, but this attempt to prosecute Gómez Farías proved unsuccessful. The Grand Jury dismissed the proceedings against the *puro* activist because of insufficient evidence.[69]

The court martial of General Rangel, who had been captured a few days after the revolt, further diminished the reputation of Herrera's government. When the trial began on June 14, the prosecutor asked that Rangel, who was defended by Colonel Tomás Requena, receive the death penalty. After having just one day to prepare a case, Requena argued that Rangel found out about the revolt accidentally as he walked past the Granaderos quarters. He pointed out that Rangel had been dressed as a civilian and no officer would consider wearing that type of clothing for a military operation. According to Requena, Rangel joined the mutinous troops only after failing to dissuade Captain Othón from attacking the National Palace and solely with the goal of preventing a greater tragedy. In the end, the *Consejo de Guerra* stripped Rangel of his job and sentenced him to a ten-year prison term. The *Suprema Corte Marcial* later modified the verdict to the prison term only because Rangel, as a retired officer, could not be divested of his position.[70]

These two decisions disgusted supporters of Herrera's regime. *El Siglo XIX* wrote that Rangel's judges invited "all those who stand to gain something from the chaos of our revolutions to launch them without fear."[71] Minister of Justice Mariano Riva Palacio described the *Consejo de Guerra's* verdict as "a thousand times worse than the revolt."[72] Even the usually cautious Herrera castigated Rangel's judges when he addressed Congress early in July. He publicly lamented that the magistrates had ignored legislation that designated Rangel's crime "to be so grave, so pernicious, as the first fundamental [rights] of all societies are respected and sacred." Civil war would "move forward in the most abhorrent manner" whenever tribunals acted "according to political considerations or personal opinions." Herrera added that a Congress or a government capable of forgiveness would be regarded as "sublime," but that "the foundations of the social edifice" would crumble if those "charged with making justice triumph" misused that power. In closing, Herrera noted that he could not "disregard such a deplorable event because public opinion and the republic's morality demand[ed]" that he "condemn such an error, which is even less excusable because the [conduct of the] actual administration has been conciliatory and humane."73

Why did the military courts fail to punish Rangel? Besides demonstrating esprit de corps and loyalty to a member of the military caste, the personal attributes of the judges no doubt influenced their verdicts. One Mexican commentator pointed out that some of the men who made up the *Consejo de Guerra* had committed crimes similar to Rangel's, while the magistrates of the *Suprema Corte Marcial* were hypocritical—they had accepted Judge José María Jáuregui's version of the events of June 7 (Jáuregui's son, Ignacio, had been an accomplice of the plotters). Jáuregui persuaded them that Rangel sought to defend Herrera on that afternoon. Confidential United States agent William S. Parrott echoed the opinion, reporting that public opinion in Mexico City attributed the *Consejo de Guerra's* judgment to the fact that most of its members were compromised in the revolt, and those who were not were old and afraid.74

In an attempt to play down the scandal caused by the sentences and to show its resolve, Congress dissolved the *Suprema Corte Marcial* on July 1, and one week later the minister of war brought charges before the Senate against the tribunal for its verdict in Rangel's case.75 The measures could not repair damage already done. The verdicts provided the *puros* with additional ammunition to lambaste Herrera's administration. Just as importantly, Herrera's political enemies felt free to organize more plots against the government. As Spanish Minister Bermúdez de Castro pointed out, "the scandalous impunity with which the courts have left the authors of the June 7th mutiny has singularly encouraged the rebels, and it is to be feared that a new revolt in favor of the federation will explode once the troops march to Texas."[76]

Besieged by Revolution

Bermúdez de Castro's words rang prophetically. On June 14, General Ignacio Martínez led a revolt in Tabasco. The rebellion's manifesto echoed the criticisms levied by *puro*-controlled newspapers about Texas and constitutional reform. The document also justified the uprising on two other issues: it opposed a May 10, 1845, circular letter from the Ministry of War that prohibited the army from using its right of petition *(derecho de petición)* to participate in political affairs, as well as Herrera's intention to reincorporate Yucatán into the Mexican union by military means. The rebels demanded reestablishment of the 1824 constitution "with those reforms beneficial to the nation's welfare and happiness," and the reinstatement of government officials deposed in 1834 (Santa Anna being the sole exception).[77]

Gómez Farías tried to capitalize on developments in Tabasco. Early in July he counseled General Martínez to seek support in Chiapas and Oaxaca and to disregard the entreaties of government emissaries.[78] The *puro* activist also praised Colonel Felipe Montero for doing in Tabasco "what we had long contemplated," and recommended that Tabasco's rebels adopt Articles 3 and 5 of General Rangel's plan. The articles charged the special Congress with the election of a provisional chief executive, insuring that the presidency would not automatically fall upon Gómez Farías. Politically aware Mexicans might not support the rebellion if they believed its sole aim was to place him in power.[79] Gómez Farías also tried to put several army officers who shared his ideas in contact with Tabasco's rebels but his efforts were unproductive. Nearby departments did not support the rebellion, and it collapsed in late September.[80]

Meanwhile, a variety of rumors and incidents heightened the trepidations of Mexico City's *hombres de bien*, who viewed the likelihood of a *puro*-led revolt with increasing apprehension. The return of General Anastasio Bustamante to Mexico in mid-June prompted some to speculate whether he would become the *puros'* leader. Alarmed merchants closed their shops on the afternoon of June 16 when an immense *leperada* congregated at the main plaza following gunshots near the Salto del Agua precinct.[81] Hearsay also had it that the *ayuntamiento* would lead a city-wide *pronunciamiento* in favor of the Tabasco plan.[82] The possibility, according to Bustamante, was not far-fetched. Not only did "the slightest alarm bring swarms of *léperos* out of the earth as if they were mosquitos," but the urban poor, which outnumbered the regular army troops, were heavily armed and had been encouraged with promises of plunder.[83]

The rumbling underscored the increasingly precarious position of Herrera's regime. The best indicator of its tribulations was that Herrera apparently considered resigning his post.[84] Yet the government tried to maintain its composure despite the pitfalls it faced. On July 22, Minister of Foreign Relations Cuevas wrote General Paredes that no one in Mexico City paid any attention to the "ridiculous efforts made by the ungovernable to sow discord."[85] Subsequent dispatches from Cuevas reassured Paredes that Mexico's situation improved daily due to

> the nation's good sense and, with the exception of a few rioters, everyone else is in agreement with the existing order.... Talk about [government] systems is fine; peaceful discussion is not harmful and we have seen in these eight months that reason and truth have triumphed over the exaggerations of [political] parties.[86]

The Ministry of Foreign Relations also tried to assuage the fears of departmental governors, reassuring them in late August that concerns about a coming rebellion were largely unfounded.[87]

The façade did not fool anyone, however. By August the government not only had to fear the *puros* but also had to be concerned with the possibility of a military coup. According to

Carlos María Bustamante, Paredes' expected arrival in Mexico City to outline plans for a Texas campaign only covered up his intent to "launch a revolution."[88] Other contemporaries believed that plans to establish a three-man military dictatorship were well-advanced. Although these commentators disagreed about the make-up of the triumvirate and its objectives,[89] talk of such a conspiracy heightened tensions in Mexico City and undermined public confidence in the government. Two other reports further highlight the ominous situation that Herrera's administration found itself in. On August 30 one Mexico City resident observed that in recent days "everyone became alarmed at once" on learning the slightest report about any impending *pronunciamiento*.[90] A few days later, American agent Parrott commented that the government could only stay in power if it "declare[d] for the federation, *whether prepared for the change or not*," and armed the civic militia.[91] The prevailing uncertainty increased the *puros'* chances of launching a successful coup d'état, and Gómez Farías worked to prevent Herrera from being sworn in as president.[92]

The rebellion was supposed to break out in Puebla, then Tlaxcala, Jalapa, Veracruz, and Mexico City. The rebels would reissue Rangel's plan with an additional article inviting General Canalizo to assume leadership of the movement. Three generals who had not previously assisted the *puros* threw in their lot with the conspirators—Anastasio Torrejón, Francisco Avalos, and José María Jarero.[93] The failure of the June 7 rebellion led Gómez Farías to urge the plotters to adopt one additional precaution. They were not to use Santa Anna's name. To do so, warned Gómez Farías, would "weaken the revolution and upset everything. Federalism or [the] 1824 constitution are the only things that should be proclaimed."[94]

Gómez Farías' choice of Canalizo to lead the rebellion may seem perplexing given the events of June 7 and Lafragua's assertion that Canalizo fooled the *puros* by calling for Santa Anna.[95] How could Gómez Farías write to conspirators in Puebla that Canalizo was "loyal to his words," "valiant," with "much following among the troops," which "undoubtedly meant resistance would diminish so much that there would hardly be any"?[96] Gómez Farías' decision was pragmatic. He realized that he needed the support of a prominent general to bring the *puros* to power and sought to allay any qualms his fellow plotters may have had about Canalizo's integrity. Once Gómez Farías and the *puros* had secured the reins of government, they would then try to restrain the wily officer.

Herrera was well-informed about Gómez Farías' intentions and foiled his plans. The *puro* leader believed he needed between 8,000 and 10,000 pesos to insure victory. Prospects for obtaining this sum were encouraging, for one Juan Pereda had contributed 3,500 pesos by mid-September. The plotters, however, were left short of money when General Jarero failed to capture a government silver convoy. By September 20 Gómez Farías bemoaned the fact that those who had promised 200,000 pesos by the time the new government was installed refused to contribute just 8,000 to back the uprising in Puebla. The rebellion's chances for success also dwindled because several plotters had been arrested by late September, including Guadalupe Perdigón Garay and General Jarero.[97]

Financial problems and the government's energetic pursuit of the conspirators were not the only factors that sabotaged the revolt. Those career army officers who hoped to set up a triumvirate also set back Gómez Farías' expectations of toppling Herrera. The *puro* leader noted that several generals (whose names he did not mention, but which included "A." [probably Juan Nepomuceno Almonte]) wished to expatriate Canalizo so "they could take his place and force us to accept their conditions, including that of desisting from the federation." Despite the obstacles, Gómez Farías believed that carrying on with his plans would facilitate the task of collecting the money.[98] Thus, he urged Canalizo:

escape and hide while I start the revolution; its resources still endure and soon will come together again; and since everything is becoming complicated, the government commits more errors every day and its enemies increase daily, once the movement starts it will spread with the speed of lightning. Hear what I have to say, do not disregard my advice. . . . [A] brave soldier should not become discouraged despite the disgraces [that may have befallen him].[99]

Canalizo did not heed Gómez Farías' advice. He left Mexico in late September because of the "treacheries and broken promises of some commanders."[100] According to General Basadre, who also sailed into exile at the same time, responsibility for both his and Canalizo's banishment fell upon "P."[101] "P." was most likely (Gómez) Pedraza.

Gómez Farías' next step was another practical move to secure military support for the *puros*. Early in October he wooed Paredes, Mexico's strongman, by telling him that they should cooperate to prevent the country's "complete and total ruin." The numerous plots then in circulation only sought to consolidate "opposing interests," which would undoubtedly reap havoc in Mexico. In Gómez Farías' opinion, all Mexicans had to embrace a constitution that fulfilled the popular will and wage an "eternal war" against countries that did not respect Mexico's rights.[102] The *puro* leader requested that Paredes not sign his response and to address it to a pseudonym—Sebastián Perreault. Paredes, who had plans of his own, answered that he would not communicate with someone hiding behind a false name.[103]

Gómez Farías had developed an alternate plan to unseat Herrera by the time his correspondence with Paredes began. He had been exchanging letters with General Joaquín Rangel since early September to capitalize on regional chieftain Juan Alvarez' good will and stir things up in the *tierra caliente*. Rangel met with Alvarez on September 3, and Alvarez offered to put all his resources at Gómez Farías' disposal. Alvarez proved to be helpful indeed, for he personally spoke with Rangel's prison guards to insure that Rangel was well-treated.[104] Approximately two weeks later, Alvarez disregarded governmental orders to transfer Rangel to Tuxpan and arranged for the captive to serve his jail sentence in a private home in Acapulco.[105]

But Alvarez' kindness toward Rangel ended by late September. Rumor had it that Rangel had been appointed Alvarez' personal secretary, and Alvarez probably discontinued assistance because he feared that Herrera's government would retaliate.[106] This development killed Gómez Farías' plans for a rebellion in the *tierra caliente*. In fact, on October 7 he wrote Rangel that he was "impatient to know when that which you have announced to me will take place" and urged him to get on with his efforts.[107] But Rangel's alliance with other potential rebels was limited by that time and nothing of magnitude unfolded in Acapulco. Nonetheless, the letters emphasize the frantic reliance that Gómez Farías and the *puros* placed on knavish military leaders from 1845 on.

Despite the setbacks, the mid-October 1845 results of elections for a new Congress that was to assemble in January 1846 bolstered the *puros*' spirits. Based on Santa Anna's electoral law of December 10, 1841, which preserved the income requirements for voters, electors, and deputies stipulated in the *Bases Orgánicas*, the balloting insured that the *hombres de bien* would prevail in the Senate. The departments of Mexico, Puebla, Morelia, Querétaro, Zacatecas, and Guanajuato, however, elected *puros* to the Chamber of Deputies. It appears that the *puros* won in other departments as well, and thus obtained a majority in the chamber.[108] Their political enemies were quick to condemn the possibility that lower classes would hold political sway. A friend of Paredes noted that the "common people, naked and badly dressed, but with expensive dresscoats and frockcoats," had taken over the Chamber of Deputies.[109] Carlos María Bustamante's prognosis was even more ominous. The *puros*' rise to power meant that the country was "lost without remedy unless Providence wished to save it through unforeseen devices."[110]

The election results also shook the government's confidence. At a little-known meeting held around October 22, Gómez Pedraza and other statesmen (including conservative leader

Lucas Alamán, former Minister of War Pedro García Conde, and Archbishop Manuel Posada y Garduño) advised Herrera that he could only remain in power by proclaiming federalism. Although Gómez Pedraza's and García Conde's urgings were probably sincere, Alamán and Archbishop Posada y Garduño clamored for a federation for opportunistic reasons. Such a step would hasten Herrera's downfall and help insure the success of the monarchist plot. Regardless, Herrera tried to implement the proposal to enhance his popularity and shortly thereafter asked departmental governors to advise him on the possibility of restoring federalism. In the end, Herrera did not act on the issue,[111] and his indecisiveness cost the government an excellent opportunity to gain public support.

As public-spirited Mexicans became increasingly disillusioned with Herrera's regime, newspapers and contemporary pundits of every political belief reported that an uprising against the government was imminent.[112] By early December, five different groups intended to launch a final assault in their bid for political supremacy. Paredes, plotting with Alamán and Spanish Minister Bermúdez de Castro to establish a monarchical regime, led one faction.[113] Generals Tornel, Bravo, Valencia, and Paredes (who evidently did not hesitate to explore any route to the presidency) made up a second camp. They planned to create a triumvirate as the executive power.[114] Manuel Gómez Pedraza represented another bloc. He distanced himself from Herrera's government because the chief executive did not heed his October 22 suggestion to restore federalism. While his objectives remained unclear, the *moderado* politician seemed mostly concerned with keeping Gómez Farías and the *puros* from power.[115] General Juan Nepomuceno Almonte saw in the imminent change in government an extraordinary opportunity to satisfy his own political appetite. Described by a foreign observer as "totally devoid of principle of any sort, and . . . devoured by the most selfish ambition,"[116] Almonte queried members of the Senate about the possibility that the new Congress, when it convened in January 1846, would appoint a new president—himself. By late December, however, lack of support for his plans forced Almonte to join Paredes' conspiracy.[117]

Gómez Farías and the *puros* opposed the four factions. The *puro* leader had declined an invitation to join the Tornel-Bravo-Valencia cabal, which had offered him one of the three executive positions to minimize turmoil resulting from a change in government. Gómez Farías' refusal may seem somewhat illogical in light of his efforts to unseat Herrera. Why would he turn down an opportunity to hold the reins of power? Gómez Farías realized that a "badly-disguised dictatorship" stood behind this offer and did not wish to discredit the *puros'* political credo. While he wanted to bring the *puros* to power with the military's help, he was unwilling to share political authority with generals who had little intention of implementing a liberal agenda.[118]

After rejecting the Tornel-Bravo-Valencia faction, on December 3 Gómez Farías introduced the *puros'* latest plan, which called for overthrowing the executive and legislative powers, suspending the *Bases Orgánicas*, reestablishing federalism, immediately prosecuting the Texas war, and excluding all who had favored a peaceful solution to the Texas issue from the new government. Keeping in line with the strategy adopted for the June 7, 1845, revolt, the plan was intended to appeal to high-ranking ecclesiastical and army leaders by promising to preserve the clerical and military *fueros*.[119] Gómez Farías claimed that his scheme had one important advantage over previous manifestoes: it would uphold the will of the people through primary elections to select the legislators entrusted with the drafting of a new constitution.[120]

Given the *puros'* fear that the army would crush their scheme,[121] Gómez Farías sought Paredes' help again and sent him a copy of the December 3 plan. The actual contents of the letter remain a mystery, but Paredes responded to the appeal on December 10 in the most flattering terms. He maintained that his only desire was to call a Congress in which all classes of society would be represented, a measure that would fulfill "the views of those worthy liberals that, like yourself, distinguish themselves by the steadfastness of their beliefs." Paredes also noted that a "complete fusion" between them would be possible if each one made the "small sacrifice of yielding slightly" in their convictions. To convince Gómez Farías of his good faith, Paredes noted that Mexico should unleash a "sweeping attack against the insolent invaders" that trampled its soil. Last, Paredes tried to impress on Gómez Farías his lack of political ambition, writing that he would be happy if the chiefs of any upcoming revolt did not have a voice in the formation of the ensuing government.[122]

Paredes did not wait for Gómez Farías to respond. On December 14, the commandant general of San Luis Potosí, Manuel Romero, asked Paredes to lead a "glorious and purifying" movement to end the maladies brought on Mexico by the nefarious Herrera administration. Romero charged that Herrera had betrayed the nation's trust: Herrera attempted "to establish the most ridiculous political extravaganza as a form of government" with the *Bases Orgánicas*; he avoided a "glorious and necessary war through concessions that undermined our dignity"; he revived the civic militia through a "most heinous law designed to arm and let loose upon society masses of the most thoughtless, immoral, and peace-hating men"; Herrera tried to disband the army; and he was willing to receive United States Envoy John Slidell. To correct these abuses, the army would occupy Mexico City and call for a special Congress with full powers to reorganize the government.[123]

On the following day, Paredes issued a manifesto accepting the invitation to lead the movement. He first compared the "halcyon days" of the post-independence period with the ruinous and lethargic conditions that besieged the country in 1845. The decline was due to impotent governments. Paredes argued that lack of a strong central authority had nearly ruined Mexico, which was on the verge of collapse.[124] He then went on to berate the government that emerged from the December 6, 1844, rebellion. Although that movement had been the "most popular" in the history of Mexico, it failed to improve the country's situation or meet its needs. According to Paredes, Herrera's regime was to blame for the threat the *puros* posed to Mexico's stability. He argued that

> the demagogic party has come to believe it should inherit power from General Santa Anna. Dissatisfied with the important concessions made by the government, it preaches war to arm its partisans while it works feverishly to destroy the army. Concealing under the mantle of a wanton federalism its well-known projects of revenge and its proven anarchical instincts, it cares very little if it provokes the ruin of a nation with which it lacks links of any sort. . . . The government, either because it is dominated by them or because it is afraid of their boldness, grants concession after concession: defamation, calumnies, and threats wrest from it the most pernicious measures, while the forces of anarchy organize themselves to annihilate the country... once again.[125]

Paredes would not allow Mexico to surrender "defenselessly to the tyranny of the demagogues." His revolt aimed to prevent power from falling into the "hands of the rabble" so the country would never again be "scandalized by their excesses."[126]

To resist Paredes, who was at the head of an army of several thousand soldiers, Herrera's administration once again called on the civic militia for its defense. But the regime's disdain for the militia, coupled with at least one gross error in judgment, prevented this force from being as effective as in 1844. On December 20, the government asked the department of Puebla to send 5,000 *cívicos* to defend the capital. A force of that size did not exist, however. Further hampering the government's call was the reluctance of Puebla's militiamen to leave their homes to fight in Mexico City, and their commander's fear that they might plunder the capital if left unsupervised. Four days earlier, the government committed a major gaffe when it disbanded a unit of 1,000 men raised by Manuel Reyes Veramendi, a *regidor* of the Mexico City *ayuntamiento*. Confusion and disorder thus surrounded

Herrera and his supporters as they prepared for a struggle against Paredes.[127]

On December 27, Herrera moved to correct the deficiencies and to fortify his regime's military position. He authorized the Mexico City *ayuntamiento* to organize the civic militia. It is difficult to determine exactly how many men joined this military force. José Fernando Ramírez remarked that nearly 3,000 *cívicos* enlisted in the capital, while Carlos María Bustamante noted that 7,000 muskets were distributed among the Mexico City militia and the civil population. Although Bustamante's aversion for the *puros* and the urban poor probably led him to embellish his figures, the arming of the populace disturbed several special-interest groups and institutions, effectively negating the government's latest effort to organize the civic militia and hastening Herrera's downfall.[128]

Merchants were alarmed, for they remembered the atrocities perpetrated during the 1828 Parián riot. Therefore, the *Junta Mercantil de Fomento* called for its members to take up arms and to be ready to resist any outburst on the part of the people.[129] The regular army also viewed Herrera's orders with suspicion. According to "A." (Almonte), the arming of the rabble had

> excited and angered the troops. My greatest worry now is how to control the situation so that there will not be a clash. Since no judgment was used in arming the people, I have very grave fears that they will indulge in all kinds of excesses, thus repeating the scenes of 1828. In that event, I shall be occupied in controlling the mob and I shall even send troops against them if need be.[130]

On December 30, the members of the Council of State, fearing a popular rebellion headed by the civic militia, implored its president, General Gabriel Valencia, to take control of the situation. Valencia, who also tried to outwit Paredes and seize control of the revolt, visited Herrera and forcefully complained that the arming of the civil population threatened security and order in the capital. By the end of the day, Herrera had resigned his office and the Mexico City militia had laid down its arms.[131] This force would not be revived until Gómez Farías and the *puros* assumed power in August 1846.

Although the civic militia ultimately failed to check Paredes' rebellion, Gómez Farías had one more opportunity to bring his political ideas to fruition. Strange as it may seem, a plan was underway to have him join with his old enemy, Gómez Pedraza.[132] In mid-December Gómez Farías met with the *moderado* leader's ally, Minister of War Pedro María Anaya, and they agreed that the government should reestablish the Constitution of 1824 as soon as it received word of Paredes' uprising. The agreement failed. Shortly after two o'clock on December 20, Anaya read Paredes' plan to Congress and declared that the government "was resolved to pursue a constitutional course and bury itself beneath the ruins of the *Bases [Orgánicas]*."[133]

Responsibility for the failure of the arrangement between Gómez Farías and Anaya fail seems to fall on Gómez Pedraza's shoulders. On December 27, several anonymous *puro* deputies were overheard criticizing Herrera's administration for its inefficiency and deceit. They claimed that the *escoceses* dissuaded the government from restoring federalism on December 6 because it was "a bad example to set at the very time legal means were being sought to maintain public order." The *escoceses* had promised to work through Congress to establish federalism at a later date "so that everything would be strictly legal." *Puro* congressmen also emphasized that the *escoceses* would not "*choose sides*" on the issue of constitutional reform.[134] Since the *puro* press had labeled Gómez Pedraza and his backers as the "*equilibristas*" (those who perform a balancing act) by December 1845,[135] it is reasonable to assume that the term *escoceses* as used in this context refers to Gómez Pedraza and his *moderado* supporters and that Gómez Pedraza sabotaged Anaya's mid-December stratagem of having the government join with the *puros* to reestablish federalism.

Stymied by Herrera's administration and unable to mount effective resistance against Paredes, Gómez Farías and the *puros* could not act. Paredes made his triumphant entry into Mexico City shortly after Herrera resigned from the presidency. His success proved to be short-lived, however. Paredes' administration could not avoid military defeat at the hands of the United States as well as widespread domestic opposition. Gómez Farías and the *puros* capitalized on this turn of events to seize power in August 1846.

IV

The Republican Challenge

As January 1846 dawned upon Mexico, many public-spirited Mexicans hoped that the San Luis Potosí rebellion would fulfill its promise of halting the early republic's unsteady political course. The regime of General Mariano Paredes y Arrillaga, who served as Mexico's chief executive between January and August 1846, quickly moved to carry out such expectations. Paredes unequivocally stood for "the values of the *hombre de bien* . . . [he] believed that only property owners . . . were fit to govern . . . [and] despised both the proletariat and especially those renegades of his own social class who advocated popular suffrage or sovereignty."[1] Paredes, however, soon discovered that it was easier to topple governments than to establish a firm and stable regime. Diplomatic complications, domestic unrest, and military defeats gradually debilitated Paredes' administration. A coalition of *puros*, *moderados*, and *santanistas* capitalized on this turn of events to overthrow Paredes, restore the Constitution of 1824, and bring about the return of General Antonio López de Santa Anna from his exile in Cuba. Whether or not the unwieldy alliance could endure and rally the Mexican public into supporting the war effort remained to be seen.

Paredes' Vacillations

Immediately after his victorious entry into Mexico City in early January, Paredes called a meeting of army officers to establish the new government that would rule Mexico until the special Congress called for by the Plan of San Luis met. The military chiefs made several complementary propositions to the plan at a conference held on the evening of January 2. One of these stipulated that a *junta* of representatives from Mexico's departments, chosen by the leader of the San Luis rebellion, would select an interim president. To no one's surprise, Paredes was appointed chief executive on January 3.[2]

As Mexico's head of state, Paredes manipulated the issue of constitutional reform to insure the success of the monarchist scheme. The plot's groundwork was well-established by January 1846. Spanish royalists directed Salvador Bermúdez de Castro, who had been appointed minister to Mexico in May 1844, to foment a monarchist revolt. Bermúdez de Castro assumed his post in mid-March 1845 and reported to his superiors in late August that the time had come to carry out his instructions. Bermúdez de Castro gained Paredes' trust with the help of Lucas Alamán and other politically conscious Mexicans. Paredes agreed to take power, convene a Congress where Mexico's most conservative thinkers would prevail, and invite Spain to name a monarch for Mexico.[3]

To give the movement the appearance of spontaneity, the plotters kept their intentions secret throughout 1845. Indeed, the Plan of San Luis and Paredes' December 15, 1845, manifesto made no references—direct or indirect—to the establishment of a monarchy. The two documents left the door open for the adoption of a monarchical regime by stating that the special Congress would have ample powers to rebuild the nation's political structure. Despite these careful preparations, Paredes astounded the plotters when he agreed, upon becoming interim president, to uphold the additions that were made to the Plan of San Luis on January 2, 1846—one clause bound the executive to uphold the republican system of government.4 Bermúdez de Castro promptly admonished Paredes, whose January 10 manifesto made it clear that only Congress could decide what kind of political structure Mexico needed.5 However Paredes maneuvered, Carlos María Bustamante astutely recognized his objectives, noting that "the means of introducing a monarchy into Mexico are being prepared, and time will tell."6

Monarchist efforts intensified soon after. On January 24, Alamán and other *hombres de bien* introduced a daily known as *El Tiempo*. The newspaper did not openly endorse monarchist ideas at first, but on February 12, 1846, exactly one year after *La Voz del Pueblo* clamored for the restoration of the 1824 constitution, *El Tiempo* began to campaign for a monarchy.7 A January 27 decree calling for elections to Congress complemented *El Tiempo's* efforts to shape public opinion. According to Justo Sierra, the most distinguished man of letters in late nineteenth-century Mexico, the law sought to "establish an aristocracy in preparation of a monarchy,"8 and many Mexicans believed that Paredes supported the monarchical proposal of Alamán, Archbishop Manuel Posada y Garduño, and others.9

In light of the uneasiness that these developments created, Paredes abstained from making public statements that might link him to the monarchist plot. In fact, Paredes instructed at least one departmental governor to deny any rumors which tied him to the conspiracy. His silence, however, led the Spanish and British ministers to call on Paredes to inquire about his intentions. The Mexican president assured Bermúdez de Castro of his willingness to push ahead with the plot, but he gave Charles Bankhead, the British representative, a more evasive response. Congress, he said, would determine whether Mexico should adopt a monarchical regime. Paredes clearly did not wish to make such a controversial and unpopular decision by himself, and sought to delegate to the legislature some of the burden.[10]

Paredes' conduct during the following months provided further evidence of his unwillingness to act alone. To stall the attacks which Mexico City's newspapers directed against his government, he portrayed himself in a March 21 proclamation as the most renowned defender of republicanism. Who, if not he, had proposed in the December 2 *junta* that Mexico's future chief executive should swear to maintain its republican institutions?[11] Moreover, the manifesto dictated that Mexico would keep such a political system as long as Congress wished, and that Paredes would support the decision. Nevertheless, he added that responsibility for such an "interesting and vital question" remained with the legislature.[12] Paredes again left the door open for change, and Bankhead's comments following a late April interview with the Mexican president confirms the possibility. According to the British diplomat, Paredes hoped to convince the soon-to-be installed deputies to adopt a monarchist constitution. Although he did not support a Spanish prince for Mexico's throne, Paredes added that he would not oppose the national legislature if the members decided to welcome a foreign king, regardless of his nationality.[13]

But Congress never had an opportunity to act on the matter. The survival of Paredes' administration, the president's political prestige, and the success of the monarchist plot depended on the progress of the war with the United States.[14] Unfortunately for the conspirators, Mexico's armies were soundly defeated at Palo Alto and Resaca de la Palma in early May 1846 and reports of the battles had filtered back into Mexico City by the end of the month. These developments, in conjunction with several revolts against Paredes' regime, shattered the conspirators' hopes. Paredes informed Bankhead that a monarchical regime was the answer to Mexico's problems, but he doubted whether Congress would move to establish it in the near future. Indeed, several deputies of the constituent Congress told the British minister they would not back a monarchy unless they were certain of receiving foreign assistance.[15]

The death blow to the monarchist conspiracy was not long in coming. The much-anticipated Congress finally convened on June 6. In his inaugural speech, Paredes embraced republicanism in a desperate bid to retain power. He confirmed that Mexico hungered to preserve republican institutions, and that the legislature would earn Mexico's gratitude if it acquiesced.[16] Paredes' support for a monarchy disappeared. Alleging that its "dignity" left it no other option, *El Tiempo* closed its doors on the following day.[17] Alamán then tried to undermine Paredes' political agenda for the remainder of his presidency.[18]

Paredes was no more successful than former President José Joaquín Herrera in dealing with the thorny issue of Texas. Since the authors of the Plan of San Luis had criticized Herrera's irresolute policies toward Texas acridly, many Mexicans hoped that the new regime would adopt a belligerent attitude. The editors of *La Reforma* declared the war with Texas to be:

> the first duty of the actual government...[and] the most urgent need of the nation.... The triumph over the Texans will strengthen our respectability, eliminate an object of greed over which various nations speculate today, and provide ... a title of absolute glory for our army.[19]

But the statements that Paredes issued after mid-December 1845 were limited to criticizing Herrera's vacillations, and never promised an aggressive policy against the United States. Such ambiguity discredited Paredes' government, and the defeats suffered by Mexican armies in May 1846 undermined his administration even more. Indeed, the situation in Mexico was so precarious that in many eyes Santa Anna's return became an appealing possibility — "only a man with his heroic halo could inspire a shred of hope."[20]

Paredes' views on the Texas issue began to take shape during the fall of 1845. Despite having first-hand knowledge of the deplorable condition of the Army of the North, Paredes wrote his fellow monarchist conspirators in early October that they needed to call for the reconquest of Texas. Alamán and Bermúdez de Castro both rejected the strategy as preposterous. An armed confrontation with the United States would be fatal for Mexico, but Paredes ignored their warnings. The documents issued to accompany the San Luis Potosí revolt were adorned with warlike overtones. The *puros*' war cries in Mexico City scared Paredes; he would be branded a traitor if he looked for a peaceful solution to the Texas issue. Paredes also needed the army's support to insure the triumph of his rebellion, so he promised to prosecute the Texas campaign vigorously. Such rhetoric appealed to his officers' aspirations for fame, glory, and prestige; war would provide them with an excellent opportunity to fulfill their ambitions.[21]

Paredes, nonetheless, never closed the door on the possibility of negotiating a bloodless settlement. Although the Plan of San Luis accused then President Herrera of avoiding a "necessary and glorious war," and of receiving a commissioner with whom it tried to "reconcile the ignominious loss" of the nation's territorial integrity, the eight articles in the plan did not mention rebel intentions to reconquer Texas.[22] Paredes' December 15, 1845, manifesto, while blaming Mexico's previous "weak and improvident" governments for the loss of its former province and recognizing that Mexico faced a possible war if it wished to retake Texas, did not promise to reclaim the territory. The manifesto emphasized the country's calamitous internal situation and stated that Paredes would "march to the frontier to fight like a soldier" only when the nation was no longer in danger of disintegration.[23] The tone of Paredes' December 25 military order was similar. It was more concerned with justifying his revolt than in making promises about the Texas campaign.[24]

The initial measures taken by Paredes' government suggest that other prominent Mexicans shared his desire to avoid war with the United States. The *junta* that named Paredes interim president included conservative politicians Alamán and Carlos María Bustamante, as well as Generals Juan Nepomuceno Almonte, José María Tornel, and Pedro Ampudia. All held strong anti-American feelings. Yet the *junta* ignored Bustamante's suggestion that the presidential oath of office contain a clause obliging Paredes to stave off the United States invasion. Instead, the *junta* proclaimed that such a pledge would be equivalent to a declaration of war, which exceeded its powers.[25] Furthermore, when Paredes set forth his political agenda in the January 10, 1846, manifesto, he merely pointed out that Herrera's "indecision and weakness" had encouraged the United States to commit the "scandal of usurping Texas" and did not include any threatening declarations toward Mexico's northern neighbor.[26]

Paredes' hope for a peaceful solution to the Texas question remained alive through the early spring of 1846 thanks to the continued presence in Mexico of United States representative John Slidell. Indeed, Slidell confided to his superiors in early February that an offer of money might induce Mexico to reach a desirable boundary agreement with the United States.[27] The Paredes administration most likely never had the opportunity to consider this thinly veiled bribe, but any hope for a peaceful settlement vanished quickly. By March 1, the Polk administration had authorized Slidell to present himself before Paredes' government as a minister plenipotentiary. In December 1845 the Mexican Council of State had rejected Slidell for appearing in that capacity before Herrera's regime, so the council rebuffed him again for lack of proper credentials. Although Bermúdez de Castro believed that the

Mexican rejection "had not closed the door to the decorous means of conciliation that could later be used to settle the pending differences between both nations," Slidell's response to Mexico's snub suggests otherwise. On March 17 he requested his passports so he could leave the country.[28]

Despite these setbacks, Paredes not only continued to search for a way to avoid a military confrontation with the United States, but he also sought to lay responsibility for such a decision with the constituent Congress. His March 21 manifesto set a framework for an aggressive policy toward the United States. After defending his government's decision to reject Slidell, Paredes affirmed that Mexico would protect its "invaded property" and would not allow the United States to launch any new conquests. Such bellicosity notwithstanding, Paredes ignored the provisions of both the *Bases Orgánicas* and the Plan of San Luis. The former still operated as Mexico's constitution and authorized the executive to declare war if necessary; the latter granted him the authority as president to use necessary military force to maintain Mexico's territorial integrity, and did not place any restrictions on his ability as chief executive to declare war. Paredes announced that he lacked the option to proclaim war on the United States and that such a decision would be reached by the Congress when it convened. In the meantime, Mexico would repel any attack but would not launch one.[29]

Three additional examples illustrate the reluctance of Paredes' administration to enter into a disastrous war with the United States. The president's April 23 manifesto trumpeted that a "defensive war" against the United States had begun, but it also reiterated that only the legislature could declare war.[30] In mid-May, an anonymous member of Paredes' cabinet, concerned over Mexico's recent defeats at the battles of Palo Alto and Resaca de la Palma (which were then unknown to the public), informally suggested that Mexico receive an "ad hoc" envoy to discuss the Texas question. The envoy might have additional—and secret—powers to solve other pending issues.[31] Finally, the most warlike document to emerge from the constituent Congress, the decree of July 2, 1846, did not include an explicit declaration of war. It only authorized Mexico's chief executive to resist the American invasion.[32]

In a desperate effort to shore up his regime, Paredes sought and received permission from Congress in mid-June to assume command of Mexico's armed forces, and he issued a manifesto proclaiming the need to withstand the United States invasion. But the measures did not suffice, and by late July American troops had begun to march on Monterrey.[33] Paredes' two-faced policies and military failures were not, however, the only reasons that brought his government to an end. The biting condemnations of Mexico City's daily journals also contributed to Paredes' downfall.

The Duel with the Press

The triumph of the December 1845 San Luis revolt gave rise to new hope for Mexico's future. Even those newspapers that eventually became Paredes' most rancorous critics lauded the uprising at first. *Don Simplicio* pointed out that the recent political change marked "the point of departure for a new direction for the country," and hoped that its leaders would protect Mexico from "anarchy and the danger of losing its nationality."[34] *La Reforma* expressed a similar opinion. Its editors commented that the San Luis revolt was the antithesis of all others, for Paredes had recognized that he was "a soldier and a subject of the nation who was obliged to respect and maintain its sovereign will, submitting himself to its laws, and pledging not to step beyond them except to defend the integrity of the national territory."[35]

If such dreams were to become a reality, Mexico needed a stable government. *Puro*-controlled newspapers, as Paredes well knew, had been a significant destabilizing force during Herrera's regime. Paredes could not allow the press to criticize him as bitterly as it had censured his predecessor, especially since he harbored dreams of a monarchy. Paredes took steps to neutralize all potential journalistic opponents. Among the first reporters to be compromised was Agustín Franco, the former editor of *La Voz del Pueblo*. Franco assumed responsibility for publishing the *Diario Oficial del Gobierno Mexicano*. Franco's abrupt switch stemmed from his opportunistic temperament. As Guillermo Prieto noted, Franco's desire "to be first in everything" meant that "neither political convictions nor beliefs mattered." This character trait, as well as his desire to avoid another jail term (he was arrested by Herrera's agents in late December 1845), and the closing of *La Voz del Pueblo* allowed Paredes to gain Franco's allegiance.[36]

Paredes may not have threatened Franco in order to quiet his pen, but he most certainly tried to intimidate other prominent journalists. During a January 12 meeting with José María Lafragua, Mariano Otero, and Ignacio Cumplido, Mexico's chief executive, delivered a blunt message to his three guests:

> I am aware, gentlemen, that my government is unconstitutional [*de puro hecho*]; but I warn you . . . that I will humiliate you if you disturb the peace with your writings; so go away, and remember to be cautious.[37]

Paredes' warning could not be ignored. Rumors abounded that he intended to send those "types of gentlemen" to fight in the Texas campaign, where they would have "ample opportunities to develop their patriotism."[38]

The government's intent to suppress all dissents became even clearer when it distributed two circular letters in late January. The first was issued by the Ministry of Foreign Relations to coincide with the appearance of *El Tiempo*, no doubt because the government anticipated a strong reaction against this daily and wished to protect it. The circular announced that no abuse of the freedom of the press would be tolerated, but it did not specify what constituted such an abuse. The Ministry of Justice subsequently declared that no one could be persecuted for his political beliefs and that all such prisoners were to be released immediately. In the final analysis, both circulars attempted to make journalists uncertain about how much liberty they would have, and Paredes would be able to identify his enemies more easily.39

Paredes' strategy failed. Otero, Cumplido, and Lafragua did not heed to his warning and publicly criticized his January 10 manifesto with "an irony so biting that [it] could only be expected of men willing to bear a cruel persecution."40 In addition, the appearance of *El Tiempo* gave birth to a heated debate about the most convenient form of government. *El Tiempo* and the *Diario Oficial del Gobierno Mexicano* defended monarchism, while *La Reforma, Don Simplicio, El Republicano, La Época, El Contratiempo,* and *El Monitor Republicano* became the champions of republicanism.41 Unlike 1845, none of the newspapers served as the exclusive standard-bearer of the *puros,* yet this did not hamper their goals during the Paredes administration. *Puros* and *moderados* had no choice but to set aside their political differences to resist the monarchist threat posed by Paredes' regime.

Republican newspapers fiercely attacked the idea of a monarchy. They argued that the time to establish a monarchical regime in Mexico had long gone by, and they turned to the past in search of evil monarchies to butress their argument. Even conservative politician Carlos María Bustamante, who launched countless invectives against the *puros* between 1845 and 1847, participated in the journalistic campaign to oppose monarchism. As a result of these biting attacks, the Ministry of Foreign Relations finally prohibited "all discussions about governmental systems," and on March 14 ordered strict observance of all laws dealing with freedom of the press.42 The measure proved as ineffective as Paredes' admonitions. From then on, the front pages of republican newspapers included a declaration against such a restriction; the journals also featured articles attacking both the government and the men who supported a monarchy.43

Paredes began to use repression to stem the growing tide of criticism. On March 10, Paredes dismissed General José Vicente Miñón from the army. The discharge appears to have been the culmination of a dispute that started when Miñón, who had been one of Valentín Gómez Farías' principal allies in 1845, refused to sign the complementary propositions made to the Plan of San Luis on the evening of January 2.44 Two days later, the publisher of the anti-monarchical broadside *"Venida de un príncipe extranjero y embarque del general Santa Anna"* was impressed into an infantry regiment, while *puro* advocate Agustín Buenrostro was deported to Veracruz for collaborating in the production of the broadside.45 In late March, Captain Francisco Schiafino, who collected signatures endorsing a letter sent by several army officers to *El Monitor Republicano* that declared the army favored republicanism, was arrested and sent to the San Juan de Ulúa dungeon. The names of the signees were not made public, but *La Reforma* reported that they included some of Mexico's "most accredited generals and leaders"; one of them, General Lino Alcorta, received orders to march to Oaxaca.46 Shortly after, government agents imprisoned Luis Espino, a writer for *El Contratiempo,* and ordered the arrest of Anastasio Zerecero, a former correspondent of *La Voz del Pueblo.* Paredes' men also confiscated *La Reforma's* editions of March 24, 25, and 27 and broke into its printing house, hoping to find several letters that linked General Juan Nepomuceno Almonte—who was rumored to be *La Reforma's* main sponsor—to a conspiracy to overthrow Paredes.47

Paredes' hard-line measures worked. He first cowed the editors of *El Republicano,* who announced on April 7 that they had met with the interim president and had agreed to support the government fully despite some minor differences of opinion. Mexico City's remaining newspapers remained active, but only briefly. A few days later, Paredes argued furiously with Vicente García Torres, who in 1845 published *El Estandarte Nacional* and now edited both *El Monitor Republicano* and *El Contratiempo*. Paredes exiled García Torres to Monterrey. *Puro* activist Juan José Baz, who authored an article entitled *"Firmeza en principios políticos"* that appeared in *La Reforma* on March 10, was arrested on April 16. Paredes had completely crushed all journalistic opposition two days later. An April 18 decree authorized departmental governors to punish the authors, editors, and printers of any articles that directly or indirectly protected the aims of any of the republic's invaders, abetted any change in the established order, or slandered the national or departmental authorities. Shortly after, two of the most vocal critics of Paredes' regime, *Don Simplicio* and *La Reforma*, ceased publication.[48]

Paredes may have restricted freedom of the press, but censorship could not halt the deterioration of the public image or the declining prestige of his government. Republican newspapers that were still operating in late March generally agreed that his administration had erred in many ways. The editors of *La Reforma*, for example, noted that the government's support of *El Tiempo*, its disregard for freedom of the press, as well as the January 1846 call for a special Congress, had brought down "the creation of the San Luis revolt."[49] Both *La Reforma* and *Don Simplicio* believed Paredes' choice of ministers was another serious mistake; they were largely responsible for the evils that had fallen on Mexico.[50] The chief culprit was Minister of War General José María Tornel, who became the target of *La Reforma's* unceasing attacks. The editors criticized him for having authored the March 21 manifesto, forcing Almonte's resignation from the cabinet, persecuting innocent civilians, failing to adopt the necessary measures to wage war effectively, and provoking several upheavals in the army and the navy.[51]

Paredes could only have overcome these condemnations by waging a successful war against the United States, but

Mexico's military shortcomings sealed the fate of his regime. Conditions were ripe for a coup and the *puros*, whose endeavors to seize power had not stopped since Herrera's downfall in December 1845, saw their efforts rewarded thanks to their alliance with a most unlikely figure: General Antonio López de Santa Anna.

The Odd Couple

Presiding over the coalition was Manuel Crescencio Rejón, Santa Anna's minister of foreign relations in 1844. He had stayed in hiding in Mexico while Congress prepared the case against Santa Anna and his cabinet in early 1845 but had sailed for Havana on April 20. Shortly after his arrival, Rejón learned of the May 24, 1845, decree granting general amnesty for political crimes. Rejón, however, did not receive an unconditional pardon. He would not be exonerated unless he left Mexico for ten years and asked for a stay of the charges. The decree raised Rejón's hatred for Herrera's administration. Moreover, by 1843 Rejón had come to believe that Mexico needed to act firmly against the United States. Herrera's vacillating policies toward Texas distressed him further.[52] Rejón's rancor made him an ideal conspirator against Herrera, a fact that Santa Anna recognized and capitalized on. Aware that the failure of General Joaquín Rangel's June 1845 coup d'état had crushed any chance for a glorious return to Mexico, Santa Anna turned Rejón into a political asset.

It was Rejón, therefore, who first planted the seed for reconciliation between Valentín Gómez Farías and Santa Anna. Rejón wrote the *puro* leader on July 7, 1845, justifying his 1844 conduct as a cabinet member and indicating that he desired to declare war on Texas. But Congress not only failed to provide Santa Anna's government with the necessary financial support, it also nearly made public its intention of recognizing Texas' independence. That would have been reason enough to dissolve the legislature, but Rejón's decision was influenced by Santa Anna's "irrevocable intention of stepping down from power [and] . . . limiting himself to defending [the republic] as a soldier in its foreign disputes." The former minister added that he had presented his ideas to Santa Anna, who replied that the interim government could act as it believed proper. Only then did Rejón shut down Congress. Later events, however, led to the December 6, 1844, revolt.53

Rejón's apologetic remarks were followed by an attempt to restore Santa Anna's public personae. The exiled general remained "firm in his decision not to return to rule the republic." He wanted to contribute to Gómez Farías' "splendid plans, acting as a soldier and helping with all influence that he had, provided only that he be allowed to spend the rest of his days on the small piece of land he selected some time ago to repose in his old age." Santa Anna recognized that the *escoceses* were his real enemies and would have nothing more to do with them. In sum, Santa Anna had been the victim of much deception and the time was ideal for a reconciliation. Together they would save Mexico from the dangers that threatened it.54

Gómez Farías' response to Rejón has not survived, but it appears that Rejón's letter had the desired results. Available documentation shows that the *puro* leader's attitude toward Santa Anna in late 1845 lacked much of the earlier antagonism. Gómez Farías did not want Santa Anna's name linked with the revolt he planned for September 1845, but he showed some concern over Santa Anna's fate when Mexico City's newspapers reported that a Spaniard had been sent to Havana to assassinate the exile. The culprit was captured and confessed to the charges. The *puro* chief blamed *moderado* politician Manuel Gómez Pedraza for attempting the "horrible" deed, but Santa Anna may have fabricated the episode to discredit Gómez Pedraza, believed by Carlos María Bustamante to be the major obstacle to Santa Anna's return to Mexico. Certainly the stories brought Santa Anna new sympathizers and strengthened the link between the exiled general and Gómez Farías.55

Another sign of Gómez Farías' changing attitude toward Santa Anna can be gleaned from Rejón's next letter. No comment suggests that Gómez Farías was reluctant to enter into another alliance with the general.56 Instead, Rejón impressed on Gómez Farías the need to work on behalf of a coalition, for the "inevitable triumph of federalism" had led "the servile ones" to seek Santa Anna's support. Rejón urged Gómez Farías to *"move ahead, for you are safe everywhere,"* and warned him to "keep the most profound silence about this [union], since it is convenient to work with the greatest caution." Rejón implored the *puro* leader to use his influence so that Mexico City's newspapers did *"not attack or hurt don Antonio,"* and, to assuage Gómez Farías' apprehensions, Rejón also assured him of Santa Anna's "good faith."57

Rejón's letter served its purpose. Although Gómez Farías did not mention Santa Anna in his reply, the *puro* statesman did express the hope that God would grant Mexico a man that ruled "with a spirit of unity, justice, and beneficence . . . who will not be insensitive to public misery, who does not call the people's feigned silence the national will . . . who will not cut any deals at his fellow countrymen's expense."58 It is reasonable to assume that Gómez Farías was referring to Santa Anna. Carlos María Bustamante maintained in mid-November that the Havana exile would be "greeted with applause" should he return,59 and others believed that General Anastasio Parrodi's support would enable Santa Anna to disembark safely in Tampico.60 By late 1845, the alliance between Santa Anna and the *puros* began to take shape.

Despite signs of an impending agreement with Santa Anna, the *puros'* prospects were not bright early in 1846. They remained estranged from the *moderados*, who appeared to be close to an alliance with Paredes. Both Paredes and many *moderados* espoused the values of the *hombres de bien*, and in late December 1845 Paredes sought to reconcile with Gómez

Pedraza. After delivering a scathing condemnation of the San Luis rebellion at the December 20 session of Congress, Gómez Pedraza had taken refuge in a small town on the outskirts of Mexico City. Paredes advised Gómez Pedraza that he could return to the capital in complete safety.[61] Paredes seemed to have achieved his goal on January 2, 1846. He met with "P." (probably Gómez Pedraza), who was "quite enthusiastic over the repeated assurances [from] Paredes . . . about his good intentions and his desire to consult with persons able to advise him about the proper steps to take for the welfare and prosperity of the nation."[62]

In the end, however, no deal was struck. The "unwise severity" of Article One of the January 2 additions to the Plan of San Luis caused a minor rift between Paredes and P. The clause mandated that members of the past legislative and executive branches resign their duties if they had not "responded to the desires and needs of the nation," had failed to sustain "its dignity," and had not "secured the integrity of its territory."[63] In P.'s opinion, any outgoing legislator (like himself) would be hesitant to accept a seat in the soon-to-be-installed *junta* of representatives from Mexico's departments because "it would be tantamount to confessing that he deserves the criticism he gets in the new session."[64] But Paredes' monarchist plans were what turned P., like so many other Mexican statesmen, against the interim president. Late January 1846 found P. assisting other *moderados* in their efforts to organize resistance to Paredes' regime.

The *moderados* must have begun the attempt in high spirits, as Lafragua had returned to their fold. Lafragua later explained that the ties that bound him to the *puros* in 1845 had been purely circumstantial. The *moderado* party disdained federalism and favored re-establishment of the *Bases Orgánicas* after Santa Anna's downfall in 1844, so Lafragua felt compelled to break away because his "companions [had] separated themselves from the road . . . [he] had always followed."[65] But the monarchist plot made the issue secondary, and Lafragua and other prominent *moderados* such as Gómez Pedraza, Mariano Otero, Luis de la Rosa, and Juan Bautista Ceballos hastened their efforts to depose Paredes. Despite their resolve, the *moderados'* lack of financial resources and military support limited their endeavors to "writing to the states and feeding the liberals' hopes with pompous words."[66]

By late February, however, *puros* and *moderados* had set aside their differences to overthrow Paredes' government. Rejón invited Lafragua to work against Paredes; the *moderado* leader accepted after Santa Anna pledged to reestablish federalism upon returning to Mexico. Lafragua then procured the support of well-known civilians and army officers. The former included *puro* advocates José María del Río, Francisco Modesto Olaguíbel, and Guadalupe Perdigón Garay. Generals Juan Morales, Santiago Blanco, José G. Partearroyo, José Frontera, and José Vicente Miñón lent their names to the movement.[67] Both *puros* and *moderados* understood the dangers inherent in an alliance with Santa Anna, but they also knew that they needed his aid to depose Paredes. Even Gómez Farías' most zealous supporters realized that the coalition was an evil to be endured. Zacatecas politician Manuel González Cosío, his hate for Santa Anna notwithstanding, declared that he would "gladly throw himself in [Santa Anna's] arms if he desired to return and battle the baneful faction" that was ruling the nation.[68]

At the same time that *puros* and *moderados* joined Santa Anna's movement, the Havana exiles launched a publicity campaign to garner sympathy to their cause. Rejón sent Gómez Farías a long letter to vindicate his conduct during Santa Anna's previous presidency and to argue that a federalist regime suited Mexico best. It was published by *El Republicano* in early March.[69] *La Reforma* printed a petition that Rejón and General José Ignacio Basadre addressed to Paredes' government, withdrawing a request for permission to return to Mexico to answer the charges levied against them for having authorized the November 29, 1844, decree. Rejón and Basadre noted that they were indignant about essays in several newspapers (undoubtedly *El Tiempo*) and the convocation of the new Congress. They refused to return to Mexico until the nation had a government that reflected national interests and did not taint them with "ignominy."[70]

But the man who most needed to redeem himself to politically conscious Mexicans was Santa Anna. Help to regain his former prestige gathered momentum in mid-February 1846. The *Memorial Histórico* published a manifesto in which Santa Anna denied rumors that he would lead Cuban soldiers in an invasion of Mexico and that he endorsed the monarchist plot. Santa Anna portrayed himself as a patriot incapable of "stabbing a dagger in his country's entrails." He preferred exile in foreign lands or to die far from Mexico than to "return to its bosom by relying on violence, open insults, and opprobrium."[71] The proclamation was successful. Even Carlos María Bustamante was forced to admit that Santa Anna would be well-received if he disembarked in Veracruz.[72]

La Reforma provided an additional boost to Santa Anna's image when its editors lobbied for his return. Numerous articles listed his virtues and portrayed him as the only man capable of saving the republic. One such essay stated that Santa Anna's

> private conversations and letters speak the language of disillusionment, and make manifest his repentance at having abandoned the people, whom he is now willing to support until his death. Come, then, he who had the courage to lead our troops to the Sabine [River]; he who lost a limb fighting a foreign enemy in Veracruz; he who affirmed [our] independence and conquered trophies of glory on the Pánuco's edges that constitute our pride. Come and help us defend the right of universal suffrage and the dogma of popular sovereignty which have been trampled upon by the present administration. Come and

save us from the monarchist Congress. Come and save our nationality and sustain the independence of our politics from any foreign influence. Come, in short, and be reconciled with the nation and the army, as Napoleon reconciled himself with France when he returned from the island of Elba.73

At least one other Mexico City newspaper joined this crusade. *El Contratiempo* pointed out that Mexico needed a man whose "feats and services made him deserving of the popular goodwill" if it wished to obtain order and freedom. Its editors argued that only Santa Anna possessed such abilities.74

As the exiled *caudillo* became a viable opponent to Paredes, Santa Anna and his supporters quickened their efforts to return to Mexico. In early March, Rejón stressed Santa Anna's renewed belief in democracy and federalism to *puro* statesman Crescencio Boves, who had been a member of Congress in 1844 and 1845. Rejón noted that Santa Anna was determined to *"proclaim and sustain [the federal republic], and he would have done so sooner if you and the others had not insisted on your ill-starred revolution of December 6, 1844."* Rejón's letter included a statement of even greater significance; according to Santa Anna, Gómez Farías was *"the most important man for bringing order to the affairs of the republic."*75

At the same time, Santa Anna espoused his dedication for democracy, assuring several allies that he intended to support "the pretensions of the masses" and allow the people "complete freedom" to constitute a government. Santa Anna wrote of his willingness to die for these causes and to guarantee their fulfillment; his only reward would be to sign the new federal constitution. He promised not to remain in power once this was done, for his "irrevocable purpose" was to serve Mexico as a soldier. The letter provides further insights about the exiles' plans. "We must work with the greatest caution in all this," added Santa Anna, "for if our project is discovered by the army, which is shy of federalism, it will be difficult for us to establish it. For this reason we must prepare opinion astutely, and adopt a plan in which the word [federal] is not mentioned, but [one that] will lead us nonetheless to our desired end."[76]

Santa Anna's revitalized public image and the newly found harmony between *puros* and *moderados* set the groundwork for several high-ranking military officials to plan an uprising for the early spring of 1846. The rebellion was to start in Veracruz, where two senior army leaders gave departmental authorities reasons for concern. Veracruz' commandant general reported that General Ventura Mora, who was regarded as a *santanista*, showed "great imprudence in his conduct," and that the arrival of General Juan Soto, whom he considered to be the leader of the demagogic party, might lead to a coup.[77] The anxieties were justified. Mora and Soto were to assist General Juan Nepomuceno Almonte, who had accepted an offer to champion Santa Anna's cause.

By the spring of 1846 two circumstances had forced Almonte into Santa Anna's camp: his differences of opinion with Paredes and the realization that his own aspirations for power were at risk. Almonte's relationship with Paredes began to deteriorate not long after being named minister of war in early January. When republican newspapers responded to *El Tiempo's* pro-monarchical arguments, Almonte drafted a circular letter indicating that the government was pro-republican. Paredes did not approve of the letter, and an irate Almonte tore it to shreds and threw it on the ground in the president's presence. The breaking point came on February 18. Almonte arrived late at his office, and Paredes cynically commented that "at that rate very little would be accomplished." Almonte resigned from the cabinet the next day and his public appeal went into a meteoric rise. Encouraged, he drew up a plan similar to one that Gómez Farías would propose on August 4, 1846. Almonte invited regional chief General Juan Alvarez and *moderado* leader Lafragua to join him. Their refusal to back him, however, left Almonte no choice but to give up his scheme and to seek refuge with Santa Anna.[78]

Although his political ambitions may have been dampened, Almonte still represented a threat to Paredes' regime, so Minister of War Tornel was given the task of engineering his exile from Mexico. Since Mexico's representative in France was gravely ill, Tornel alleged that a new appointment was a matter of the utmost urgency. Thus, the government named Almonte extraordinary envoy to France, and he left Mexico City on March 27. As soon as Almonte departed, postal administrators at Jalapa and Veracruz received orders to intercept at Puebla special mail deliveries from Veracruz. The purpose was to prevent *santanistas* in Mexico City from learning of their *caudillo's* return. In addition, troop movements in the nation's capital increased noticeably, a obvious sign of government concern. Soldiers were placed on the roof of the National Palace and in the tower of the Cathedral, while the guard in Paredes' home was reinforced. The situation apparently unnerved Paredes—several reports indicate he was drinking excessively.[79]

The preparations proved unnecessary in the end, for the uprising never broke out. While Carlos María Bustamante suggested that Almonte may have had a number of personal reasons for not staging a coup d'état,[80] two other factors help to explain Almonte's failure to act. First, he lacked military assistance. On March 11, General Pedro Ampudia cut short a potential army mutiny in San Luis Potosí that may have been intended to pave the way for Almonte's uprising. A small number of units rebelled because they allegedly did not want to fight in Texas without adequate supplies, but several observers suggested that the upheaval was intended to bring Santa Anna back and restore federalism. Almonte also did not find sufficient military support in other key locales. Army leaders in Veracruz and Puebla were not unanimously in favor of an uprising, while the garrisons in both cities remained loyal to the government.[81]

Paredes' government also weathered the crisis at Veracruz because Santa Anna and his allies did not agree on the plan for the rebellion. Santa Anna's version, which had been forwarded to Mexico in early March, focused on three points: Santa Anna claimed that the January 27, 1846, decree threatened Mexico's sovereignty because it called for a foreign prince; the plan called for a popularly elected Congress to meet within four months to provide the nation with a new constitutional framework (except for a monarchy) and to deal with the Texas question; and, keeping in line with the 1845 manifestoes issued by the *puros*, the document guaranteed the army's existence and upkeep.[82]

Despite Santa Anna's earlier admonitions, Almonte and Manuel Baranda encouraged several influential *santanistas* to make a number of additions to Santa Anna's plan. Their version openly called for Santa Anna's return and named General Gabriel Valencia interim president until Santa Anna arrived in Mexico.[83] An anonymous correspondent of Gómez Farías explained the reasons for the changes—launching "a revolution of principles without even mentioning the name of a prestigious person" would make it difficult "to gain the support of a powerful class [the army]."[84] The modifications frustrated Santa Anna's attempt to return, however, for they proved to be unacceptable to Santa Anna, Gómez Farías, and General Juan Soto.[85] As United States' Consul John Black pointed out, the alterations "disfigured [Santa Anna's plan] throughout in its sense and object."[86]

Cognizant that the life of his administration had been extended because Santa Anna and his allies worked at cross-purposes, Paredes sought to broaden his base of support through an alliance with the *moderados*. To that end, the Mexican president arranged to meet with Gómez Pedraza, Otero, and two former members of Herrera's cabinet, Mariano Riva Palacio and Pedro García Conde, on April 2. According to *La Reforma*, Paredes was ready to yield on two issues: he was willing to modify the decree calling for elections to the special Congress, and he offered to abrogate the circular letters that restricted freedom of the press.[87] Despite the concessions, Paredes' plan to rally the *moderados* proved unsuccessful. On this occasion, Gómez Pedraza decided to skip the meeting. He later explained that the gathering was scheduled to begin at noon, but the invitation was delivered to his home at 10 A.M., and he was not there. His absence, he claimed, was unintentional.[88] Gómez Pedraza's excuse was without merit. He must have found out about the encounter ahead of time and hid to prevent the *moderados* from supporting the tottering regime. Paredes' subsequent efforts to link his political fortunes with this group proved equally futile. The Mexican president met with Otero in mid-May and made "many well-deserved accolades" of Riva Palacio. Paredes then asked Otero to arrange a conference between himself and Riva Palacio.[89] It is unlikely that the meeting ever took place.

Paredes' administration received another blow when General Juan Alvarez pronounced against the government in mid-April. Alvarez' federalist inclinations suggest that he would have been receptive to the *santanistas'* message, so Santa Anna's agents acted quickly to gain Alvarez' allegiance. In early March 1846, Santa Anna urged Manuel Feulet to impress on Alvarez the "necessity of uniting so as to destroy the advances of tyranny."[90] To convince Alvarez of the merits of their cause and gain his loyalty, *santanista* emissaries paid him $30,000.[91] Alvarez, who was also influenced by peasant demands in the territory that now forms the state of Guerrero, issued the Plan of Acapulco, which denounced Paredes' regime, asked for the ratification of a republican government, and recognized Santa Anna as president.[92] Although Paredes' supporters sought to discredit Alvarez by arguing that his only objective was to "satisfy his well-known aspirations of committing robberies and assassinations with impunity," the government needed more than flattery and moral support to survive.[93] Alvarez' revolt, as the minister of foreign relations later acknowledged, delivered a severe blow to the Paredes government.94

As Paredes' regime began to fall, the Havana exiles renewed their efforts to court Gómez Farías. On April 8, Rejón wrote the *puro* leader that Almonte's personal secretary was returning to Mexico "under the pretext of taking some sealed documents, but with the real objective of talking with you and other friends to finish arranging our things."95 Rejón added that Santa Anna only wished to *"renew the former friendly political relationship which existed in [18]33 and [18]34 because both agree with the ideas they supported at that time."* According to Rejón, Santa Anna wanted to join Gómez Farías *"and follow his advice"* to pull the country out of the embarrassing situation that it found itself in.96

Santa Anna wrote Gómez Farías two weeks later to consummate their rapprochement. After pointing out the need to establish a "frank, loyal, gentlemanly, and eminently patriotic friendship," Santa Anna promised to give him

> the affection of the army, in which I have many good friends, and you will give me the masses over whom you have so much influence, not because I desire to return to power, which I will need only for a brief time to become reconciled with my country and belie with greater deeds that I never intended to oppress it or tyrannize it . . . but to cooperate efficiently for the republic's salvation and to put it on the road to prosperity and glory.

Only by cementing the "intimate union" between the people and the army could Santa Anna and Gómez Farías end the manifold abuses and interests that precluded the establishment of "a prudent democracy" and "political liberty." Santa Anna remarked that they had to "wrest power from the detestable *hombres de bien*," whom Gómez Farías had "so justly challenged" and whom Santa Anna had "thoughtlessly protected since 1834."97

The die was cast. Gómez Farías had decided to tie his fate to his former ally, but he also understood the need to alleviate the fears that conservative and *moderado* statesmen harbored about the *puros*, their goals, and their popularity among the urban poor. Gómez Farías rejected an earlier suggestion by Santa Anna which advanced the idea of including all classes of Mexican society in the Congress that would be called after the *puros* took power. The *puro* leader wrote that the social classes were "so varied and diverse, and very few of them have people of sufficient aptitude and understanding to be able to carry out the arduous and difficult task which has to be entrusted to their care." Gómez Farías was not likely to have acted in this manner out of solidarity with the *hombres de bien,* as one historian recently noted, but because pragmatic political considerations required him to temper his convictions.98

By the time Santa Anna's reply reached Gómez Farías, Paredes' regime was near collapse. He had been warned that the men of the garrison in the port of Mazatlán—a key city because its customs office could provide an economic boost for the political faction that controlled the port—openly supported an uprising in favor of Santa Anna. The revolt broke out on May 7 with the rebels denouncing Paredes' government and the January 27, 1846, decree that called for elections to the constituent Congress. They also demanded a republic as the only form of government that suited the country, guaranteed the army's existence, and called for Santa Anna's return to the presidency.99 Two weeks later, on May 20, Colonel José María Yáñez headed a rebellion in Guadalajara with goals similar to those advocated by Mazatlán's garrison. Plans were underway for Gómez Farías' followers in Guanajuato, Zacatecas, Durango, and Puebla to join the struggle against Paredes.100

But *santanistas* and *puros* were were not able to strike the final blow in Mexico City at this time. Government agents intercepted the correspondence of various plotters and arrested several of them, including Gómez Farías, between May 17 and May 20.[101] Despite the setback, Santa Anna maintained an attitude of kindness and concern toward his new allies. Upon hearing of Gómez Farías' arrest, Santa Anna expressed his grief to the *puro* leader's children and reiterated that genuine friendship linked him and their father. As evidence of his good faith, he sent the renowned financier Cayetano Rubio a letter of credit to alleviate the Gómez Farías family's economic problems.[102] After spending nearly two months in jail, Gómez Farías was cleared of the charges levied against him on July 13 and resumed plotting to overthrow Paredes.[103]

The *moderados'* intrigues gave *puros* and *santanistas* a suitable pretext to launch what proved to be the decisive blow against the government. Aware of the weaknesses of Paredes' regime and yearning to prevent Santa Anna's return, several anonymous *moderado* congressmen moved to "restore the affairs and persons of December 6."[104] Their ill-fated attempt to short-circuit the *puros'* political aspirations began after General Nicolás Bravo replaced Paredes—who vacated the presidency to assume command of Mexico's armies—as chief executive on July 27. The legislators spread rumors that Bravo was "determined to do well, arm the nation, and adopt other popular measures."[105] On August 3, Bravo's government forwarded to Congress a proposal demanding the immediate reestablishment of the *Bases Orgánicas*. It has been suggested that Bravo did so at the suggestion of Paredes, which raises the possibility that Paredes struck a deal with the *moderados* in a final effort to save his crumbling presidency.[106] Bravo's proposal, however, was anathema to the *puros*, who moved to shatter the hopes of the *moderados* and perhaps those of Paredes as well.

On August 4, General José Mariano Salas, a long-time enemy of Paredes, announced the Plan of the Ciudadela, a manifesto similar to the one Santa Anna sent to Mexico in early March. There was one important addition, however: the new Congress, besides having the capacity to issue a constitution, would be in charge of all measures relative to the war with the United States.[107] Bravo's administration resorted to dilatory tactics over the next two days to stall the uprising, but the rebels had triumphed by August 6. The question that remained unanswered, however, was whether the rebellion of August 4 would provide Mexicans with the much-needed harmony required to face the foreign threat.

V

"A Most Fearful State of Anarchy"

"I say again," wrote the perceptive José Fernando Ramírez early in August 1846, "that I still cannot get a clear idea of the state of things." Indeed, Ramírez correctly assessed the confused political circumstances that prevailed in Mexico City shortly after the triumph of the rebellion of the Ciudadela. The Valentín Gómez Farías-led *puros* won a resounding victory and took the reins of government with great hope. Not only had they defeated General Mariano Paredes y Arrillaga's attempt to revive a monarchical regime, but General Antonio López de Santa Anna was on his way back to Mexico to lead military resistance against the American forces. Just as importantly, Santa Anna appeared determined to uphold the *puros'* political ideology. He had enhanced Gómez Farías' clout by ordering "that everything be carried out in agreement with [his] wishes."[1]

Despite this auspicious state of affairs, Ramírez also feared that the immediate future would bring "a period of absolute intolerance, boundless envy, and an eruption of whetted passions."[2] In fact, the stumbling blocks in the road which the *puros* had to take to assert themselves as Mexico's dominant political faction made Ramírez' words come true. First, Santa Anna had directed that nothing was to be done until he arrived, not even the organization of a provisional government, indicating his unwillingness to grant his new allies full control over domestic affairs. Second, members of the *moderado* party worked to sabotage the *puros'* goals by refusing to endorse the Plan of the Ciudadela unanimously and by disregarding all the *puros'* efforts to effect a reconciliation. The dangers inherent in this situation became more serious as 1846 moved along because at times the *moderados* counted on Santa Anna's assistance. Third, the attempt to bridge the chasm that divided Mexican society proved to be nearly impossible. Conservative and *moderado* statesmen, as well as senior army officers, saw traces of demagoguery in the *puros'* activities. They opposed Gómez Farías because they feared that the *puros* would give free rein to the *leperada*.

Uncertain Optimism

As soon as the August 4 rebellion was underway, Gómez Farías and General José Mariano Salas (who became provisional president) issued a manifesto to explain their conduct and to sway public opinion in favor of the uprising. After blaming the monarchist plotters for Mexico's numerous problems, the proclamation stated that the Plan of the Ciudadela had

> as its fundamental basis the sincere union of the people and the army. . . . The democratic principle is completely saved in our plan; the entire nation, and not a ridiculous oligarchy, will decide the destinies of this unfortunate nation; and the army, commanded by the hero of Tampico and Veracruz [Santa Anna], will

undoubtedly be the constitution's most resolute sup-
porter.3

Salas published a similar proclamation two days later. Since
the uprising that began in San Luis Potosí in December 1845
tried to "completely destroy the organization of society," it was
necessary to summon the nation according to the law that in
1823 had created Mexico's second constituent Congress. Salas
also argued that it was imperative to name Santa Anna gen-
eral-in-chief of the armed forces. His "unquestionable prestige
in the army will be the best guarantee of the union of this mer-
itorious class with the people, while his devotion to republican principles" made him the "firmest support of that system
against the perfidious plans of the monarchist party."4

These phrases, as others that had accompanied past insurrections, promised the dawn of an auspicious era for Mexico.
To make clear the character of the August 4 revolt, however,
Salas and Gómez Farías backed up their rhetoric with deeds
during the following days. The government published a
decree calling for elections for a new Congress, repealed all
restrictions on freedom of the press, and abolished a May
1846 edict that had reduced the salaries of public employees
by twenty-five percent. Meanwhile, Gómez Farías restored
efficiency to daily bureaucratic operations, visiting the
national treasury to supervise a payroll disbursement and
ordering government workers to return to their posts. Salas
did not lag behind. He announced that he would not accept
a salary increase while serving as provisional chief execu-
tive.5

Mexico City's newspapers—namely *El Republicano, El
Monitor Republicano,* and *Don Simplicio,* which eventually
became the public voices of the *moderados*—praised the government's eloquent declarations and initial actions. The same
periodicals, however, lambasted the Plan of the Ciudadela.
According to *El Republicano,* the plan did not authorize Salas
to serve as provisional executive, nor did it reserve that posi-

tion for Santa Anna. The Plan of the Ciudadela had other drawbacks. It did not specify the president's powers and their limitations, it failed to guarantee individual rights, and it did not address the way in which the internal administration of Mexico's departments was to be organized. *El Monitor Republicano* only discerned confusion and a military take-over, while *Don Simplicio,* with its characteristic sarcasm, commented that the Plan of the Ciudadela's best features were its omissions.[6] In response to the attacks of these newspapers, Salas ordered *moderado* politician José María Lafragua to draft a bill limiting the executive's authority and guaranteeing individual rights. Lafragua complied with the request, but the later reestablishment of the Constitution of 1824 made its publication unnecessary.[7]

The opposition of *moderado* journals, however, was not the only troublesome element facing the new government. A more serious problem confronting Gómez Farías and the *puros,* as following verse vividly illustrates, was that many politically conscious Mexicans questioned the sincerity of Santa Anna's latest promises of his republican faith.

AN OMEN FROM *DON SIMPLICIO*
The stupid servile regulation
Issued by the clumsy monarchist faction
Speeded up the splendid victory
Of the brave liberal federalist [party].
It is headed for the temple of glory;
But federalists and *santanistas* beware
Together they will descend into the deep abyss
If don Antonio returns the same as always.[8]

Santa Anna acted ambiguously from the day he set foot in Mexico. Although he hinted at being willing to fulfill the promises made during his 1845-1846 exile in Cuba, he also refrained from wholeheartedly supporting the *puros* on more than one occasion. Santa Anna, as it became clear in 1847, was only trying to set the framework for him to betray Gómez Farías as he had done in 1834.

Since the date of Santa Anna's arrival remained unknown, Gómez Farías sent his three sons to Veracruz to welcome him. Their reports clearly depicted apprehension about Santa Anna. Fermín wrote that "some timidity and perhaps distrust" were evident in the city of Jalapa, while Casimiro noted that several individuals in Veracruz doubted Santa Anna's good faith. The most extensive report came from Benito, who said he had worked unceasingly to "unite everyone" in Veracruz. Although the Veracruz councilmen were "very distrustful" of Santa Anna's return, he told them that Gómez Farías took part in the August 4, 1846, revolt "with the greatest loyalty, and not because of a trade-off, as many believed." Benito's arguments were persuasive, for he wrote that "everyone became perfectly convinced that it was necessary to pursue a union between the people and the army."9

Gómez Farías' sons did not have time to dispel any lingering suspicions. An artillery salvo on the morning of August 16 announced that Santa Anna's ship had been sighted off Veracruz. The exiled hero remarked that he disembarked at one o'clock "amidst the applauses of the people and Ulúa's garrison." A British observer, however, noted that he "looked anything but pleased" with the lack of applause and that his wife "pouted at the cool reception, for not one *viva* was heard." The lukewarm welcome seemed to indicate that Mexico remained unwilling to forgive Santa Anna's past abuses.10

Santa Anna quickly assessed the state of public opinion, and he sent to the printers a proclamation that sought to "dissipate any distrust" caused by a past that filled him with bitterness. He blamed the monarchist plotters for bringing about Mexico's current domestic and foreign difficulties. Their attempt to impose their "baneful beliefs" had prevented Mexico from a major constitutional reorganization and had provoked the American invasion. Santa Anna argued that "republicans of all parties, the masses, and the army" had to unite to "insure the country's independence, putting it at liberty to choose the form of government that best suited her, and with everyone sacrificing his own convictions to the will of the majority."[11]

Santa Anna's manifesto included two modifications to the Plan of the Ciudadela. Since Congress' faculties were limited to providing the country with a new constitutional structure and handling every aspect of the war with the United States, the provisional regime would be obliged to rule arbitrarily, turning it into "a dictatorship, always hateful even if there are imperative circumstances which may make it necessary." Thus, Congress should be authorized to deal with all branches of public administration that were of the "general interest and competence of the legislative power, while the republic's interim executive would act with complete subjection to its decisions." Santa Anna also called for the immediate reestablishment of the 1824 constitution. This charter would function as a "beacon" that would guide the president and "regulate the internal administration of the departments." To eliminate all doubts about his new convictions, Santa Anna portrayed himself in the manifesto's conclusion as a "slave of public opinion." He only wished to retake "the enviable title of soldier of the people" and "defend the republic's independence and liberty until his death."[12]

Santa Anna displayed other signs of his apparent political regeneration and willingness to collaborate with the *puros* shortly thereafter. He congratulated Gómez Farías on August 17 for the manner in which he had guided the rebellion of the Ciudadela. The conduct of the *puro* leader would allow him to preside over "the glorious enterprise" of creating a constitutional framework for the nation. Mexico would then regain the "respectability that the previous iniquitous administration made it lose" and it would soon figure "among the world's most advanced countries." Santa Anna added that he was certain they would be able to "overcome everything, *uniting* with our respective influences the people and the army. For this, I implore you, do not omit any means or effort, in calming the passions that excite the masses, and I will do my part to allay any fears they may induce in the military. You know what my principles are, and deeds will demonstrate if I know how to live up to my word."[13] Two days later, Rejón wrote Gómez Farías that Santa Anna had *"arrived with the best intentions and determined to work in agreement with you, whom he considers his best friend and the staunchest supporter of public liberties."*[14] Any doubts that may have remained in Gómez Farías' mind about Santa Anna's intentions diminished considerably.

Despite these encouraging words, there was soon reason to be suspicious of Santa Anna. Instead of hastening to Mexico City, he stopped at his hacienda El Encerro. Santa Anna allegedly needed to rest the leg that had been wounded fighting the French during the 1838 "Pastry War"; he claimed that the limb had become irritated during the voyage from Cuba. It seems, however, that Santa Anna was already scheming to break his alliance with the *puros*. According to British Minister Charles Bankhead, Santa Anna had decided to wait until a dominant party emerged in the capital. He would then ally himself with that group and make a triumphant entry into Mexico City.[15]

The British representative's conjecture becomes more viable in light of Santa Anna's decision to send General Juan Nepomuceno Almonte to the capital on August 17. Almonte was "universally thought of as Santa Anna's advance agent, or at least as a champion of his political theories," and had been "commissioned to explore the situation to see what course [Santa Anna] should pursue."[16] Although Almonte had joined Santa Anna's camp in the spring of 1846, the animosity which Gómez Farías harbored toward him could have undermined the success of the mission. Thus, Santa Anna implored Gómez Farías to act in accordance with his emissary, for Almonte was a person of "complete confidence whose cooperation would be extremely valuable."[17] Santa Anna's caution proved unnecessary at the time. Almonte's arrival coincided with the publication of an August 22 decree reestablishing the Constitution of 1824, which convinced Almonte that Santa Anna should not yet reveal his true intent. Almonte limited his activities, therefore, to emphasizing Santa Anna's conversion to republicanism. In doing so, Almonte managed to persuade José Fernando Ramírez that Santa Anna had "made up his mind, at least for the present, to identify himself with the democratic party"—Gómez Farías and the *puros*.[18]

But several developments forecast difficulties for the *puros*. One was Lafragua's decision to nominate fellow *moderado* Manuel Gómez Pedraza for the post of first director of the departmental assembly of Mexico. Elections for that body were to be held on August 18. Gómez Pedraza's selection caused a stir among *puro* supporters, one of whom described it as an "insolent idea" that had caused "real alarm."[19] The reason behind Gómez Pedraza's designation is a matter of debate. Lafragua's retrospective chronicle claims that Gómez Farías had suggested the appointment to insure a degree of cooperation with the *moderados*, for a few days earlier Gómez Pedraza had refused to join forces with the *puros*. On the other hand, at least two *puro* advocates believed that Lafragua's nomination of Gómez Pedraza was an attempt to undermine the goals of the rebellion of the Ciudadela.[20] In the end, Gómez Pedraza won the election, but the reestablishment of the Constitution of 1824 made installation of the departmental assembly unnecessary.[21] It was, nevertheless, a sign of things to come.

Organizing the cabinet also provoked intrigue and uncertainty. Provisional President Salas named his ministers on August 15. Gómez Farías would be in charge of finance, Lafragua would head the Ministry of Foreign Relations, fellow *moderado* Luis de la Rosa would take over the Ministry of Justice, and General Lino Alcorta was appointed minister of war. This cabinet was never installed, perhaps due to the opposition of several army officers or possibly because Lafragua refused to occupy his post, arguing that another cabinet was inevitable since Santa Anna had not yet arrived. Regardless, Salas decided to wait further instructions from Santa Anna before moving ahead.[22]

Santa Anna gave notice on August 25 that he had named the men who would make up his cabinet—Rejón (foreign relations), Almonte (war), Gómez Farías (finance), and José Ramón Pacheco (justice)—and they assumed their posts three days later. The new ministers gave the impression of harmony. They made public their desire to implement the Plan of the Ciudadela, to abolish internal customs duties gradually, to reduce fees on foreign commerce, to promote European migration, to undertake the necessary reforms in all branches of public administration, to help raise resources to wage war, and to bolster the union of the people and the army.[23] A clerk in the Ministry of Foreign Relations commented that Santa Anna was extremely pleased with the declaration. The cabinet's principles, according to the informant, were "entirely in conformity" with those Santa Anna judged "conducive to the republic's welfare and prosperity."[24] Santa Anna also praised Gómez Farías for "his decisiveness, laboriousness, and distinction." Santa Anna hoped that those traits would allow the new finance minister to gather sufficient resources to cover the war's expenses.[25] The statements seemed to augur an era of friendly relations between the cabinet, Santa Anna, and Provisional President Salas. That, however, was not to be. The ministers had "nothing in common and distrust[ed] one another,"[26] and mutual suspicions soon hindered the *puros'* attempts to solidify their hold on power.

The *puros'* attempt to purge those bureaucrats who did not share their political ideas contributed to the prevailing unrest. Article Five of the August 22 decree (which declared that the Constitution of 1824 was in effect) stated that departmental authorities did not have a legal right to their positions. Such claims rested on the August 4 movement. Consequently, the interim chief executive could dismiss them if he deemed it convenient to the national welfare. The proviso allowed Gómez Farías, Rejón, Lafragua, and Francisco Modesto Olaguíbel to demand in late August 1846,

> a clean sweep of state governments and assemblies to rid them, as they say, of Monarchists, Decembrists and Pedracistas.... Almonte did not mention any names nor did he discuss the crux of the matter, but he did explain the general idea.... He added that the dismissals from office were part of the general plan.[27]

The *puros'* scheme became reality on August 31. A decree issued that day warned that public employees who refused to render services demanded during the war with the United States without showing just cause (to be determined by the government) would be removed from their posts and declared ineligible to solicit other positions. In addition, those bureaucrats would be subject to legal penalties.[28]

On balance, existing conditions in Mexico City may have impressed on Gómez Farías and his associates the need to crush their enemies with one swift blow. The capital was awash with rumors that troops stationed in San Luis Potosí would rebel against the government and that General Gabriel Valencia, who earlier in the month had emphasized he would never ally himself with the *puros*, planned to proclaim Santa Anna's dictatorship.[29] Nonetheless, the August 31 decree gave rise to a burning animosity against Rejón—its supposed author—and provided the *moderados* with another pretext to attack their political rivals. *El Republicano* editorialized that the law was "arbitrary, unjust, and exceedingly impolitic"; *Don Simplicio* declared it to be "an assault against property [rights] and the guarantees granted by the laws." The protests proved effective in the end, and the decree was abrogated in early November.[30]

Two other measures adopted by Interim President Salas

and his advisers insured that political passions reached a fever pitch. One was the decision to hold public meetings—the contrivance of Rejón. During his 1845-1846 exile in Havana, Rejón became convinced that Mexico could not sustain a military campaign against the United States *"purely with arms."* Since the conflict would be *"a war of principles,"* he believed it necessary to develop *"institutions similar to those of that nation, which will allow us to stop him at our frontiers, and prevent him from absorbing us."*[31] Thus, Rejón and others set about to organize a federalist society similar to those in Great Britain and the United States. *Every Mexican* was encouraged to participate.[32]

Expectations for the meetings were high at first; even the editors of *El Republicano* commented that they hoped the meetings would stir public spirit and help to introduce measures beneficial to the republic.[33] A September 10 decree listed the advantages of the open meetings. The sessions would allow the nation to "meet head on the dangers that it faced, to find the remedy of the evils that afflict it, and to deploy the energy of free nations to constitute and save itself." The law also noted that those Mexicans who wished to congregate peacefully to discuss the reforms that should be incorporated into the country's institutions, send "respectful petitions to the authorities, or cooperate to their mutual enlightenment" were free to do so.[34]

Despite these admirable intentions, meetings were soon hampered by partisan differences. The prolific contemporary journalist Guillermo Prieto stated that public gatherings attempted to counter the intrigues of the clerical party (the conservatives). José Fernando Ramírez agreed, affirming that the meetings clearly indicated the *puros'* determination "to make a clean sweep of everything." Speakers at the proceedings lambasted conservative statesmen such as Lucas Alamán and institutions like the Catholic Church. They called for beheading Alamán as well as those believed to be monarchist sympathizers and argued that it would be desirable to seize

Church properties and abolish the Church's special privileges. These orators alarmed observers like Carlos María Bustamante, who claimed that public rallies gave rise to a "frightful disorder" because they only brought together "crazy persons."35 As a result, meetings came to be perceived as potentially dangerous to the established social order. They had lost much of their initial appeal by the end of 1846.36

The second significant measure taken by Salas' administration that paved the way for future animosities in Mexico was revival of the civic militia. The editors of Mexico City's newspapers had clamored for this force since mid-June 1846. They believed that it would allow Mexico to organize a more effective resistance against the United States.37 During his presidency, Paredes had disregarded such demands because he feared his political enemies would use the militia to overthrow him. His caution was of no avail. The uprising on August 4, 1846, was partially successful due to the great number of men who took up arms spontaneously in Mexico City.38 Later that month Salas ordered Generals Joaquín Rangel and Ignacio Sierra y Rosso, civilians Francisco Carbajal and Anastasio Zerecero, and Minister of Justice Pacheco, to draw up an ordinance for the civic militia. The ordinance became law on September 11, establishing the civic militia in Mexico's states, districts, and territories.39 The victory proved to be fleeting, as the strife between *puros* and *moderados* soon found its way into this military force. Civic militia units became divided along partisan and social lines, and the *cívicos* turned into yet another pawn in the factional struggle.

Santa Anna's reluctance to make his entry into Mexico City further complicated the *puros'* attempt to establish themselves after the August 4 rebellion. Although Santa Anna told Gómez Farías that he had recovered from his leg injury by early September and was ready to depart for the capital, he abruptly changed his mind. Two events probably caused his change of heart. One was receiving a petition from Generals José Vicente Miñón and Juan Morales stating that the reestab-

lishment of federalism would make the army's continued existence impossible. The two officers, it must be remembered,
had assisted Gómez Farías in his schemes in 1845 and 1846, so
their appeal to Santa Anna again illustrated the fragile character of the *puros'* alliance with the military. Santa Anna's
behavior may also be explained by several remarks made at
the inaugural public meeting held on September 8. Some
orators suggested that the civic militia be given greater recognition, and Santa Anna doubtless construed these comments
as indicative of the *puros'* and the populace's desire to diminish the army's importance.[40] Santa Anna was growing increasingly worried about the consequences of an affiliation with
the *puros* and decided to play for time.

Santa Anna's decision to postpone his entry "placed the
government in a most embarrassing position," and the ministers' lack of confidence in each other made the situation more
difficult. No one wanted to travel to Santa Anna's hacienda,
since "those who remained behind mistrusted the one who
left, while the latter was fearful of what the others would do in
his absence." To break the deadlock, the government dispatched General Manuel Baranda to convince Santa Anna to
take charge of the government, and that he should not fix his
residence at Tacubaya. To force Santa Anna's hand, Gómez
Farías "especially urged Baranda to tell Santa Anna that it
would be considered an open act of hostility toward the people if he did not come into the city." Santa Anna would
assume the presidency as soon as he arrived.[41]

Baranda's mission met with partial success. Santa Anna
agreed to enter Mexico City, but he refused to comply with
the additional conditions and told Minister of War Almonte
that he would take charge of the army immediately.[42] Santa
Anna stated that it would be "most degrading" to hold the
presidency when duty called him to fight the enemies of the
republic. "Neither my honor nor my loyalty"—wrote Santa
Anna—"demand that I abandon interests that are so dear."[43]
Thus, Santa Anna once again proved his sagacity. Any doubts

that his previous vacillations may have awakened were now of secondary importance. These words made Santa Anna a most worthy recipient of his countrymen's trust.

Santa Anna's much anticipated entry into Mexico City began around 1:30 P.M. on September 14. The festive atmosphere and the decorations that adorned the streets did not fool two keen observers. Their impressions of the affair noted the incongruity and frailty of the alliance between Santa Anna and Gómez Farías. José Fernando Ramírez wrote that "the whole affair was eminently democratic: not a frockcoat nor a carriage other than those of the officials." Nonetheless, he remarked that both Santa Anna and Gómez Farías "seemed more like victims than conquerors." The scene so disturbed Ramírez that he complained of a headache that left him dizzy for the rest of the day.[44] The comments of Carlos María Bustamante were in a similar vein. In his opinion, Gómez Farías' decision to make Santa Anna hold a copy of the 1824 constitution in their carriage was akin to "giving [Santa Anna] a sack of scorpions."[45]

The distrust was even more evident that evening. Santa Anna had earlier announced that he would not attend a sumptuous banquet that had been prepared in his honor, and would instead dine in Tacubaya with several close friends. Rejón, however, insisted on surrounding him with the "chiefs of the people," and invited to Tacubaya *puro* politicians such as Francisco Carbajal, Vicente Romero and his son Eligio, and Juan José Baz, who had been one of the outspoken orators at the September 8 public meeting.[46] Their company surely must have spoiled Santa Anna's appetite.

The animated events of September 14 ended with what must be considered a moral triumph for the *puros*. Nonetheless, it would be one of the few duels with Santa Anna that the *puros* would win. Santa Anna remained in Mexico City two weeks to raise funds for his army, but that was not the only matter that occupied his attention. Before leaving for San Luis Potosí on September 28 with his troops,[47] he orchestrated a plan to undermine the political influence of Gómez Farías and the *puros*.

"This Useless and Ridiculous Organism"

Santa Anna implemented his scheme through the establishment of a Council of State. The Constitution of 1824 stipulated the existence of this body, specified its duties, and determined its organizational structure. The council was to be formed by half the members of the Senate (one per state), and Mexico's vice-president would sit at its head. Since Mexico did not have a congress nor a vice-president in September 1846, the decree (issued on September 20) that created the council justified its existence because of the country's "eccentric situation." The council, while not endowed with specific powers by the legislation, was authorized to advise the government on the nation's problems. Finally, the September 20 decree provided that the president of the council would govern Mexico when the chief executive was absent. The real purpose of this body, however, was to abort Gómez Farías' appointment to the cabinet.[48]

Success would require the *moderados'* support, which called for Santa Anna to put aside his differences with Gómez Pedraza. Santa Anna met with the *moderado* leader within a few days of arriving in Mexico City, and they reached a mutual understanding. Gómez Pedraza agreed that the *moderados* would join forces with the *puros*. In return, Santa Anna promised not to take such unlimited power as in 1844.[49] Santa Anna's ability to extract such a promise from Gómez Pedraza gave him the wherewithall to carry out his design, which began to unfold on September 19—before publication of the decree.

On that date, Santa Anna sent Rejón a list of the individuals who would make up the Council of State. To showcase Mexico's newly fashioned domestic harmony, members of various political factions were invited to join the council. Ignacio

Trigueros, Francisco Lombardo, and General Martín Carrera represented the *santanistas*. At Gómez Farías' behest, *moderado* statesmen Lafragua, Mariano Otero, and Luis de la Rosa had agreed to join, and two of them offered to talk to Gómez Pedraza into doing so as well. The presence of the dispassionate statesman José Fernando Ramírez in this association was intended to mitigate any animosities that might emerge between his fellow *moderados* and the *puros*. Finally, since Gómez Farías was to assume the presidency of the council, Santa Anna also recommended that the new minister of finance be Antonio Haro y Tamariz, a former *santanista* loyalist who had apparently reconciled with Gómez Farías.[50] But Santa Anna's mandate had a hidden goal: start a dispute that would compromise the *puros'* dominance in public affairs.

The impending removal of Gómez Farías from the cabinet startled the *puros*, who moved quickly to gain the upper hand. Rejón and Gómez Farías threatened Santa Anna with the resignation of the entire cabinet. Santa Anna, however, replied that Gómez Pedraza would occupy the presidency of the Council of State only if Gómez Farías refused to take the position. Santa Anna had played his cards perfectly. First, if Gómez Farías remained minister of finance, his archenemy would be a heartbeat away from the presidency. Second, although acceptance of the leading post in the Council of State would put Gómez Farías closer to Mexico's executive power, his ability to shape governmental policy would be severely restricted. The council could only be as influential as Santa Anna allowed, and members from the *moderado* and *santanista* factions were likely to block Gómez Farías' directives. In the end, Gómez Farías had little choice but to retreat. By September 25 he had resigned from the cabinet—because of rheumatism, he claimed—and accepted the presidency of the Council of State.[51]

The imbroglio over the Council of State also illustrated the *moderados'* unwillingness to reconcile with the *puros*. No sooner had the creation of the committee been announced than *moderado*-sponsored newspapers began a publicity campaign to discredit it. According to *El Republicano*, there was no "need to infringe the constitution nor to create a council without any fixed faculties, nor to burden the moribund state treasury with a heavy expense to pay for *opinions* the government can hear for *free* if it calls to its side those and other citizens, nor was it…necessary to insist on a *dictatorial* decree only to satisfy a whim."[52] *Don Simplicio* opposed the September 20 law for similar reasons. Its editors pointed out that it was misleading to think that the political goals of the decree could be realized. The Council of State was "an anomalous and vicious institution, impotent to promote the general welfare, and dangerous if its majority bowed to the will [of the person] in power." Members of the *moderado* party would provide "evidence of a repugnant inconsistency" if they joined the ranks of the council.[53] Given that Article Four of the September 20 decree stated that the law would remain in force as long as most states did not repudiate it, the *moderados* requested several state leaders to ask for a veto of the legislation.[54]

Jeopardizing the *puros'* political position further, five *moderado* councilmen broke a pledge that they would not resign their appointments and vacated their posts before the Council of State's scheduled October 1 installation.[55] The first to quit was Gómez Pedraza, who alleged he did not know about his nomination until he read the September 21 issue of the *Diario del Gobierno de la República Mexicana*. He indicated he lacked "the necessary qualifications to carry out such a difficult task."[56] Juan Rodríguez Puebla, Lafragua, and Otero grounded their resignations on the council's dubious constitutional status.[57] De la Rosa noted that he "would derive immense satisfaction" in carrying out his appointment. Nonetheless, his deteriorating health and his personal affairs, which he had unattended to for some time, dictated that he leave the capital for an indefinite period. *Santanista* advocate Trigueros also resigned because he planned to be away from Mexico City during the following months.[58]

The excuses had little justification. Gómez Pedraza's reasoning might be expected of someone who was making his first venture into the turbulent world of Mexican politics, but not from a man whose career as a statesman included stints as president of the republic, minister of war, and senator. Gómez Farías correctly pointed out that the *moderados'* "opposition had no other objective than to get rid of him."59 In the end, although only five of the original nominees occupied their positions, replacements were found and the Council of State was installed on the scheduled date.60 It is clear, though, that the *moderados* and some *santanistas* betrayed the *puros* in an attempt to crush them.

Santa Anna sought to prevent the estrangement in a bid to cover his actions, dispatching Rejón on September 26 to remind Gómez Pedraza he could not break his promises. The maneuver did not bring about the expected results, however. Otero assured Rejón, on Gómez Pedraza's, de la Rosa's, and his own behalf, that the decision to resign was irrevocable. Ramírez found such intransigence to be appalling. He believed the Council of State to be "one of the most vital elements in our social order, especially under such scatterbrained systems as ours, where men appear on the political scene and then disappear, like the fleeting figures thrown on the screen by the magic lantern." More importantly, Ramírez concluded that Gómez Pedraza and the other *moderados* had "put the capstone to our misfortunes by refusing to help the government, which they ought to uphold in this crisis."61 In fact, the matter of the creation of the Council of State was just one of the many instances where *puros* and *moderados* clashed, and their skirmishes in other arenas confirmed the impossibility of a rapprochement.

Primary Electors and Embraces

The bitter antagonism that characterized relations between *puros* and *moderados* emerged again over the question of choosing primary electors to the upcoming constituent Congress. An August 6, 1846, decree stipulated that elections to choose these individuals would be held on September 27, and that the voting would not be limited by income or property qualifications.[62] As the date for the tally drew near, a correspondent for *Don Simplicio* warned that one did not need "a great talent to foresee that the party known as *puro* would dominate them without any effort and rivals.... The opportunity which the regulations give to the shepherds of forty or fifty sheep to decide where and how they want to hold the voting has turned the election's terrain into forbidden ground for the friends of order."[63] These concerns apparently became a reality. Carlos María Bustamante noted that Gómez Farías may have "stirred the masses so that they voted for the lists that his supporters printed,"[64] while the editors of *El Republicano* remarked that the casting of ballots had been characterized

> by an extraordinary disorder: in many booths there were sixty or eighty men of the people devoted to some of those pure liberals, whose decency has never been doubted, and who entered the booth as many times as necessary and left handfuls of lists, and that iniquitous party triumphed as a result.[65]

Whether true or not, these comments vividly illustrated the prevailing distrust between *puros* and *moderados*. The *puros'* electoral victories in other parts of Mexico (San Luis Potosí, Puebla, Oaxaca, and Guadalajara)[66] enhanced their chances of dominating affairs in the legislature that was scheduled to be installed by the end of the year. This circumstance was yet another reason why *puros* and *moderados* refused to reach an agreement.

Despite the bitterness, at least one more attempt to patch up relations between factions was made in the fall of 1846. At an October 2 public meeting, Lafragua encouraged *puros* and *moderados* to join together to save the country from internal and external dangers. The speech inspired several listeners to ask Gómez Farías and Gómez Pedraza to forget their past differences, work on behalf of the public welfare, and embrace each other on the balcony of the National Palace as a sign of their reconciliation.[67] Gómez Farías, knowing that the *puros'* political survival required easing *moderado* opposition, immediately agreed.[68] Gómez Pedraza, however, rejected the invitation. The *moderado* leader wrote that it was not logical to suppose that the embrace would produce unity. Instead, Mexicans would probably suspect he was "conceited and priggish." Moreover, even if the episode turned out to be a success, both he and Gómez Farías would look "ridiculous" and invite "universal deprecation."[69] Gómez Farías was frustrated by this turn of events, describing his rival's response as "insulting"[70] and as a "censure to General Santa Anna's conduct and mine, for when [Santa Anna] returned to this capital he only wanted to enter it with me in order to give public testimony of our reconciliation."[71] The *puros'* struggle with the *moderados* continued in October and briefly weakened the *puros'* influence in Mexican affairs.

"This Capital is Pandora's Box"

Political discord also grew as the relationship between Gómez Farías and Acting President Salas deteriorated. There had been little or no evidence of dissent between them as of late August 1846. Santa Anna, in fact, congratulated Salas for the "harmony" that existed between the two. Gómez Farías had even stated that the interim chief executive was both "an honest man and a patriot" who did not take any action without consulting him.[72] By early October, however, when Gómez Farías described Salas as "a man of limited knowledge who lacked experience in public affairs," cordial relations were a thing of the past. Salas needed "to be taken by the hand so he did not stumble at each step," according to Gómez Farías, and the provisional president did not "have any fondness for democracy and progress." He would have wielded power like a despot "if the torrent of [public] opinion had not dragged him to the side of liberty, and if the illustrious General Santa Anna, faithful to his pledges, had not proclaimed the federation" in the "memorable manifesto" he published after disembarking at Veracruz.73

The reasons for Gómez Farías' change in attitude can be inferred from a letter written by then Minister of Foreign Relations Manuel Crescencio Rejón in late October 1846. According to Rejón, Salas was determined to uphold "the persons and objects most opposed to the ideas of the [August 4] revolution."74 To implement his plan, Salas enlisted the support of the minister of justice, José Ramón Pacheco, and General José Gómez de la Cortina, governor of the Federal District. Gómez Farías' comments about the ruses instigated by the governor were sparse, but he did not mince words when criticizing Pacheco's conduct. The minister of justice was a man "without any political beliefs" who took possession of his post "through craftiness and lies." Pacheco paid "little attention to his chores" and "spent long hours daily with Salas. His pleasantness and his adulating disposition gave him so much superiority over his colleagues that he came to resolve affairs which belonged to other ministers."75 One example of how Pacheco contributed to undermine the *puros'* influence was his role in the militia committee. That assignment even befuddled *Don Simplicio*, which poetically editorialized about Pacheco's new duties:

MILITIA
The minister of justice
Gathers around him talented persons
And among them busies himself
With the militia's arrangement
All that is missing is for the [minister of] war to realize
[That] his powers have been nullified
[And begin to] talk about bishops and [papal] bulls

What things about our country![76]

There was, however, a simple explanation for Pacheco's membership on the board. Salas and the *moderados* wished to prevent the *puros* from turning the civic militia into a tool for their own partisan ambitions.

Although Pacheco's appointment to the cabinet helped drive Salas and Gómez Farías apart, it was Cortina who provided the spark that lit the fuse for a showdown between *puros* and *moderados*. Cortina's previous political affiliations shed light on why the *puros* viewed him suspiciously. He had been a member of both the Assembly of Notables, which drafted the 1843 charter known as the *Bases Orgánicas*, and of the Senate that spearheaded the December 6, 1844, movement.[77] Thus, on September 22, 1846, nine *regidores* of Mexico City's *ayuntamiento* visited Santa Anna requesting Cortina's removal as governor of the Federal District. They argued that the capital's residents viewed his appointment with "repugnance," and that his lack of "liberal ideas" was notorious. Santa Anna ignored the petitioners. He admitted that the rumors about Cortina's unpopularity were true, but the governor had already visited him to discuss the matter and he did not distrust him.[78] Before long, however, the governor confirmed *puro* suspicions.

Animosities surfaced on October 6 when Cortina apprehended *puro* partisan Francisco Próspero Pérez on the grounds he had threatened domestic tranquility. Not only was Próspero Pérez suspected of authoring leaflets inciting the populace to loot the capital, but at a public meeting held earlier that day he had called Gómez Pedraza a traitor for refusing to embrace Gómez Farías publicly. Both incidents raised the specter of the 1828 Parián riot among Mexico City's *hombres de bien*, and Cortina ordered Próspero Pérez' arrest. The governor of the Federal District added to the conflict when he disbanded the 4th Battalion of the civic militia on the same day.[79]

The *puros* moved quickly to frustrate Cortina's plans. They objected to Próspero Pérez' arrest on the grounds that it infringed upon his right to free speech and secured his release. The fate of the 4th Battalion, however, proved to be a more consequential issue. The battalion colonel enlisted the support of General Pedro Lemus, then commandant general of the State of Mexico, to block Cortina's directive. Lemus refused to implement Cortina's order on the grounds that the governor had committed an error of judgment. Lemus further justified his determination not to disband the 4th Battalion by indicating that Cortina's decision overstepped Lemus' powers as commandant general. The battalion was under Lemus' command in accord with the circular letter issued by the Ministry of War on October 1, 1846, that placed the civic militia under the authority of commandant generals (state governors had supervised militia units until then).[80]

In the end, Minister of Foreign Relations Rejón supported Lemus and overturned Cortina's order,[81] but the solution pleased no one. *Moderado* newspapers reacted angrily. *El Monitor Republicano* argued that Cortina's actions sought to assuage public anxiety about that unit's "lack of morality," while *El Republicano* noted that the 4th Battalion's intentions to upset public tranquility prompted Cortina's behavior.[82] On the other hand, the *puros* were disappointed because several men asked Rejón to dismiss Cortina, but Interim President Salas ignored the requests.[83] As a result, tensions between *puros* and *moderados* continued to increase to the point of explosion.

Indeed, a few days later another incident involving Cortina stirred additional discord. On October 1, Rejón had exhorted Cortina to adopt the necessary measures to preserve public security in the capital. One week later, influenced by the events of October 6, Cortina organized a civic militia unit supported by a merchant group, the *Junta Mercantil de Fomento*. Enlistment in this unit was widespread, even attracting students from the secondary schools of San Ildenfonso, San Juan de Letrán, and San Gregorio.[84] In his report, Cortina lavishly praised the force, suggesting that its members were "persons of morality, decisiveness, and valor beyond any doubt," and that "the estimable class of merchants, property owners, and capitalists...[had] armed itself at its own expense, and given itself regulations which are proof of the most noble selflessness." Cortina also noted that the measure inspired a "sense of general confidence" and cut back on the arduous tasks that were required of the capital's corps of public security, allowing it to "direct its attention to other, no less important, objectives."[85] Cortina's report, however, was nothing but a façade designed to obscure its real objective: raising a civic militia battalion to protect *moderado* interests. This prompted *puro* sympathizer Anastasio Zerecero to collect signatures in support of a petition to oppose the merchant unit.[86] Rejón, in turn, ordered Cortina to suspend "every proceeding in this matter...abstaining from promulgating measures that were not in the province of his powers and...cannot be approved."[87]

The efforts of Zerecero and Rejón not only failed to prevent organization of the *Junta Mercantil de Fomento's* militia unit, but also brought *puros* and *moderados* to the brink of civil war in the midst of a foreign conflict. On the evening of October 10, Cortina and Rejón engaged in a heated discussion:

> Rejón said he supported the rights of the people.... I sustain the same (said Cortina) with the distinction that I regard as the reunion of men of property and [Rejón] that of rabble.... Rejón said he wanted [Cortina] to resign his post, but Cortina said he would only stop being governor when he was deposed through violent means.[88]

In light of Cortina's defiance, several men met the next evening at the home of *puro* supporter Vicente Romero, a *regidor* of Mexico City's *ayuntamiento*, to discuss the best way to dissolve all aristocratic militia units.[89] On October 12,

Romero asked the *ayuntamiento* to "deal with an *urgent matter that is of interest to the public cause*" and proposed a prohibition against arming the well-to-do. Romero pointed out that "the procedures which have been carried out to organize some units have had as their sole objective arming the wealthy and aristocratic class against the people, and, since that [class] has the means to arm and defend itself, the people would undoubtedly succumb in the event of a struggle." According to Romero, "the only remedy that will prevent these evils is to form the civic militia in accordance with the law."[90] In the end, the *ayuntamiento* approved Romero's proposal. A compromise was out of the question and the stage was set for skirmishes between *puros* and *moderados* that nearly resulted in chaos in Mexico City.

Indeed, *El Republicano* pointed out that since the morning of October 14 "nothing other than agitation among individuals could be seen" in the capital and most shops closed by one o'clock that afternoon.[91] "There was talk of sacking the city [wrote José Fernando Ramírez] an occurrence not at all improbable once the lower classes were given free rein." The reason for such commotion was that *puros* and *moderados* were on the verge of an armed clash. The *puros* sought to dissolve the militia units formed by the well-to-do and to oust Interim President Salas, while the *moderados* hoped to seize Rejón and Gómez Farías "and immediately ship them out of the country."[92]

The *puros* tried to strike first. Rejón threatened to attack Salas with 4,000 militiamen if he did not resign his post. Salas was not intimidated, however, and *moderado* militia forces met in their respective headquarters, took up arms, and prepared for battle that afternoon. Gómez Farías and Cortina prevented the affair from ending in violence. Gómez Farías convinced members of the *Junta Mercantil de Fomento's* battalion to return to their homes, then appeared at one of the balconies in the National Palace to calm the people. Cortina traveled the capital's main streets, spreading the word that there was no reason for alarm. He later gave General Lemus a conciliatory embrace.[93] Tranquillity seemed to have returned to the city, but a new crisis was not long in emerging.

The *puros* appeared poised to destroy the *moderados* by October 17. Not only had both Pacheco and Cortina resigned their posts, depriving Salas of two of his main collaborators,[94] but the peripatetic Santa Anna had apparently decided that it would be prudent to support the *puros*. He warned Rejón on October 15 not to abandon the Ministry of Foreign Relations, even if Salas ordered him to do so. Santa Anna added that he would tell Salas of his displeasure with certain measures that "tended to start a reaction"; Santa Anna also wished to "stop the snubs that are being directed against my friends."[95] Indeed, there is evidence that Rejón was preparing a decree that ratified the appointment of Santa Anna as commander-in-chief of the army, placed Santa Anna in charge of the executive branch, and nullified Salas' authority.[96] The *puros* were also counting on General Lemus to help them oust Salas. Lemus had taken up a position at the convent of San Francisco, where Rejón, who had been appointed colonel of the "Guerrero" civic militia artillery brigade, "had two cannons…guarded by a group of scantily clothed rabble who were at his orders."[97] A revolt against Salas, supported by the *puros'* civic militia units, was underway.

Salas, however, moved first. As colonel of the "Hidalgo" civic militia battalion, he engineered his own coup d'état before the *puros* could act. On October 17 he summoned his battalion to the Ciudadela, the central military fortress, armed his men with new muskets, and ordered other elite militia units to assemble.[98] After fortifying his position, Salas dispatched regular army troops to the National Palace to arrest Gómez Farías and Rejón, but the *puro* leaders had already assembled a considerable number of loyal militiamen. Neither faction gained an advantage and both sides agreed that Salas should leave his troops in the Ciudadela and return alone to the National Palace.[99] It was also decided, in an attempt at reconciliation, that Gómez Farías would try to convince Salas that he did not seek to depose him. But the *puro* leader did not comply. He met Salas at the Palace's main entrance, "looked at him with disdain," and withdrew.[100]

Although no clear winner emerged from the confrontation, Salas' energetic response allowed him to capitalize on the situation. On October 19, Rejón was asked to resign his cabinet post because his presence did not suit "public tranquillity."[101] Lafragua replaced him, Almonte and Haro kept their posts, while Joaquín Ladrón de Guevara became minister of justice. The purge headed by the *moderados* did not end there. Salas also deposed Lemus from his post as commandant general because Lemus, according to authorities, had been obliged to "reestablish his health." On October 21, Salas replaced Agustín Buenrostro (who had succeeded Cortina as governor of the Federal District three days earlier, then began plotting against Salas) with José Lázaro Villamil. Salas also had plans to remove Gómez Farías from public affairs by dissolving the Council of State.[102] Within a few days of the *puro*-led attempted coup of October 17, the political situation in Mexico had changed dramatically. Salas and the *moderados* had gained the upper hand in the struggle.

What factors brought on this reversal? Why did the *puros*, who appeared to count on Santa Anna's support, fail to apprehend Salas when he returned to the National Palace on the evening of October 17? Why did they allow Salas to remove Rejón, Lemus, and Buenrostro from their posts? The most likely explanation is that Rejón and Gómez Farías were aware on October 17 of the "weaknesses and impotence of their forces, and of the great superiority of Salas'."[103] The *puros* had no choice but to bow to the *moderados'* will, especially since Santa Anna was in San Luis Potosí and could not intercede on their behalf. Gómez Farías and the *puros*, however, did not wait long before launching a counterattack. On October 22, Manuel Othón, governor of San Luis Potosí, decreed that his state would only obey Santa Anna's orders if a rebellion broke out in the nation's capital. This was a necessary step because the recent turmoil in Mexico City might preclude the upcoming Congress from meeting and adopting measures to counter the United States invasion.[104] The *puros'* luck, it seemed, was about to change.

Various accounts point to Santa Anna as the inspiration behind the San Luis Potosí coup. Lafragua's retrospective chronicle mentions that Salas received a letter on October 21 from San Luis Potosí reporting that "Rejón's dismissal had made Santa Anna furious, and that a revolt was going to explode." Carlos María Bustamante indicated that the five days which passed between the October 17 uprising in Mexico City and the publication of the San Luis Potosí manifesto were "insufficient" to plan, print, and issue the legislation. He also noted that it was "hardly believable that the paltry governor of San Luis . . . could dictate such an accord unless he was secretly obliged to by Santa Anna," and that Santa Anna had announced, even before Governor Othón published the law, that he would send 2,000 soldiers to help preserve order in Mexico City.[105]

In the end, the San Luis Potosí *pronunciamiento* failed in a matter of days. Inadequate regional support was one factor that undermined its chances. Even though state authorities in Querétaro and Jalisco issued laws in support of the San Luis Potosí decree,[106] there was little backing in other locations. Francisco Modesto Olaguíbel, then governor of the state of Mexico, announced that he had strong reservations (which he did not reveal) about San Luis coup.[107] Zacatecas Governor Manuel González Cosío could not understand the motives behind the attempt to depose Salas; after all, Santa Anna had publicly expressed his satisfaction with the way Salas had handled executive power.[108] Durango's chief executive thought "that any type of a revolution in the present circumstances would consummate" Mexico's disgrace. He had "the highest opinion about the intentions of Salas and the men who surround[ed] him."[109] The governor of Puebla, Domingo Ibarra, had also promised to support the San Luis Potosí movement, but Lafragua apparently convinced him to change his mind.[110]

The main factor that worked against the *puros*, however, was Santa Anna's reluctance to accept the invitation that the October 22 decree offered—to take charge. Gómez Farías pleaded with Santa Anna to back the San Luis Potosí rebellion quickly and actively; it would be the only way "to end the alarms and confusion that prevail in all branches of administration. Otherwise, more and more misfortunes will befall our unfortunate country, which today more than ever needs to direct its attention to the war." Salas, Gómez Farías wrote, was "devoted to the *decembrista* party, to the clergy, and the aristocracy, which have joined together, [and Salas] only acts according to their suggestions." It was "absolutely necessary" that Santa Anna take executive power and appoint a provisional ministry in San Luis to help him run governmental affairs until Congress met in December.[111] Santa Anna ignored Gómez Farías' pleas, probably because his informants warned him that the October 22 decree had not been well-received across Mexico. Santa Anna soon began to distance himself from Rejón and Gómez Farías.

Santa Anna's new political agenda became evident immediately. Neither Gómez Farías nor Rejón received letters from Santa Anna between October 19 and 26, but the last special mail from San Luis Potosí brought letters from Santa Anna to men like Haro, Trigueros, Almonte, Salas, and Rangel—all of whom Gómez Farías and Rejón considered personal enemies. Moreover, Santa Anna approved of Rejón's removal from the cabinet in one of the dispatches.[112] Another indication of Santa Anna's reversal was his October 23 manifesto, which denied that he intended to oust Salas from the presidency. Santa Anna admitted addressing letters to Rejón and Salas on October 15, explaining that those communications had been necessary because he felt accountable to the people of Mexico, who had trusted him to safeguard their interests. Silence or indifference in these crucial days might cause some to question his conduct or give the impression that Salas only acted with his consent. Santa Anna noted, therefore, that he did not want responsibility for the actions of others, nor to give the impression that his silence proved he had fooled the nation.[113]

Santa Anna's reticence and the October 23 proclamation were but two steps in his new course. A third, more private, measure was a letter he sent to Gómez Farías and Rejón on October 28. Santa Anna wrote that Salas had acted sensibly when he tried to arrest them on October 17 and that the publication of his October 15 dispatch to Rejón had "displeased" him. Given that the letter was confidential, Gómez Farías and Rejón should have known that:

> those who did not wish me well would have a pretext to berate me. I will never regret what I do in keeping with my convictions, but you know how delicate those affairs are and the strict confidence in which they must be dealt so as not to go astray.

The October 23 manifesto had been only been issued to:

> clear up the facts, deprive my enemies of their weapons, and ratify my political faith, which was none other than the consummation of the program of August's revolution. I am determined not to betray my feelings, which oblige me to pay attention to the people's opinion and reciprocate the trust they have generously put in me.[114]

Ironically, although Santa Anna did not feel the slightest remorse at having abandoned his allies, Mexico's highly volatile political situation forced him to seek shelter in the arms of the *puros* once again.

The December 1846 Presidential Elections

Santa Anna did not take long to mend his fences with

Rejón and Gómez Farías. On November 4, he reiterated to Gómez Farías that his friendship was sincere and denied that he had ever intended to abandon him. Santa Anna explained that his sole purpose during the previous crisis had been to spare Mexico City the horrors of a civil war and to preserve the federal system.[115] Six days later, Santa Anna echoed those feelings and gave a more complete explanation of his mid-October actions. He argued that he had not backed Rejón's continued presence in the cabinet because Lafragua had already replaced him by the time he became aware of the *moderado*-led purge of October 19. In this light, Santa Anna questioned the wisdom of the *puros'* wishes that he turn against Salas, especially since the interim president was only exercising his constitutional right to remove the cabinet members. Had he separated himself from his mission at the head of the army, he would have emulated Paredes' actions of December 1845 and stirred up public indignation. Santa Anna beseeched Gómez Farías not to characterize him "so carelessly, nor indiscretely provide our rivals with weapons that might be used to batter us."[116]

Santa Anna again portrayed himself an innocent victim of circumstance. As the facts suggest, however, his pronouncements were not sincere. Santa Anna's shift in disposition no doubt was influenced by the appearance of *El Federalista Puro*, a newspaper that began publication in late October 1846. Edited by Rejón, Anastasio Zerecero, and Miguel Buenrostro, the journal unleashed a piercing attack against Santa Anna for his failure to assist the *puros* during the events of mid-October.[117] Of even greater significance were the results of the elections for the constituent Congress. Contemporary accounts suggest that the *puros* would have at the very least a significant amount of clout in the legislature. Although Lafragua remarked that "Congress was perfectly divided between *puros* and *moderados*," the opinion of José Fernando Ramírez was more categorical. He commented that Rejón's banner would "go on waving without opposition" in the assembly.[118] Since Congress was to elect an interim president and vice-president, Santa Anna opted to seek Gómez Farías' forbearance until a more propitious opportunity to get rid of him arose. Santa Anna's strategy had the desired effect; the *puro* leader promised to make "his friend" Santa Anna chief executive.[119]

By the time Congress assembled on December 6—a date that, ironically, marked the second anniversary of the movement to overthrow Santa Anna in 1844—the *moderados* agreed with the *puros* that Santa Anna should be president. The *moderados*, however, wanted to deny Gómez Farías the vice-presidency and resorted to several tricks to accomplish their goal.[120] On December 15, the Committee on Governmental Affairs (*Gobernación*), which included former President José Joaquín Herrera and his one-time cabinet member Mariano Riva Palacio, presented a bill stipulating that Congress should elect an interim president on the day after the decree was published. The proposal was supported by *moderado* Mariano Otero, who, with Rejón and Gómez Farías, belonged to the Committee on Constitutional Affairs. Rejón and Gómez Farías correctly interpreted the *Gobernación* proposal as a ruse by the *moderados* to exclude Gómez Farías from the incoming government. They issued a dissenting opinion, proposing that Congress elect both an interim president and vice-president on December 16, and that state legislatures choose the lawful president and vice-president in voting scheduled for January 17, 1847.[121]

As Congress debated these proposals on December 17, it seemed that the *moderados* would prevail. But Herrera made a surprising announcement. He declared that he agreed with Rejón's and Gómez Farías' proposal on one point: to elect both a president and a vice-president. Herrera also refused to withdraw his signature from the *Gobernación* report, and it became doubtful whether a majority opinion existed. *Puro* Deputy Juan Othón took advantage of the uncertainty to suggest that Gómez Farías' and Rejón's idea be given preference in the discussion. Othón's proposition was approved, and Gómez Farías' and Rejón's report became the basis for the December 22, 1846, decree. The legislation mandated that Congress elect both an interim president and vice-president on the following day.[122]

The *moderados* countered with tactics to reduce Gómez Farías' influence in the new government. Some offered to support Gómez Farías for the vice-presidency if he turned against Santa Anna and backed the presidential candidacy of Francisco Elorriaga, Durango's ex-governor.[123] The *moderados* also attempted to turn public opinion against Gómez Farías and the *puros*. *El Republicano* commented that the "horrible evils that would follow a bad appointment" gave everyone reason to worry. Federalism would never be firmly established if public affairs were directed by "men whose ideas of agitation are notorious; by men hankering to seize [private] property, who have announced that the people will take out the money from the coffers of the wealthy; by men determined to banish their enemies; by men, in short, whose unbridled ambition hardly recommends them." *El Republicano's* subsequent editorials targeted Gómez Farías exclusively. The authors argued that his candidacy lacked "sympathies among Mexicans with the exception of his tiny circle [of friends]. His system of *rapid and radical progress* unfolded in his understanding with the most beautiful colors, and he always tended to carry it out without considering any type of obstacles." His rise to power would be a "public calamity." *El Republicano* only hoped that those deputies who voted for Gómez Farías did not "regret their mistake amidst the disgrace of a domestic revolution that might ruin the republic."[124]

The denunciations had the opposite effect of what the *moderados* intended on at least one deputy, Durango's José Agustín de Escudero. Escudero originally planned to vote, together with four deputies from Durango and Zacatecas, for two candidates whose selection would clear them from the insinuation that they cast their votes with partisan motives.

Their initial choice had been Elorriaga, but they dropped him after *puro* Deputy Guadalupe Perdigón Garay passed around a leaflet accusing Elorriaga of having failed to support the August 1846 revolt of the Ciudadela and of favoring peace with the United States. Escudero then met secretly with two unknown men to discuss the virtues of Santa Anna and Gómez Farías. Escudero returned to his quarters and decided, after reading the December 20 issue of *El Republicano*, to vote for Gómez Farías if the *puro* leader assured him—as he did—that his agenda as chief executive would "serve as a guarantee to quiet the disaffected ones and keep every plausible pretext for a revolution at a distance."[125] If Escudero was so influenced by the *El Republicano* article, it is reasonable to assume that other deputies who found themselves in a similar quandary acted accordingly.

In the end, the *moderados'* tactics did not succeed; Santa Anna and Gómez Farías were elected president and vice-president on December 23. Gómez Farías became acting chief executive in Santa Anna's absence while the general commanded the army in San Luis Potosí. These results raised the possibility that a civil war might engulf Mexico. Carlos María Bustamante, in fact, feared the army would stop Gómez Farías from taking his post and that Gómez Farías would resist by calling on the *léperos* and those departments loyal to him.[126] Such fears did not materialize as 1846 came to a close. Santa Anna and Gómez Farías seemed to be staunch allies once again, and Santa Anna remarked that he had the utmost confidence that the *puro* leader would guide the ship of state "to a safe haven."[127] But appearances proved deceptive and the opposite would prevail.

VI

A Question of Survival

Conventional historical wisdom views the acting presidency of Valentín Gómez Farías (late December 1846 to March 1847) as a period that confirmed the apprehensions of many public-spirited Mexicans about the *puros*. In mid-January 1847, Gómez Farías attacked a sacrosanct Mexican institution, the Catholic Church, when he decreed the appropriation of Church property to finance the war effort against the United States. His domestic enemies organized a February 1847 armed uprising commonly known as the "rebellion of the *polkos*," which erupted just a few days before General Winfield Scott and the United States expeditionary army landed in Veracruz. Gómez Farías mobilized the *puro*-controlled civic militia units to withstand the revolt, but the specter of armed *léperos* being set loose upon the Mexican capital precluded any type of reconciliation. In the eyes of Gómez Farías' political opponents, the *puros* threatened Mexico with chaos, anarchy, and social dissolution.

A more profound analysis of Gómez Farías' acting presidency belies this perspective. Gómez Farías sought a rapprochement with rival factions until such a course was no longer practical. He also did not act arbitrarily, impulsively, or whimsically in turning to the Church for financial support. Gómez Farías was under pressure from General Antonio López de Santa Anna to find economic resources that would allow Mexico to wage war against the American armies. The *puros* could not remain in power without Santa Anna's support. In the end, Gómez Farías' efforts were null. He lacked the means to fight back when in late March 1847 Santa Anna broke off his ties with the *puros*.

"Resources, Resources, Resources for the Government!"

"Will we, my dear friend, perform that drama once again and portray the role of victims?" Zacatecas' Governor Manuel González Cosío posited to Gómez Farías after learning the results of the December 1846 presidential elections. They brought back "the fateful remembrance of the years [18]34 and [18]35, and the similarity of the present circumstances with the ones of those ill-fated days."[1] Such uneasiness could not be dismissed as sheer speculation. Santa Anna's puzzling conduct since his return to Mexico in August 1846, the burden of a penurious treasury that could not cover wartime expenses, and the *moderados'* growing strength—evidenced by their strong showing in December's tally along with the existence of *moderado* civic militia units—combined to cast a cloud over the future of Gómez Farías' regime.

Gómez Farías realized that his grasp on power was precarious at best. In keeping with the promise he had made to Durango Deputy José Agustín Escudero shortly before the December elections, he tried to dispel concerns that his "exalted ideas" and "iron will" aroused among politically conscious Mexicans.[2] The conciliatory tone of a speech he delivered upon being sworn in as vice-president on December 24, 1846, clearly indicated his desire to accommodate political rivals. Gómez Farías' discourse did not contain any potentially inflammatory remarks. He merely declared that his government would foster the growth of industry, agriculture, and commerce, preserve the federal system, and prosecute the war with the United States. Gómez Farías provided additional evidence of his compromising attitude two days later when he issued a proclamation endorsing the 1824 constitution and swearing to protect individual rights.[3]

Gómez Farías' selection of cabinet members also revealed uncharacteristic restraint. For instance, *puro* advocate Manuel Crescencio Rejón publicly declined the position of minister of foreign relations. Although he commented that he did not feel it necessary to surround "a distinguished patriot" such as Gómez Farías with men willing to carry on the goals of the August 1846 revolt of the Ciudadela (as had been the case with General José Mariano Salas), Rejón's decision intended to allay public anxiety about the *puros'* plans.[4] The appointment of General Valentín Canalizo as minister of war proved to be another wise political move. Not only did it scuttle a coup scheduled for the day Gómez Farías was sworn in as vice-president,[5] but it also slowed Santa Anna's machinations. Santa Anna had recommended General Joaquín Rangel for minister of war, no doubt expecting that his appointee would obstruct the *puros'* efforts to achieve their political and economic goals.[6] Thus, the appointment of Canalizo, Pedro Zubieta (finance), José Fernando Ramírez (foreign relations), and Jesús Ortiz (justice) impressed contemporary observers such as Alejandro Arango y Escandón, who would achieve notoriety in Mexican political and literary circles by the 1860s. Arango y Escandón remarked that Gómez Farías had "assumed a moderate approach that was not expected of him," and that his choice of his ministers had diminished, at least temporarily, the fears that the "scenes of [18]33 would be repeated."[7]

But the government's inability to collect funds necessary to provision and supply the Mexican army compromised Gómez Farías' ability to steer this middle-of-the-road course successfully. The *puros* and their erstwhile allies had tried to raise money to wage war against the United States in a variety of ways since coming to power in early August 1846. A few days after his triumphant September 14 entry into Mexico City, Santa Anna met with several businessmen to solicit loans that would allow him to undertake the military campaign; government officials held other similar meetings on October 1 and November 25, 1846.[8] Then, on September 17, Congress decreed that the national treasury would take in all port taxes, a four percent tax on coinage, the revenue from land sales, the tobacco monopoly, the lottery, the salt deposits, official paper, and the mints. The national government would also receive all monies from the Federal District, national territories, and Church property in government hands, as well as a payment (*contingente*) of 1,011,000 pesos from the states. The decree also abolished the sales tax (*alcabala*) and reimposed taxes on property as well as a fifty percent surcharge on businesses, income, and luxury taxes collected by the states. In addition, an October 2 law mandated that all owners of urban real estate were to yield one month's income to the government. The efforts, however, proved unsuccessful. The taxes decreed on September 17 were repealed shortly thereafter, probably because of bribes paid to then Minister of Finance Antonio Haro y Tamariz. The October 2 law was doomed from the start. The government had no way of collecting revenue and most property owners lacked liquid assets.[9]

Mexico City's newspapers also offered various suggestions on how to raise money during the fall of 1846. The editors of *El Republicano* noted that a prudently negotiated foreign loan would be beneficial; they also listed the advantages of voluntary donations. *Don Simplicio* pointed out that the tobacco monopoly, if properly managed, could furnish the government with 100,000 pesos a month.[10] The *Diario del Gobierno de la República Mexicana*, however, issued a highly contro-versial recommendation that cast doubt on the *puros'* inten-tions. One of its writers (apparently Anastasio Zerecero) sug-gested that:

> money was to be obtained wherever there was any; the poor and the middle class will present their persons. The wealthy, following General Santa Anna's noble example, should hand over their treasures without delay, lest the people, who know well where their coffers are, fling themselves upon them, extract the money, and carry it to our soldiers.[11]

Such posturing alarmed the *hombres de bien* by raising the specter of the urban masses joining the *puro* movement, and, consequently, another episode of devastation and pillaging like the 1828 Parían riot.[12] The *Diario's* admonition made it increasingly difficult for the *puros* to find a middle ground with their political rivals and jeopardized their ability to maneuver in Mexico's political arena.

Meanwhile, the army remained without resources and Santa Anna repeatedly urged the government to come to its aid. Writing on November 9, 1846, Santa Anna argued that it was "absolutely indispensable" that he receive 150,000 pesos to cover the November budget; he could not tell his officers that there was "no money, and much less that everyone should look for it wherever he could find it." Since the government had not filled his requests, Santa Anna threatened to issue a manifesto claiming not to be "responsible for the evils that befall public service if this army was left to its own devices." Repeating the warning one week later, Santa Anna wrote that he would protect his own reputation by publishing the amount of money that had been forwarded to him in the past six weeks, the way that it had been distributed, and the result-ing deficit.[13]

Santa Anna's appeals tested the limits of Gómez Farías'

patience. The Spanish minister in Mexico wrote that the vice-president grew "tired of watching considerable sums [of money] going to waste," and proposed to the cabinet that the army be ordered to immediately march on Tampico or Monterrey. Gómez Farías' tenuous control over affairs of state prevented him from carrying out this idea, for its implementation most likely would have "put an end to the administration."[14] The only way to prevent Santa Anna from acting on his thinly veiled threats was to appeal to the Catholic Church for money to fight the American invaders. This proved to be another stumbling block that prevented Gómez Farías from carrying out the moderate policies he pledged to adopt when he was sworn in as vice-president in late December 1846. His political enemies did not see any patriotic motives in this plea; rather, they erroneously interpreted it as a senseless attempt to repeat the ill-fated reforms of 1833, and they did not waste time in moving against Gómez Farías.

The January 11, 1847, Decree and its Aftermath

A central question among historians of the Mexican War has been the role of the Catholic Church in the war effort. The Church was supposed to be in position to supply the financial aid that was so desperately needed. No other institution could give immediate cash loans at low interest rates. In addition, should the Church prove unwilling or unable to provide loans without delay, clerical property and goods could be used by the government as security to repay funds raised from moneylenders (*agiotistas*). Since the war was being fought against Protestant Americans, various newspapers began to hint that the Church should provide Santa Anna with fewer prayers and more aid. Despite the arguments, the Catholic Church proved to be more concerned with holding off its domestic enemies and safeguarding Church assets. Not only did it fail to contribute to the war effort as the *puros* hoped, but it provided financial support for the anti-Gómez Farías February 1847 revolt of the *polkos*.[15]

The idea of divesting the Church of its wealth to secure funds to wage war against the United States was first discussed during the final months of General José Joaquín Herrera's administration. On November 27, 1845, Deputy Luis Palacios recommended authorizing the government to mortgage one fourth of clerical property held in mortmain to raise four million pesos for the campaign. Deputy Gabriel Sagaceta's objections forced Palacios to withdraw his proposal, but Palacios had reserved the right to submit it at a later date. Palacios most likely planned to present the bill to the Congress scheduled to convene in January 1846. Chances that the legislature would approve the law were good, for the *puros* held a majority in the Chamber of Deputies. Palacios' plans, however, never came to fruition. The December 1845 revolt headed by General Mariano Paredes y Arrillaga prevented that legislature from meeting, but it did not take long for this highly controversial question to come up again.[16]

Paredes' regime had next asked the Catholic Church for financial support to prosecute the war, but its efforts to solicit a loan in mid-May 1846 also proved unsuccessful. Then, both *puro* and *moderado* statesmen held negotiations with Church leaders in the late summer and early fall of 1846. During his brief tenure as minister of finance, Gómez Farías attempted to convince leading clergymen to allow its property to be used as a guarantee for loans raised among civilians, but the overtures failed to produce results. Gómez Farías' successor, Haro y Tamariz, suggested a bill (authored by *moderado* José María Lafragua) ordering the sale of all clerical property in early October 1846; the proposal resembled the 1856 Lerdo Law. Church officials promised to name a commission to study the measure, a response that amounted to a polite refusal. Frustrated by the Church, Salas' government took more drastic action in mid-November 1846 when it issued a decree mortgaging Church property for two million pesos. Although

Church resistance forced the government to annul the law shortly thereafter, ecclesiastical authorities agreed to endorse an 850,000 peso loan, to be raised by the sale of bonds to private citizens. Those bonds were probably sold at a considerable discount and the measure failed to remedy the situation in the treasury.[17] More extreme proceedings would be necessary to alleviate the government's financial needs.

Expropriation of Church property seemed to be the most suitable, yet potentially dangerous, way of raising money for the war effort. Several advisers had encouraged Gómez Farías to expropriate the assets ever since the *puros* had come to power in August 1846. Angel Binaghi wrote in mid-September that Church holdings had to be seized "now more than ever," and that it would be prudent to get Rome's sanction to "avoid outcries and revolts on the part of the clergy or [the] people."[18] A month later, José María Luis Mora noted that it was "indispensable to wipe out the clergy as soon as possible, taking away their *fuero* and their belongings."[19] Meanwhile, José de Arrillaga urged Gómez Farías to build up Mexico's treasury with the "numerous [clerical] property held in mortmain."[20] Any reluctance or misgivings that Gómez Farías may have had disappeared as Mexico's financial situation worsened. He wrote on November 10 that "the fanatic Salas is resisting the occupation of [clerical] property held in mortmain to cover the expenses that the republic's actual situation requires; but with or without his will, Congress will adopt this measure."[21]

The stage was set for the *puros* to launch an attack on the Church's assets in late December 1846. At the time, Congress' Commission on Finance was debating whether to permit the executive branch to negotiate a loan for 500,000 pesos. During the discussion, Rejón pointed out that such an amount would not suffice and that new sources of funding would have to be found quickly. After the minister of finance corroborated this opinion, Rejón stated that the war would not end soon and that the executive should be empowered to manage the war with honor. He suggested that the Commission on Finance find the means for the government to sustain the war for at least six months and that Congress should declare itself in permanent session to resolve the issue. In the end, Congress merely authorized the government to negotiate a one million peso loan.[22]

Rejón undoubtedly favored the nationalization of clerical assets, but he did not openly state so because Santa Anna had not yet consented. Santa Anna's blessing, however, did not take long in coming. On January 2, 1847, Santa Anna wrote he had "carefully examined" a proposal submitted by Rejón and had come to the conclusion that the government had "no other recourse to obtain the money necessary to maintain independence." In Santa Anna's opinion, a twenty million peso loan, guaranteed by Church property, is what

> Congress should deal with today, because any other artifices will only be mere talk, and there is no time to lose. It is not unusual for the clergy to come to the rescue of the state's expenses with its income and possessions. . . . I had my doubts and for ten years I staunchly resisted dictating any measure against Church property, and I even assured the cabinet many times that I would rather have my hand cut off than to sign a decree that would dispose of those possessions: the country's resources were more or less abundant, the treasury was not as drained as it is today. . . .
>
> As a result of these considerations I am not opposed to the loan being carried out under the aforementioned basis, and if such is Congress' august will, I will support it.[23]

Santa Anna appeared to have given the *puros* permission to execute the risky process, but he had also put his allies in a quandary. The general knew that widespread hostility toward Gómez Farías' government would follow, and, as in 1834,

Santa Anna would have an ideal excuse to nullify the *puros'* influence.

The *puros* had no time to assess Santa Anna's motives. On January 3 they attempted to pass legislation confiscating the Church's holdings. Although Congress voted against the proposal on the following day (forty-six votes to thirty-two), events during the next two days made it clear that the government could only sustain the war effort if it seized and sold the Church's property. On January 5, the minister of finance informed deputies that he could not negotiate the loan decreed on December 30. Congress then approved Alejo Ortiz de Parada's proposal ordering the Commission on Finance to present within three days a bill that would provide enough resources to subsidize the war's expenses for six months. The need to solve Mexico's monetary crisis became more evident one day later. The entire cabinet appeared before the legislature and presented several letters from Santa Anna requesting urgent assistance.[24]

The government tried to circumvent its predicament on January 7. On that day, a report authored by Minister of Finance (and *puro* supporter) Pedro Zubieta was read to Congress. It stated that Mexico, while practically bankrupt, possessed great material elements (clerical wealth) with which to wage war. The president had not issued a bill on the matter so as not to deprive the legislature of the glory it would earn by fulfilling its chief obligation. Zubieta's report, in short, was trying to shield Gómez Farías from any future upheavals by asking Congress to assume responsibility for enacting a law that would result in the expropriation of Church property. In keeping with the strategy, *puro* deputies filed two similar proposals at a secret session of Congress that did not rule out the controversial measure. The first requested that the government be authorized to obtain twenty million pesos as long as it did not encumber private property and impose new taxes. The second asked that the government be given permission to provide the national treasury with the necessary resources to carry out the war as long as it did not impose forced loans, exact new taxes, or raise current ones. After pondering the proposals, the Commission on Finance authorized the government to obtain up to fifteen million pesos by any means deemed convenient, including mortgaging or selling clerical property held in mortmain.[25]

Legislators debated the measure for the next three days. The discussion on January 7 saw *puro* congressmen Rejón, Tiburcio Cañas, Domingo Arriola, Alejo Ortiz de Parada, as well as *moderado* José Fernando Ramírez, speak in favor of the measure. They argued that private citizens should not bear the burden of new taxes, and that failure to seize Church assets would result in the loss of national sovereignty. Mariano Otero elaborated the *moderados'* position. In his opinion, the law not only represented a dangerous relinquishment of important congressional powers to the executive branch, but the taking of Church property would ruin the economy and further divide Mexican society. As the war of words continued, *moderado* legislators managed to exclude certain properties from the proposed law, but they could not prevent it from passing. Deputies approved the bill by a narrow margin, forty-four votes to forty-one. On January 11, Vice-President Gómez Farías signed a decree authorizing the government to raise fifteen million pesos by mortgaging or selling ecclesiastical property; a set of bylaws to regulate the legislation was issued four days later.[26]

The January 11 decree was not received warmly. State legislatures in Querétaro, Guanajuato, and Puebla called for its repeal, and those in Durango and Mexico suspended enforcement. Prominent clergymen and their ecclesiastical allies also protested vigorously. Bishop Juan Manuel Irrizarri, the head of Church funds in Mexico City, asked for its revocation, Catholic newspapers criticized the law, and the bishops of Guadalajara, Michoacán, and Oaxaca wrote letters of protest to Congress. The decree proved so controversial that even one staunch *puro* supporter, Vicente Romero, then governor of the Federal District, refused to publish the edict. By January 14, leaflets reading "Death to Congress!" and "Death to Farías!" were on the streets of Mexico City while the National Palace's balconies were pelted with stones. All churches in Mexico City closed their doors and a multitude gathered in front of the National Cathedral to hear a priest harangue the government. Rumor also had it that the *moderado*-controlled "Independencia" and "Victoria" civic militia battalions would soon revolt.[27]

Gómez Farías' government moved quickly to restore public tranquillity and implement the January 11 law. On January 13 the minister of finance sent Bishop Irrizari a copy of the circular letter of October 31, 1833, which prohibited the clergy from discussing political affairs from the pulpit. The ban would be enforced anew by January 16, but it is difficult to ascertain the effects, if any, that it had.[28] The selection of *puro* sympathizer Juan José Baz to replace Romero as governor of the Federal District further showed the government's resolve. Baz "did not hesitate to make public his lack of religiosity, which was astounding in those days when public officials called themselves ultra-Catholic." It is not surprising, then, to find that Baz disregarded some of the exemptions established in the January 11 decree and ordered the seizure of clerical assets from hospitals, houses of charity, and Church-affiliated institutions such as lay brotherhoods (*cofradías*).[29] On January 14 Baz issued an edict prohibiting groups of eight or more from meeting during the day on the streets of Mexico City; nighttime encounters of three or more persons were also banned. Domestic gatherings that had not been approved either by Baz himself or the military commandant general would also be ordered to disperse immediately.[30] Finally, in early February Gómez Farías established a committee whose sole responsibility was to carry out the complex provisions of the January 11 decree.[31]

But the *puros'* best chance to restore calm and rally public opinion was Santa Anna's approval of the law.[32] Thus, the

Diario del Gobierno de la República Mexicana published Santa Anna's January 2, 1847, letter to Rejón as well as other dispatches in which Santa Anna praised the legislature's resolve. A note directed to Minister of War Canalizo confirmed that the January 11 decree showed Congress' patriotism, while another message to Rejón characterized the legislation as a "lifesaver and eminently patriotic."33 Santa Anna also informed Deputy Crescencio Gordoa that the national legislature could now count on the army's support "for the fulfillment of its decisions."34 These declarations, however, could not halt the prevalent unrest and agitation that the January 11 decree had unleashed.

Gómez Farías' struggle to keep a cabinet together compounded his difficulties. On January 16, *moderado* Mariano Otero and Alejo Ortiz de Parada (who supported the January 11 decree) accused Minister of Foreign Relations José Fernando Ramírez of breaking the September 1846 law permitting public meetings because he authorized Baz' January 14 edict. They also denounced Ramírez for disregarding the clerical *fuero* when he ordered that clergymen who led the January 14 disturbances be tried in state courts.35 The insinuations disturbed Ramírez and he resigned his post, lamenting to Gómez Farías that he would "help and serve him insofar as I am useful, remaining, if need be, at your side; but not as a minister, and if possible far removed from the matters which have disgraced me."36 Yet Ramírez' decision only encouraged the *moderados* to step up their attacks on the *puros*, and their newspapers trumpeted the idea that Ramírez quit the cabinet because he disapproved of Gómez Farías' policies. Congress exonerated Ramírez of the charges in late January, but the *moderados'* denunciations served their purpose. They deprived the *puros* of the services of a perceptive statesman and hurt Gómez Farías' efforts to stabilize administrative affairs.37

Pedro Zubieta's case also distinctly exemplifies the obstacles that the *puros* faced. Although the reasons that led to his resignation on January 19 as minister of finance remain unknown, Zubieta probably stepped down because he found it impossible to fill the national coffers. Gómez Farías' enemies had yet another weapon to bear. The conservative writer Carlos María Bustamante attributed Zubieta's resignation to an unwillingness to "tolerate [Gómez] Farías' follies and haughtiness,"[38] an assessment that surely influenced the opinion that other *hombres de bien* held about the vice-president. Three men subsequently held the cabinet post in the next two months: Ignacio Piquero, Antonio María Horta, and Francisco Suárez Iriarte.[39] Such instability provided the *moderados* with more opportunities to vilify the *puros*.

Gómez Farías faced similar problems in the other two ministries. Jesús Ortiz wrote on January 5 that illness prevented him from occupying his chair in the Ministry of Justice. Andrés López de Nava replaced him on January 14, but he remained in office for just five days. Joaquín Ladrón de Guevara took over next but resigned after one week.[40] Bustamante again blamed the events on "Gómez Farías' vile treatment." He commented that if "[Francisco] Próspero Pérez presented himself whenever the ministers met, [the vice-president] would abandon them to listen to this evildoer's gossip."[41] López de Nava assumed the post once again, but he left it on February 10.[42] Last on the list, Canalizo asked to be relieved from his duties as minister of war in late January to rejoin the army. Gómez Farías refused at first, but he bowed to Canalizo's wishes two weeks later.[43]

Gómez Farías attempted to turn the situation to his advantage. He tried to orchestrate a reconciliation by inviting several *moderados* to fill the cabinet vacancies, but they spurned his overtures. Juan Bautista Ceballos rejected an invitation to become minister of justice. Joaquín Cardoso, Cayetano Ibarra, and Juan Rodríguez Puebla refused to replace Ramírez, while Javier Echeverría, Octaviano Muñoz Ledo and Manuel Baranda declined the minister of finance's chair. The letters that Rodríguez Puebla and Baranda wrote to excuse themselves have survived and their pleas can only be construed as frivolous. The former alleged he could not become minister of foreign relations because he had been away from politics for several years and did not know English or French. The latter simply argued that he would not be useful as minister of finance. By mid-February 1847, Gómez Farías did assemble a cabinet that included Rejón (foreign relations), Suárez Iriarte (finance), General Antonio Vizcaino (war), and José María Jáuregui (justice), but this ministry fared little better than its predecessors. For instance, Suárez Iriarte resigned on February 19 because his economic proposals failed to win Gómez Farías' approval. The constant changes and reluctance of many to serve cast serious doubt about the stability of Gómez Farías' government.44

Meanwhile, tensions ran so high that even harmless measures stirred partisan hatreds. On January 20 Congress debated a bill sponsored by the Commissions on Governmental and Constitutional Affairs. Article Two of the legislation stipulated that Congress would not be able to confer extraordinary powers on the executive branch. Nonetheless, the rumor quickly spread through Mexico City that Gómez Farías had requested the legislature to grant him such capabilities. Surprisingly, the *moderado* controlled *El Republicano* tried to allay fears by noting that the bill under discussion did not threaten constitutional guarantees. The reasons for this uncharacteristic remark remain unknown, but the writer may not have been willing to support those who would take up arms against Gómez Farías.45 Regardless, Carlos María Bustamante, in an effort to discredit the *puros*, did not hesitate to present his opinion about the measure. Bustamante claimed that the bill was couched "in vague and confusing terms, without indicating the objective it hoped to accomplish; of course, everyone realized that it was designed to violently carry out the law that expropriated church property, to incarcerate and destroy its enemies, and to consummate [Gómez Farías'] characteristic tyranny."46

These problems notwithstanding, the deteriorating relations between Santa Anna and Gómez Farías proved to be the most devastating blow to the *puros'* position. Santa Anna chastised Gómez Farías for his inability to provide the army with resources. On January 7 Santa Anna reprimanded Gómez Farías because he had been in power for fifteen days and had not forwarded any money. Testing the limits of Gómez Farías' patience, the denunciations continued even after the enactment of the January 11 decree.47 In response, Gómez Farías told Santa Anna that the states of San Luis Potosí, Zacatecas, and Guanajuato had each sent him between eleven thousand and twenty thousand pesos, and that revenue from the tobacco monopoly constantly flowed into his coffers. Gómez Farías also detailed some of the difficulties he had encountered as he tried to provision Santa Anna. One setback proved to be the doing of General Ventura Mora in Mazatlán, Sinaloa. According to Gómez Farías, cargo on two ships that had recently docked at Mazatlán should have yielded a "respectable" sum of money in custom duties. The funds should have gone to the national treasury, but Mora struck a deal with "interested" parties and pocketed fourteen thousand pesos.48

In light of Gómez Farías' resolve and the obstacles strewn before the government as it tried to carry out the January 11 decree, Santa Anna decided to distance himself from the *puros*. He informed Congress that his January 2 letter to Rejón had no other purpose than to express his beliefs about the means to raise money. Santa Anna did not intend for his ideas to be construed as decisions, much less for them to be adopted as law, for he could be wrong and Congress should not be influenced by anyone's opinion. Santa Anna argued that:

> if the measure adopted in that law is not the only one that exists; if my relentless enemies wish to say that it is the outcome of my suggestions once its results have been seen, and that they only wish to carry it out because I approved it, I beg the sovereign Congress...that if it is

not convinced of the disposition to which I have made reference, to modify it as it believes convenient so that it may produce the desired effects.49

Santa Anna left San Luis Potosí for Saltillo in search of the United States army two days later.50 As he marched north, the political storm clouds that had been gathering since December 1846 threatened even more. Santa Anna and the *moderados* would press on with their plans to oust the *puros* from the government.

"Don Valentín Has Ruined Us"

Mexico City's gossip mill kept busy with news of plots against Gómez Farías' administration even before the enactment of the January 11, 1847, decree. One of the first stories to circulate said that Gómez Farías had avoided a coup by appointing General Valentín Canalizo minister of war. Nonetheless, the government was not out of danger, since several men would try to convince Canalizo to abandon the cabinet and turn the army against the vice-president. To avoid a revolt, Gómez Farías should send General Mariano Arista— the only alleged conspirator whose last name appeared in the letter—far from Mexico City as soon as possible.51 Rumors such as this did not bode well for the *puros'* political future.

Indeed, the January 11 law and subsequent public ferment provided fertile ground for plots against Gómez Farías. On January 21, *El Republicano* commented that various letters from San Luis Potosí announced that the army would soon rebel and proclaim a military dictatorship. It also mentioned that articles published by newspapers in the cities of Puebla and Morelia agitated in favor of a rebellion.52 Carlos María Bustamante gave credence to these assertions two days later when he noted that schemes in favor of a Santa Anna dictatorship were moving along quite rapidly. A secret lodge known as the "Red Comet" worked toward that goal in San Luis

Potosí, while General Rangel did the same in Mexico City.[53] Bustamante's opinion about the "Red Comet" may have been mistaken, for another contemporary analyst noted that its members were "viewed as a group of convivial officers who sought in this society a larger field for amusement."[54] Subsequent developments, however, revealed that the same could not be said about Rangel. Just as importantly, the rumors illustrated the fragility of the much-acclaimed union of the people and the army—one of the *puros'* key principles since 1845 and the foundation for the August 1846 Plan of the Ciudadela. That alliance was on the verge of crumbling.

Developments in Sinaloa confirmed that Santa Anna wanted to break off relations with the *puros*. In late January 1847, probably after pilfering the money from the two ships that had docked in Mazatlán, General Ventura Mora launched a rebellion to establish a Santa Anna dictatorship, an uprising unquestionably organized by Santa Anna himself. Santa Anna had informed Gómez Farías in late December 1846 that General Anastasio Bustamante, the recently appointed commander-in-chief of Mexico's Army of the West, planned to head an uprising in Guadalajara and Mazatlán. These designs could be foiled if Mora, who "deserved our complete confidence," replaced General Bustamante.[55] In the end, Mora's *pronunciamiento* collapsed shortly after it began. The states of Jalisco, Mexico, Michoacán, Querétaro, San Luis Potosí, and Zacatecas had formed a coalition to defend federal institutions. More importantly, Santa Anna behaved as "always in similar cases," issuing a manifesto that denounced the insurrection and abandoned General Mora to his own fate.[56]

Gómez Farías' presidency was also threatened by growing dissent within his own party. In late January, twenty anonymous *puro* deputies sought to oust him from power by framing a petition that would have declared him "inept and incapable of governing"; *yorkino* legislators had filed a similar accusation against President Vicente Guerrero in 1829.[57]

Several unidentified *moderados* kept the document from being brought before Congress, but they did not act to promote national welfare. The *moderados* wanted to reorganize and control the cabinet with the promise that Gómez Farías would "follow blindly the voting of their majority." Gómez Farías refused to accept these conditions; they would have turned him into a mere figurehead.[58] His obstinacy on the occasion may have precluded a chance for internal peace, but the *moderados* were also to blame for their inability to rise above partisan politics.

More trouble for the *puros* occurred in mid-February when Mexico City's *moderado*-controlled newspapers, spearheaded by *El Republicano*, began to censure Gómez Farías' administration. Their articles gradually moved from imploring Gómez Farías to mend his ways, especially in relation to Mexico's precarious financial situation, to ruthless personal attacks demanding his resignation. On February 13 *El Republicano* alleged that the government was incapable of conducting daily administrative affairs because Gómez Farías could not fill the cabinet, even while "searching for [appointees] with a lantern in the middle of the day." The paper maintained that past regimes had met public expenses without resorting to extraordinary measures, but that the present administration had not been able to fill the treasury's coffers despite being favored by Congress with two loan decrees. In the minds of *El Republicano's* editors, Gómez Farías and his appointees should "leave their posts so they could be occupied by persons who may have more public sympathies, and who were capable of finding both ministers and money."[59]

Relative newcomer *El Federalista* adopted an even more caustic stance toward the vice-president. One of its correspondents remarked that Gómez Farías' health and morals had been "debilitated by the passage of time, and perhaps the sufferings he had tolerated on his country's behalf had shortened his life." He no longer possessed "the acuity and ease to reason, nor the energy to act that he once had [in 1822, 1824, and from 1832 to 1834], and, far from that, he had decayed to such a degree that he was truly incapable of governing." To support its allegations, *El Federalista* compared the regimes of General Salas and Gómez Farías, and portrayed the former in a favorable fashion. While Salas had been in charge of affairs of state, "public spirit grew, love for independence became widespread . . . and one only saw troops marching, enrollments in the [National] Guard, donations, weapon factories, everything, in short, indicating that the country was preparing to repulse the invaders." On the other hand, "public spirit suddenly extinguished itself" once Gómez Farías became president. Those "who previously were full of ardor and enthusiasm became timid and sluggish; the poor and the middle class no longer volunteered their personal services, nor did the wealthy cede their resources." Discrediting Gómez Farías further, *El Federalista* stressed the uncertain situation that prevailed in the cabinet and Mexico's lack of money. The writer concluded that Gómez Farías' continued presence in power was "an obstacle" that prevented the republic from functioning properly. He should give public testimony of his patriotism by renouncing his post immediately.[60]

As Mexico City's journals distorted both Gómez Farías' accomplishments and his public image, *moderado* politicians, army chiefs, and prominent Church leaders began planning the "revolt of the *polkos*." Preparations for the uprising probably began in late January when Santa Anna dispatched General José Ignacio Basadre to Mexico City to reach an accord with Manuel Gómez Pedraza about the political future. Basadre helped the *moderados* define their plans in the frequent meetings with Gómez Pedraza, Otero, and José Guadalupe Covarrubias. Others joined the conspiracy, including Generals Matías de la Peña y Barragán, José Gómez de la Cortina, Juan Nepomuceno Almonte, Salas, and Rangel, as well as civilians Manuel Eduardo Gorostiza, Guillermo Prieto, Manuel Payno, Vicente García Torres, Lafragua, and Bishop Juan Manuel Irrizari.[61]

The plotters were not tight-lipped and their plans soon became public knowledge. On February 9 one member of the "Iturbide" civic militia battalion wrote Gómez Farías that his political rivals could count on support from the "Hidalgo," "Victoria," "Bravos," and "Zapadores" civic militia battalions, "Mina's" artillery, and the 6TH Infantry Regiment. He advised that the first two units be transferred to Veracruz as soon as possible. Eight days later, three deputies from Oaxaca, including the future chief executive of Mexico Benito Juárez, noted that members of the clergy and several *moderados* actively sought to replace Gómez Farías with the president of the Supreme Court of Justice and two associates. Yet another rumor hinted at a scheme to place General José Joaquín Herrera in the presidency, something of a reenactment of the *moderado*-led December 6, 1844, revolt.[62]

Gómez Farías recognized how precarious his position was and tried to solidify his grip on domestic affairs. In late February he announced to Congress the terms of a secret peace proposal delivered by Alexander J. Atocha, who in February 1846 had approached United States President James K. Polk with a message from Santa Anna—then in Havana in exile—advising the Polk administration on a military strategy that would bring peace. The concessions in Atocha's offer were similar to those that several Mexican aristocrats and clergymen had submitted during the late summer of 1846 to United States confidential agent Moses Y. Beach, who was living in Mexico City in February 1847. By exposing the peace plan, Gómez Farías hoped to discredit defenders of the Church and consolidate his political authority.[63]

The *puros* took action on two other fronts to strip their enemies of military power and ward off a revolt. Orders went out on February 24 and 25 calling for the banishment or imprisonment of those senior army chiefs who conspired against Gómez Farías. The tactic, however, proved futile. Almonte, told to march to Chihuahua, disobeyed. Peña y Barragán evaded the government agents sent to arrest him, while other

army chiefs who were instructed to leave the capital—
Generals Rómulo del Valle, Ignacio Falcón, Cosme Furlong,
and Basadre—most likely did not do so. [64]

The *puros* also tried to weaken their rivals by attacking the
moderados' civic militia units. Efforts to reduce the numerical
strength of these corps had been underway since early
January. At that time Federal District Governor Baz dismissed
those individuals who worked in his office from the ranks of
the "Hidalgo" battalion. Baz followed this measure with a
January 23 edict which stated that men exempted from militia
service by the September 11, 1846, bylaws had been delinquent
in paying their dues; funds to create the militia, therefore,
were lacking. The edict imposed a February 1 deadline for
offenders to pay their obligations; failure to do so would subject them to the penalties established in the September 11
ordinance. The editors of *El Monitor Republicano* were quick
to chastise Baz and point out the edict's true intent. They
reported that Baz violated its terms by exempting from service
men who were already enrolled in two other *moderado* battalions—the "Victoria" and "Independencia." Given that enlistees in other militia units were denied a similar privilege, the
January 23 edict was a subtle move designed to strengthen the
puros' militia corps. [65]

By late February, however, the unstable political situation
forced the *puros* to adopt harsher procedures toward the *moderados'* militia units. On February 22, on learning that several
members of the "Independencia" battalion had spoken out
against him, Gómez Farías ordered his son Fermín, colonel of
the "Libertad" battalion, to occupy the "Independencia's"
quarters at the National University. The venture proved
unsuccessful after energetic protests by General Pedro María
Anaya, who told the vice-president that his troops
("Independencia") would take up arms if government forces
had not vacated the premises by ten o'clock that evening.[66]
Gómez Farías and his advisers countered on another tack. On
February 23, the minister of war, arguing that Mexico City's

militia units contributed to public unrest by gathering on days they were not supposed to, prohibited such meetings—even on the assigned dates—unless the office of the commandant general received twenty-four hours advance notification. [67] One day later, Gómez Farías ordered the transfer of the "Independencia" battalion from its quarters to the hospital of Terceros. The order proved to be an omen. A large crowd, cheering loudly and crying out "Death to the *Puros*! Death to Don Valentín Gómez Farías!" accompanied the men of "Independencia" as they marched to their new lodgings. [68]

The government again found itself in a quandary. Although the threat of a *moderado*-led revolt warranted the measure Gomez Farías had taken, [69] he had also delivered to his enemies yet another opportunity to criticize his administration. *El Republicano* argued that the government had grossly abused the rights specified in a February 3, 1847, decree; that law empowered the federal government to deploy the country's civic militia with the sole object of sustaining the national defense in the war against the United States. Actions such as the transfer of the "Independencia" battalion not only threatened to "denaturalize" the civic militia, but to destroy such a "beloved institution." [70] Just as importantly, the public demonstrations of support for the "Independencia" battalion made it clear that relocating the unit would not quiet the *moderados*. Gómez Farías then decided to remove the *moderados'* militia corps from Mexico City. On February 25, acting on the February 3 legislation, Gómez Farías ordered the "Independencia," "Hidalgo," "Bravos," "Victoria," and "Mina" battalions to march to Veracruz within twenty-four hours to aid in the resistance against an expected American invasion. [71]

Gómez Farías' mandate spurred the *moderados* into action. On February 27 they launched the "revolt of the *polkos*." The plan issued by the rebels severely criticized both the national legislature and the executive branch for disregarding the spirit of the August 4, 1846, movement. Congress, they argued, was made up of "men blinded by exaltation" who had usurped the state legislatures' prerogative of naming the president and vice-president.[72] In addition, the national legislature had not paid heed to comments which had forewarned that the January 11, 1847, decree would foster internal discord and leave "the hungered-for resources . . . in the range of a mere scheme." Framers of the February 27 plan also alleged that Gómez Farías was "incapable of holding [the reins of government] with any skill," for he often acted whimsically and surrounded himself with the "most wretched and despicable [men] from among the dregs of all factions." According to the rebels, neither Congress nor the vice-president could save the country from ruin. Their plan promised the immediate suspension of the acting legislative and executive powers. It also called for the repeal of the January 11 and February 4, 1847, decrees in return for the financial aid that the Catholic Church had extended to the plotters.[73]

The rebels' grand proclamations did not bring instant success. First, the Mexican national legislature did not acquiesce to their demands. Congress immediately countered by granting Gómez Farías' administration the authority to enact any measures deemed necessary to reestablish order. The legislature also offered the *polkos* amnesty if they laid down their arms within two hours. The *polkos* rejected the offer.[74] Then, on March 1, Gómez Farías refused to resign as demanded by rebel commander General Peña y Barragán.[75] Both sides refused to compromise, thus exacerbating political instability in the capital.

Since finding a middle ground proved impossible, the Gómez Farías administration adopted several measures to thwart the *polko* threat. It requested district heads in the neighboring territory of Tlaxcala, as well as in the states of Mexico and Puebla, to send their civic militia units to Mexico City. Armed troops would impress upon the rebels the fact that the government had abundant military resources at its disposal.[76] Gómez Farías and his advisers again tried to deprive *moderado* militia units of manpower, ordering all employees of the Ministry of Foreign Relations to assemble. Failure to comply would result in unspecified penalties. The government then decreed that any employee from the ministry who took up arms on behalf of the *polkos* would lose his post and would be subject to prosecution. Finally, Federal District Governor Baz was told to transfer discreetly to the Portaceli convent any clerics suspected of disturbing public order.77

Besides encountering determined resistance, the *polko* rebels were surprised by several unexpected problems. The plotters had bribed General Rangel, who commanded the Ciudadela and had 1,000 soldiers and various artillery pieces at his disposal, with 8,000 pesos. Rangel could have turned the tide of the uprising in the *polkos'* favor. On the same day that the coup d'état broke out, however, Almonte disrupted rebel plans. He visited the Ciudadela and convinced Rangel not to aid the insurrection. The pleas of both the *santanistas* and Gómez Farías also persuaded Rangel not to join the *polkos.* The *santanistas* argued that the rebels were trying to undo their *caudillo's* political influence. At the same time, Gómez Farías, fearing Rangel's defection, flattered the general "to the utmost degree" to keep him loyal to the government.78

The failure of the February 27 plan to unify the *puros'* enemies proved to be a far more serious predicament for the insurgents than Rangel's last-minute reticence. Few conspirators were acquainted with the plan before it was published.79 Once the contents were made public, most of the remaining plotters, who "were sincere republicans," realized that the Church only wanted to preserve its holdings. Consequently, many who had either assisted the rebellion or remained neutral decided to support the government, a turn that discouraged leading *moderado* politicians. Some went into hiding. Others went to the Academy of San Carlos to condemn the same men they had incited into rebelling. In the words of a contemporary observer, the rebels had been "delivered over to the major-domos of the monks, and other mystical personages of that nature, who insisted that the plan should in no way be changed."[80]

The revolt received a lukewarm reception in two nearby states, further hampering its chances. When the uprising began, *puro* advocate Francisco Modesto Olaguíbel, governor of the state of Mexico, offered to serve as a mediator to end the fighting. Yet Olaguíbel acted more as Gómez Farías' "auxiliary" than as a man "proposing a middle ground" between the belligerents.[81] In Puebla, state Governor Domingo Ibarra led efforts to crush a rebellion that broke out on March 2 in support of the *polkos*. Authorities in other states also frowned on the motivation behind the February 27 uprising. The rebels simply failed to secure nationwide support.[82]

The plotters also did not expect to face a better armed *puro* force in Mexico City. General Rangel's betrayal and the decision by the commander of the 6th Infantry Regiment (whose 700 men were supposed to join the rebels) to remain neutral left the *polkos* short-handed. According to one source, Gómez Farías had twenty-two cannons and 3,300 troops. The *polkos* did not have any artillery but could count on 3,250 fighters. The result was a standoff. "Both parties," wrote one eyewitness, "kept their respective positions, very few were killed or wounded, and more injuries were received by the people, who from necessity or curiosity passed through the streets."[83]

In this unsettled situation, General Peña y Barragán sought to broaden the rebels' base of support. Santa Anna's report about the February 22-23, 1847, Battle of Buena Vista, which portrayed the encounter as a Mexican victory, reached Mexico City on March 1. Since it would have been political suicide to continue attacking the man who appeared to be Mexico's savior, Peña y Barragán courted the *santanistas* by eliminating the reference in the February 27 plan to the alleged unconstitutionality of Santa Anna's presidency. Peña y Barragán publicly recognized Santa Anna as chief executive on March 2. His proclamation, however, did not appease the *santanistas* because it confirmed to them that the revolt had been fueled by a hatred for Santa Anna.[84]

The March 5 arrest of *moderado* leader Gómez Pedraza was the beginning of the end to the stalemate in Mexico City. The editors of *El Republicano* commented that the apprehension took place as Gómez Pedraza, who was travelling on horseback with his wife, accidentally wandered near a building occupied by government troops. The *puro*-controlled *Boletín de la Democracia* recorded, however, that Gómez Pedraza was in disguise at the time of his capture and had attempted to bribe the armed forces that supported the government.[85] *Moderado* advocate Juan Bautista Ceballos and conservative Carlos María Bustamante—no friends of Gómez Farías— raised another possibility. They suggested that General Rangel ordered Gómez Pedraza's arrest and also prevented Manuel Baranda, whom Gómez Farías commissioned to free the *moderado* leader, from carrying out his charge. The supposition is not far-fetched. By arresting Gómez Pedraza, Rangel could discredit Gómez Farías and simplify Santa Anna's return to power.[86]

Regardless of which account is true, Gómez Pedraza's incarceration—he remained in jail until a letter from Santa Anna ordering him to be set free arrived in the capital on March 20—forced *moderado* statesmen to retaliate. These politicians, "who cared little for the fate of many who were exposed to the shock [of the rebellion], conceived a great apprehension for the life of [Gómez] Pedraza" and devised two strategies to solve their party's and Gómez Pedraza's dilemma.[87] On April 9, with the religious issue meaningless, the *moderados* reduced the rallying cry for the revolt to a single issue—Gómez Farías would have to go.[88] The strategy failed. The *moderados* almost forfeited the backing of the Church, which threatened to withhold further monetary resources from the rebels. Although Guillermo Prieto and Manuel Payno convinced Bishop Irrizari not to act so hastily, the rebels had to contend with a new hindrance—diminished public support—as hostilities continued.[89]

Since the change in plans did not end the impasse, on March 11 forty-one deputies (advised by *moderado* leaders Lafragua, Riva Palacio, Otero, and General Anaya) issued a brief public manifesto. The document reasoned that Congress could not meet to restore internal peace and organize the national defense because *puro* deputies did not attend legislative sessions. In light of the situation the *moderados* called on Santa Anna to return to the capital, take on the presidency, and reestablish public order.[90] *Puro* legislators countered with a proclamation the following day. They argued that they did not attend Congress because they had no liberty to express their opinions and cast their votes. The claims were only partially true.[91] *Puro* deputies feared that their attendance in Congress would result in Gómez Farías' resignation, or at the very least "deprive him of the few means of defense that he had left, since new obstacles would be placed in his path."[92] Another line of battle had been drawn. Both factions then dispatched representatives to meet with Santa Anna in an attempt to maximize their position.

Santa Anna's Double Game

Santa Anna first heard about the revolt of the *polkos* as he retreated toward San Luis Potosí in late February following the Battle of Buena Vista.[93] His first known reaction to the turmoil in Mexico City was to stand by Gómez Farías. On March 6, Santa Anna claimed to be "profoundly affected by the scandal." He announced that he would send 4,000 soldiers to support the government and care for defenses outside Veracruz. Furthermore, he promised to leave the country if the mutineers went unpunished.[94] Santa Anna arrived in San Luis Potosí three days later and immediately sent Gómez Farías two letters confirming his determination to back the *puros*. The first message stated that he would take over the government to end the unrest and that Gómez Farías could be sure that "no motive nor pretext would cause him to be harmed."[95] His second dispatch urged the acting chief executive to proceed

> with firmness and energy so that the time may come when the rebels are made to feel all the consequences of their acts. To be weak at this time would deliver us into the arms of the factions, who would then also tear the nation apart. The moment has come to terminate the revolt, but this will not come about amidst unsteadiness.[96]

All signs indicated that the rebels would soon feel Santa Anna's ire and that the *puros* would emerge the victors.

Santa Anna being Santa Anna, it did not take long for him to reveal his true intent. Shortly thereafter, Santa Anna received a bulletin that included a marginal note in Gómez Pedraza's handwriting stating that the rebels' plan had been changed. He also got letters from other individuals who did not sympathize with the government.[97] Although these messages are unavailable, they doubtless contained stock condemnations of Gómez Farías' acting presidency. More importantly, the letters probably included remarks similar to those of Salvador Bermúdez de Castro, the Spanish minister to Mexico, who characterized the rebellion as a class war that threatened to plunge Mexico City into turmoil and social upheaval.

Bermúdez de Castro's portrayal of the troops that supported Gómez Farías was not laudatory. He first described the soldiers as "proletarians and vagabonds," and the leaders as "enraged men and demagogues."[98] In a subsequent dispatch, the Spanish minister contrasted the conduct of the *polko* and government militia units during the insurrection. After praising the "dexterity" of *polko* troops in handling firearms, he commented that they "demonstrated such firmness and steadiness as could not have been expected from troops so inexperienced." These units, in short, were "an excellent model" of what the civic militia should be. On the other hand, Bermúdez de Castro reiterated his belief that "the defenders of the government belonged to the most despicable and miserable classes of the population." Moreover, these men "had turned the political question into a social question: at all hours they shot at any person who was dressed with any decency, and [they] often amused themselves by firing [their guns] at the women and children who appeared on the rooftops or ventured out into the streets."99 If the reports that reached Santa Anna in early March also emphasized the danger in which the populace had placed Mexico City, his subsequent decision to reevaluate the situation in the capital before casting his lot with the *puros* seems all the more reasonable.

On March 10, therefore, Santa Anna ordered both Gómez Farías and rebel leader General Peña y Barragán to cease hostilities.100 The message, which greatly disturbed Gómez Farías, reached Mexico City three days later. According to one observer, the vice-president "attempted to call a *junta* that would approve the proposal to prevent Santa Anna's entrance into Mexico [City], and . . . he wanted to make him march to defend the coast of Veracruz."101 Gómez Farías' scheme, however, went awry because two of his presumed allies proved to be turncoats. Rangel had pledged his undivided loyalty to the vice-president several times during the uprising, but he and Canalizo—who had commanded the government's forces during the "rebellion of the *polkos*"—refused to obey Gómez Farías' orders. They informed him that they would merely preserve the status quo until Santa Anna's arrival.102

This grim panorama led Gómez Farías to search for an honorable escape. First, he drafted a letter on March 13 resigning from office on account of his "broken health."103 He then advised Santa Anna, probably on the same day, that:

the lessons of experience had proven fruitless; the country's politics will become much more complex than at the present moment, and without fear of being wrong I will tell you that you have not become friends with those who are not and cannot be [your supporters]; and you have alienated many of your true friends. Misgivings and disgust have spread in all directions; two generals have asked me to relieve them from service; several units attempted to withdraw [from their positions] yesterday, and if they have not done so it is because they have been denied permission. I am going to resign the post convinced that I have held it with dignity, because I do not wish to be so poorly rewarded by those who should appreciate my services because of their many qualifications.[104]

Yet a postscript to Gómez Farías' letter of resignation (probably his own) indicates that the message never reached Congress. Thirty deputies—*puro* congressmen determined to prevent a recurrence of the events of 1834—blocked the resignation.[105] Despite the display of resolve, the bonds between Santa Anna and Gómez Farías would be completely severed within three weeks.

The first official from Mexico City to reach Santa Anna as he marched south was San Luis Potosí Deputy Juan Othón, a Gómez Farías agent. They met at the town of San Miguel el Grande. Othón's words "were well-received" and Santa Anna appeared willing to side with the *puros*. Santa Ana allowed Othón to sit in his carriage on resuming the trek and listened to him with the "utmost satisfaction." But two *moderados*, former Minister of Justice José Ramón Pacheco and Eugenio María Aguirre, joined Santa Anna's retinue in the village of Santa Rosa and interrupted this intimate soiree. Their version of what had happened in Mexico City differed markedly from Othón's. From that point on, Santa Anna showed himself "less obsequious" with Othón and even forced Othón to continue the journey on horseback. Four other *moderados* awaited

Santa Anna in Querétaro—General Salas, José María and José Guadalupe Covarrubias, and Joaquín Ladrón de Guevara. Santa Anna seemed "highly pleased with the reasons expounded by the [*moderados*] . . . and from that time on he favored the insurgents' plan, and manifested himself very obsequious with their envoys, treating them with the greatest signs of distinction, although without openly opposing the government."[106]

The courting of Santa Anna continued when he reached the village of Guadalupe on the outskirts of Mexico City on March 21. Although the national legislature rejected a summons to meet with him, it dispatched a commission that included such *moderado* luminaries as Lafragua and Otero, who were to swear him in as president. Rejón led a contingent of *puros* to congratulate Santa Anna on the following day, but some members of the party already realized that Santa Anna was, in fact, scheming against them. Federal District Governor Baz greeted Santa Anna with a speech condemning the *moderados* and warned him that he would be their next victim. Baz' admonition, however, had no discernible effect. Santa Anna had made up his mind to abandon the *puros*.[107]

Santa Anna's sympathies were clear as soon as he entered the capital on March 23. He promptly chose a cabinet that included three *moderados*—Otero (foreign relations), Juan Rondero (finance), and General José Ignacio Gutiérrez (war).[108] Another *moderado* whose stock rose was the new commandant general of Mexico, General Pedro María Anaya, while the governor of the Federal District, Ignacio Trigueros, was a devoted *santanista*.[109] As Santa Anna took charge, he also ordered that some of the barricades used by *puro* militia units against the *polkos* should be torn down and he dispatched the same troops that had defended the government to Veracruz, where they were to fight against the Americans. Santa Anna also made improvements in the lodgings of the *moderado* militia units, flattered their leaders, and took steps to augment their rosters.[110] The *moderados* did not waste time in following Santa Anna's lead. They assigned the task of guarding Mexico City and the National Palace to the militia units that led the rebellion. To humble the *puros* further, the "Hidalgo," "Victoria," and "Independencia" battalions paraded through the capital.[111] Bystanders greeted their march with standing ovations as "the most distinguished ladies . . . threw crowns of laurel and roses . . . at the soldiers."[112]

Santa Anna took two more steps to finalize his break with the *puros*. First, he had to have the Church's economic support to continue the war against the United States, and he initiated negotiations with Church leaders on March 28. On the following day, in return for a 1,500,000 peso loan, he abolished the decrees relative to the expropriation of Church property.[113] Finally, Santa Anna had to force Gómez Farías out of public office. The surrender of Veracruz in late March required that Santa Anna leave the capital to halt the advance of United States troops into central Mexico, and it would have been awkward to leave Gómez Farías—running a *moderado* cabinet—as interim president.[114] In the words of Carlos María Bustamante, that would have been like handing over the Catholic Church to Martin Luther.[115]

Lafragua had the solution: abolish the vice-presidency and replace it with a substitute president. He argued that the most practical way to do this was to abolish the December 22, 1846, decree that provided for an *interim vice-president*. The action would be legal because in December 1846 Congress had not been bound by the 1824 constitution. Congress could appoint both an *interim* president and *vice-president*. On February 10, 1847, however, the national legislature decreed the 1824 constitution to be in force. Article Three of the law stated that Congress had to abide by the charter in all matters except in those that pertained to it as a constituent body. Lafragua thus contended that since the Constitution of 1824 did not provide for an interim *vice-president*, only a president, Gómez Farías could be legally suspended from office, clearing the way for the election of a substitute.[116]

The *puros* made one final effort to derail Lafragua's plan. They designated Almonte as their candidate for substitute president. Despite his earlier intrigues against the *puros* when the "rebellion of the *polkos*" broke out, Almonte's political laurels made him a suitable choice for the occasion. The *puros* came close to victory, but they erred by refusing to attend the session of Congress when the decree that dealt with the abolition of the vice-presidency was discussed. *Puro* legislators believed that their absence would "embarrass Santa Anna" and force him to leave Mexico City with the issue unresolved. In that case, Gómez Farías would be able to return to his government post, since he was the only person who could legally replace Santa Anna. But the *puros* did not persist. Opinion makers openly discussed dissolving Congress because it had become an "obstacle" in the way of Mexico's welfare, and Santa Anna threatened not to join the army if the election was not held or if Almonte was elected.[117]

Other factors weakened the *puros'* position. The most significant was that *moderado* and *santanista* advocates convinced many deputies to oppose Almonte's election. Just as importantly, Gómez Farías went along with this line of reasoning, and his cryptic declarations further impaired the *puros'* chances for victory. He made it known that he disapproved of Almonte as chief executive. Gómez Farías' correspondence does not reveal the reason for this stance, but it proved costly. As one eyewitness put it, this "new note of disorganization decided the contest."[118] Congress abolished the vice-presidency and appointed General Anaya (the *moderado's* candidate) as substitute president on April 1.[119]

The ouster of Gómez Farías disheartened at least one Mexican statesman who believed that national unity was more important than partisan politics. José Fernando Ramírez commented that he did not "recall ever having seen a spectacle that was sadder, more distressing or more foreboding." He had witnessed "the dying gasps of the nation."[120] The defeats that the Mexican army suffered in the coming weeks were an omen that Ramírez' fears would come true. The setbacks, however, allowed the *puros* to revitalize their political aspirations. As both Santa Anna and *moderado* statesmen began to consider negotiating an end to the conflict with the United States, the *puros* clamored for war in a last-ditch attempt to regain their former influence.

VII

An Unsuccessful Comeback

The future of the Valentín Gómez Farías-led *puros* looked bleak in April 1847. Military backing had all but disappeared. Generals Valentín Canalizo and Joaquín Rangel, among other senior officers for example, had turned their backs on *puro* endeavors. Moreover, not only did the *moderados* enjoy Santa Anna's endorsement and hold the reins of government, but Gómez Farías and Manuel Crescencio Rejón had been forced out of public affairs. Health problems prevented the former from assuming his seat in the national legislature, while the latter did not return to Congress after a mob tried to lynch him because he allegedly tried to arrange peace with the United States.[1]

Despite the disheartening signs, Vicente and Eligio Romero, Guadalupe Perdigón Garay, and Juan Othón tried to fill the void, and by June 1847 circumstances had helped the *puros* regain some of their political influence. The *moderados'* fortunes sagged after General Pedro María Anaya gave up the presidency in mid-May. Although General Antonio López de Santa Anna reclaimed his post as chief executive at the time, his political power had declined. The *puros* capitalized by again backing Santa Anna, who needed allies desperately.

The *puros* also tried to regain their former influence by calling for the continuation of hostilities against the Americans. *Moderado*-controlled newspapers had attempted to rally public-spirited Mexicans into supporting the war effort during the spring of 1847, but the military defeats that the United States had inflicted upon Mexico by late August ended the publicity campaign.[2] The *puros*, however, continued to agitate for war, especially after the United States Army occupied Mexico City in September 1847. The *puro* attitude was best exemplified by Zacatecas' Governor Manuel González Cosío, who contended that "the horrors of the most disadvantageous war and the disasters of the most awful anarchy were one thousand times [preferable] to the loss of national honor and to the scorn and vilification that will be the immediate consequences of an dishonorable peace."[3]

The *puros*, however, faced a much different situation in 1847 and 1848 than the one they had confronted when Gómez Farías returned to Mexico from New Orleans in 1845. They could not count on influential newspapers like *La Voz del Pueblo* or *El Estandarte Nacional* to arouse public support for their bellicose rhetoric. Partisan hatreds in the national legislature also hampered *puro* efforts to articulate a systematic and coherent response to the war effort. One contemporary observer, in fact, commented that the prevailing antipathy prevented Congress from "seeing anything clearly, except when it wish[ed] to discredit its opponents."[4] Furthermore, most states responded to the *puros'* hawkish cries with apathy. Peace between Mexico and the United States finally came in early February 1848.

A Brief Resurgence

News of the capitulation of Veracruz to General Winfield

Scott, which reached Mexico City on March 31, 1847, awakened patriotic feelings among both *puro* and *moderado* legislators. Deputies immediately proposed a flurry of combative pieces of legislation. *Puros* Vicente Romero, Juan Othón, and three other congressmen suggested that hostilities continue even if the United States army occupied Mexico City; they also wished to brand as a traitor any Mexican who sought peace while United States troops occupied any part of Mexican territory. Vicente Romero further urged that the government be authorized to buy weapons and to arm the citizenry. On April 2, Ramón Gamboa demanded that Mexico City be prepared at once to resist the invasion. Three days later, *puro* Eligio Romero advised protesting any treaty that Mexico signed with the United States as long as American troops remained in any part of the national territory as defined by the 1824 constitution. The bill also offered various rewards to Spaniards, Irishmen, and slaves if they served in the military on Mexico's behalf and labeled any Mexican who favored or provided assistance to the United States a traitor.[5]

A special commission of Congress created on April 1 to determine what needed to be done to insure the republic's salvation debated the legislation. *Moderados* held four of the five seats on the commission (Mariano Otero, José María Lafragua, General José Joaquín Herrera, and Miguel Lazo de la Vega), and the deliberations resulted in the decree of April 9, 1847. The law authorized the government to organize the civic militia and to secure arms to defend the country's independence against the United States.[6] The *moderados* seemed on the verge of putting partisan concerns aside to join the *puros* in support of the war effort.

As the national legislature discussed these matters, residents of Mexico City anxiously awaited word from Santa Anna, who had marched east in early April to meet the American army along the road to the capital. A victory over General Scott's troops would provide a much-needed morale boost and stem the United States advance into central Mexico. These hopes vanished when the Mexican army suffered a devastating defeat at the Battle of Cerro Gordo on April 18. News of the loss reached the capital two days later, and the *moderado*-controlled commission presented Congress with a bill that became law immediately. An April 20 decree gave Anaya's administration the power to take all measures necessary to prosecute the war. The legislation also prohibited the executive branch from: 1) arranging a peace treaty with the United States; 2) concluding negotiations with foreign powers; 3) disposing of any portion of the national territory; and 4) it branded as a traitor any individual who entered into treaties with the United States government.7 Every article was approved either unanimously or by an overwhelming majority of Congress. Once again, all signs seemed to indicate that *puros* and *moderados* were willing to set aside their differences to prosecute the war vigorously.

Several developments, however, indicated that the factions had not reconciled. One such instance was the late March proposal by *puro* Deputies Pedro Zubieta and Ramón Reynoso to transfer the seat of government to the city of Celaya in the state of Guanajuato. The tactic had a dual purpose. One was to allow the *puros* to gain a majority in Congress because they suspected that *moderado* deputies would not abandon Mexico City. The other objective was to support the coalition that the states of Jalisco, Mexico, Michoacán, Querétaro, San Luis Potosí, and Zacatecas had organized to withstand General Ventura Mora's January 1847 uprising in Mazatlán. The latter prospect worried two of Santa Anna's correspondents, who noted that the coalition might challenge Anaya's claim to the presidency and thus negate efforts to prosecute the war. In the end, the apprehension proved unwarranted; Zubieta and Reynoso's petition was not passed. Deputies finally agreed that Congress would leave Mexico City when the United States army reached a defensive line set at the fortress of Perote, near Jalapa in Veracruz, and that thirty legislators would be enough to carry on deliberations.8

This arrangement did not end the bickering between the *puros* and their political opponents. Great Britain's offer to arrange a peace treaty between Mexico and the United States provided *puros* and *moderados* with another opportunity for dispute. Charles Bankhead, the British minister to Mexico, had first made an overture in August 1846, but neither *puros* nor *moderados* had been willing to jeopardize their political futures by taking on such an explosive issue. In fact, then-Minister of Foreign Relations Rejón had responded that such a grave matter should be resolved by Congress in its December session. Lafragua, who succeeded Rejón, did the same when confronted with a similar proposal two months later. José Fernando Ramírez subsequently brought this matter to Congress' attention, but the legislature did not issue a report until late February 1847. Its Committee on Foreign Relations decided that the matter did not fall within Congress' responsibility and recommended rejecting any arbitration.9

Santa Anna's defeat at Cerro Gordo, however, revived the idea of British mediation. On April 24, despite his earlier support for legislative measures designed to promote a vigorous pursuit of the war effort, Otero suggested to Congress that the government be allowed to use its constitutional right—with the limitations that the April 20 decree placed on negotiations with foreign powers—to discuss the proposal. Although this was merely a procedural matter, *puro* deputies responded with a "furious storm of insults" and threatened advocates of the measure with a charge of treason. The protests forced Otero to vote against the proposal and legislators shelved the matter. In the end, however, little was accomplished. Congress did not seat a quorum until April 29, as both *puro* and *moderado* deputies abandoned the chambers when it came to a vote on whether to admit Otero's motion for debate. At that time legislators finally agreed to consider the British mediation offer by a tally of thirty-six to thirty-five, but deputies rejected the proposition by over twenty ballots on the following day. The bill returned to the Commission on Foreign Relations, which decided not to act on the controversial matter.[10]

The stalemate prompted *moderados* to search for a way to accept Great Britain's bid. First, they trusted General José Ignacio Basadre with the mission of convincing state authorities not to oppose the British offer. Then, on May 1, Mariano Riva Palacio, Manuel Gómez Pedraza, and Juan Rodríguez Puebla asked Otero to arrange for a congressional recess in order to nullify *puro* opposition. But at that moment Otero began to maneuver "in all imaginable ways" and declared that Congress would continue to meet. Otero's unexpected conduct was prompted by his desire to get legislative approval for what would be known as the *Acta de Reformas*, a bill to sanction some minor modifications to the 1824 constitution. Anaya's ministers then tried to bribe several deputies to leave the capital so that Congress would lack a quorum—a tactic that failed.[11]

Despite the setbacks, developments in Oaxaca revived the *moderados'* hopes of dissolving Congress. On February 15, a revolt in Oaxaca—a reaction to the January 11, 1847, anticlerical decree—ousted state authorities who had come to power as a result of the rebellion of the Ciudadela. Federal deputies from Oaxaca asked the national government late in April to reinstate the deposed officals, but Anaya disapproved. The request made by Oaxacan legislators could only be implemented forcefully, but the troops were needed in the war against the United States. Supporting the Oaxacan deputies would have also deprived Anaya's administration of the financial assistance it received from the government installed in that state by the mid-February uprising. Available documentation suggests that by late April this regime had collected between 6,000 and 20,000 pesos to defray the expenditures of the army in Veracruz. Other considerations, however, determined the course that the Mexican government would pursue.[12]

Primary among these concerns was Anaya's responsibility for insuring that Santa Anna remain in power. Santa Anna's victory in the presidential elections scheduled for May 15 was not certain. His tenure in office would continue, however, if legal elections were not held. Article 81 of the 1824 constitution stipulated that three-fourths of the state legislatures had to vote for an election to be considered legitimate. Since Mexico consisted of twenty-three states at the time, elections would be null if less than eighteen state legislatures cast ballots. If Oaxaca's former officials were not reinstated there would be no legislature in the state and Oaxaca could not hold presidential elections. Other states faced the same problem, so Anaya had a vested interest in keeping Oaxaca's deposed authorities from their posts. On May 6, the Mexican government turned down a proposal to reinstate the Oaxacans, and the Oaxaca delegation prepared to leave Mexico City.[13] Anaya's plan seemed on the verge of success.

But there would be another obstacle to Anaya's scheme — the issue of Otero's constitutional reform bill came up unexpectedly. Debate on the law had nearly ended by this time, and Otero became almost "frantic" on learning of the government's May 6 resolution. Thinking that his efforts would be wasted if Congress adjourned, he offered to assist the Oaxaca deputies in their attempt to reinstate the deposed state authorities if they attended congressional sessions and voted for the *Acta de Reformas*.[14] In the end, Otero emerged victorious. The Oaxacans did not abandon the assembly and on May 11 Congress called the administration installed in Oaxaca by the February 15 revolt "subversive" and "contrary to the federal constitution."[15] One week later the Mexican national legislature approved the *Acta de Reformas*.[16]

Otero's strategy did not prevent other Mexican statesmen from trying to revive the *moderado* administration's plan to dissolve Congress so Mexico could consider the British mediation. Minister of Foreign Relations Manuel Baranda, an advocate of peace who had recently encouraged José Fernando Ramírez to write for the antiwar newspaper *El Razonador*, resigned his portfolio on May 10. Three days later, Baranda told Anaya and other prominent *moderados* that he would only return to his post on two conditions: the ministers of justice and war had to go (*puro* supporter Francisco Súarez Iriarte, who supposedly "would not listen to the Americans," held the former post);[17] and Congress would have to recess by May 15. In the end, Baranda returned to the cabinet, but he could not bring about suspension of Congress. *Puro* deputies remained a staunch source of opposition to the *moderados*, leaving both the Mexican government and British Minister Bankhead with little choice but to look for other avenues to conduct peace negotiations.[18]

As these events unfolded, word of Santa Anna's impending return to the capital reached Mexico City on May 17. The news set off a chain of events that temporarily blocked the *moderado* political reign; Santa Anna thought that he would benefit from the developments, but it was the *puros* who capitalized instead. Whereas Santa Anna remained in power legally because only fifteen state legislatures held presidential elections,[19] his decision to return to Mexico City jeopardized a scheme by Baranda to entice Irish-born soldiers in the United States armed forces to desert and join the Mexican regular army unit known as the San Patricio Battalion. Baranda's plot also required that Santa Anna remain at the head of Mexican troops on the outskirts of Puebla, which had been captured by Scott's forces on May 15. Santa Anna was to protect the deserters and, with the aid of Puebla's 80,000 inhabitants, attack that city.[20]

On May 18, Ramírez, Baranda, and Ignacio Trigueros traveled to Ayotla, approximately twenty miles from Mexico City, to apprise Santa Anna of the recruiting strategy. On their way, however, the men ran into a throng of soldiers "in the most wretched condition" who informed them that the army was marching back to the capital. Ramírez, Trigueros, and Baranda realized that it would be impossible to convince Santa Anna to remain near Puebla, so they scrambled for a way to keep Anaya in power. Santa Anna was to draft a letter stating that Mexico faced an imminent rebellion that could only help the invaders. To forestall such a calamity, Santa Anna should resign both as chief executive and as commander-in-chief of the army.[21]

No sooner had the retinue returned to Mexico City than Santa Anna changed his mind. General José María Tornel and other army leaders, as well as Rejón and several *puros*, convinced Santa Anna that the sole purpose of Ramírez, Baranda, and Trigueros' visit had been to deprive him of his presidential powers. Santa Anna reconsidered his actions and wrote Congress a second letter, arguing that public outcry had been such that he had no choice but to withdraw his resignation. After meeting with his generals and deciding to defend the capital against the United States forces, Santa Anna took the presidency on May 20.[22]

The new chief executive could not have been at ease in this situation. By reassuming the presidency Santa Anna had broken with the *moderados*. In fact, Santa Anna's decision so disturbed Anaya that "he would have opposed it forcefully had he been able to do so."[23] Moreover, Santa Anna's decision to fortify Mexico City alienated politicians fearful of a Santa Anna dictatorship (under the extraordinary powers granted the government by the April 20 decree), as well as clergymen, advocates of peace, and property owners who feared the consequences of a United States siege of the Mexican capital. In addition, Generals Juan Nepomuceno Almonte, Mariano Arista, and Pedro Ampudia took advantage of this turn of events to plot against Santa Anna, while Generals Nicolás Bravo and Manuel Rincón, who commanded the Army of the East, showed their discontent by resigning their posts.[24]

Santa Anna first tried to assuage the growing dissatisfaction by arresting Generals Almonte and Arista and exiling General Ampudia to Cuernavaca.[25] But the tactics did not work. Opposition to Santa Anna only increased. In a desperate attempt to regain control, Santa Anna opted to abandon the presidency on May 29. The Spanish minister in Mexico remarked that Santa Anna portrayed himself in his letter of resignation as "a victim of his irrevocable determination to fight" the Americans. Congress could, therefore, be blamed for wanting peace if it endorsed Santa Anna's actions.[26]

Santa Anna hoped that his dismissal would provoke public demonstrations against the legislature, and he would be able to remain as chief executive with even greater power. The gamble backfired. Although the Commission on Constitutional Affairs refused to accept Santa Anna's resignation, his followers discovered that Congress planned to set aside the commission's recommendation and ask him to renounce the presidency. After learning this, Santa Anna withdrew his resignation on June 2. He argued that news of his ouster had led the American troops to begin their march upon Mexico City. This had increased public agitation, which would add to the national woes. Santa Anna would make yet another sacrifice to Mexico and remain as president.[27] Despite allegations that Santa Anna "again became a . . . dictator,"[28] he did not govern as an autocrat. Santa Anna had little choice but to indulge his many adversaries to rule the country during the summer of 1847.

The *puros* benefited from Santa Anna's predicament. By June 4 gossip in Mexico City proffered that Santa Anna had decided to surround himself with the *puros* and name Rejón minister of foreign relations.[29] Not long after, the editors of *El Republicano* pointed out that Rejón had become a member of Santa Anna's clique. They also wrote that friends of Rejón boasted of his status as "the man of the moment, [as] the one who will fix everything."[30] Rejón did not join the cabinet, but his new influence was immediately evident. Rejón believed that Minister Baranda had instigated the events in Ayotla in mid-May, so he asked Congress on June 5 to abolish the decree of May 17, 1847, which was written by Baranda and prohibited the Church from demanding immediate repayment of its loans to urban and rural property holders. Abrogation of the law also benefited the government; it received money from the Bishop of Michoacán to purchase muskets.[31]

The *puros'* growing strength became more apparent on June 6 when they kept the *moderados* from regaining access to Santa Anna's inner circle. On learning that Santa Anna intended to appoint Lafragua as minister of foreign relations, Rejón, José María del Río, Fernando Ortega, and Vicente and Eligio Romero staged "a near mutiny" in Santa Anna's office, declaring that it "would have been better if Lucas Alamán had been named." Rejón later said that he would support Lafragua as long as the *moderado* politician acted in accordance with his orders, but Lafragua refused to join the cabinet under the conditions.[32] The invitation extended to Vicente Romero to become minister of justice provided further evidence that *puros'* political fortunes were on the rise — at least for the time being.[33]

Moderado leaders retaliated, using Articles Six and Seven of the April 20, 1847, decree to end the *puros'* ascent. If Congress could not meet, the clauses provided for a committee of the senior members of each state's delegation to the legislature to carry out the duties of the Council of State.[34] In mid-June, thirty-six deputies requested then president of Congress, *moderado* politician Luis de la Rosa, to establish the committee. After consulting with senior legislators de la Rosa agreed to do so. General Anaya would preside; the vice-president and two secretaries were also well-known *moderados*.[35]

Puro deputies moved to foil the tactic. They informed de la Rosa that the commission violated Articles 69 and 113 of the 1824 constitution, as well as Articles 21 and 30 of the *Acta de Reformas*. *Puro* legislators charged that dissolving Congress in this manner would be a "demagogic act," and promised to hold accountable those responsible for such "a flagrant offense."[36] Santa Anna, however, prevented both factions from airing their differences. On June 21, then Minister of Foreign Relations Domingo Ibarra told the secretaries of the permanent commission that Santa Anna did not think that it was proper to establish the committee, much less name its members. Santa Anna wanted only for Congress to convene.37

Santa Anna's decision to push for a meeting of the legislature was inspired by his "secret, yet constant" desire to make peace with the United States.38 A new opportunity to end hostilities had presented itself; Santa Anna would put responsibility for the delicate matter in the hands of Congress. The issue influenced political developments in Mexico during the next two months. At first *puro* and *moderado* legislators clashed over the question in an attempt to insure their party's dominance, but late in August, as Mexicans prepared to defend the capital, congressmen from both factions cooperated in a bid to thwart Santa Anna's dictatorial ambitions. In the end, however, domestic solidarity proved impossible to achieve.

On June 22, Minister Ibarra wrote James Buchanan, United States secretary of state, that he would inform the national legislature of the arrival of Commissioner Nicholas P. Trist, who was to submit peace proposals to the Mexican government.39 But Congress again proved hesitant to handle the issue. For the next three weeks the legislature lacked a quorum, and when it met the *moderados* foiled Santa Anna's plans. On July 13 three members of the Commission on Foreign Relations (Otero, Lafragua, and Juan Bautista Ceballos) issued a resolution suggesting that proclamation of the *Acta de Reformas* had implicitly revoked the April 20, 1847, decree. The declaration indicated that the Constitution of 1824 authorized the president to oversee diplomatic negotiations and arrange treaties. Since Congress only had to approve these agreements before ratification, the question of negotiating peace with the United States fell under the president's jurisdiction. The committee pointed out that the special powers conferred on Congress by the August 4, 1846, Plan of the Ciudadela and the August 6, 1846, decree ceased to be in effect once the *Acta de Reformas* sanctioned the constitution.40

Congress overwhelmingly approved the report, fifty-two to twenty-two. Voting followed partisan lines, which strongly suggests that the *puro* deputies who rejected the proposal did so in an attempt to stand behind Santa Anna, extend their party's political standing, and nullify the *moderados'* influence. Moreover, the *puros'* vote implied that the national legislature, not Santa Anna, had the right to hear United States peace propositions. If Congress entertained peace overtures, the *puros* could brand the *moderados* as traitors for having voted in favor of such a proposal.[41] On July 16, *moderado* José Ramón Pacheco, who had recently replaced Ibarra as minister of foreign relations, requested that the legislature reconsider their decision to revoke the April 20, 1847, decree. Pacheco's appeal (which aimed to protect Santa Anna) fell upon deaf ears. Neither Santa Anna nor Congress wanted to confront the matter directly and the possibility of opening peace negotiations with the United States was temporarily shelved.[42]

Debate was renewed three weeks later, but Mexico then found itself in less favorable circumstances. American troops won victories at the Battles of Contreras and Churubusco on August 20, and everything seemed to indicate that the United States army would soon enter the capital. On the following day, however, General Ignacio Mora y Villamil visited the American camp and presented General Scott with two letters, one from Bankhead and one from Pacheco. The former requested that Scott not pillage the city, while the latter indicated that the Mexican government would hear Trist's proposal and negotiate a treaty within a year. Scott, who had already discussed ways of arranging peace with *santanista* agents, agreed to an armistice.[43]

In essence, Pacheco's note meant that Santa Anna recognized that implementing the *Acta de Reformas* revoked the April 20, 1847, decree. Mexico's chief executive would decide whether to continue the war. Santa Anna, nevertheless, remained unwilling to bear full responsibility. Again he tried to force Congress into sharing the burden. Pacheco notified then president of Congress Antonio Salonio of Santa Anna's decision to hear out Trist's proposals, and urged him to call the deputies to a special session that was to begin at noon. But only twenty-six deputies had assembled by mid-afternoon. The attendees agreed to summon again those who had not attended and to press the president to call on state governors to help assemble the national legislature.44

The deputies, however, refused to be cowed by Santa Anna. Several *puro* and *moderado* statesmen momentarily put aside their differences and worked feverishly on a statement to insure that Congress met in the city of Querétaro, where Santa Anna could not influence the debate. Eight congressmen who had moved to Toluca signed the petition, among them Gómez Farías, de la Rosa, and Mariano Otero. They explained that "the actual circumstances of Mexico City would not grant the legislature the freedom it needed for its discussions and deliberations." As a result, the "dignity of the republic" would be tarnished if its representatives discussed a peace treaty in such a setting. Moreover, they believed that any foreign relations agreement that Congress did not ratify would be "improper . . . entirely null as well as unconstitutional, and would turn whoever endorsed it into a traitor." The legislators would not return to the capital, but they were willing to travel to Querétaro.45

Meanwhile, about thirty deputies—including *puro* advocate Perdigón Garay, who was concerned that the enemies of Congress could "brand it a *junta* of rebels and introduce anarchy" if the legislature moved without legal authorization—remained in the capital and worked to relocate to Querétaro. Perdigón Garay hoped to gather enough deputies in Mexico City to form a quorum and lawfully sanction the legislature's transfer.46 Another group of deputies who lingered in Mexico City tried another strategy: they hoped to circumvent the lack of a quorum and to pass a proposal that authorized the president of Congress or the permanent commission to sanction the move.47

All efforts came to naught. The record is unclear as to why

the endeavors of the Toluca-based legislators failed, but some evidence suggests that the *moderados* worked to defeat those deputies who remained in Mexico City. Otero, his endeavors in Toluca notwithstanding, did not approve of the step advocated by Perdigón Garay. Otero remarked that many petty questions might be debated once enough deputies assembled, delaying discussion of Trist's proposals and possibly killing an armistice. In that case, Congress would bear the blame for all the disasters that befell Mexico once hostilities broke out again.[48] Lafragua may have also supported Otero's efforts, albeit for different reasons. While he expressed a willingness to go to Querétero if fighting broke out again, he also believed that duty called on him to remain in the capital as long as it was "morally possible." Lafragua had explained that congressional decisions might be disregarded if not made in Mexico City, thus providing Santa Anna with a convenient pretext to declare a dictatorship.[49]

The maneuvers of Congress did not prevent Santa Anna from continuing to negotiate with Trist, but the talks ended on September 6 without a mutually satisfactory arrangement. Hostilities resumed two days later, and United States troops defeated the defenders at Molino del Rey and Chapultepec Castle. The Americans pressed on into Mexico City, which surrendered on September 14. Santa Anna resigned the presidency two days later, declaring that executive authority should lay with the president of the Supreme Court of Justice, Manuel de la Peña y Peña, and two associates—Generals José Joaquín Herrera and Lino Alcorta. Santa Anna also ordered that the seat of government be moved to Querétaro.[50] As Mexican statesmen then debated the question of war or peace, *puros* and *moderados* continued to bicker even more acridly than before.

"The Battlefield is in Querétaro"

On September 18 Peña y Peña learned of his new charge at

his hacienda near Toluca. The situation across Mexico was grim and he was reluctant to assume the presidency. Peña y Peña, in fact, took four days to acknowledge Santa Anna's decrees and five more to accept the post of chief executive. Once Peña y Peña made his decision public on September 27, he took steps to end the conflict with the United States. Peña y Peña appointed Luis de la Rosa—a dove—as minister of foreign relations. The new Mexican president arrived in Querétaro on October 12 and, nine days later, selected General Ignacio Mora y Villamil as minister of war. Mora y Villamil—another dove—had participated in the peace negotiations with Trist. Like Peña y Peña, Mora y Villamil did not want to join the government in an official capacity, but he assumed the cabinet post after being assured that every possible effort to arrange a peace treaty would be made.[51]

A second priority of the new *moderado* administration was to insure the meeting of the legislature.[52] Congress was the only body that could confirm Peña y Peña in his post and determine whether the prohibition on peace negotiations with the United States stipulated by the April 20, 1847, decree remained in effect. Both Congress and Santa Anna had agreed that the decree was meaningless but it had never been struck down formally. Therefore, Peña y Peña thought it necessary to determine the law's validity once and for all. Antonio Salonio ordered deputies to Querétaro by October 5, including the thirty-seven legislators who remained in Mexico City and those who were in Toluca. The result of a consultation that Peña y Peña held with the forty or so deputies already in Querétaro appeared to presage the change. When he asked if the Council of State referred to in the April 20 decree should be installed, they opposed the measure.[53]

Yet several obstacles remained in Peña y Peña's way. Again it was the time-honored scenario—chronic political upheaval caused by the ambitions of senior army officers. General Almonte had decided that the time was right to plot his way into the presidency. General Mariano Paredes y Arrillaga, who allegedly intended to volunteer his military services to the government, was returning to Mexico from exile; in truth, Paredes hoped revitalize his plans to establish a monarchy. Tornel and former Minister of Finance Francisco Lombardo tried to instigate a Santa Anna dictatorship. Given that Santa Anna's supporters represented the most serious of the threats, Peña y Peña moved quickly to thwart the *santanistas* and assert his own authority. He dismissed Santa Anna as commander-in-chief of the army on October 7 and, in essence, placed him under house arrest to await court-martial.[54]

Peña y Peña and the *moderados* also had to contend with the Valentín Gómez Farías-led *puros*, who still wanted to rally Mexicans in the war effort. At least two witnesses have questioned the motives for this policy, maintaining that all *puros* favored Mexico's annexation to its northern neighbor. United States Colonel Ethan Allen Hitchcock wrote that the *puros'* desire to fight sprang from the conviction that hostilities would annihilate the Mexican army and insure "an adequate civilian government" similar to that in the United States.[55] Commissioner Trist offered a similar opinion, noting that the *puros* desired to prosecute the war as long as necessary to make "a connection of some sort . . . between the two countries . . . which shall suffice to secure among them the predominance of those political principles to which our country is indebted for the happiness which reigns there."[56] Mexican historian José Fuentes Mares also casts doubts on the *puros'* motives. He claims that they presented themselves "as champions of an armed struggle against the invaders, but only to obtain Mexico's final annexation to the United States."[57]

There is no doubt that several *puro* politicians advocated establishment of a United States protectorate, but it is difficult to identify the majority who concurred since Trist did not refer to them by name in his correspondence. Nonetheless, the case of Francisco Carbajal, who had been an important correspondent at the bellicose *puro* newspaper *El Estandarte Nacional* in 1845, sheds light on why some *puros* broke away from Gómez Farías. Carbajal was one of four *puros* with whom Colonel Hitchcock discussed a protectorate in the fall of 1847 (the other three were José María Benítez, Tiburcio Cañas, and José María Sánchez Espinosa). By that time Carbajal edited *La Razón,* a journal that called for peace.[58] Carbajal must have been convinced of the futility of carrying on the war, and, fearful that Mexico would lose its sovereignty, decided to break ranks with his associates. Carbajal wanted the United States Army to remain in Mexico. Such a guardianship would ease the establishment of trial by jury and freedom of religion, as well as the abolition of internal custom duties and military and ecclesiastical *fueros*—reforms essential to rejuvenate Mexico's political, economic, and social development.[59] The goals of other *puros* were even more dramatic. Several unidentified men asked General Scott to become dictator of Mexico. Although the proposition was not as fanciful as it might appear, Scott turned down the invitation.[60]

The members of the Mexico City *ayuntamiento* who took office on December 24, 1847, may also have had annexationist inclinations. Francisco Suárez Iriarte, who had served as minister of finance under Gómez Farías earlier that year, headed this body. Other former collaborators of Gómez Farías who sat on the *ayuntamiento* included Tiburcio Cañas and Miguel Buenrostro.[61] In a manifesto that publicized their views about the war, as well as their agenda for Mexico's political and economic future, they argued that the United States invasion was both a consequence of the natural development of an active and industrious nation, and of the Mexicans' incapacity to govern themselves. Like Carbajal, the councilmen endorsed reforms such as the abolition of internal customs duties and *fueros,* as well as the establishment of trial by jury. But it would be two other propositions that illustrated the *ayuntamiento's* intent to incorporate Mexico into the United States. One stated that the Federal District had the potential of forming a "perfect political body"; the second declared that if national authorities could not defend Mexican institutions—a possibility that was not far-fetched—Mexico City should enter into a confederation that would grant it respectability, peace, order, and freedom of thought and conscience.[62]

In the public's mind, subsequent actions of the *ayuntamiento* were also indicative of its annexationist views. In early January 1848, the *moderado* national government appointed Manuel Gómez Pedraza director of the national pawnshop *(Monte de Piedad)* in Mexico City. The *ayuntamiento*, however, denied the legality of the nomination. It has been argued that the *ayuntamiento*, by rejecting an order from the national government, insinuated that Mexico lacked a central authority that all citizens should obey. If that was the case, annexing the Federal District to the United States would surely follow. Annexationist tendencies were also ascribed to the *ayuntamiento's* sanction of a set of bylaws to organize a rural police force; these troops were to apprehend deserters from the American army and turn them over to their superiors. One historian characterized this as an "unpatriotic" measure, for most of those American soldiers intended to join the Mexican forces. Finally, a January 29, 1848, banquet held on the outskirts of Mexico City at the Desierto de los Leones also foretold the *ayuntamiento's* desire to attach Mexico's fate to its northern neighbor. The luncheon honored several United States army officers for having completed a survey to establish the level of the lakes surrounding the city. It is said, however, that during the course of the afternoon a toast was offered calling for Mexico's annexation to the United States.[63]

An alternative interpretation of these events is more judicious. The *moderado* national government sought to use Gómez Pedraza's designation as director of the *Monte de Piedad* to regain control over affairs in the capital. The *ayuntamiento's* stand on the Gómez Pedraza appointment, thus, was nothing more than a party move aimed at preventing a *moderado* politician from being in charge of the *Monte de Piedad*. The views on the activities of the Mexico City *ayuntamiento*, which reflect the perspective of several Mexican scholars, may have been influenced by their deep-seated nationalism. Another historian who studied the council posits a different interpretation of their actions, and suggests that Mexico City's *ayuntamiento* only sought to create a highly decentralized state. The *ayuntamiento* would have broad enough powers to make Mexico City and the Federal District almost sovereign, but it would be linked to other states in a confederation—the Mexico of the future. Finally, since the lakes surrounding Mexico City frequently overflowed into the capital during the rainy season and the city lacked the necessary resources for the survey, the banquet at the Desierto de los Leones may well have been "a deserved courtesy."[64]

The opinions of contemporary observers like Colonel Hitchcock and Trist about the *puros* are also flawed. They failed to recognize the factionalism—which puzzled many politically conscious Mexicans—within the party in late 1847. For example, *moderado* leader Mariano Riva Palacio commented that he did not understand "the double conscience of the *puro* party, in Mexico in favor of annexation and in Querétaro for a war without respite."[65] Although some of Gómez Farías' backers harbored annexationist ideas as 1847 came to an end, most *puros* followed Gómez Farías' leadership. Gómez Farías' contingent made every effort to insure that hostilities continued with the United States to avoid what they considered to be a dishonorable peace.

Gómez Farías' Yankeephobia, in fact, remained as resolute in the fall of 1847 as in the more visionary days of 1845. He indicated in an undated letter (probably written in September 1847) that the armistice's failure filled him with joy. Nonetheless, he would be more content if no new negotiations were held until United States troops left Mexican soil. It was preferable to perish, according to Gómez Farías, than to accept a compromise. Gómez Farías later wrote that only a "continuous and determined war, a war without respite, and an eternal war if necessary," would restore Mexican honor and "remove the stigma" that hung over its people.[66] But Gómez Farías met with failure during the following months despite Herculean efforts to make his hopes come true.

As soon as he learned of Peña y Peña's accession to the presidency, Gómez Farías left Querétaro for the city of Lagos, Jalisco, justifying his departure on the grounds that his enemies would interpret his permanence in Querétaro as an implicit recognition of the new *moderado* government. That, he argued, was impossible. Gómez Farías had more important objectives in mind. He wanted to support Jalisco politician Juan N. Cumplido in organizing a coalition of several states that included Mexico, San Luis Potosí, Aguascalientes, Zacatecas, Querétaro, and Jalisco.[67] The Lagos coalition would resist "all tendencies toward centralism" and reject any "shameful [peace] treaties or preliminary agreements."[68] Its ultimate goal may have been to name Gómez Farías chief executive.[69]

Gómez Farías had great faith in the coalition. Not only did Cumplido's followers greet him "warmly," but they agreed with his political ideas. The *puro* leader commented that "several measures [which he did not identify] have been adopted that could offer some hope to the nation if the members of the coalition realize the gravity of the situation and what is expected of them."[70] Nonetheless, Gómez Farías' expectations never materialized. The coalition alarmed the *moderados* because it threatened to provide the *puros* with sufficient regional support to overthrow the Peña y Peña administration. *El Republicano's* editors launched a campaign to discredit the Lagos bloc, declaring that it threatened to "offer new proposals to the anarchy" that was destroying the country.[71] *Moderado* journalists may have cast doubt on the coalition's merits, but the response of state authorities proved to be a more important factor in explaining its eventual collapse. Francisco Modesto Olaguíbel, governor of the state of Mexico and a devoted collaborator of Gómez Farías, simply did not allow the state Congress to publish a decree that recognized any federal authority save that of the Lagos confederacy.[72] The historical record is scanty on this topic, but it is reasonable to assume that other state governors followed Olaguíbel's example. The *puros*, thus, had to find other instruments with which to contest Peña y Peña's regime.

The *puros* did not have to wait long for another opportunity to discredit the *moderados*. The constituent Congress finally assembled in Querétaro on November 2. Eight days later, it decreed that a tally to elect an interim president would be held on November 11 in accordance with the 1824 charter and the *Acta de Reformas*. The winner would stay in office until January 8, 1848.[73] The *puros* initially considered backing one of three candidates: Cumplido, Zacatecas' Governor González Cosío, or General Almonte. Events forced the *puros* to champion Cumplido. González Cosío withdrew from contention for reasons unknown, while Almonte's well-known hate for Santa Anna spoiled his aspirations. Fearing that Almonte would seek revenge against Santa Anna if elected, pro-Santa Anna deputies struck a bargain with the *puros*. They would vote for Cumplido if the *puros* promised not to bring Santa Anna to trial and to restore his position as commander-in-chief of the army.[74]

At the same time that the *puros* mapped out their strategy for the presidential elections, they continued to criticize the *moderado* regime for its prosecution of the war. On November 4, Vicente and Eligio Romero declared before Congress that every state desired to pursue the war at all costs and accused the government of failing to raise the means for the operation. They requested that the ministers of foreign relations and war reveal what steps had been taken to wage war, or whether those measures were "the halfhearted [steps] between war and peace" that President Peña y Peña had mentioned in a recent manifesto.[75] *Puro* legislators denounced the *moderado* regime for the next two days. Guadalupe

Perdigón Garay accused the minister of war of high treason and José María del Río asked that the government declare whether it had entered into new negotiations with the United States.[76]

Two other proposals further highlight *puro* belligerence. On November 4, Mariano Otero suggested that the government should not entertain any peace negotiations that might lead to the loss of territory held by Mexico before the war. The legislature threw out Otero's bill when it came up for discussion two days later, but *moderado* newspapers in Mexico City took advantage of the events: twenty-two of the forty-six deputies who opposed the bill were *puros*, who, it could be said, supported an ignoble peace.[77] *Puro* congressmen published a pamphlet later that month to belie the allegations, arguing that Otero's proposal was inadmissible because it tacitly consented to the annexation of Texas and the territories north of the Rio Bravo to the United States.[78] Then, on November 8, Deputy Miguel García Vargas urged the government to promote all those measures "that were sufficient and within its capacity to carry on the war."[79]

Despite their efforts, the *puros* failed. Congress threw out the motions submitted by the Romeros, Perdigón Garay, del Río, and García Vargas, and the *puro* coalition with the *santanistas* did not bring victory in the presidential elections. The *moderados* settled on General Pedro María Anaya as their candidate, and he prevailed in the November 11 tally.[80] Anaya kept de la Rosa and Mora y Villamil in their cabinet posts and named Peña y Peña minister of foreign relations.[81] The *moderados*, for the third time since 1845, were in charge of public affairs and facing the aggressive policies of the United States.

Puro deputies made one last try to use the constituent Congress to break the *moderado* grip on power. On November 19, Pedro Zubieta presented a bill declaring that the federalist pact of 1824 was broken. Zubieta's proposal authorized the states to adopt the political system that suited them best and to organize their own resistance against United States forces.

By a vote of fifty-six to eighteen, Congress rejected the bill.[82] By mid-December, many deputies from both parties had left Querétaro and, without a quorum, Congress had no choice but to suspend sessions. Preparatory meetings for the next national legislature—to be installed on May 3, 1848—began at the same time.[83] The *puros* would not enjoy a majority in the upcoming assembly and they turned to armed force to thwart *moderado* policies.

During his term as president, Peña y Peña had summoned state governors to Querétaro for a conference scheduled to begin on November 10, and leading public officials from Puebla, Mexico, Querétaro, Michoacán, Guanajuato, Jalisco, San Luis Potosí, and Zacatecas responded. Minister of War Mora y Villamil told participants that they had been called to advise the cabinet, which, however, was not obliged to adopt their suggestions. Mora y Villamil also briefed state governors on Mexico's discouraging military situation, the costs of carrying on the war, and the need to make peace. The conference ended in mid-December and, in a gesture designed to help President Anaya avoid the problems that the April 20, 1847, decree stipulated about peace negotiations, the governors declared that they would help the *moderado* regime fulfill its duties as specified in the constitution.[84]

The governor of San Luis Potosí, however, dissented. Ramón Adame walked out in late November when he realized that the government had no intention of considering the governors' opinions.[85] This turn of events lifted Gómez Farías' spirits. One correspondents wrote in early December 1847 that public opinion in San Luis Potosí favored prosecution of the war. He added that efforts were underway to summon the state legislature, which would publicly object to peace talks and give Adame a public testimonial in appreciation of his stand in Querétaro.[86] As 1847 drew to a close, Gómez Farías and other *puros* began plotting a rebellion against Anaya.[87]

The state of Zacatecas was to play a major role in the enterprise. On December 21, Governor González Cosío informed Gómez Farías that *puro* Deputy Perdigón Garay had purchased seventy-nine English muskets from a Mr. Veyna and had donated 250 more to the state. The weapons would be used to arm the Zacatecas civic militia. Since most of the guns were stored in Cuautitlán, Mexico, and its surroundings, Gómez Farías' son Casimiro was instructed to transport them to Zacatecas. Gómez Farías urged his son to be careful and not to go near Mexico City on the assignment. He also told Casimiro to ship the muskets as soon as possible, to make sure that they worked properly, and that they were of the same caliber.[88]

Preparations for the rebellion moved along in San Luis Potosí and other states. On January 1, 1848, Governor Adame addressed the state legislature, telling them that the *moderado* government gave little evidence of carrying on the war against the Americans. Adame urged delegates to continue fighting; duty called them to prevent San Luis Potosí from falling into the same dismal condition as other states. Some military setbacks were inevitable, but they would prevail over the United States if they fought with the "valor and steadfastness" of the heroes of Mexico's war of independence. Lending a dramatic element to his speech, Adame resigned from office.[89] To rally public opinion in the region, the newspapers *El Voto de Gracias* in Querétaro and *La Atmósfera* in San Luis Potosí began to censure the *moderado* government; Adame, who at the time probably busied himself with details for the uprising, is likely to have helped the journals get started.[90]

The coup d'état commenced on January 12, only four days after the installation of Manuel de la Peña y Peña as chief executive in accordance with the November 10, 1847, decree.[91] The *puros* hoped to capitalize on the regime's newness and on the resumption of discussions with Trist—these had begun on January 2—to propel its downfall. To justify the rebellion, San Luis Potosí Vice-Governor Mariano Avila

issued a nine-article plan, damning the Querétaro government because it had disregarded the national will by failing to
engage in war against the United States. Avila invited state
authorities to send two representatives to a convention that
would name a new chief executive and take steps to continue
hostilities against the American army. Since military support
was essential to the revolt's success, Avila asked General
Anastasio Bustamante, who was in Guanajuato as the commander of a reserve division *(ejército de reserva)*, to lead the
coup.[92]

According to Percy Doyle, who replaced Bankhead as the
British representative in December 1847, the San Luis Potosí
rebellion caused "great consternation" among the leading
moderado statesmen. He remarked that the Mexican government had neither the "money nor [the] means of resisting this
movement," and that other states would imitate San Luis.
Doyle believed that any chance of ending hostilities with the
United States would vanish if the rebellion proved even partially successful. In that case General Scott planned to march
to San Luis to defend the Mexican regime, an event that
might prove "fatal" to the *moderados*. Not only would the public conclude that the *moderado* administration depended on
the support of the United States, but the Mexican government
would also find it "most difficult" to remain at Querétaro as
the American forces marched past the city.[93] The *puros* could
argue that the country lacked a stable central authority. Such
a cry might help them rally Mexicans and organize an effective defense against the United States.

Several events, however, killed the San Luis Potosí movement. The state legislature refused to make Avila's initiative
law, General Bustamante remained loyal to the national government, and the commandant general of San Luis had
arrested both Avila and Adame by January 20. In addition
authorities in Guanajuato, Jalisco, Michoacán, Morelia, and
Querétaro did not take up the banner.[94] The response from
Guanajuato and Morelia must have perplexed the rebels. In

early January, Almonte met frequently with Guanajuato Governor Lorenzo Arellano in an attempt to secure support for the coming rebellion.[95] The bellicose disposition of Morelia Governor Melchor Ocampo, who advocated a guerrilla war because it would ultimately grant Mexico victory over the Americans, also seemed to bode well for the conspirators.[96] In the end, however, these considerations proved secondary to Arellano's and Ocampo's belief that Mexico required a strong central authority. Arellano stated that Guanajuato would never disavow or withdraw its support from the country's "center of union," while Ocampo described Avila's plan as "repugnant" because it sought to divide the republic in order to prosecute the war.[97]

The collapse of the San Luis Potosí rebellion brought to an end the most serious threat against Peña y Peña's second wartime administration. While the *puros* regrouped, Peña y Peña's regime continued discussions with Trist that culminated with the signing of the Treaty of Guadalupe Hidalgo on February 2, 1848. Mexican and American statesmen deliberated on the treaty's contents until late May, and, in spite of *puro* efforts to derail the talks, approved the treaty.

"The Infamous Peace Treaty"

On February 6, 1848, Minister of Foreign Relations Luis de la Rosa began the groundwork for the ratification of the Treaty of Guadalupe Hidalgo. He notified state authorities of the signing and told them that its terms would not be made public until it had been considered by Congress. Preparatory meetings for the new legislature had begun and early indications of its membership did not bode well for the *puros*. Neither Gómez Farías nor Rejón were elected, and it soon became apparent that partisans of war would not make up a majority. The process leading to the ratification of the treaty in the United States moved along more swiftly. By mid-March the Senate had voted to confirm a slightly different version of the treaty that President James K. Polk had submitted for its consideration in late February. [98]

The *puros* persisted in trying to halt the inevitable, but by the spring of 1848 Gómez Farías and his followers lacked effective support. Gómez Farías feared that Mexico would fall into chaos unless the states assumed "a respectable attitude to detain the [American] invasion," but state governments either refused or proved unable to assist in the war effort. Guillermo Prieto commented that all states by late 1847 "suffered on account of the war; revenues hardly covered the most basic necessities, bank drafts were completely paralyzed, the countryside was in a state of abandonment, [and] roads were deserted."[99] The situation did not improve over the next few months. A correspondent from Toluca wrote that the state of Mexico could not offer help because it found itself in a "most deplorable situation." The same despair engulfed Zacatecas' Governor González Cosío, who indicated that public spirit in his state was either "completely dead, or so listless or disconcerted that it offers no hope." The failure of *puro* supporters in Jalisco to launch a "relentless struggle" against the *moderado* government by the end of March further exemplified the *puros'* predicament.[100]

Gómez Farías became increasingly depressed at the turn of events. To buoy *puro* hopes during the spring of 1848, he sponsored a Querétaro newspaper, *El Progreso,* and argued that new negotiations with the Americans would be necessary because of changes made in the United States to the Treaty of Guadalupe Hidalgo. Neither action proved effective. In his desponded state, Gómez Farías hoped for entirely unrealistic goals. In mid-March he speculated that Mexico's debt to Great Britain would leave the British with no choice but to intervene in the war on Mexico's behalf. Yet to expect any help from Great Britain was nothing but a remote fantasy. The British had not granted the Mexicans aid since 1845 and none came in 1848.[101] A month later, Gómez Farías observed that the 1848 revolution in France, in which the common people took up arms to overthrow Bourbon monarch Louis Philippe and establish a republic, would set an example that revitalized enthusiasm among the *puros*.[102] The events of 1848 in France, however, did not renew the zeal that the *puros* had demonstrated three years earlier, and Gómez Farías' efforts to rally his partisans proved unsuccessful.

Meanwhile, preparations for the meeting of the new Mexican Congress were underway. The *puros*, led by Manuel Crescencio Rejón, attempted to stimulate discussion about the merits of sustaining the war with the United States to make the legislature's duty—ratifying the Treaty of Guadalupe Hidalgo—more difficult. On April 17, Rejón submitted a sealed document at the preliminary meetings with his thoughts on the treaty. The position paper forcefully took exception to both the pact and to the way Mexico's negotiators arrived at its terms.[103]

Rejón believed that the treaty would have several detrimental consequences. He argued that it would cause Mexico's economic subordination to the United States and that American racism would not allow Mexican citizens in the ceded territories to be treated justly. Even more threatening to Rejón was that the treaty would not prevent future territorial losses; in fact, he believed that it would only delay the demise of Mexico's "political existence as a republic." Rejón advocated several legal arguments to buttress his objections to the treaty, declaring that the Mexican government should not have signed it without congressional approval. By doing so, the government had gone beyond the letter and the spirit of its constitutional rights. Moreover, neither the chief executive nor Congress had the power to cede any part of the nation to another country.[104] In conclusion, Rejón made three suggestions that, if adopted, would allow Mexico to emerge from the "mortal position" that the *moderado* government had put it in by signing the treaty. He argued that Congress should elect a president whose intelligence and patriotism would allow him to gather and develop the resources necessary to save the country from ruin. The president should reject the treaty and bring to trial those who had agreed to make such unacceptable concessions. Finally, Rejón demanded that Mexico not enter into further negotiations until it could do so with honor.[105]

When Congress convened on May 7, 1848, the *moderados* launched an offensive to counter Rejón's challenge. Legislators first listened to President Peña y Peña outline the reasons why he favored ratification of the Treaty of Guadalupe Hidalgo. Three days later, to persuade the legislators to ratify, the *moderado* regime also asked them to consider three reports in favor of a peaceful solution to the war. Minister of War Anaya described the deplorable conditions of the Mexican army and the impossibility of continuing hostilities. He explained that some governors did not even publish a mid-December 1847 decree requesting that the states of Mexico, Michoacán, Jalisco, Puebla, Guanajuato, Oaxaca, San Luis Potosí, Zacatecas, and Querétaro raise 16,000 men to reorganize the regular army. Minister of Foreign Relations de la Rosa discussed Mexico's precarious financial situation and the reasons that had led the government to endorse the treaty. Finally, the commissioners who signed the agreement indicated that they had gotten as many concessions as circumstances had allowed. The strategy succeeded. On June 13, the Chamber of Deputies' Commission on Foreign Relations declared that it favored approval of the treaty.[106]

In response, the *puros* resorted to desperate measures. They attempted to organize a revolt during the evening of May 10 to scare away deputies from Querétaro. If enough delegates left, Congress would lack a quorum and could not vote to ratify. But the tactic failed and Congress met to consider the recommendation issued by the Commission on Foreign Relations. The Chamber of Deputies reflected on the matter first. Nine deputies, including José María Cuevas, whose brother Luis had signed the settlement, spoke out against the pact. Deputy Cuevas, who was ill, entered the chambers on a

stretcher and delivered a discourse that earned a standing ova-
tion. Despite the rousing display, legislators met on May 19
and voted fifty-one to thirty-five for ratification. Five days later,
the Mexican Senate endorsed the Chamber of Deputies' resolution and approved the treaty, thirty-three to four.[107]

Most legislators, in voting for ratification, hoped to end
American military occupation, as well as avoid the ongoing
economic crisis and a likely loss of additional territory. Yet
contemporary accounts of the debates do not mention
another concern that led representatives to accept the treaty.
Recent scholarship has pointed out that these men were
"freshman deputies and senators whose future political life
might depend on their alliance with the president."[108] The
legislators did not want to jeopardize these aspirations by
opposing the treaty and, thus, cast their ballots to end the war.

Despite the turn of events, Gómez Farías and the *puros*
made another attempt to rally enough public support to carry
on with the war effort. First they tried legal means. On June 1,
two days after Mexico and the United States exchanged signatures, eleven *puro* deputies brought a petition to the
Mexican Supreme Court. They argued that congressional ratification of the Treaty of Guadalupe Hidalgo was unconstitutional; the legislature had violated several clauses of the *Acta
Constitutiva* of 1824, the Constitution of 1824, and the 1847
Acta de Reformas. The petitioners requested that the Supreme
Court of Justice order that the treaty be submitted to individual states for approval. The scheme proved futile when the tribunal denied the appeal in early July.[109]

Other *puros* strove to organize armed resistance. In late
May, Eligio Romero headed efforts to stage a rebellion in
Mexico City against the *moderado* government as soon as
United States troops left the capital. The possibility of an
uprising concerned several observers. Not only might a clash
lead to a renewal of hostilities with the Americans, but
Mexico City could find itself in the midst of a class war. The
puros, it was said, had armed the populace and were inciting

rebellion with promises of plunder. In the end the plot failed; the government crushed the uprising and jailed several conspiritors.[110] Shortly after, Gómez Farías tried to boost his sons' spirits by writing that if "a respectable person" attempted to renew the fighting he would become "very popular among the people and the middle class; and even the clergy would support it because both country and religion are in danger at the same time."[111] But Gómez Farías, like his confederates in Mexico City, could not attract widespread backing. The *puros* had little choice but to abandon their fight.

"There Has Not Been...A National Spirit"

Historians agree that by the mid-1840s Mexicans had come to view the United States with "outright, near unanimous hostility." The territorial ambitions of Mexico's northern neighbor had prepared Mexican public opinion to "oppose American encroachments" and Mexican leaders were "forced to fight rather than make concessions."[1] In the words of David Pletcher, "a national impulse toward self-immolation" had taken hold of Mexico as the specter of war with the United States loomed over the country in 1845. Some statesmen, like José Joaquín Herrera, did not know how to restrain the impetus, while others, such as *puro* leader Valentín Gómez Farías, "plunged into the flames with the rest."[2]

This assessment of Gómez Farías as an imprudent man who ill-advisedly attempted to halt aggressive United States expansionism merits reconsideration. Gómez Farías was "more genuinely committed to a war with the United States than any other prominent Mexican of the period." The battle cry that he devised to rally the *puro* faction—*"Federación y Tejas"*—aspired to consummate the "regeneration of Mexico" and should have garnered nationwide support in 1845. Not only was federalism (in the form of the 1824 constitution) the only political alternative that promised future stability, but restoration of the federal system also augured the reconquest of Texas, an issue that had figured in the programs of all political factions since 1836.3

Gómez Farías and his supporters, however, could not act on their own to bring their plans to fruition. The *puros'* control over Mexico's destiny even when they held power (August 1846-March 1847) was tenuous at best. Numerous factors hindered Gómez Farías' efforts to establish the *puros* as Mexico's dominant faction during the war with the United States: the country's fiscal insolvency and regional divisions, General Antonio López de Santa Anna's deceitfulness, the refusal of Manuel Gómez Pedraza and the *moderados* to cooperate, the Church's lack of patriotism, and the *puros'* ties to the urban poor. These elements compromised the *puros'* ability to gain the full-fledged support of the army and to develop a strong civic militia; the *puros* needed the latter to restrain the former and consolidate their grip on Mexican politics.

Mexico's lack of a sense of national identity made the *puros'* task even more difficult. *Moderado* statesman Mariano Otero wondered why Mexicans did not rise up in defense of their homeland as the Spaniards had done during the Napoleonic invasion of 1808. After analyzing the ills that afflicted Mexican society, Otero concluded that Mexico's military fiasco in 1847 could only be attributed to the fact that *"there has not been, nor could there have been, a national spirit, for there is no nation."*4 The United States, on the other hand, did not face such a severe handicap in the mid-1840s. Manifest Destiny served as a guiding ideology that allowed the United States to surmount, if only temporarily, sectionalism and internal political conflict.

In the final analysis, the blame for Mexico's inability to organize an effective resistance against the United States should not rest solely on the shoulders of Gómez Farías and the *puros*. Their goals may have been far-fetched and somewhat utopian, and they may have promoted their political agenda recklessly and in less than ideal circumstances. At times Gómez Farías lacked the necessary sophistication to judge and appraise the hopes and motivations of the United States and of other Mexican military and civilian leaders. Nonetheless, Gómez Farías and his political associates promoted specific solutions to Mexico's problems in the mid-1840s that did not conceal self-seeking aims as did men like Gómez Pedraza, Santa Anna, and General Mariano Paredes y Arrillaga. The *puros'* political enemies must also bear responsibility for the tragedy of 1846-1848.

The pain of invasion, however, left a deep impression on Mexican society. Articulate Mexicans feared that national existence was in jeopardy. The United States could take over Mexico at any moment, and ethnic conflict—the Caste War of Yucatán and the Sierra Gorda rebellion—threatened the country as well. Pundits pressed for a better understanding of the political and social ills that affected the republic. In the opinion of a new generation of *puro* and *moderado* thinkers, the country's main problem was that independence had failed to abolish the Spanish colonial legacy in Mexico. On the other hand, conservatives, led by Lucas Alamán, advocated the idea of a monarchical government for Mexico in the postwar era. Intellectual debate grew increasingly rancorous and turned to open political conflict shortly after Santa Anna returned to Mexico from yet another exile in April 1853. Alamán had brought him back to hold power while conservative envoys searched Europe for a royal prince to take a throne in Mexico. The death of Alamán in June, however, removed the only hand that could have restrained Santa Anna, and his regime degenerated into dictatorship. This turn of events led *puros* and *moderados*—whose rivalry did not end after the

Mexican War—to close ranks and launch the Ayutla Rebellion in March 1854. Within two years Santa Anna had again been ousted from power and forced into exile. Mexico headed toward the era known as the *Reforma*.5

Mexico's leaders then had to grapple with many of the issues that Gómez Farías and the *puros* struggled with during the mid-1840s. But the experience of the Mexican War helped shape their response to problems such as the structure of national power, the relationship between the state, the Church, and the military, and the country's association with the United States. Many *puros* concluded that federalism had caused Mexico's defeat and loss of territory. They believed it would be prudent to create a strong central government. Thus, the Constitution of 1857 provided for a federal republic, but on several key issues the charter took powers away from the states and granted them to the national government. *Reforma* leaders also tried to negate the influence of the Church and the army. The Juárez Law of 1855 restricted both military and clerical *fueros*. Politicians sought to reduce military authority further by trusting the civic militia with the maintenance of internal peace and security. The Lerdo Law of 1856, which forced the Church to sell all its urban and rural real estate not directly used in day-to-day operations, sought to end Church economic power and hence reduce its political and social influence. *Reforma* statesmen also initiated a program of economic reform and modernization in which the United States played a significant role.6

Efforts to implement these changes, as *Reforma* politicians found out, was not an easy task. In fact, their endeavors triggered yet another round of political strife in Mexico—the Three Years' War (1857-1860) and the French Intervention (1862-1867). Although the *puros* prevailed against the conservatives and their French allies, they could not solve the problems of political order and the need for economic growth. Those questions remained and bedeviled Mexico's political leaders until well past the Revolution of 1910. This only serves to highlight the difficulty of the task for Gómez Farías and the *puros* while confronting a foreign invasion in the mid-1840s. The political, ideological, social, and economic realities of Mexico practically insured that he and the *puros* would fall short of their expectations.

In the end, the objectives, motivations, and statesmanship abilities of Valentín Gómez Farías and the *puros* during the war with the United States are perhaps best summarized by José Fernando Ramírez, who referred to the *puro* leader's proclivity for "imprudence" and "obstinacy," and also remarked that "anyone who knows how irritable and peremptory [Gómez Farías] can be will understand that he is a man who cannot be scorned with impunity." But Ramírez also praised Gómez Farías, commending him for discharging his duties as chief executive during the "revolt of the *polkos*" with "such dignity and valor" that "even his enemies" had no choice but to "admire him." Seen in this light, Ramírez' estimate of Gómez Farías as a "fanatical politician with . . . good intentions" seems a most fitting appraisal.7

Notes

"Crisis to Crisis": A Preface

1. David Brading, *The First America: The Spanish Monarchy, Creole Patriots, and the Liberal State, 1492-1867* (New York: Cambridge University Press, 1991), 640.

2. Timothy Anna, "Demystifying Early Nineteenth-Century Mexico," *Mexican Studies/Estudios Mexicanos*, 9:1 (Winter 1993), 119-122.

3. According to one nineteenth-century Mexican politician, the nickname *"puro"* emerged during a popular demonstration on October 14, 1838, when a mob continually clamored that it wanted "a constitution without a tail and [a] pure federation." José María Bocanegra, *Memorias para la historia de México independiente, 1822-1846*, 2 vols. (Mexico City: Imprenta del Gobierno Federal, 1892), 2: 760-761. Another eyewitness asserted that the *puro* sobriquet was first used in October 1846 as a result of the appearance of a newspaper entitled *El Federalista Puro*. José María Lafragua, "Miscelánea de política," in *Memorias de la Academia Mexicana de la Historia* (1943-1944), 42. Although the origins of the *moderado* and *puro* factions of the federalist party can be traced to the late 1820s and early 1830s, it seems likely that the nickname *"puro"* was used with increasing frequency in 1846.

4. Donald F. Stevens, *Origins of Instability in Early Republican Mexico* (Durham: Duke University Press, 1991), 29-31, 34-36, 111. The civic militia was also known as the national guard, national local militia, or local militia. To avoid confusion in this volume they are referred to as the militia or civic militia, and their members are designated as *cívicos* or militiamen.

5. Michael P. Costeloe, *The Central Republic in Mexico, 1835-1846: Hombres de Bien in the Age of Santa Anna* (New York: Cambridge University Press, 1993), 267-268; Stevens, *Origins of Instability*, 29-31, 34-36, 111.

6. Michael P. Costeloe, "Federalism to Centralism: The Conservative Case for Change, 1834-1835," *The Americas*, 45:2 (Oct. 1988), 182-183; Miguel Soto, *La conspiración monárquica en México, 1845-1846* (Mexico City: EOSA, 1988), 73-74; Stevens, *Origins of Instability*, 29, 37-38, 110-111.

7. Gene M. Brack, *Mexico Views Manifest Destiny, 1821-1846: An Essay on the Origins of the Mexican War* (Albuquerque: University of New Mexico Press, 1975), 171.

8. José María Luis Mora, *Obras sueltas* (Mexico City: Editorial Porrúa, 1963), 10, quoted in Costeloe, *The Central Republic*, 28.

9. Will Fowler, "Valentín Gómez Farías: Perceptions of Radicalism in Independent Mexico, 1821-1847," *Bulletin of Latin American Research*, 15:1 (1996), 45.

10. Reynaldo Sordo Cedeño, *El congreso en la primera república centralista* (Mexico City: El Colegio de México and Instituto Tecnológico Autónomo de México, 1991), 297. Gómez Pedraza's efforts to reestablish federalism in 1838 came to be known as the "moral" or "philosophical" revolution, and contemporaries nicknamed him the "philosopher." *Puro* newspapers relied on the name to ridicule Gómez Pedraza's conduct during the war with the United States.

11. Guillermo Prieto, *Memorias de mis tiempos* (Mexico City: Editorial Porrúa, 1985), 252.

12. David Pletcher, "United States Relations with Latin America: Neighborliness and Exploitation," *The American Historical Review*, 82:1 (Feb. 1977), 45.

13. For analysis of the plot, see Jaime Delgado, *La monarquía en México, 1845-1847* (Mexico City: Editorial Porrúa, 1990), and Soto, *La conspiración monárquica*.

14. On the *hombres de bien*, see Costeloe, *The Central Republic*. The distinctions between political factions were put forth by Stevens, *Origins of Instability*, 28-45. My earlier description of the differences and similarities between *puros*, *moderados*, and conservatives is based largely on Stevens' account.

15. Costeloe, *The Central Republic*, 18, 29-30.

16. Barbara Tenenbaum, "The Emperor Goes to the Tailor," in *Mexico in the Age of Democratic Revolutions, 1750-1850*, ed. Jaime E. Rodríguez O. (Boulder: Lynne Rienner Publishers, 1994), 299.

17. Mariano Cuevas, *Historia de la nación mexicana* (Mexico City: Editorial Porrúa, 1967), 636-684.

18. Donathon Ollif, *Reforma Mexico and the United States: A Search for Alternatives to Annexation, 1854-1861* (Tuscaloosa: University of Alabama Press, 1981), 15.

19. Prieto, *Memorias*, 250.

20. Josefina Zoraida Vázquez, *Don Antonio López de Santa Anna: Mito y enigma* (Mexico City: Centro de Estudios de Historia de México Condumex, 1987), 21.

21. José Fernando Ramírez, *Mexico During the War with the United States* (Columbia: University of Missouri Press, 1950), 109.

22. Richard Sinkin, *The Mexican Reform, 1855-1876: A Study in Liberal Nation Building* (Austin: University of Texas Press, 1979), 23.

23. Ramón Alcaraz, et. al., *The Other Side: or Notes for the History of the War Between Mexico and the United States* (New York: Burt Franklin, 1970), 456.

I—The Seeds of Dissension

1.Josefina Zoraida Vázquez, "Los años olvidados," *Mexican Studies/Estudios Mexicanos*, 5:2 (Summer 1989), 314.

2. Alexander Freiherr von Humboldt, *Ensayo político sobre el reino de Nueva España* (Mexico City: Editorial Porrúa, 1966), 7; George Rives, *The United States and Mexico, 1821-1848*, 2 vols. (New York: Charles Scribner's and Sons, 1913), 1: 51.

3. José Valadés, *Orígenes de la república mexicana. La aurora constitucional* (Mexico City: Editores Mexicanos Unidos, 1972), 422-423.

4. Stephen H. Haber, "Assessing the Obstacles to Industrialization: The Mexican Economy, 1830-1940," *Journal of Latin American Studies*, 24:1 (Feb. 1992), 2-4; Mary Helms, *Middle America: A Cultural History of Heartland and Frontiers* (Englewood Cliffs: Prentice-Hall, 1975), 177, 180, 186-187; David Pletcher, *The Diplomacy of Annexation: Texas, Oregon, and the Mexican War* (Columbia: University of Missouri Press, 1973), 31-33; Lesley Bird Simpson, *Many Mexicos* (Berkeley: University of California Press, 1960), 4.

5. The Bourbon kings excluded New Spain's sparsely populated northern provinces from the arrangement. Cognizant of the threat that several European powers posed to this region, they removed the area from the viceroy's jurisdiction in 1776 and placed it under the authority of a military

commandant general. Richard Graham, *Independence in Latin America: A Comparative Approach* (New York: McGraw Hill, 1994), 11.

6. Charles Gibson, *Spain in America* (New York: Harper & Row, 1966), 171; Stanley C. Green, *The Mexican Republic: The First Decade, 1823-1832* (Pittsburgh: University of Pittsburgh Press, 1987), 13; Edmundo O'Gorman, *Historia de las divisiones territoriales de México* (Mexico City: Editorial Porrúa, 1966), 4-6, 10-12, 21, 24-25. Historians disagree over the intendancies' role in Argentina. Some claim that they fostered development of a spirit of provincial and municipal autonomy. See John Lynch, *Spanish Colonial Administration, 1782-1810: The Intendant System in the Viceroyalty of the Río de la Plata* (London: Athlone Press, 1958). Others contend that intendancies in Argentina helped bring on centralism. See Claudio Véliz, *The Centralist Tradition of Latin America* (Princeton: Princeton University Press, 1980), 82-83. It has been suggested that intendancies were the "ultimate antecedent for Mexican federalism." Charles A. Hale, *Mexican Liberalism in the Age of Mora, 1821-1853* (New Haven: Yale University Press, 1968), 80, n. 17.

7. Nettie Lee Benson, *The Provincial Deputation in Mexico: Harbinger of Provincial Autonomy, Independence, and Federalism*, (Austin: University of Texas Press, 1992), 61-62. The quotation is from *El Sol*, Aug. 1, 1823. Unless otherwise noted, all newspapers were published in Mexico City.

8. Benson, *The Provincial*, 4-6, 32, 59-60; Hale, *Mexican Liberalism*, 79-80.

9. Christon I. Archer, "Insurrection—Reaction—Revolution—Fragmentation: Reconstructing the Choreography of Meltdown in New Spain during the Independence Era," *Mexican Studies/Estudios Mexicanos*, 10:1 (Winter 1994), 63-98.

10. Jan Bazant, *A Concise History of Mexico: From Hidalgo to Cárdenas* (New York: Cambridge University Press, 1977), 27-28; John Lynch, *The Spanish American Revolutions, 1808-1826* (New York: W. W. Norton, 1986), 323.

11. Timothy E. Anna, "The Rule of Agustín Iturbide: A Reappraisal," *Journal of Latin American Studies*, 17:1 (May 1985), 86-93; William Spence Robertson, *Iturbide of Mexico* (New York: Greenwood Press, 1968), 164-172. The quotation is from Anna, "The Rule of Agustín," 86. For the role of Iturbide's popular following in his rise to power, see Richard Andrew Warren, "Vagrants and Citizens: Politics and the Poor in Mexico City, 1808-1836" (Ph.D. diss., University of Chicago, 1994), 96-109.

12. Timothy E. Anna, *The Mexican Empire of Iturbide* (Lincoln: University of Nebraska Press, 1990), 88-89; Nettie Lee Benson, "The Plan of Casa Mata," *Hispanic American Historical Review*, 25:1 (Feb. 1945), 47-48. For details on Iturbide's unpopular actions and the disparate proclamations that Santa Anna issued when he rebelled against Iturbide (only one of

which mentioned a republic), see Anna, "The Rule of Agustín," 96-104. Santa Anna most likely did not have a clear idea of what type of government he was fighting for. Many years later he stated that a lawyer from Jalapa had taught him all he knew about a republic. Wilfrid H. Callcott, *Santa Anna: The Story of an Enigma Who Once Was Mexico* (Norman: University of Oklahoma Press, 1936), 42.

13. Anna, *The Mexican Empire*, 167-169; Anna, "The Rule of Agustín," 105, 108; Benson, *The Provincial*, 73; Benson, "The Plan of Casa Mata," 48-52.

14. Michael P. Costeloe, *La primera república federal de México, 1824-1835: Un estudio de los partidos políticos en el México independiente* (Mexico City: Fondo de Cultura Económica, 1975), 23-24; Jaime E. Rodríguez O., "The Struggle for the Nation: The First Centralist-Federalist Conflict in Mexico," *The Americas*, 49:1 (July 1992), 9; Anna, "The Rule of Agustín," 101-102; Benson, *The Provincial*, 78, 82, 85.

15. Benson, *The Provincial*, 92; Green, *The Mexican Republic*, 37-38; Rodríguez O., "The Struggle for the Nation," 8-9, 13, 18-19.

16. Timothy E. Anna, "Inventing Mexico: Provincehood and Nationhood After Independence," *Bulletin of Latin American Research*, 15:1 (1996), 15-16.

17. John Lynch, *Caudillos in Spanish America, 1800-1850* (New York: Oxford University Press, 1992), 118; Michael C. Meyer and William E. Sherman, *The Course of Mexican History* (New York: Oxford University Press, 1995), 314; Vicente Riva Palacio, ed., *México a través de los siglos*, 5 vols. (Mexico City: Editorial Cumbre, 1956), 4: 101.

18. "Discurso que pronunció el presidente del supremo poder ejecutivo, general don Guadalupe Victoria, después de haber jurado en el salón del soberano Congreso la constitución federal," Mexico City, Oct. 4, 1824, in *El Aguila Mexicana*, Oct. 6, 1824.

19. Romeo Flores Caballero, *La contrarevolución en la independencia: Los españoles en la vida política, social y económica de México (1804-1838)* (Mexico City: El Colegio de México, 1969), 29-31; Doris Ladd, *The Mexican Nobility at Independence, 1780-1826* (Austin: University of Texas Press, 1976), 133-149; Barbara A. Tenenbaum, *The Politics of Penury: Debts and Taxes in Mexico, 1821-1856* (Albuquerque: University of New Mexico Press, 1986), 10-11, 19; Lynch, *The Spanish American*, 326.

20. Harold D. Sims, *La expulsión de los españoles de México (1821-1828)* (Mexico City: Fondo de Cultura Económica, 1974), 22-23; Costeloe, *La primera república*, 20-22; Green, *The Mexican Republic*, 89-90; Warren, "Vagrants and Citizens," 120.

21. Silvia M. Arrom, "Popular Politics in Mexico City: The Parián Riot, 1828," *Hispanic American Historical Review*, 68:2 (May 1988), 245, 267-268;

Warren, "Vagrants and Citizens," 110-156. The quotation appears in page 149 of Warren's dissertation.

22. Stevens, *Origins of Instability*, 36-37.

23. Prieto, *Memorias*, 190.

24. Carlos María Bustamante, "Memorándum, o sea, apuntes para escribir la historia de lo especialmente ocurrido en México," June 9, 1845 (Bancroft Library, University of California at Berkeley [microfilmed in six reels consulted at El Colegio de México]). Bustamante recorded daily those events he witnessed or which were reported to him in the diary. Bustamante's dates are cited hereafter. The names "Carlos María de Bustamante" and General "Anastasio Bustamante" appear throughout. To avoid confusion, the latter is referred to as General Bustamante.

25. Jan Bazant, "From Independence to the Liberal Republic, 1821-1867," in *Mexico Since Independence*, ed. Leslie Bethel (New York: Cambridge University Press, 1991), 10-11; Lorenzo de Zavala, *Ensayo histórico de las revoluciones de México desde 1808 hasta 1830* (Mexico City: Editorial Porrúa, 1969), 469; Costeloe, *La primera república*, 240-246.

26. David Bushnell and Neill Macaulay, *The Emergence of Latin America in the Nineteenth Century* (New York: Oxford University Press, 1988), 68; Manuel Dublán and José María Lozano, eds., *Legislación mexicana*, 42 vols. (Mexico City: Imprenta del Comercio, 1876-1904), 2: 49-51; Costeloe, *La primera república*, 155-156, 252, 257, 260, 279, 298-301; Green, *The Mexican Republic*, 187.

27. Frank N. Samponaro, "La alianza de Santa Anna y los federalistas, 1832-1834. Su formación y desintegración," *Historia Mexicana*, 30:3 (Jan.-Mar. 1981), 360, 370-371; Bazant, "From Independence," 14; Costeloe, *La primera república*, 300-301, 316-317; Mora, *Obras*, 28-29, 33-37, 43-44, 51.

28. Frank N. Samponaro, "Santa Anna and the Abortive Federalist Revolt of 1833 in Mexico," *The Americas*, 40:1 (July 1983), 96-100; Samponaro, "La alianza," 372-377, 382-383; Costeloe, *La primera república*, 424, 428-429.

29. Josefina Zoraida Vázquez, "The Texas Question in Mexican Politics, 1836-1845," *Southwestern Historical Quarterly*, 89:3 (Jan. 1986), 311; Costeloe, *The Central Republic*, 40, 46; Costeloe, "Federalism to Centralism," 175-179; Dublán and Lozano, *Legislación*, 3: 38; Samponaro, "La alianza," 384, 384, n. 70.

30. Ramón Eduardo Ruiz, *Triumphs and Tragedy: A History of the Mexican People* (New York: W. W. Norton, 1992), 179; Costeloe, *The Central Republic*, 62-63, 101; Samponaro, "La alianza," 384-385, 385, n. 76; Sordo Cedeño, *El congreso*, 174-181; Tenenbaum, *The Politics of Penury*, 41-42; Vázquez, "The Texas Question," 313.

31. Michael P. Costeloe, "The Triangular Revolt in Mexico and the Fall of Anastasio Bustamante, August-October 1841," *Journal of Latin American Studies*, 20:2 (Nov. 1988), 338; Brack, *Mexico Views*, 97; Tenenbaum, *The Politics of Penury*, 42-45; Vázquez, "The Texas Question," 314-315.

32. Michael P. Costeloe, "A *Pronunciamiento* in Nineteenth Century Mexico: '15 de julio de 1840,'" *Mexican Studies/Estudios Mexicanos*, 4:2 (Summer 1988), 259-260; Josefina Zoraida Vázquez, "La Supuesta República del Río Grande," *Historia Mexicana*, 36:1 (July-Sept. 1986), 51.

33. Michael P. Costeloe, "Generals versus Politicians: Santa Anna and the 1842 Congressional Elections in Mexico," *Bulletin of Latin American Research*, 8:2 (1989), 259-260; Costeloe, "The Triangular Revolt," 345; Jesús Reyes Heroles, *El liberalismo mexicano*, 3 vols. (Mexico City: Fondo de Cultura Económica, 1982), 2: 306-307, 313, 316-317. The quote, which is taken from a November 19, 1842, circular letter issued by then-Minister of War General José María Tornel, appears in Costeloe, *The Central Republic*, 210.

34. Tenenbaum, *The Politics of Penury*, 45-46, 53. Paredes' participation in this uprising was in part motivated by his desire to exact revenge from Santa Anna, who had publicly humiliated him in early March 1843. For an account of this incident, see Michael P. Costeloe, "Los generales Santa Anna y Paredes y Arrillaga en México, 1841-1843: Rivales por el poder, o una copa más," *Historia Mexicana*, 39:2 (Oct.-Dec. 1989), 417-440.

35. Fernando Díaz Díaz, *Caudillos y caciques: Antonio López de Santa Anna y Juan Alvarez* (Mexico City: El Colegio de México, 1972), 177; Niceto de Zamacois, *Historia de México desde sus tiempos más remotos hasta nuestros días*, 22 vols. in 25 (Barcelona: J. F. Parres y Cía., 1878-1902), 12: 333-334; Callcott, *Santa Anna*, 206-207; Costeloe, *The Central Republic*, 253-255.

36. Pedro Pascual de Oliver to Primer Secretario de Estado, Mexico City, Dec. 28, 1844, in *Relaciones diplomáticas hispano-mexicanas (1839-1898)*, 4 vols. (Mexico City: El Colegio de México, 1949-1968), 3: 132.

37. Díaz Díaz, *Caudillos y caciques*, 179.

38. Valadés, *Orígenes*, 431, 440.

39. José Fuentes Mares, *Génesis del expansionismo norteamericano* (Mexico City: El Colegio de México, 1980), 149.

40. Lester D. Langley, *America and the Americas* (Athens: University of Georgia Press, 1991), 44, 58; Josefina Zoraida Vázquez and Lorenzo Meyer, *The United States and Mexico* (Chicago: University of Chicago Press, 1985), 21.

41. James M. McCaffrey, *Army of Manifest Destiny: The American Soldier in the Mexican War, 1846-1848* (New York: New York University Press, 1992), 1-2; Langley, *America*, 58-59; Meyer and Sherman, *The Course*, 335-336.

42. Ruiz, *Triumphs and Tragedy*, 206.

43. Nettie Lee Benson, "Territorial Integrity in Mexican Politics, 1821-1833," in *The Independence of Mexico and the Creation of the New Nation*, ed. Jaime E. Rodríguez O. (Los Angeles: UCLA Latin American Center Publications, 1989), 286-287; Curt Lamar, "A Diplomatic Disaster: The Mexican Mission of Anthony Butler, 1829-1834," *The Americas*, 45:1 (July 1988), 1-2, 9-10.

44. W. Dirk Raat, *Mexico and the United States: Ambivalent Vistas* (Athens: University of Georgia Press, 1992), 64; Brack, *Mexico Views*, 62; Green, *The Mexican Republic*, 119; Lamar, "A Diplomatic Disaster," 9-10; McCaffrey, *Army of Manifest Destiny*, 1-2.

45. Benson, "Territorial Integrity," 301.

46. Lamar, "A Diplomatic Disaster," 14; McCaffrey, *Army of Manifest Destiny*, 2-5.

47. Lamar, "A Diplomatic Disaster," 14-15.

48. Bernardo González to the United States' secretary of state, Mexico City, Jan. 24, 1833, in *Niles' Weekly Register*, Apr. 20, 1833.

49. Lamar, "A Diplomatic Disaster," 15-16; McCaffrey, *Army of Manifest Destiny*, 4; Meyer and Sherman, *The Course*, 338-340; Vázquez and Meyer, *The United States*, 35-36.

50. Cecil Allan Hutchinson, "Valentín Gómez Farías and the 'Secret Pact of New Orleans,'" *Hispanic American Historical Review*, 36:4 (Nov. 1956), 473-474; Benson, "Territorial Integrity," 280.

51. Vicente Fuentes Díaz, *Valentín Gómez Farías, padre de la reforma* (Mexico City: Edición del Comité de Actos Conmemorativos del Bicentenario del Natalicio del Dr. Valentín Gómez Farías, 1981), 140-154; Hutchinson, "Valentín Gómez Farías and the 'Secret Pact,'" 471-489; Pletcher, *The Diplomacy*, 68, n. 11; Cecil Robinson, *The View from Chapultepec: Mexican Writers on the Mexican-American War* (Tucson: University of Arizona Press, 1989), xxv.

52. Manuel Urbina, "The Impact of the Texas Revolution on the Government, Politics, and Society of Mexico, 1836-1846" (Ph.D. diss., University of Texas at Austin, 1976), 164, 171; Brack, *Mexico Views*, 97-98, 107-108, 112, n. 40, 126; Vázquez, "The Texas Question," 326.

53. Valentín Gómez Farías to Francisco Modesto Olaguíbel, New Orleans, May 3, 1844, Valentín Gómez Farías Papers (Nettie Lee Benson Collection, University of Texas; hereafter cited as VGFP) 5221, f. 65 B. Unless otherwise noted, other personal papers cited in subsequent notes are located in the same collection. Reference is made to the correspondence of Gómez Farías' sons—Benito, Fermín, and Casimiro. To avoid confusion, subsequent citations designate their father as Gómez Farías and allude to his offspring by their full names.

54. Josefina Zoraida Vázquez, "Santa Anna y el reconocimiento de Texas," *Historia Mexicana*, 36:3 (Jan.-Mar. 1987), 553-554.

55. Gómez Farías to Olaguíbel, New Orleans, Apr. 26, 1844, VGFP 5220, f. 65 B.

56. Gómez Farías to José María Luis Mora, New Orleans, May 3, 1844, in *Documentos inéditos o muy raros para la historia de México*, ed. Genaro García (Mexico City: Librería de la Vda. de Ch. Bouret, 1906), vol. 6: *Papeles inéditos y obras sueltas del doctor Mora*, 48.

57. Gómez Farías to anonymous, no place, no date (probably mid-1844), VGFP 5169, f. 65 B.

58. Gómez Farías to José María Jáuregui, New Orleans, July 27, 1844, VGFP 5225, f. 65 B.

59. Rives, *The United States*, 1: 478.

60. *Documentos inéditos o muy raros para la historia de México*, ed. Genaro García (Mexico City: Editorial Porrúa, 1974), vol. 56: *La situación política, militar y económica en la república mexicana al iniciarse la guerra con los Estados Unidos, según el archivo del general Paredes*, 521-639; José María Roa Bárcena, *Recuerdos de la invasión norteamericana (1846-1848)*, 3 vols. (Mexico City: Editorial Porrúa, 1947), 1: 249.

61. Lafragua to Manuel de la Peña y Peña, Querétaro, Nov. 25, 1847, in "Miscelánea," 50.

II— "Great Evils Will Befall The Nation"

1. Prospectus, *La Voz del Pueblo*, late Jan. 1845.

2. Jesús Velasco Márquez, *La guerra del 47 y la opinión pública (1845-1848)* (Mexico City: Secretaría de Educación Pública, 1975), 15.

3. *El Siglo XIX*, Jan. 19, 1845.

4. Charles Bankhead to the Earl of Aberdeen, Mexico City, Jan. 29, 1845, in Public Record Office/Foreign Office, Series 50/Mexico (hereafter cited as PRO/FO, 50/M), vol. 184, 4-5; Riva Palacio, *México a través*, 4: 531.

5. Thomas Ewing Cotner, *The Military and Political Career of José Joaquín Herrera* (Austin: University of Texas Press, 1949), 110. The quote is from Ruiz, *Triumphs and Tragedy*, 181.

6. Pletcher, *The Diplomacy*, 193, 277.

7. Ramírez, *Mexico During the War*, 11.

8. *Ibid.*, 48.

9. Juan A. Mateos, *Historia parlamentaria de los congresos mexicanos de 1821 a 1857*, 25 vols. (Mexico City: Imprenta Madero, 1895), 17: 214.

10. "El general D. José Joaquín Herrera, al jurar como interino, en 15 de diciembre de 1844," in *Informes y manifiestos de los poderes ejecutivo y legislativo*, 3 vols. (Mexico City: Imprenta del Gobierno Federal, 1905), 1: 284.

11. "El general Herrera, al abrir las sesiones del primer período, en 1° de enero de 1845," in *Informes y manifiestos*, 1: 291.

12. *Diario del Gobierno de la República Mexicana*, Jan. 19, 1845.

13. *Ibid.*, Jan. 27, 1845. Articles similar in tone appear in issues for Jan. 30, Feb. 8, Mar. 13, Apr. 15 and 16, 1845.

14. These proclamations, except for the last two, can be found in the *Diario del Gobierno de la República Mexicana*, Feb. 9, Mar. 16 and 21, Apr. 15 and 20, May 2, 5, 6, 15, 16, 17, 18, 19, 20, and 21, 1845. The latter two appear in *El Monitor Constitucional Independiente*, Mar. 28 and 29, 1845.

15. *El Monitor Constitucional Independiente*, Apr. 19 and June 3, 1845.

16. "El general Herrera, al abrir las sesiones del segundo período, en 1° de julio de 1845," in *Informes y manifiestos*, 1: 302. The quote is from "El general D. J. Joaquín de Herrera, al jurar como presidente constitucional, en 16 de septiembre de 1845," in *Informes y manifiestos*, 1: 305.

17. Cotner, *The Military*, 119.

18. Francisco Cuevas Cancino, in the prologue of Luis Gonzaga Cuevas' *Porvenir de México* (Mexico City: Editorial Jus, 1954), xii.

19. Brack, *Mexico Views*, 136-137, 152-157; Costeloe, *The Central Republic*, 267; Cotner, *The Military*, 119.

20. *Memoria del ministro de Relaciones Exteriores y Gobernación leída en el Senado y en la Cámara de Diputados el 12 de Marzo de 1845* (Mexico City: Imprenta de Ignacio Cumplido, 1845), 20; Alcaraz, *The Other Side*, 22-24; Cotner, *The Military*, 125-126; Riva Palacio, *México a través*, 4: 538-539.

21. Felipe Tena Ramírez, *Leyes fundamentales de México, 1808-1982* (Mexico City: Editorial Porrúa, 1982), 420; Circular letter of the Ministry of Foreign Relations, Mexico City, May 6, 1845, in *El Monitor Constitucional Independiente*, May 13, 1845; Dublán and Lozano, *Legislación*, 5: 17. The quote is from "El general Herrera, al cerrar dichas sesiones, en 30 de mayo," in *Informes y manifiestos*, 1: 302.

22. Riva Palacio, *México a través*, 4: 543.

23. Salvador Bermúdez de Castro to Primer Secretario, Mexico City, July 29, 1845, in *Relaciones diplomáticas*, 3: 196.

24. The quote appears in "El general D. José Joaquín Herrera, al jurar como presidente constitucional," in *Informes y manifiestos*, 1: 309-310. See also Pletcher, *The Diplomacy*, 258.

25. William S. Parrott to James Buchanan, Mexico City, Aug. 26, 1845, Justin Smith Papers (hereafter cited as JSP), 6: 66; Pletcher, *The Diplomacy*, 260, 274-276. The quote is from Manuel de la Peña y Peña to John Black, Mexico City, Oct. 15, 1845. It can be found in Zamacois, *Historia de México*, 12: 392.

26. Pedro Fernández del Castillo to Peña y Peña, Mexico City, Nov. 11, 1845; Pedro María Anaya to same, Mexico City, Dec. 2, 1845, in *Algunos*

documentos sobre el tratado de Guadalupe y la situación de México durante la invasión norteamericana (Mexico City: Secretaría de Relaciones Exteriores, 1930), 27-33.

27. *Comunicación circular que el Exmo. Sr. D. Manuel de la Peña y Peña extendió en el año de 1845 como ministro de Relaciones, para dirigirla a los gobiernos y asambleas departamentales, sobre la cuestión de paz o guerra, según el estado que guardaban en aquella época* (Querétaro: Imprenta de J. M. Lara, 1848), 1-8, 10-14, 16-18.

28. Pletcher, *The Diplomacy*, 276-277, 290, 355-356; Riva Palacio, *México a través*, 4: 545; Zamacois, *Historia de México*, 12: 394.

29. Ramírez, *Mexico During the War*, 44. Financial sponsors included Francisco de Paula Mora and Yucatán Deputy Crescencio Boves. Autobiographical statement by Anastasio Zerecero, Mexico City, Sept. 30, 1845, Archivo General de la Nación, México, Ramo de Gobernación (here-after cited as AGNM/RG) box 168, leg. 104, exp. 34; Bustamante, "Memorándum," Mar. 27, 1845.

30. *La Voz del Pueblo*, Feb. 1, 1845.

31. *Ibid.*

32. *Ibid.*

33. *Ibid.*, Feb. 12, 1845.

34. *Ibid.*

35. *Ibid.*

36. This remark may have had some validity. Although the Mexican peo-ple rejoiced when war was declared and many asked the *ayuntamientos* to supply them with arms and military instructors, few militia units were orga-nized and they did not play a prominent role in the war. The government did not deem them trustworthy, for it feared they would use the resources placed at their disposal to proclaim federalism. Riva Palacio, *México a través*, 4: 422-423.

37. *La Voz del Pueblo*, Feb. 12, 1845.

38. *Ibid.*

39. *Ibid.*, Feb. 15, 1845.

40. *Ibid.*, Feb. 19, 1845.

41. *Ibid.*, Feb. 26, 1845.

42. *El Estandarte Nacional*, Apr. 12, 1845. Vicente García Torres, one of the outstanding printers of mid-nineteenth century Mexico, was in charge of the paper. Its writers included three close collaborators of Gómez Farías throughout 1845: Francisco Modesto Olaguíbel, José María Lafragua, and Francisco Carbajal. Bustamante, "Memorándum," Apr. 6, 1845; Velasco Márquez, *La guerra del 47*, 17.

43. *La Voz del Pueblo*, Mar. 26, 1845.

44. *Ibid.*, Apr. 12, 1845.

45. *Ibid.*, May 3, 1845.

46. *Ibid.*, Mar. 26, 1845.

47. *El Estandarte Nacional*, May 3, 1845.

48. Writers for the newspaper were a mixed group. Some sympathized with Santa Anna and others came from the ranks of *El Monitor Constitucional Independiente*. That journal had been founded in March 1845 after a difference of opinion among the editors of *El Monitor Constitucional*, but it folded three months later for unknown reasons. *El Monitor Constitucional Independiente*, June 22, 1845; Ramírez, *Mexico During the War*, 49; Riva Palacio, *México a través*, 4: 555; Stevens, *Origins of Instability*, app. A, 123.

49. *El Amigo del Pueblo*, July 7, 1845. For articles of a similar nature, see the editions of Sept. 11, Oct. 7, Nov. 1 and 18, 1845.

50. *Ibid.*, Aug. 2, 1845.

51. Mariano Riva Palacio to Mariano Paredes y Arrillaga, Mexico City, Aug. 13, 1845, Mariano Paredes y Arrillaga Papers (hereafter cited as MPAP) 99, f. 143.

52. On this matter, see the comment by Antonio de la Peña y Reyes in *Lord Aberdeen, Texas y California* (Mexico City: Secretaría de Relaciones Exteriores, 1930), xiii.

53. The governor of the department of Nuevo León to Pedro María Anaya, Monterrey, Aug. 20, 1845; Anaya to the governor of Nuevo León, Mexico City, Sept. 2, 1845, in *El Amigo del Pueblo*, Sept. 11, 1845.

54. The article went on to blame Manuel Gómez Pedraza for the cabinet's ill-advised decision. Its author pointed out that both councils had been "influenced by the same baneful man that, representing one faction, is the *primeval origin* of all our maladies; that shallow and superficial philosopher who has been the plaything of all petty tyrants." *El Amigo del Pueblo*, Sept. 11, 1845. *Puro*-sponsored newspapers launched a bitter campaign against him. See *El Amigo del Pueblo*, Sept. 16 and 18, Nov. 18, 20, and 22, and Dec. 4, 1845; *La Voz del Pueblo*, Sept. 6, 10, 13, and 20, Oct. 1, 8, and 22, Nov. 1 and 22, 1845.

55. *La Voz del Pueblo*, Oct. 4, 1845.

56. Pletcher, *The Diplomacy*, 258.

57. Parrott to Buchanan, Mexico City, Oct. 11, 1845, JSP 6: 85-86.

58. *La Voz del Pueblo*, Oct. 15, 1845.

59. "Exposición que dirigen a la augusta Cámara de Diputados los ciudadanos que abajo firman," Mexico City, Apr. 5, 1845, in *El Estandarte Nacional*, Apr. 5, 1845. The signees were so numerous that their names were published in two separate editions—April 16 and 23, 1845. The persons interested in signing the document were invited to visit the registers that had been opened in the homes of Lafragua, Olaguíbel, Carbajal, José María del

Río, and Mariano and Joaquín Navarro. *El Estandarte Nacional*, Apr. 16, 1845; José Miguel Quintana, *Lafragua, político y romántico* (Mexico City: Editorial Academia Literaria, 1958), 18, n. 26.

60. Archivo del Ayuntamiento de la Ciudad de México, Actas de Cabildo (hereafter cited as AACM/AC), vol. 167-A, meeting of Aug. 1, 1845; *La Voz del Pueblo*, May 7, 1845. The petitions are in *El Estandarte Nacional*, Apr. 23, 26, and 30, May 3, 24 and 27, 1845, and addendum to *El Estandarte Nacional*, May 3, 1845; *El Monitor Constitucional*, May 16, 1845; *La Voz del Pueblo*, July 23, Aug. 6 and 27, 1845; and VGFP 1181, f. 48.

61. Juan Bautista Morales to Riva Palacio, Guanajuato, Apr. 4, 1845, Mariano Riva Palacio Papers (hereafter cited as MRPP) 1672.

62. Bautista Morales to Riva Palacio, Guanajuato, Apr. 14, 1845, MRPP 1692; *El Siglo XIX*, Apr. 22, 1845.

63. *El Estandarte Nacional*, May 21, 1845; *La Voz del Pueblo*, May 7, 1845.

64. Anonymous to Bautista Morales, Puebla, Apr. 24, 1845, in *El Estandarte Nacional*, Apr. 30, 1845.

65. *El Estandarte Nacional*, May 14, 1845. A rough draft of the article can be found in the Biblioteca Nacional de México/Colección Lafragua (hereafter cited as BNM/CL), vol. 398.

66. *El Estandarte Nacional*, May 14, 1845.

67. Christon I. Archer, *The Army in Bourbon Mexico, 1760-1810* (Albuquerque: University of New Mexico Press, 1977), 1-3; Lyle McAlister, *The "Fuero Militar" in New Spain, 1764-1800* (Gainesville: University of Florida Press, 1957), 1, 98, app. 1, table 5; Frank Safford, "Politics, Ideology and Society in Post-Independence Spanish America", in *The Cambridge History of Latin America*, ed. Leslie Bethel, 9 vols. (Cambridge, U. K.: Cambridge University Press, 1985), 3: 379; Hale, *Mexican Liberalism*, 141.

68. Dublán and Lozano, *Legislación*, 1: 619-626; Hale, *Mexican Liberalism*, 142-144.

69. For a brief examination of the civic militia's history in the 1830s and early 1840s, see Pedro Santoni, "A Fear of the People: The Civic Militia of Mexico in 1845," *Hispanic American Historical Review*, 68:2 (May 1988), 272-273.

70. Jorge Alberto Lozoya, *El ejército mexicano* (Mexico City: El Colegio de México, 1976), 27-28; Costeloe, *The Central Republic*, 8-9; Green, *The Mexican Republic*, 82.

71. Costeloe, *The Central Republic*, 265-266.

72. *La Voz del Pueblo*, Feb. 1, 1845.

73. *El Estandarte Nacional*, Apr. 5, 1845.

74. José María Castaños to Mariano Otero, Tepic, Feb. 18, 1845, in Archivo Histórico Nacional de Madrid, Mariano Otero Correspondence,

microfilm reel 2, 299. Microfilm of this archive is at the Nettie Lee Benson Collection, University of Texas (hereafter cited as AHNM/MOC; the microfilm reel upon which the citation appears will be included). See also Bankhead to Aberdeen, Mexico City, Jan. 29, 1845, PRO/FO, 50/M, vol. 184, 10.

75. *La Voz del Pueblo*, Feb. 15, 1845.

76. *Ibid.*, Mar. 26, 1845.

77. *La Marcha del Siglo* (Zacatecas), Apr. 4, 1845, in *La Voz del Pueblo*, Apr. 12, 1845.

78. Plan of the June 7, 1845, revolt, in *La Voz del Pueblo*, July 5, 1845.

79. David Brading, *The Origins of Mexican Nationalism* (Cambridge, U.K.: Centre of Latin American Studies, 1985), 68.

80. Camilo to his father, Villa de Pozos, Aug. 12, 1845, AHNM/MOC, microfilm reel 2, 412-415; Vicente Filisola to Paredes, Ciudad de Hidalgo, Aug. 17, 1845, MPAP 112, f. 143.

81 . Josefina Zoraida Vázquez, "Political Plans and Collaboration Between Civilians and the Military, 1821-1846," *Bulletin of Latin American Research*, 15:1 (1996), 32-33.

82. *La Voz del Pueblo*, Aug. 27, 1845.

83. *El Amigo del Pueblo*, July 26, 1845.

84. *Ibid.*, Nov. 18, 1845.

85. Anonymous to the editors of *El Amigo del Pueblo*, San Luis Potosí, no date, in *El Amigo del Pueblo*, Oct. 2, 1845.

86. *La Voz del Pueblo*, Oct. 4, 1845.

87. Callcott, *Santa Anna*, 210-211; Cotner, *The Military*, 110; Dublán and Lozano, *Legislación*, 4: 769; Riva Palacio, *México a través*, 4: 592. The quote is from Zamacois, *Historia de México*, 12: 363. Herrera's government publicly lauded the efforts of Puebla's *cívicos*. Mexican Foreign Relations Minister Cuevas praised their bravery on March 11 and 12, 1845. See *Memoria del ministro*, 116. The legislature belatedly acknowledged the gallantry of Puebla's militia in the December 6, 1844, revolt through the decree of September 6, 1845. This law granted Puebla the nickname "Unconquerable" and ordered a monument in the city with the names of the siege's casualties. The legislation also exempted militiamen from service in the army and awarded them diplomas recognizing their actions, which were to help them advance their military or civilian careers. Dublán and Lozano, *Legislación*, 5: 34-35. In the end, the measures only reflected the inability of Herrera's administration to articulate a clear policy toward the civic militia.

88. "Proposiciones presentadas al ayuntamiento de México en el cabildo de 14 de actual por el regidor don Francisco Carbajal," in *El Siglo XIX*, Jan. 16, 1845; *El Siglo XIX*, Feb. 5, 1845. The *cabildo extraordinario* was in effect

the same as what was most often known in the colonial period as the *cabildo abierto*. Clarence Haring, *The Spanish Empire in America* (Gloucester: Peter Smith, 1973), 160-161.

89. Circular letter of the Ministry of War, Mexico City, Jan. 15, 1845, in *El Monitor Constitucional*, Jan. 17, 1845. Puebla, at least for some time, disobeyed the order and did not disband its units. *El Monitor Constitucional Independiente*, Mar. 5, 1845.

90. Prieto, *Memorias*, 236; Lynch, *Caudillos*, 345.

91. Bustamante, "Memorándum," Jan. 14, 1845.

92. *El Monitor Constitucional*, Jan. 23, 1845.

93. *El Siglo XIX*, Jan. 23, 1845.

94. *Ibid.*, Feb. 15, 1845.

95. Bustamante, "Memorándum," Feb. 3 and 6, 1845; *El Siglo XIX*, Feb. 28, Mar. 12, 1845. Although *El Siglo XIX* published the abstracts of the proceedings of that chamber, this author has not found any reference to Alas' February 28, 1845, proposal in the paper or in other sources. In addition, a document titled "Lista del número de expedientes que han pasado a las respectivas comisiones en el mes de marzo próximo pasado, del que en dicho mes se han despachado y del que les quedan pendientes" reveals that the various committees of the Chamber of Deputies had 339 proposals pending at the end of February 1845. Since forty-seven other projects were received during March and only thirty were dispatched, the Chamber of Deputies probably decided not to act on a controversial matter like establishment of the civic militia. See *El Siglo XIX*, Apr. 24, 1845.

96. Parrott to Buchanan, Mexico City, June 10, 1845, JSP 6: 37; *El Siglo XIX*, Feb. 6, 14, and 16, 1845; Pletcher, *The Diplomacy*, 258; Valadés, *Orígenes*, 431.

97. *El Siglo XIX*, Mar. 26, 1845.

98. *Ibid.*

99. AACM/AC, vol. 166-A, meeting of Apr. 1, 1845.

100. *Ibid.*, Apr. 1, 4, and 25, 1845. Otero's vote was published in *El Siglo XIX*, Apr. 27, 1845.

101. Archivo del Ayuntamiento de la ciudad de México, Milicia Cívica (hereafter cited as AACM/MC), vol. 3275, exp. 117.

102. Departmental assembly reports appear in *El Siglo XIX*, Mar. 18, Apr. 17 and 27, and May 4, 9, 18, 19, 20, 21, 22, 23, 24, 25, 1845.

103. "Exposición que dirigen," Mexico City, Apr. 5, 1845, in *El Estandarte Nacional*, Apr. 5, 1845; *El Monitor Constitucional Independiente*, Mar. 5 and 18, Apr. 13, May 30, 1845.

104. *El Estandarte Nacional*, May 27, 1845.

105. *Ibid.*, June 4, 1845.

106. *El Monitor Constitucional Independiente*, Apr. 9, 1845; Dublán and Lozano, *Legislación*, 5: 19-20.

107. Plan of the June 7, 1845, revolt, in *La Voz del Pueblo*, July 5, 1845.

108. Luis G. Cuevas to the President of the Council of State, Mexico City, June 20, 1845, and Gabriel Valencia to the minister of foreign relations, Mexico City, July 1, 1845, AGNM/RG, box 277, leg. 189, exp. 3; Dublán and Lozano's *Legislación* (5: 20-22) dates the bylaws June 7, 1845. Other sources make clear that the government did not issue them until July 7.

109. *La Marcha del Siglo* (Zacatecas), Aug. 15, 1845, in *El Amigo del Pueblo*, Aug. 23, 1845.

110. *El Centinela* (Puebla), July 17, 1845, in *El Amigo del Pueblo*, July 22, 1845. Article 18 of the *Bases Orgánicas* stipulated that an individual had to be eighteen years old and married, or twenty-one if single, and have an annual income of at least 200 pesos, to meet this criterion. Tena Ramírez, *Leyes fundamentales*, 409.

111. Parrott to Buchanan, Mexico City, July 15, 1845, JSP 6: 50.

112. Costeloe, *The Central Republic*, 258, 264.

113. Circular letters of the Ministry of Foreign Relations, Mexico City, July 16 and Aug. 23, 1845, in *El Amigo del Pueblo*, July 22 and Aug. 30, 1845.

114. "Noticia del número de Defensores de la Independencia y las Leyes que según las constancias que hay hoy en este ministerio se han alistado en los departamentos que se citan," AGNM/RG, box 277, leg. 189, exp. 3.

115. Bautista Morales to the minister of foreign relations, Guanajuato, Aug. 29, 1845; José María Flores to same, San Luis Potosí, Sept. 3, 1845; Victorino F. Canales to same, Ciudad Victoria, Sept. 4, 1845, in AGNM/RG, box 277, leg. 189, exp. 3.

116. AACM/MC, vol. 3275, exp. 119; *El Siglo XIX*, Aug. 22, 1845.

117. Bustamante, "Memorándum," Sept. 2, 1845.

118. *La Voz del Pueblo*, Sept. 3, 1845.

119. This had already been suggested by del Río during Mexico City's *ayuntamiento* August 1 meeting. The *ayuntamiento*, however, refused to discuss his proposal. AACM/AC, vol. 167-A, meetings of Aug. 1 and 5, 1845.

120. This paragraph synthesizes the principal complaints and suggestions made by governors regarding organization of the militia. The most useful letters were those of Manuel Rincón (Mexico), Antonio Escobedo (Jalisco), José María Flores (San Luis Potosí), Marcos Esparza (Zacatecas), Basilio Mendarrozqueta (Durango), Victorino F. Canales (Tamaulipas), Santiago Rodríguez (Coahuila), Antonio Domínguez (Querétaro), Juan Bautista Morales (Guanajuato), Juan González Cabofranco (Puebla), Juan Soto (Veracruz), and Francisco Moreno (Aguascalientes). They are located in AGNM/RG, box 277, leg. 189, exp. 3.

121. *El Amigo del Pueblo*, Oct. 25, 1845.

122. AGNM/RG, box 277, leg. 189, exp. 3; *El Siglo XIX*, Nov. 24, 1845.

123. Ignacio Inclán to the minister of war, Puebla, Sept. 11, 1845; minister of war to Inclán, Mexico City, Sept. 12, 1845, in *La Voz del Pueblo*, Sept. 24, 1845.

124. *Periódico de a Cuartilla* (Puebla), Sept. 20, 1845, in *La Voz del Pueblo*, Sept. 24, 1845. For further criticism of Anaya's answer, see *La Voz del Pueblo*, Oct. 4, 1845.

125. Gómez Farías to Manuel González Cosío, Mexico City, Oct. 25, 1845, VGFP 1291, f. 48.

III—A Call to Arms

1. Costeloe, "A *Pronunciamiento*," 260.

2. Mora, *Obras sueltas*, 153-154.

3. Costeloe, *The Central Republic*, 227-228; Fowler, "Valentín Gómez Farías," 47.

4. Gómez Farías to José Joaquín Herrera, New Orleans, no day, Jan. 1845, VGFP 1047, f. 48. Herrera sought to mend fences with Gómez Farías at some point in 1845. Since the president was reportedly in the "best disposition to talk," Gómez Farías should announce the day he wished to visit the National Palace for a private interview. B. Haro to anonymous, no place, no date, VGFP 1410, v. 1409, f. 49. Genaro García dated this letter late March 1845, but his reasons for doing so are not clear. It is possible that Herrera extended this invitation at a later date, perhaps in the fall of 1845 when the *puros'* bitter attacks against his government led him to consider a rapprochement with Gómez Farías. Such a reconciliation had to be kept secret because of its political repercussions, as it would have augmented Herrera's public image as a feeble chief executive. Available documentation does not reveal whether Gómez Farías accepted Herrera's invitation.

5. Gómez Farías to Antonio Canales, New Orleans, Jan. 9, 1845, VGFP 1053, f. 48.

6. Gómez Farías' colleagues tried to capitalize on the triumph of the December 6 movement to hasten their leader's return to Mexico. Francisco Modesto Olaguíbel suggested to Mexico's minister of justice that Herrera should welcome Gómez Farías back. It is difficult to determine whether the petition influenced the Mexican president, but Gómez Farías arrived in Veracruz on February 11, 1845, and made his entry into Mexico City nearly one month later. Olaguíbel to Riva Palacio, Mexico City, Dec. 19, 1844, MRPP 1521; Gómez Farías to Olaguíbel, Veracruz, Feb. 27, 1845, VGFP 1090, v. 1088, f. 48; *El Veracruzano Libre* (Veracruz), Feb. 12, 1845, in *La Voz del Pueblo*, Feb. 22, 1845; Cecil Allan Hutchinson, *Valentín Gómez Farías.*

La vida de un republicano (Guadalajara: Unidad Editorial de la Secretaría General del Gobierno de Jalisco, 1983), 276-277.

7. Gómez Farías to Canales, New Orleans, Jan. 9, 1845, VGFP 1053, f. 48; Josefina Zoraida Vázquez, "La crisis y los partidos políticos, 1833-1846," in *America Latina: Dallo stato coloniale allo stato nazione*, ed. Antonio Annino, 2 vols. (Milan: Franco Angeli, 1987), 2: 562.

8. Mariano Arista to Paredes, Monterrey, Aug. 24, 1845, MPAP 174, f. 143. Arista's other letters to Paredes, dated July 13 and 26, Sept. 5, and Oct. 5, 1845, convey the same message. MPAP 18, 58, 231, and 331, f. 143.

9. The quote is from a letter written by Bernardo Othón on Oct. 31, 1844, in Fuentes Díaz, *Valentín Gómez Farías*, 188.

10. Gómez Farías to Luis Gago, Mexico City, April 8, 1845, VGFP 1133, f. 48.

11. Canales to Gómez Farías, Camargo, Apr. 20, 1845, VGFP 1155, f. 48.

12. José María Carvajal to Gómez Farías, Camargo, April 20, 1845, VGFP 1152, f. 48.

13. Núñez de Cáceres to Gómez Farías, Ciudad Victoria de Tamaulipas, Apr. 24 1845, VGFP 1162, f. 48; *Ibid.*, May 19, 1845, VGFP 1174, f. 48.

14. José Fernando Ramírez to Gómez Farías, Durango, May 9, 1845, VGFP 1169, f. 48.

15. Bernardo González Angulo to Gómez Farías, Puebla, May 10, 1845, VGFP 1171, f. 48.

16. Pedro Zubieta to Gómez Farías, Guadalajara, May 16, 1845, VGFP 1172, f. 48.

17. González Cosío to Gómez Farías, Zacatecas, May 19, 1845, VGFP 1176, f. 48.

18. Francisco Vital Fernández to Gómez Farías, Ciudad Victoria de Tamaulipas, May 20, 1845, VGFP 1178, f. 48.

19. Edmund Fontall to Ashbell Smith, no place, Apr. 18, 1845, Ashbell Smith Archives, in Hutchinson, *Valentín Gómez Farías*, 280. The governor of Texas was later warned of this development, probably so he would advocate annexation to the United States. Smith to Anson Jones, Boston, May 1, 1845, in *Memoranda and Official Correspondence Relating to the Republic of Texas, its History and Annexation* (Chicago: The Rio Grande Press, 1966), 456.

20. Cecil Allan Hutchinson, "Valentín Gómez Farías and the Movement for the Return of General Santa Anna to Mexico in 1846," in *Essays in Mexican History*, eds. Carlos Castañeda and Thomas E. Cotner (Austin: University of Texas Press, 1958), 174; Costeloe, *The Central Republic*, 260, 265-266, 277; Cotner, *The Military*, 117, 122-123. The quoted phrase is from Costeloe, *The Central Republic*, 305.

21. Callcott, *Santa Anna*, 214-215; Costeloe, *The Central Republic*, 259-260.

22. *El Monitor Constitucional*, Mar. 11, 1845. For similar articles, see *Ibid.*, Mar. 14, 1845, and *El Siglo XIX*, May 2, 1845.

23. Bankhead to Aberdeen, Mexico City, Mar. 31 1845, PRO/FO, 50/M, vol. 184, 225; *El Jalisciense* (Guadalajara), Feb. 28, 1845, in *Diario del Gobierno de la República Mexicana*, Mar. 10, 1845; José Ramón Malo, *Diario de sucesos notables de José Ramón Malo (1832-1853)*, 2 vols. (Mexico City: Editorial Patria, 1948), 1: 273; Bustamante, "Memorándum," Mar. 28, 1845. Perdigón Garay argued his innocence, a claim that his relations with Gómez Farías proved false. "Al público," in the addendum to *La Voz del Pueblo*, Apr. 2, 1845.

24. Olaguíbel to Gómez Farías, Mexico City, Feb. 22, 1845, VGFP 1255, f. 48; Gómez Farías to Olaguíbel, Veracruz, Feb. 27, 1845, VGFP 1090, v. 1088, f. 48; Bustamante, "Memorándum," June 7, 1845.

25. Bautista Morales to Riva Palacio, Guanajuato, Apr. 4, 1845, MRPP 1672.

26. *Ibid.*, May 2, 1845, MRPP 1724.

27. Juan González Cabofranco to the minister of foreign relations, Puebla, May 6, 1845, AGNM/RG, box 301, leg. 203 (3), exp. 1.

28. Ramón Muñoz Muñoz to the minister of foreign relations, Veracruz, May 3 and 8, 1845, AGNM/RG, box 301, leg. 208 (3), exp. 1.

29. Juan Alvarez to Olaguíbel, La Providencia, Apr. 22, 1845, VGFP 1158, f. 48.

30. González Angulo to Gómez Farías, Puebla, May 10, 1845, VGFP 1171, f. 48.

31. Brack, *Mexico Views*, 138.

32. Agustín Suárez de Peredo to Paredes, Mexico City, June 7, 1845, MPAP 446, f. 142.

33. Lafragua, "Miscelánea," 33.

34. Gómez Farías to González Angulo, Mexico City, May 2, 1845, VGFP 5209, f. 65 B.

35. Gómez Farías to José Vicente Miñón, Mexico City, May 20, 1845, VGFP 1179, f. 48.

36. Miñón to Gómez Farías, Puebla, May 25, VGFP 1187, f. 48.

37. Bustamante, "Memorándum," May 6, 1845.

38. Gómez Farías to Francisco Pablo de Vázquez, Mexico City, May 28, 1845, VGFP 1189a, f. 48.

39. Malo, *Diario*, 1: 279.

40. Gómez Farías to Vital Fernández, Mexico City, June 4, 1845, VGFP 1194, f. 48.

41. Bustamante, "Memorándum," May 2 and 6, June 2, 1845; Malo, *Diario*, 1: 277. The quote is from Bustamante, "Memorándum," May 2, 1845.

42. Bustamante, "Memorándum," June 7, 1845; Callcott, *Santa Anna*, 219. Santa Anna never reached his destination. He stated that the obsequiousness of Cuba's captain-general when his ship called in Havana left him no choice but to fix his residence in Cuba. Antonio López de Santa Anna, *The Eagle: The Autobiography of Santa Anna*, ed. Ann Fears Crawford (Austin: The Pemberton Press, 1967), 88. Subsequent events make it clear that Santa Anna wanted to remain near Mexico should a revolt on his behalf prove successful.

43. Personal note of Francisco M. Lombardo, Mexico City, Oct. 28, 1846, AGNM/RG, box 186, leg. 104, exp. 34; Lafragua, "Miscelánea," 33.

44. Reynaldo Sordo Cedeño, "El general Tornel y la guerra de Texas," *Historia Mexicana*, 42:4 (Apr.-June 1993), 920; Bustamante, "Memorándum," June 7, 1845; Lafragua, "Miscelánea," 33.

45. Carlos María Bustamante, *El nuevo Bernal Díaz del Castillo, o sea, historia de la invasión de los anglo-americanos en México* (Mexico City: Secretaría de Educación Pública, 1949), 18; Lafragua, "Miscelánea," 33.

46. José Ignacio Basadre to José María García Figueroa, Chapultepec, June 2, 1845, and José María Lafragua to the Supreme Court of Justice, Mexico City, June 2, 1845, in the *Diario del Gobierno de la República Mexicana*, June 11, 1845; Lafragua, "Miscelánea," 33; Malo, *Diario*, 1: 278-279.

47. Plan and manifesto of the June 7, 1845, revolt, in *La Voz del Pueblo*, July 5 and 19, 1845. Gómez Farías authored the document. His personal archive contains a copy of the manifesto in his handwriting. See VGFP 1323, f. 48, and VGFP 5205, f. 65 B. A June 4, 1845, decree had authorized the government to arm the civic militia under the name "Voluntarios de la Independencia y de las Leyes." Dublán and Lozano, *Legislación*, 5: 19-20. This measure proved to be tardy, for the plot to overthrow Herrera was already moving to its inexorable conclusion.

48. Joaquín Rangel to the editors of *La Voz del Pueblo*, Mexico City, Mar. 27, 1845, in the addendum to *La Voz del Pueblo*, Apr. 16, 1845; Rangel to the secretary of Congress, Huichapan, Apr. 13, 1845, in the addendum to *La Voz del Pueblo*, May 14, 1845; Costeloe, *The Central Republic*, 272; Lafragua, "Miscelánea," 33. For the January 17, 1845, reports of two physicians about Rangel's illness, see the addendum to *La Voz del Pueblo*, May 14, 1845.

49. Francisco Mejía, *Epocas, hechos y acontecimientos de mi vida y de los que fuí actor y testigo, 1822-1878* (no date, no place), in Genaro García Collection at the University of Texas at Austin, # 402, 2; Bustamante, "Memorándum," June 30, 1845; Bustamante, *El nuevo Bernal*, 21.

50. J. Miguel Arroyo to Paredes, Mexico City, June 7, 1845, MPAP 445, f. 142; Mejía, *Epocas, hechos*, 2-3; Riva Palacio, *México a través*, 4: 541.

51. Bustamante, *El nuevo Bernal*, 21.

52. Gómez Farías to Mora, Mexico City, July 24, 1845, in *García, Documentos*, 6: 52. Gómez Farías subsequently indicated that the plotters should have waited at least three more days to strike, but other available evidence suggests June 7 to have been the scheduled date for the uprising. Gómez Farías to Ignacio Martínez, Mexico City, July 4, 1845, VGFP 1221, f. 48.

53. Mejía, *Epocas, hechos*, 2-3; Riva Palacio, *México a través*, 4: 541.

54. *La Voz del Pueblo*, addendum to its edition of June 7, 1845.

55. *Ibid.*, June 11, 1845.

56. *El Siglo XIX*, June 8, 1845.

57. *El Monitor Constitucional Independiente*, June 8, 1845; *El Amigo del Pueblo*, June 28, 1845.

58. *El Siglo XIX*, June 16, 1845.

59. Bustamante, "Memorándum," June 9, 1845.

60. Bankhead to Aberdeen, Mexico City, June 8, 1845, PRO/FO, 50/M, vol. 185, 175-176.

61. Bustamante, *El nuevo Bernal*, 44.

62. Atilano Sánchez to Riva Palacio, no place, June 10, 1845, MRPP 1798.

63. Francisco Facio to Paredes, Mazatlán, June 18, 1845, MPAP 476, f. 142.

64. Paredes to Riva Palacio, Lagos, June 12, 1845, MRPP 1801.

65. Bustamante, "Memorándum," June 8, 1845. Both Tornel and the president of the Council of State, General Gabriel Valencia, unsuccessfully protested Tornel's innocence. José María Tornel to the editors of *El Siglo XIX*, National College of Mining, June 8, 1845, in *El Siglo XIX*, June 8, 1845; Gabriel Valencia to the minister of foreign relations, Mexico City, June 17, 1845, AGNM/RG, box 298, leg. 207, exp. 1.

66. *El Siglo XIX*, June 10, 1845; *La Voz del Pueblo*, June 14, 1845; *Documentos inéditos o muy raros para la historia de México*, ed. Genaro García (Mexico City: Editorial Porrúa, 1974), vol. 59: *Memorias del coronel Manuel María Giménez*, 320; Bustamante, "Memorándum," June 10, 1845; Malo, *Diario*, 1: 280.

67. Bustamante, "Memorándum," June 21, 1845; Bustamante, *El nuevo Bernal*, 20.

68. Lafragua to Riva Palacio, Mexico City, June 12 and 16, 1845, MRPP 1802, 1811; Lafragua to Gómez Pedraza, Mexico City, June 12, 1845, MRPP 1803; Quintana, *Lafragua*, 17.

69. Gómez Farías to the minister of foreign relations, Mexico City, June 18, 1845, VGFP 4631, v. 4629, f. 62; Gómez Farías to the departmental

assemblies of Coahuila, Sinaloa, Durango, and Nuevo León, Mexico City, June 20, 1845, VGFP 1205, f. 48; Personal note of Gómez Farías, no place, no date, VGFP 5186, f. 65 B; Costeloe, *The Central Republic*, 273; Hutchinson, *Valentín Gómez Farías*, 284, 284, n. 115.

70. *Defensa que el Sr. General Don Tomás Requena hizo en favor del Sr. General Don Joaquín Rangel, en la causa que se le ha instruido por la revolución del día 7 de Junio de 1845* (Mexico City: Imprenta de J. M. Lara, 1845), 4, 9-10; *La Voz del Pueblo*, June 18, 1845; Riva Palacio, *México a través*, 4: 547.

71. *El Siglo XIX*, July 2, 1845.

72. Riva Palacio to Paredes, Mexico City, June 18, 1845, MPAP 475, f. 142.

73. "El general Herrera, al abrir las sesiones del segundo período, en 1° de julio de 1845," in *Informes y manifiestos*, 1: 303.

74. Parrott to Buchanan, Mexico City, June 17, 1845, in *Diplomatic Correspondence of the United States: Inter-American Affairs, 1831-1860*, ed. William R. Manning, 12 vols. (Washington: Carnegie Endowment for International Peace, 1932-1939), 8: 727; Bustamante, "Memorándum," June 14, 25, and 30, 1845. A list of the members of the *Consejo de Guerra* and the *Suprema Corte Marcial* can be found in *El Siglo XIX*, June 15, 1845, and Bustamante, "Memorándum," June 25, 1845.

75. Dublán and Lozano, *Legislación*, 5: 25-26. *El Amigo del Pueblo*, July 8, 1845. On April 1, 1845, Congress had abolished the *Suprema Corte Marcial*, but the legislation was not enforced. An eyewitness characterized the government's conduct as "a real imprudence, since it knew very well the character, circumstances, and way of thinking of its directors [which was] similar, if not identical to the ones who made up the *Consejo de Guerra*." Perhaps Herrera failed to act so that departmental assemblies would vote for him in the upcoming August elections; any undue zeal might have earned him the "hate of the factious party *[puros]*" and ended in defeat. Dublán and Lozano, *Legislación*, 5: 12-13. The quotes are from Bustamante, *El nuevo Bernal*, 30, and Bustamante, "Memorándum," June 21, 1845.

76. Bermúdez de Castro to Primer Secretario, Mexico City, June 29, 1845, in *Relaciones diplomáticas*, 3: 199. For articles critical of the government in *puro* newspapers, see *La Voz del Pueblo*, July 5, 9, and 12, 1845.

77. "Acta de la guarnición del estado libre y soberano de Tabasco," San Juan Bautista de Tabasco, June 14, 1845, in *La Voz del Pueblo*, addendum to its June 28, 1845 edition.

78. Gómez Farías to Martínez, Mexico City, July 4, 1845, VGFP 1221, f. 48.

79. Gómez Farías to Felipe Montero, Mexico City, July 11, 1845, VGFP 1227, f. 48.

80. Gómez Farías to José María Muñoz, Mexico City, July 12, 1845,

VGFP 1228, f. 48; José Víctor Jiménez to the minister of foreign relations, San Juan Bautista de Tabasco, Sept. 28, 1845, in *El Siglo XIX*, Nov. 7, 1845.

81. Bustamante, "Memorándum," June 16 and 19, 1845; *El Siglo XIX*, June 17, 1845.

82. Bankhead to Aberdeen, Mexico City, June 29, 1845, PRO/FO, 50/M, vol. 185, 250; Otero to Manuel Reyes Veramendi, Mexico City, June 29, 1845, in *El Siglo XIX*, July 11, 1845. A variant of this rumor stated that seven congressmen would petition the national legislature to restore federalism. Deputies would enjoy the support of the *ayuntamiento* and the populace, which would be led by Gómez Pedraza and Lucas Balderas. Bautista Morales to Riva Palacio, Guanajuato, July 4, 1845, MRPP 1852; Teófilo Romero to Paredes, Guanajuato, July 7, 1845, MPAP 6, f. 143.

83. Bustamante, "Memorándum," June 30, 1845.

84. Parrott to Buchanan, Mexico City, July 11, 1845, JSP 6: 45.

85. Cuevas to Paredes, Mexico City, July 22 1845, MPAP 42, f. 143.

86. *Ibid.*, Aug. 13, 1845, MPAP 100, f. 143.

87. Circular letter of the Ministry of Foreign Relations, Mexico City, Aug. 29, 1845, in *El Amigo del Pueblo*, Sept. 4, 1845.

88. Bustamante, "Memorándum," Aug. 7, 1845.

89. One pundit believed that Gómez Farías and Generals Nicolás Bravo and Gabriel Valencia would compose the three-man *junta*. Bautista Morales to Riva Palacio, Guanajuato, Aug. 11, 1845, MRPP 1924. Another writer mentioned that Paredes would be one of its members, joined by either Valencia and Bravo, or by Herrera and Tornel. Monterola to Paredes, Mexico City, Aug. 30, 1845, MPAP 206, f. 143. Finally, one observer stated that Paredes, Tornel, and Valencia would head a dictatorship that would restore federalism. If Paredes' objections to federalism could not be over-come, his fellow leaders were to try to control him, although the means to do so were not specified. The plotters could count on the army's support, which the recent mutiny at the hacienda of the Peñasco seemed to bear out. Bankhead to Aberdeen, Mexico City, Aug. 29, 1845, PRO/FO, 50/M, vol. 186, 113-115. See also Parrott to Buchanan, Mexico City, Aug. 29, 1845, JSP 6: 67; Romero to Paredes, Guanajuato, Sept. 5, 1845, MPAP 227, f. 143; Monterola to Paredes, Mexico City, Oct. 29, 1845, MPAP 419, f. 143; José de Ugarte to Paredes, Morelia, Nov. 5, 1845, MPAP 435, f. 143.

90. Monterola to Paredes, Mexico City, Aug. 30, 1845, MPAP 206, f. 143.

91. Parrott to Buchanan, Mexico City, Sept. 2, 1845, JSP 6: 70-71 (emphasis added).

92. J. Miguel Arroyo to Paredes, Mexico City, Aug. 30, 1845, MPAP 205, f. 143.

93. Gómez Farías to Juan Pereda, Mexico City, Sept. 5, 1845, VGFP 1246, f. 48; Herrera to Paredes, Mexico City, Sept. 13, 1845, MPAP 272, f. 143;

Gómez Farías to One Poblano, no place, around Sept. 20, 1845, VGFP 1262, f. 48.

94. Ruperto Atenójenes (Valentín Gómez Farías) to José Garrido de Sandoval, Mexico City, Sept. 11, 1845, VGFP 1252, f. 48.

95. Lafragua, "Miscelánea," 33.

96. Gómez Farías to One Poblano, no place, around Sept. 20, 1845, VGFP 1262, f. 48.

97. Gómez Farías to Francisco de Paula Mora, Mexico City, Sept. 12, 1845, AGNM/RG, box 168, leg. 104, exp. 34; Gómez Farías to One Poblano, no place, around Sept. 20, 1845, VGFP 1262, f. 48; Herrera to Paredes, Mexico City, Sept. 13, 1845, MPAP 272, f. 143; *La Voz del Pueblo*, Sept. 24, 1845; Bustamante, "Memorándum," Sept. 13, 1845.

98. Gómez Farías to One Poblano, no place, around Sept. 20, 1845, VGFP 1262, f. 48.

99. Hermenegildo (Valentín Gómez Farías) to Canalizo, no place, Sept. 22, 1845, VGFP 1263, f. 48.

100. Canalizo to Gómez Farías, Perote, Sept. 28, 1845, VGFP 1269, f. 48.

101. Basadre to Gómez Farías, Veracruz, Sept. 27, 1845, VGFP 1267, f. 48.

102. Gómez Farías to Paredes, Mexico City, Oct. 4, 1845, VGFP 1297, f. 48.

103. Paredes to Gómez Farías, San Luis Potosí, Oct. 14, 1845, VGFP 1329, f. 48.

104. Rangel to Gómez Farías, Acapulco, Sept. 9, 1845, VGFP 1250, f. 48.

105. Alvarez to Riva Palacio, La Providencia, Sept. 16, 1845, MRPP 1972.

106. Rangel to Gómez Farías, Acapulco, Sept. 30, 1845, VGFP 1273, f. 48. Earlier that year, Alvarez had pledged his support to Herrera. He responded to rumors that placed him at the helm of a federalist insurrection by stating his determination to "uphold the present federation." Alvarez to the minister of war, Chilapa, Feb. 19, 1845, in *El Siglo XIX*, Mar. 10, 1845.

107. Gómez Farías to Rangel, Mexico City, Oct. 7, 1845, VGFP 1281, f. 48.

108. Those who had been chosen included Manuel González Cosío, Gómez Farías, Olaguíbel, and Lafragua. Monterola to Paredes, Mexico City, Oct. 8, 1845, MPAP 339, f. 143; Tornel to Paredes, Mexico City, Oct. 31 1845, MPAP 347, f. 143; Parrott to Buchanan, Mexico City, Oct. 11, 1845, JSP 6: 85-86; Bustamante, "Memorándum," Oct. 6, 9, and 13, 1845; Costeloe, *The Central Republic*, 275-276; Hutchinson, "Valentín Gómez Farías and the Movement," 177.

109. F. Ml. de San Juan Crisóstomo to Paredes, Mexico City, Oct. 7, 1845, MPAP 338, f. 143.

110. Bustamante, "Memorándum," Oct. 6, 1845.

111. "Illegible" to Paredes, Mexico City, Oct. 22, 1845, MPAP 392, f. 143;

José María Mestes to Otero, Guadalajara, Nov. 7, 1845, AHNM/MOC, reel 2, 464. Paredes' correspondent added that several individuals, whose spokesman was Lombardo (probably Francisco de Paula), met on another occasion to invite General Pedro Ampudia to head a movement that would restore federalism in Santa Anna's name. Ampudia decided not to compromise himself until he found out how Paredes would react, but the government feared Ampudia and ordered him to leave Mexico City in mid-November. "Illegible" to Paredes, Mexico City, Oct. 22, 1845, MPAP 392, f. 143; *El Amigo del Pueblo*, Nov. 20, 1845.

112. Several of Paredes' correspondents discussed these rumors. See their letters in MPAP 435, 452, 459, 470, 473, 475, 477, 487, 501, f. 143. One may also consult *El Amigo del Pueblo*, Nov. 18, 20, and 22, 1845, and *El Siglo XIX*, Nov. 12, 14, 15, 16, 20, 22, and 25, 1845.

113. Bankhead to Aberdeen, Mexico City, Dec. 6, 1845, PRO/FO, 50/M, vol. 187, 246; Soto, *La conspiración*, 51-62.

114. Gómez Farías to anonymous, Mexico City, early Dec. 1845, VGFP 1326, f. 48; Soto, *La conspiración*, 64-65. The text of their plan can be found in *El Siglo XIX*, Nov. 25, 1845.

115. Gómez Farías to anonymous, Mexico City, early Dec. 1845, VGFP 1326, f. 48; *El Amigo del Pueblo*, Dec. 4, 1845; Ramírez, *Mexico During the War*, 11-12, 29-30.

116. Nicholas P. Trist to Buchanan, Mexico City, Oct. 25, 1847, Nicholas P. Trist Papers, Library of Congress (hereafter cited as NPT/LC) microfilm reel 8.

117. Romero to Paredes, Guanajuato, Nov. 16, 1845, MPAP 477, f. 143; Procopio de Sanvictores to Paredes, Mexico City, Dec. 20, 1845, MPAP 579, f. 143; Ramírez, *Mexico During the War*, 27-29. Sanvictores has been identified as General Tornel, one of the monarchist revolt's chief conspirators. Soto, *La conspiración*, 76, 96, n. 86.

118. Gómez Farías to anonymous, Mexico City, early Dec. 1845, VGFP 1326, f. 48.

119. "Plan de los liberales verdaderos," in *La Voz del Pueblo*, addendum to its Dec. 3, 1845, edition. Gómez Farías surely authored this plan; his personal papers contain a draft of the document. VGFP 4549, f. 62 (2).

120. Gómez Farías to González Cosío, Mexico City, Dec. 4, 1845, VGFP 1321, f. 48.

121. Francisco Pacheco to Paredes, León, Nov. 28 1845, MPAP 515, f. 143; Luis Robles to Paredes, Mexico City, Dec. 3, 1845, MPAP 532, f. 143.

122. Paredes to Gómez Farías, San Luis Potosí, Dec. 10, 1845, VGFP 1329, f. 48.

123. Plan of San Luis Potosí, San Luis Potosí, Dec. 14, 1845, in *El Siglo XIX*, Dec. 20, 1845.

124. "A la nación mexicana," San Luis Potosí, Dec. 15, 1845, in *El Siglo XIX*, Dec. 20, 1845.

125. *Ibid.*

126. *Ibid.*

127. Sanvictores to Paredes, Mexico City, Dec. 20, 1845, MPAP 579, fol. 143; Anonymous to Paredes, Mexico, Dec. 23, 1845, MPAP 596, fol. 143; [Bermúdez de Castro] to Paredes, Dec. 25, 1845, MPAP 606, fol. 143. While the reasons for this decision remain unknown, *puro* newspapers blamed Gómez Pedraza for having influenced the government. See *La Voz del Pueblo*, Dec. 17, 1845.

128. *El Siglo XIX*, Dec. 26 and 28, 1845; Bustamante, *El nuevo Bernal*, 77; Ramírez, *Mexico During the War*, 13, 28.

129. Ramírez, *Mexico During the War*, 29; Costeloe, *La primera república*, 306-307.

130. Ramírez, *Mexico During the War*, 27.

131. *Ibid.*, 31, 35. Valencia's conduct during the last days of December is explained in Soto, *La conspiración*, 79-83.

132. Sanvictores to Paredes, Mexico City, Dec. 23, 1845, MPAP 586, f. 143; *El Amigo del Pueblo*, Dec. 9, 1845.

133. Ramírez, *Mexico During the War*, 12-13.

134. *Ibid.*, 25.

135. Costeloe, *The Central Republic*, 277.

IV—The Republican Challenge

1. Costeloe, *The Central Republic*, 284.

2. Bustamante, *El nuevo Bernal*, 93-95; Hutchinson, "Valentín Gómez Farías and the Movement," 181-182; Soto, *La conspiración*, 101-102; Zamacois, *Historia de México*, 12: 404, 408-409.

3. Pletcher, *The Diplomacy*, 358; Soto, *La conspiración*, 49-52; *Relaciones diplomáticas*, 3: 310, n. 55. Besides Miguel Soto's and Jaime Delgado's exhaustive analysis of the plot, others who have examined the monarchist scheme are Frank N. Samponaro, "Mariano Paredes y el movimiento monarquista mexicano en 1846," *Historia Mexicana*, 32:1 (July-Sept. 1982), 39-54, and Frank Sanders, "Proposals for Monarchy in Mexico, 1823-1867," (Ph.D. diss., University of Arizona, 1967).

4. Samponaro, "Mariano Paredes," 43; Soto, *La conspiración*, 101-102; Zamacois, *Historia de México*, 12: 400.

5. "El presidente interino de la república a la nación," Palacio Nacional de México, Jan. 10, 1846, in *Memorial Histórico*, Jan. 12, 1846.

6. Bustamante, *El nuevo Bernal*, 103-104.

7. Soto, *La conspiración*, 104-105.

8. Justo Sierra, *The Political Evolution of the Mexican People* (Austin: University of Texas Press, 1969), 236. The decree appears in Dublán and Lozano, *Legislación*, 5: 105-119.

9. Samponaro, "Mariano Paredes," 44-45.

10. José María Flores to Paredes, San Luis Potosí, Feb. 25, 1846, MPAP 3, f. 144; Bankhead to Aberdeen, Mexico City, Mar. 10, 1846, PRO/FO, 50/M, vol. 196, 15; Soto, *La conspiración*, 126-127.

11. Although the proclamation indicated that the meeting was held on December 2, it most likely referred to the one held on January 2, 1846. The discrepancy was probably intentional. It implied that Paredes had backed republicanism during Herrera's presidency and events would be different under his administration. Soto, *La conspiración*, 168, n. 63.

12. "Manifiesto del Exmo. sr. presidente interino de la república, a sus conciudadanos," Mexico City, Mar. 21, 1846, in *El Tiempo*, Mar. 25, 1846.

13. Bankhead to Aberdeen, Mexico City, Apr. 29, 1846, PRO/FO, 50/M, vol. 196, 265-270.

14. Bermúdez de Castro to Primer Secretario, Mexico City, Apr. 28, 1846, *Memorándum*, dispatch no. 238, f. 25, cited in Soto, *La conspiración*, 178.

15. Bankhead to Aberdeen, Mexico City, May 30, 1846, PRO/FO, 50/M, vol. 197, 109-110; Pletcher, *The Diplomacy*, 442-443.

16. "Discurso pronunciado por el Exmo. sr. presidente interino de la república, en la solemne apertura del Congreso General Extraordinario el día 6 del presente julio," in *Informes y manifiestos*, 1: 319.

17. *El Tiempo*, June 7, 1846.

18. On June 16, then Minister of War General José María Tornel urged the legislature to approve a bill declaring war on the United States. Alamán persuaded Congress not to issue such a declaration when it discussed Tornel's initiative twelve days later. Bustamante, *El nuevo Bernal*, 189; Riva Palacio, *México a través*, 4: 568.

19. *La Reforma*, Jan. 21, 1846.

20. Díaz Díaz, *Caudillos y caciques*, 194.

21. [Alamán and Bermúdez de Castro] to Paredes, Mexico City, Oct. 18, 1845, MPAP 370, f. 143; Brack, *Mexico Views*, 164-165; Soto, *La conspiración*, 72, 94-95, n. 75.

22. Plan of San Luis Potosí, San Luis Potosí, Dec. 14, 1845, in *El Siglo XIX*, Dec. 20, 1845.

23. "A la nación mexicana," San Luis Potosí, Dec. 15, 1845, in *El Siglo XIX*, Dec. 20, 1845.

24. "Orden general del ejército," San Juan del Río, Dec. 25, 1845, in *El Tiempo*, Jan. 25, 1846.

25. Hubert Howe Bancroft, *History of Mexico*, 6 vols. (San Francisco: A.

L. Bancroft, 1883-1888), 5: 293, n. 18; Brantz Mayer, *Mexico as It Was and as It Is* (Philadelphia: G.B. Zideon & Co., 1847), 405; Brack, *Mexico Views*, 148; Bustamante, *El nuevo Bernal*, 94. Paredes named Almonte minister of war shortly thereafter, but the latter's behavior in the *junta* suggests that such an appointment did not imply the beginning of a more aggressive policy toward the United States.

26. "El presidente interino," Palacio Nacional de México, Jan. 10, 1846, in *Memorial Histórico*, Jan. 12, 1846.

27. John Slidell to Buchanan, Jalapa, Feb. 6, 1846, JSP 6: 111.

28. Bermúdez de Castro to Primer Secretario, Mexico City, Mar. 29, 1846, in *Relaciones diplomáticas*, 3: 266-269.

29. "Manifiesto del Exmo. sr. presidente interino," Mexico City, Mar. 21, 1846, in *El Tiempo*, Mar. 25, 1846; Soto, *La conspiración*, 160.

30. "Manifiesto del Exmo. sr. presidente interino de la república a la nación," Mexico City, Apr. 23, 1846, in *El Tiempo*, Apr. 25, 1846.

31. Black to Buchanan, Mexico City, May 21, 1846, JSP 6: 89-91.

32. Dublán and Lozano, *Legislación*, 5: 136.

33. Other influential politicians had caught on to Paredes' ambiguous declarations by this time. Paredes' cabinet resigned upon learning of his departure and the new ministers set as a condition for accepting their posts that Mexico negotiate peace with the United States. Bankhead to Aberdeen, Mexico City, Aug. 1, 1846, PRO/FO, 50/M, vol. 198, 227-228; *El Republicano*, June 20, 1846; K. Jack Bauer, *The Mexican War, 1846-1848* (Lincoln: University of Nebraska Press, 1992), 76.

34. *Don Simplicio*, Jan. 1, 1846.

35. *La Reforma*, Jan. 19, 1846.

36. The quote is from Prieto, *Memorias*, 247; see also *El Siglo XIX*, Dec. 25, 1845.

37. Bustamante, "Memorándum," Jan. 13, 1846.

38. *Ibid.*

39. Circular letter of the Ministry of Foreign Relations, Mexico City, Jan. 24, 1846, and circular letter of the Ministry of Justice, Mexico City, Jan. 27, 1846, in *El Tiempo*, Jan. 27 and Feb. 3, 1846.

40. Bustamante, *El nuevo Bernal*, 105.

41. Velasco Márquez, *La guerra del 47*, 18-20.

42. Circular letter of the Ministry of Foreign Relations, Mexico City, Mar. 14, 1846, in *El Tiempo*, Mar. 18, 1846. Details of the struggle between Mexico City's newspapers can be found in Soto, *La conspiración*, 147-159.

43. Soto, *La conspiración*, 157-159.

44. *El Contratiempo*, Mar. 11, 1846; *El Monitor Constitucional*, Jan. 10 and 16, 1846; Ramírez, *Mexico During the War*, 54.

45. *La Reforma*, Mar. 12, 1846.

46. "Muchos jefes y oficiales mexicanos a los redactores de *El Monitor Republicano*," *su casa*, Mar. 16, 1846, in *El Republicano*, Mar. 29, 1846; *La Reforma*, Mar. 25 and 27, 1846; *El Republicano*, Mar. 28, 1846. Alcorta, like Miñón, had refused to sanction the January 2 additions made to the Plan of San Luis. Josefina Zoraida Vázquez, "El ejército: Un dilema del gobierno mexicano (1841-1846)," in *Problemas de la formación del estado y de la nación en Hispanoamérica*, eds. Inge Buisson, Günter Kahle, Hans-Joachim Konig, and Horst Pietschmann (Bonn: Bolhau Verlag, 1984), 335.

47. *La Reforma*, Mar. 27 and 28, 1846; Bustamante, "Memorándum," Feb. 19, Mar. 27, 1846; Ramírez, *Mexico During the War*, 44.

48. *Don Simplicio*, Apr. 22, 1846; *El Republicano*, Apr. 7, 1846; *La Reforma*, Mar. 12, Apr. 16 and 22, 1846; Dublán and Lozano, *Legislación*, 5: 122; Prieto, *Memorias*, 245.

49. *La Reforma*, Mar. 21, 1846.

50. *Don Simplicio*, Apr. 8, 1846; *La Reforma*, Apr. 1, 1846.

51. *La Reforma*, Mar. 26, Apr. 1, 4, 9, and 18, 1846.

52. Sebastián Gutiérrez Estrada to Mora, Florence (Italy), June 3, 1843, in García, *Documentos*, 6: 37; Carlos Echanove Trujillo, *La vida pasional e inquieta de don Crescencio Rejón* (Mexico City: El Colegio de México, 1941), 353-354; Dublán and Lozano, *Legislación*, 5: 17-18.

53. Manuel Crescencio Rejón to Gómez Farías, Havana, July 7, 1845, VGFP 1225, f. 48.

54. Rejón to Gómez Farías, Havana, July 7, 1845, VGFP 1225, f. 48. The use of 1820s terms such as *escoceses* and *yorkinos* remained in vogue during the 1840s. In the context of this sentence, the term *escoceses* refers to the *hombres de bien* who came to power in 1834 with Santa Anna's help and to the *moderados* who led the December 6, 1844, rebellion.

55. Bustamante, *El nuevo Bernal*, 54, 54, n. 1; Callcott, *Santa Anna*, 226. The quote can be found in Gómez Farías to González Cosío, Mexico City, Oct. 25, 1845, VGFP 1291, f. 48. Gómez Pedraza denied any complicity in this affair. See the correspondence that appears in *El Republicano*, Mar. 23, 1846. At least one newspaper publicly absolved Gómez Pedraza of involvement in this incident in an effort to further cement the rapprochement between *puros* and *moderados* that was underway at the time. *El Monitor Republicano*, Mar. 24, 1846.

56. Gómez Farías' response is unavailable but Rejón refers to it in his subsequent dispatch. Rejón to Gómez Farías, Havana, Nov. 13, 1845, VGFP 1069, f. 48. Rejón's letter does not explicitly state the month in which it was issued and several historians have erroneously dated it February 13, 1845. See Callcott, *Santa Anna*, 223; Hutchinson, *Valentín Gómez Farías*, 293; and Hutchinson, "Valentín Gómez Farías and the Movement," 175. Since it refers to several events that occurred afterward—the September elections to

the Chamber of Deputies, a conversation between Rejón and General Canalizo in Havana—the letter was probably written on November 13, 1845.

57. Rejón to Gómez Farías, Havana, Nov. 13, 1845, VGFP 1069, f. 48. For a similar letter to another *puro* politician, see Basadre to Olaguíbel, Havana, Nov. 9, 1845, VGFP 1307, f. 48.

58. Gómez Farías to Rejón, Mexico City, Nov. 29, 1845, VGFP 1352, f. 48.

59. Bustamante, "Memorándum," Nov. 19, 1845.

60. "Illegible" to Paredes, Mexico City, Oct. 22, 1845, MPAP 392, f. 143; Romero to Paredes, Guanajuato, Oct. 11, 1845, MPAP 459, f. 143; Monterola to Paredes, Mexico City, Dec. 10, 1845, MPAP 542, f. 143. While Parrodi denied any complicity in this affair, another eyewitness subsequently linked him to the rebellion on behalf of Santa Anna that was to have started in Veracruz during the spring of 1846. Anastasio Parrodi to Paredes, Tampico, Nov. 17, 1845, MPAP 480, f. 143; Eligio F. Dufoó to anonymous, Puebla, Mar. 29 1846, MPAP 668, f. 144.

61. "Discurso dicho por el senador D. Manuel G. Pedraza, en la sesión del senado del día 20 de Diciembre de 1845," in *El Siglo XIX*, Dec. 27, 1845; Ramírez, *Mexico During the War*, 45.

62. Ramírez, *Mexico During the War*, 54-55. The original version of *Mexico During the War* refers to this person as "P." The editors of the English translation incorporated footnotes throughout the volume to acquaint readers with terms that they might be unfamiliar with. One annotation speculates that "P." was Gómez Pedraza. Ramírez, *Mexico During the War*, 54, n. 4.

63. "Acta general del ejército," Mexico City, Jan. 2, 1846, in *The Political Plans of Mexico*, eds. Thomas B. Davis and Amado Ricon Virulegio (Lanham: University Press of America, 1987), 427.

64. Ramírez, *Mexico During the War*, 56.

65. Lafragua, "Miscelánea," 32.

66. *Ibid.*, 37.

67. *Ibid.*, 37-38.

68. González Cosío to Gómez Farías, Zacatecas, Feb. 27, 1846, VGFP 1376, f. 49.

69. Rejón to Gómez Farías, Havana, Feb. 9, 1846, VGFP 1369, f. 49.

70. "Exposición que dirigen los ciudadanos Manuel Crescencio Rejón y José Ignacio Basadre al presidente interino de la república, y oficio con que la acompañan," Havana, Feb. 12, 1846, in *La Reforma*, Mar. 21, 1846.

71. "El general Antonio López de Santa Anna, a la nación mexicana," Havana, Feb. 8, 1846, in *Memorial Histórico*, Feb. 19, 1846. A few months later, the *Diario Oficial del Gobierno Mexicano* published an article from a French daily reporting that Santa Anna had discussed the establishment of a monarchy in Mexico with the Spanish, French, and English governments.

Santa Anna wrote a second manifesto to belie these accusations. The document was never published in Mexico, probably because agents of Paredes' government intercepted it on its way from Cuba. "Antonio López de Santa Anna, a sus compatriotas," Havana, May 2, 1846, MPAP 31, f. 146. Despite protestations of innocence, it seems likely that the ever-fickle Santa Anna made overtures in favor of a monarchy and only desisted once he recognized how unpopular such an idea had become. Soto, *La conspiración*, 199.

72. Bustamante, "Memorándum," Feb. 12, 1846.

73. *La Reforma*, Mar. 21, 1846. For other articles of this type, see editions of Mar. 24, 25, 26, 29, 31, and Apr. 1, 2, 11, and 16, 1846.

74. *El Contratiempo*, Mar. 20, 1846.

75. Rejón to Crescencio Boves, Havana, Mar. 8, 1846, VGFP 1381, f. 49.

76. Antonio López de Santa Anna to Manuel Feulet, Cerro, Mar. 8, 1846, VGFP 1377, f. 49.

77. Ignacio Mora y Villamil to Paredes, Veracruz, Feb. 19 and Mar. 26, 1846, MPAP 278, 633, f. 144.

78. Bankhead to Aberdeen, Mexico City, Feb. 27, 1846, PRO/FO, 50/M, vol. 195, 276-277; Slidell to Buchanan, Jalapa, Mar. 1, 1846, JSP 6: 113; *La Reforma*, Mar. 27, 1846; Bustamante, "Memorándum," Feb. 19 and 22, 1846; Lafragua, "Miscelánea," 38-39. The quoted phrase appears in Bustamante, "Memorándum," Feb. 19, 1846.

79. *El Monitor Republicano*, Mar. 27, 1846; *La Reforma*, Mar. 28 and 31, 1846; Bustamante, "Memorándum," Mar. 30, 1846; Hutchinson, "Valentín Gómez Farías and the Movement," 186.

80. Explanations for Almonte's lack of action included his desire to head the new government, his realization that Santa Anna would be unable to leave Havana, and his belief that leading the rebellion was a task beyond his capabilities. Bustamante, "Memorándum," Apr. 6, 1846.

81. José Cayetano de Montoya to Paredes, San Luis Potosí, Mar. 9 and 11, 1846, MPAP 480 and 499, f. 144; Pedro Ampudia to Paredes, San Luis Potosí, Mar. 11, 1846, MPAP 494, f. 144; Mariano Zavala to Paredes, San Luis Potosí, Mar. 14, 1846, MPAP 532, f. 144; Isidro Reyes to Paredes, Zacatecas, Mar. 27, 1846, MPAP 645, f. 144; Eligio F. Dufoó to anonymous, Puebla, Mar. 29 1846, MPAP 668, f. 144; Francisco Pérez to Paredes, Veracruz, Apr. 6, 1846, MPAP 59, f. 145; José F. López to Paredes, Veracruz, Apr. 18, 1846, MPAP 173, f. 145.

82. "Plan de la guarnición de Veracruz," Veracruz, probably around Mar. 8, 1846, VGFP 1378, f. 49. United States Consul John Black forwarded to his superiors a copy of Santa Anna's plan and the letters he sent to Feulet, Ignacio Trigueros, Francisco de Paula Mora, and José Julián Gutiérrez. Black to Buchanan, Mexico City, Apr. 26, 1846, JSP 4: 75. According to one of Santa Anna's biographers, it would not be far-fetched to suppose that

Gómez Farías gave the Feulet letter to Black; if not, then Feulet himself made sure that the United States kept abreast of developments. Callcott, *Santa Anna*, 229, n. 10. By late April, Santa Anna was also dealing with the United States government to return to Mexico, as several letters from Alexander Slidell Mackenzie attest. See José Fuentes Mares, *Santa Anna, el hombre* (Mexico City: Editorial Grijalbo, 1982), 185-190. Thus, it is probable that either Santa Anna or Feulet placed these documents in Black's hands, for Gómez Farías, who never showed the slightest desire to negotiate with the United States, surely did not wish to jeopardize Santa Anna's return with such actions.

83. Rejón to Gómez Farías, Havana, Apr. 8, 1846, VGFP 1394, f. 49; Gómez Farías to anonymous, no place, no date, VGFP 1426, f. 49; Black to Buchanan, Mexico City, Apr. 26, 1846, JSP 4: 75; Ramírez, *Mexico During the War*, 69.

84. Anonymous to Gómez Farías, no place, Apr. 30, 1846, VGFP 4649, f. 62.

85. Ignacia F. de Uhink to Fermín Gómez Farías, Veracruz, Apr. 2, 1846, VGFP 1391, f. 49; Rejón to Gómez Farías, Havana, Apr. 8, 1846, VGFP 1394, f. 49; Gómez Farías to anonymous, no place, no date, VGFP 1426, f. 49.

86. Black to Buchanan, Mexico City, Apr. 26, 1846, JSP 4: 82.

87. *La Reforma*, Apr. 3, 1846; Bustamante, "Memorándum," Apr. 4, 1846.

88. Manuel Gómez Pedraza to Paredes, Mexico City, Apr. 2, 1846, MPAP 8, f. 145.

89. Otero to Riva Palacio, Mexico City, May 14, 1846, MRPP 2125.

90. Santa Anna to Feulet, Cerro, Mar. 8, 1846, VGFP 1377, f. 49.

91. Bankhead to Aberdeen, Mexico City, May 30, 1846, PRO/FO, vol. 197, 108.

92. Peter Guardino, "Barbarism or Republican Law? Guerrero's Peasants and National Politics, 1820-1846," *Hispanic American Historical Review*, 75:2 (May 1995), 187-213; Díaz Díaz, *Caudillos y caciques*, 189-190.

93. Manuel María Lombardini to Paredes, Querétaro, Apr. 25, 1846, MPAP 262, f. 145.

94. *Memoria de la primera secretaría de estado y del despacho de Relaciones Interiores y Exteriores de los Estados Unidos Mexicanos, leida al soberano Congreso constituyente en los días 14, 15 y 16 de diciembre de 1846, por el ministro del ramo, José María Lafragua* (Mexico City: Imprenta de Vicente García Torres, 1847), 58.

95. Rejón to Gómez Farías, Havana, Apr. 8, 1846, VGFP 1394, f. 49. Almonte departed for Cuba shortly after his unsuccessful attempt to stage an uprising in Veracruz, but he did not continue his journey to France. Historians have speculated as to why Almonte did not proceed. According to Justin Smith and Enrique Olavarría y Ferrari, Paredes did not provide

him with the funds he needed to reach his final destination. Carlos María Bustamante indicated that Almonte learned of the death of Mexico's representative in France upon reaching Havana, and believed it would be prudent to await further instructions from the government. Hubert H. Bancroft noted that Paredes prevented him from going on to France because Almonte misappropriated some money he received before leaving Mexico. Justin Smith, *The War with Mexico*, 2 vols. (Gloucester: Peter Smith, 1919), 1: 216; Bancroft, *History of Mexico*, 6: 81; Bustamante, *El nuevo Bernal*, 577; Riva Palacio, *México a través*, 4: 576-577. As Rejón's letter indicates, none of these explanations is entirely satisfactory. Almonte did not go on because cooperating with Santa Anna and Gómez Farías was the only remaining option that would insure his political survival.

96. Rejón to Gómez Farías, Havana, Apr. 8, 1846, VGFP 1394, f. 49.

97. Santa Anna to Gómez Farías, Cerro, Apr. 25, 1846, VGFP 1400, f. 49.

98. Gómez Farías to Santa Anna, Mexico City, no date, VGFP 1427, f. 49. Either Pablo Max Ynsfran or Genaro García tentatively dated this letter June 1846, but its contents suggest that it was Gómez Farías' response to Santa Anna's April 25 letter. For the argument that Gómez Farías was at this time sympathetic to the social apprehensions of the *hombres de bien*, see Costeloe, *The Central Republic*, 18.

99. José María Castillo Iberri to Paredes, Mazatlán, May 6, 1846, MPAP 73, f. 146; "Plan de la guarnición de Mazatlán," Mazatlán, May 7, 1846, in *El Republicano*, June 6, 1846. It may well be that the Mazatlán plan was the one that disrupted Santa Anna's return to Mexico in late March. Both documents contained fourteen articles and openly called for Santa Anna's return. In addition, Article Ten stated that the interim president would be the man whom existing legislation designated while Santa Anna returned. This individual was the president of the Council of State, General Gabriel Valencia, whom Almonte had proposed for the presidency.

100. Fermín Gómez Farías to Santa Anna, Mexico City, May 29, 1846, VGFP 1412, f. 49; Bustamante, *El nuevo Bernal*, 171. The plan proclaimed by Guadalajara's garrison can be found in *Memoria de la primera*, app., 98-101.

101. Others arrested included General Ignacio Sierra y Rosso, Colonels Manuel María Giménez, Bernardino Junco and José Domingo Romero, and civilians Ignacio Trigueros, Francisco Lombardo, Anastasio Zerecero, Juan Pereda, José Lázaro Villamil, Manuel María Ituarte, and Fernando Batres. Among those plotters who managed to escape the government trap were Generals Joaquín Rangel and Ventura Mora, and civilians Bernardino Villanueva, Anselmo Cortez, and Carlos Caballero. Pedro Lemus to the commandant general of the department of Mexico, Mexico City, May 25,

1846, VGFP 4648, f. 62; García, *Documentos inéditos*, 59: 321; *El Republicano*, June 28, 1846.

102. Santa Anna to Fermín Gómez Farías, Havana, June 7 and July 7, 1846, VGFP 1417, 1431, f. 49; Santa Anna to Casimiro Gómez Farías, Havana, July 7, 1846, VGFP 1433, f. 49.

103. *El Republicano*, June 14 and 15, 1846.

104. The quote is from J. W. Richardson to Camilo Arteaga, Mexico City, July 23, 1846, VGFP 1439, f. 49. See also Delgado, *La monarquía*, 155-156.

105. Fermín Gómez Farías to Santa Anna, Mexico City, July 30, 1846, VGFP 1447, f. 49.

106. Bustamante, *El nuevo Bernal*, 194; Riva Palacio, *México a través*, 4: 569.

107. Costeloe, *The Central Republic*, 296. The Plan of the Ciudadela can be found in Dublán and Lozano, *Legislación*, 5: 143-146, n. 1. For the rivalry between Paredes and Salas, see Costeloe, "Los generales Santa Anna y Paredes," 417-440.

V—"A Most Fearful State of Anarchy"

1. Ramírez, *Mexico During the War*, 67-68.

2. *Ibid.*

3. "Proclama de Valentín Gómez Farías y José Mariano Salas," Mexico City, Aug. 4, 1846, in *El Republicano*, Aug. 6, 1846.

4. "El general en jefe del ejército libertador republicano, en ejercicio del supremo poder ejecutivo, a la nación," Mexico City, Aug. 6, 1846, in *El Republicano*, Aug. 10, 1846.

5. *Don Simplicio*, Aug. 12, 1846; *El Republicano*, Aug. 8, 1846; Dublán and Lozano, *Legislación*, 5: 146-151, 153, 155.

6. *El Republicano*, Aug. 7 and 13, 1846; *El Monitor Republicano*, Aug. 6, 1846; *Don Simplicio*, Aug. 21, 1846.

7. *Memoria de la primera*, 54.

8. *Don Simplicio*, Aug. 12, 1846.

9. Fermín Gómez Farías to Gómez Farías, Jalapa, Aug. 11, 1846, VGFP 1498, f. 49; Casimiro Gómez Farías to Gómez Farías, Veracruz, Aug. 14, 1846, VGFP 1532, f. 49; Benito Gómez Farías to Gómez Farías, Veracruz, Aug. 14, 1846, VGFP 1526, f. 49.

10. Santa Anna to Gómez Farías, Veracruz, Aug. 16, 1846, VGFP 1545, f. 49; George Ruxton, *Adventures in Mexico* (New York: Outing Publishing, 1915), 45.

11. "Exposición del general Antonio López de Santa Anna a sus compatriotas con motivo del programa proclamado para la verdadera regeneración de la república," Veracruz, Aug. 16, 1846, in *Memoria de la primera*, app.,

109-115. Rejón authored the proclamation. *Correspondencia inédita de Manuel Crescencio Rejón* (Mexico City: Secretaría de Relaciones Exteriores, 1948), 81, n. 1.

12. "Exposición del general," Veracruz, Aug. 16, 1846, in *Memoria de la primera*, app., 109-115. Two August 22 decrees implemented Santa Anna's suggestions. One empowered Congress to issue legislation on all matters that pertained to its authority and the other declared that the 1824 constitution would remain operative until a new charter was issued. The second decree, however, limited the efficacy of the 1824 code; the constitution would be binding so long as it did not clash with the goals of the Plan of the Ciudadela and only as far as Mexico's "eccentric situation" allowed. Dublán and Lozano, *Legislación*, 5: 155-156. It is important to note that neither law obligated Congress to abide by the 1824 code. This peculiarity abbetted the efforts of Santa Anna and the *moderados* to oust Acting President Gómez Farías in March 1847.

13. Santa Anna to Gómez Farías, Veracruz, Aug. 17, 1846, VGFP 1552, f. 49.

14. Rejón to Gómez Farías, Jalapa, Aug. 19, 1846, VGFP 1575, f. 49.

15. "Comunicación importante del Exmo. Sr. benemérito de la patria, general Antonio López de Santa Anna, al Exmo. general en jefe del ejército libertador republicano, don Mariano Salas," Hacienda del Encerro, Aug. 20, 1846, in *El Republicano*, Aug. 29, 1846; Bankhead to Aberdeen, Mexico City, Aug. 29, 1846, PRO/FO, 50/M, vol. 198, 352.

16. Ramírez, *Mexico During the War*, 69.

17. Santa Anna to Gómez Farías, Veracruz, Aug. 17, 1846, VGFP 1552, f. 49.

18. Ramírez, *Mexico During the War*, 71.

19. Anonymous (it can be inferred that the letter was authored by the second corporal in the office of Mexico's commandant general) to the Ministry of War, Mexico City, Aug. 18, 1846, VGFP 1567, f. 49.

20. Lafragua, "Miscelánea," 40; Ramírez, *Mexico During the War*, 67-68.

21. *Don Simplicio*, Aug. 19, 1846; *El Republicano*, Aug. 19, 1846; *Memoria de la primera*, 54.

22. Bustamante, "Memorándum," Aug. 16, 1846; Lafragua, "Miscelánea," 39.

23. Santa Anna to Gómez Farías, Hacienda del Encerro, Aug. 25, 1846, VGFP 1619, f. 49; Gómez Farías to Mora, Mexico City, Aug. 29, 1846, in *Documentos inéditos*, 6: 61; Manuel Crescencio Rejón, Juan Nepomuceno Almonte, Valentín Gómez Farías, and José Ramón Pacheco to José María Ortiz Monasterio, Mexico City, Aug. 28, 1846, in *El Republicano*, Aug. 31, 1846; Zamacois, *Historia de México*, 12: 508.

24. Ortiz Monasterio to Rejón, Almonte, Gómez Farías, and Pacheco,

Mexico City, Aug. 28, 1846, in *El Republicano*, Aug. 31, 1846.

25. Santa Anna to Gómez Farías, Hacienda del Encerro, Sept. 5, 1846, VGFP 1710, f. 50.

26. Ramírez, *Mexico During the War*, 76.

27. *Ibid.*, 71; Dublán and Lozano, *Legislación*, 5: 155-156.

28. Dublán and Lozano, *Legislación*, 5: 156-157.

29. *El Republicano*, Aug. 30, 1846; Ramírez, *Mexico During the War*, 67-68, 73.

30. *El Republicano*, Oct. 2, 1846; *Don Simplicio*, Oct. 24, 1846; Dublán and Lozano, *Legislación*, 5: 186-187.

31. Rejón to Gómez Farías, Havana, Jan. 9, 1846, VGFP 1363, f. 49.

32. *El Republicano*, Sept. 5, 1846. The emphasis is in the original.

33. *Ibid.*

34. Dublán and Lozano, *Legislación*, 5: 160-161.

35. Prieto, *Memorias*, 251; Ramírez, *Mexico During the War*, 75-76; Bustamante, "Memorándum," Oct. 4, 1846. For more detailed comments by Bustamante on the meetings, see his *El nuevo Bernal*, 220-221, and "Memorándum," Sept. 13 and 20, 1846.

36. *Memoria de la primera*, 63.

37. *Don Simplicio*, July 4 and 25, 1846; *El Republicano*, June 15, 21, and 23, 1846.

38. *El Republicano*, Aug. 21, 1846; Ignacio Jáuregui to General José Mariano Salas, Mexico City, Aug. 7, 1846, in *El Republicano*, Aug. 23, 1846; Circular letter of the Ministry of War, Mexico City, Aug. 13, 1846, in the *Diario del Gobierno de la República Mexicana*, Aug. 15, 1846.

39. Rejón to Pacheco, Mexico City, Aug. 31, 1846, in *El Republicano*, Sept. 5, 1846; Dublán and Lozano, *Legislación*, 5: 161-169. For the troubles that hindered organization of this military force in late 1846, see Pedro Santoni, "The Failure of Mobilization: The Civic Militia of Mexico in 1846," *Mexican Studies/Estudios Mexicanos*, 12:2 (Summer 1996), 169-194.

40. Gómez Farías to Santa Anna, Mexico City, Sept. 6, 1846, VGFP 1740, f. 50; Bustamante, "Memorándum," Sept. 5, 1846; Ramírez, *Mexico During the War*, 75-76.

41. Although Dublán and Lozano make no reference to a decree naming Santa Anna chief executive, the government issued some type of disposition—probably a circular letter or an edict—dealing with the matter. Santa Anna's September 14, 1846, letter to Almonte confirms this. Baranda visited Santa Anna without having any knowledge of the measure. The cabinet acted in this manner to maintain their position should Santa Anna continue to act intransigent. Ramírez, *Mexico During the War*, 76-77.

42. *Ibid.*, 77; Riva Palacio, *México a través*, 4: 578-579.

43. Santa Anna to Almonte, Ayotla, Sept. 14, 1846, in *El Republicano*, Sept. 16, 1846.

44. Ramírez, *Mexico During the War*, 77.

45. Bustamante, *El nuevo Bernal*, 216.

46. Ramírez, *Mexico During the War*, 77-78; Riva Palacio, *México a través*, 4: 578-579.

47. Ramírez, *Mexico During the War*, 78; Zamacois, *Historia de México*, 12: 521.

48. Dublán and Lozano, *Legislación*, 5: 171-172; Ramírez, *Mexico During the War*, 73; Tena Ramírez, *Leyes fundamentales*, 185.

49. Bankhead to Lord Palmerston, Mexico City, Sept. 29, 1846, PRO/FO, 50/M, vol. 199, 187; Bustamante, "Memorándum," Sept. 21, 1846; Ramírez, *Mexico During the War*, 79.

50. Gómez Farías to anonymous, no place, no date, first half of Oct. 1846, VGFP 4911, f. 51; Jan Bazant, *Antonio Haro y Tamariz y sus aventuras políticas* (Mexico City: El Colegio de México, 1985), 44-47; Dublán and Lozano, *Legislación*, 5: 171-172; Stevens, *Origins of Instability*, app. A, 120-127. The political leanings of two members of this body, Bishop Manuel Pardío and Bernardo Guimbardo, are not possible to determine. Stevens classified two other councilmen — Juan Rodríguez Puebla and Baranda — as *puro* and conservative. They, like other statesmen of the times, often switched allegiances. Both sympathized with the *moderados* during the war with the United States.

51. Gómez Farías to Rejón, Mexico City, Sept. 22, 1846, VGFP 1857, f. 50; Bazant, *Antonio Haro y Tamariz*, 47; Dublán and Lozano, *Legislación*, 5: 171-172; Ramírez, *Mexico During the War*, 80-81.

52. *El Republicano*, Oct. 2, 1846.

53. *Don Simplicio*, Sept. 23, 1846.

54. Gómez Farías to Manuel Arteaga, Mexico City, Oct. 10, 1846, VGFP 1940, f. 51; Dublán and Lozano, *Legislación*, 5: 171-172.

55. Ramírez, *Mexico During the War*, 83.

56. Gómez Pedraza to the minister of foreign relations, Tacubaya, Sept. 22, 1846, AGNM/RG, box 298, leg. 207, exp. 1.

57. Juan Rodríguez Puebla to the minister of foreign relations; Otero to same; Lafragua to same, Mexico City, Sept. 24 and 30, 1846, AGNM/RG, box 298, leg. 207, exp. 1.

58. Luis de la Rosa to the minister of foreign relations; Ignacio Trigueros to same, Mexico City, Sept. 25 and 26, 1846, AGNM/RG, box 298, leg. 207, exp. 1. The only resignation not located is that of Lombardo. Although nominally a *santanista*, it is possible that he did not renounce to slight Gómez Farías. Not only did Lombardo edit *El Amigo del Pueblo* in 1845,

but he went on to become the senior official of the Ministry of Finance in late 1846. *Don Simplicio*, Sept. 23, 1846.

59. Gómez Farías to anonymous, no place, first half of Oct. 1846, VGFP 4911, f. 51.

60. The men were Baranda, Pardío, Carrera, Ramírez, and Guimbardo. Ramírez also considered resigning but changed his mind once *El Republicano* published an article on September 26 that discredited him. The remaining posts fell on four *puros* (Miguel Arrioja, Francisco Suárez Iriarte, Manuel Eduardo de Gorostiza, and Agustín Buenrostro), one *moderado* (Bernardo González Angulo), and on Joaquín González de la Vega, whose political affiliation remains undetermined. AGNM/RG, box 298, leg. 207, exp. 1; Ramírez, *Mexico During the War*, 83-84; Stevens, *Origins of Instability*, app. A, 120-127.

61. Ramírez, *Mexico During the War*, 83-85.

62. Costeloe, *The Central Republic*, 296; Dublán and Lozano, *Legislación*, 5: 148.

63. *Don Simplicio*, Sept. 26, 1846.

64. Bustamante, *El nuevo Bernal*, 222.

65. *El Republicano*, Sept. 28, 1846.

66. Alejo O. de Pereda to Gómez Farías, San Luis Potosí, Sept. 30, 1846, VGFP 1896, f. 50; Domingo Ibarra to Rafael Q° y Molina, Puebla, Oct. 4, 1846, VGFP 1924, f. 51; Francisco Banuet to Gómez Farías, Oaxaca, Oct. 12, 1846, VGFP 1950, f. 51; Jesús Camarena to Gómez Farías, Guadalajara, Oct. 13, 1846, VGFP 1962, f. 51.

67. *El Republicano*, Oct. 4, 1846. Lafragua's oration can be found in BNM/CL, vol. 398.

68. Francisco Próspero Pérez, Tiburcio Martínez, José María Ignacio Cisneros, Irineo A. Carrillo, Nicolás Bárcela, and Pánfilo Salazar y González to Gómez Pedraza, Mexico City, Oct. 2, 1846, in *Don Simplicio*, Oct. 7, 1846.

69. Gómez Pedraza to Próspero Pérez, Martínez, Cisneros, Carrillo, Bárcela, and Salazar y González, Tacubaya, Oct. 3, 1846, in *Don Simplicio*, Oct. 7, 1846.

70. Gómez Farías to Santa Anna, Mexico City, Oct. 4, 1846, VGFP 1922, f. 51.

71. Gómez Farías to anonymous, no place, no date, first half of Oct. 1846, VGFP 4911, f. 51.

72. Santa Anna to Salas, Veracruz, Aug. 17, 1846, VGFP 1560, f. 49; Gómez Farías to Mora, Mexico City, Aug. 29, 1846, in García, *Documentos inéditos*, 6: 61.

73. Gómez Farías to Santa Anna, Mexico City, Oct. 4, 1846, VGFP 1922, f. 51.

74. Rejón to Durán, Mexico City, Oct. 20, 1846, in *El Republicano*, Oct. 23, 1846.

75. Draft of proclamation by Gómez Farías, Mexico City, late Oct. 1846, VGFP 4641, f. 62.

76. *Don Simplicio*, Sept. 2, 1846.

77. *Diccionario geográfico, histórico y biográfico de los Estados Unidos Mexicanos*, 5 vols. (Mexico City: Antigua Imprenta de Murguia, 1888), 2: 357.

78. AACM/AC, vol. 168-A, meeting of Sept. 22, 1846.

79. Francisco Calapiz to the commandant general of Mexico, Mexico City, Oct. 6, 1846, in the *Diario del Gobierno de la República Mexicana*, Oct. 10, 1846; *El Republicano*, Oct. 7, 1846; Bustamante, *El nuevo Bernal*, 236-237.

80. Pedro Lemus to Calapiz, Mexico City, Oct. 7, 1846, in the *Diario del Gobierno de la República Mexicana*, Oct. 10, 1846; Bustamante, *El nuevo Bernal*, 236-237; Hutchinson, *Valentín Gómez Farías*, 328. The October 1 circular letter of the Ministry of War can be found in *El Republicano*, Oct. 10, 1846.

81. Rejón to Gómez Farías, Mexico City, Oct. 6, 1846, VGFP 1931, f. 51.

82. *El Monitor Republicano*, Oct. 12, 1846; *El Republicano*, Oct. 9, 1846.

83. *El Republicano*, Oct. 9, 1846.

84. Bustamante, "Memorándum," Oct. 10, 1846; Bustamante, *El nuevo Bernal*, 238.

85. José Gómez de la Cortina to the minister of foreign relations, Mexico City, Oct. 8, 1846, AGNM/RG, box 348, leg. 244 (2), exp. 2. Regulations for this unit can be found in *El Republicano*, Oct. 9, 1846.

86. Bustamante, *El nuevo Bernal*, 238.

87. Ministry of Foreign Relations to Cortina, Mexico City, Oct. 9, 1846, AGNM/RG, box 348, leg. 244 (2), exp. 2.

88. Bustamante, "Memorándum," Oct. 11, 1846.

89. Zamacois, *Historia de México*, 12: 534. The civic militia units known as the *"polkos"* (which revolted against Gómez Farías in February 1847) had been organized in early October. The battalions attracted men of high-ranking social positions and of groups exempted from the civic militia by the September 11 bylaws. Its commanders included *moderados* such as Salas, Cortina, and Pedro María Anaya. *Diario del Gobierno de la República Mexicana*, Oct. 3 and 4, 1846; *Don Simplicio*, Oct. 10, 1846; *El Republicano*, Oct. 3, 4, 5, 9, and 12, 1846; Lafragua, "Miscelánea," 41. The most famous units were the "Victoria," "Independencia," "Mina," and "Bravos" battalions. They earned the sobriquet of *"polkos"* because the polka was the most popular dance in the balls held by society's elite. Prieto, *Memorias*, 252-253; Zamacois, *Historia de México*, 12: 635.

90. AACM/AC, vol. 168-A, meeting of Oct. 12, 1846.

91. *El Republicano*, Oct. 15, 1846.

92. Ramírez, *Mexico During the War*, 86.

93. Gómez Farías to Santa Anna, Mexico City, Oct. 12, 1846 VGFP 1949, f. 51; Autobiographical statement by Gómez Farías, Mexico City, Sept. 1846, VGFP 4639, f. 62. (The date listed in both these documents is erroneous for they refer to affairs that occurred at a later time). *El Republicano*, Oct. 14 and 15, 1846; Bustamante, *El nuevo Bernal*, 240-241. The cabinet met to discuss the possibility of dismissing Cortina before he embraced Lemus. These efforts were spearheaded by Almonte, who accused Cortina of alarming the populace. Either Antonio Garay or Luis de la Rosa was to have replaced him, but Cortina remained at his post a few more days. *Don Simplicio*, Oct. 17, 1846; Bustamante, "Memorándum," Oct. 18, 1846.

94. Pacheco's letter confirmed that, as a true lover of federalism, he could not be useful in the cabinet due to the "current state of affairs." His bitterness toward the *puros* was such that he did not address his letter of resignation to the minister of foreign relations (Rejón), as it was customary to do. Instead Pacheco sent it to Almonte. Pacheco to the minister of war, Mexico City, Oct. 16, 1846, in *El Republicano*, Oct. 21, 1846. The reasons invoked by Cortina to justify his resignation were more feeble. He noted that the goal of securing "order, tranquillity, and public security [in the capital] no longer required" his services, as it now rested on a "physical and moral force which had never previously existed" among Mexicans. Since his permanence as governor of the Federal District could "embarrass the general government and serve as a pretext to [increasing] the bitterness between parties"—to which he allegedly had never belonged—it was convenient to resign. Cortina to the minister of foreign relations, Mexico City, Oct. 17, 1846, in *El Republicano*, Oct. 18, 1846.

95. Santa Anna to Rejón, San Luis Potosí, Oct. 15, 1846, in *El Republicano*, Oct. 21, 1846.

96. Autobiographical statement of Rejón, no place, last trimester of 1846, VGFP 2213, f. 51. See also *El Republicano*, Oct. 19, 1846.

97. Echanove Trujillo, *La vida pasional*, 401. The quote is from Bustamante, *El nuevo Bernal*, 242.

98. Bustamante, *El nuevo Bernal*, 242.

99. Rejón to Durán, Mexico City, Oct. 20, 1846, in *El Republicano*, Oct. 23, 1846.

100. Gómez Farías to González Cosío, Mexico City, no day, Nov. 1846, VGFP 1998, f. 51.

101. Durán to Rejón, Mexico City, Oct. 19, 1846, in *El Republicano*, Oct. 23, 1846.

102. Lafragua, "Miscelánea," 41-42; Anonymous to Cumplido, Mexico

City, Oct. 21, 1846, VGFP 1993, f. 51; Bankhead to Palmerston, Mexico City, Oct. 30, 1846, PRO/FO, 50/M, vol. 200, 157; *El Republicano*, Oct. 22, 1846. The quote is from the *Diario del Gobierno de la República Mexicana*, Oct. 19, 1846.

103. Bustamante, "Memorándum," Oct. 23, 1846. Rejón gave an entirely different version of this incident. He pointed out that Salas caved in at first because he feared that the *puros'* forces would invade his hiding place at dawn on October 18. Rejón to Durán, Mexico City, Oct. 20, 1846, in *El Republicano*, Oct. 23, 1846. If Rejón's account is true, it is difficult to comprehend why the *puros* failed to capitalize on this opportunity to oust Salas. Bustamante's explanation is probably closer to the truth.

104. *Diario del Gobierno de la República Mexicana*, addendum to its edition of Oct. 24, 1846.

105. Lafragua, "Miscelánea," 42; Bustamante, "Memorándum," Oct. 24, 1846.

106. Lemus to Gómez Farías, Querétaro, Oct. 27, 1846, VGFP 2023, f. 51; Gregorio Dávila to Gómez Farías, Guadalajara, Oct. 30, 1846, VGFP 2045, f. 51.

107. Anonymous to Olaguíbel, Mexico City, Oct. 23, 1846, VGFP 2002, f. 51; *Diario del Gobierno de la República Mexicana*, Aug. 26, 1846.

108. González Cosío to Manuel Othón, Zacatecas, Oct. 29, 1846, VGFP 2039, f. 51.

109. Marcelino Castañeda to Gómez Farías, Durango, Nov. 2, 1846, VGFP 2058, f. 51.

110. Y. Guerra Manz° to Gómez Farías, Puebla, Oct. 23, 1846, VGFP 2005, f. 51; Manuel Arteaga to Rejón, Puebla, Oct. 25, 1846, VGFP 2016, f. 51. After discussing whether or not to support Othón's *pronunciamiento*, Puebla's Council of State issued an ambiguous manifesto on Ibarra's behalf. This document stated explicitly Ibarra's determination to support the principles of the rebellion of the Ciudadela, but it did not question "the path adopted by Salas." Guerra Manz° to Gómez Farías, Puebla, Oct. 23, 1846, VGFP 2005, f. 51. The proclamation appears in the *Diario del Gobierno de la República Mexicana*, Oct. 30, 1846. A few days later, however, Ibarra begged Gómez Farías' forgiveness for issuing the manifesto. Ibarra to Gómez Farías, Puebla, Oct. 27, 1846, VGFP 2030, f. 51.

111. Gómez Farías to Santa Anna, Mexico City, late Oct. 1846, VGFP 2053, f. 51. Hutchinson referred to this letter in his biography of Gómez Farías, but he did not link it with the others that implicate the *puro* leader in the revolt. Hutchinson, *Valentín Gómez Farías*, 334. Fuentes Díaz in *Valentín Gómez Farías* does not mention the affair. Both authors did so to portray him in a favorable light.

112. Gómez Farías to Santa Anna, Mexico City, late Oct. 1846, VGFP 2053, f. 51.

113. "Antonio López de Santa Anna, general de división y benemérito de la patria, a los mexicanos," San Luis Potosí, Oct. 23, 1846, in *El Republicano*, Oct. 28, 1846.

114. Santa Anna to Gómez Farías and Rejón, San Luis Potosí, Oct. 28, 1846, VGFP 2033, f. 51.

115. Santa Anna to Gómez Farías, San Luis Potosí, Nov. 4, 1846, VGFP 2064, f. 51.

116. Santa Anna to Gómez Farías, San Luis Potosí, Nov. 10, 1846, VGFP 2075, f. 51.

117. Santa Anna to Gómez Farías, San Luis Potosí, Nov. 4, 1846, VGFP 2064, f. 51; Lafragua, "Miscelánea," 42; Bustamante, *El nuevo Bernal*, 236-237. *El Federalista Puro* was one of four *puro*-sponsored newspapers that spoke out on public affairs between August and December 1846. The other three were *El Porvenir, El Restaurador,* and the *Diario del Gobierno de la República Mexicana.* Of these, the *Diario del Gobierno* was the most influential.

118. Lafragua, "Miscelánea," 44; Ramírez, *Mexico During the War*, 87. A recent study has concluded that out of the 114 deputies who attended the meetings of the legislature, fifty-five were *moderados* and forty-four were *puros*; of the remaining twelve, eleven were "independents." Reynaldo Sordo Cedeño, "El Soberano Congreso Constituyente y la Guerra con los Estadoe Unidos de América, 1846-1847," paper delivered at the Academic Symposium "Reflections on the War Between the United States and Mexico," Matamoros, Mexico, May 9, 1996.

119. Gómez Farías to Lemus, Mexico City, Nov. 10, 1846, VGFP 2077, f. 51; Alcaraz, *The Other Side*, 91-92.

120. Ramírez, *Mexico During the War*, 90.

121. *Diario del Gobierno de la República Mexicana*, Dec. 13 and 17, 1846.

122. *Diario del Gobierno de la República Mexicana*, Dec. 23, 1846; Dublán and Lozano, *Legislación*, 5: 238. Herrera's biographer did not mention this shift in opinion when discussing Herrera's term as deputy in the constituent Congress. Perhaps he could not explain it. Cotner, *The Military*, 155-156. The motivating factor may have been Herrera's concern for observing legal propriety.

123. Gómez Farías to Santa Anna, Mexico City, Dec. 22, 1846, VGFP 2149, f. 51.

124. *El Republicano*, Dec. 20 and 21, 1846.

125. *Memorias del diputado por el estado de Chihuahua, Lic. J. A. de Escudero, con documentos justificativos que pueden servir para la historia del*

Congreso constituyente mexicano del año de 1847 (Mexico City: Tipografía de R. Rafael, 1848), 11-14. The letters exchanged by Escudero and Gómez Farías can be found in *Memorias del diputado*, 42-43.

126. Hutchinson, *Valentín Gómez Farías*, 343; Bustamante, "Memorándum," Dec. 23, 1846 Santa Anna received eleven votes (Aguascalientes, Chihuahua, Oaxaca, Puebla, Querétaro, San Luis Potosí, Tabasco, Jalisco, Federal District, and the territories of Colima and Tlaxcala) while Elorriaga received nine (Chiapas, Coahuila, Durango, Guanajuato, Mexico, Michoacán, Sinaloa, Veracruz, and Zacatecas). Gómez Farías also got eleven votes (Aguascalientes, Chihuahua, Oaxaca, Querétaro, San Luis Potosí, Sinaloa, Jalisco, Zacatecas, Federal District, and the territories of Colima and Tlaxcala), Melchor Ocampo received eight (Chiapas, Coahuila, Guanajuato, Mexico, Michoacán, Puebla, Tabasco, and Veracruz), and Elorriaga received one (Durango). *El Republicano*, Dec. 24, 1846.

127. Santa Anna to Gómez Farías, San Luis Potosí, Dec. 28, 1846, VGFP 2172, f. 51.

VI—A Question of Survival

1. González Cosío to Gómez Farías, Zacatecas, Jan. 5, 1847, VGFP 2264, f. 52.

2. Antonio Haro y Tamariz to Mora, Mexico City, Oct. 29, 1846, in *Papeles inéditos*, 6: 65.

3. "El Sr. Don Valentín Gómez Farías al jurar como vicepresidente el 24 de diciembre de 1846," in *Informes y manifiestos*, 1: 329; Valadés, *Orígenes de la república*, 493-494.

4. Rejón to Ortiz Monasterio, Mexico City, Dec. 24, 1846, in the *Diario del Gobierno de la República Mexicana*, Dec. 28, 1846.

5. Anonymous to Gómez Farías, Mexico City, Jan. 4, 1847, VGFP 4655, f. 62.

6. Santa Anna to Gómez Farías, San Luis Potosí, Dec. 28, 1846, VGFP 2172, f. 51.

7. Alejandro Arango y Escandón to Mora, Mexico City, Dec. 1846, in *Papeles inéditos*, 6: 70.

8. José L. Villamil to Riva Palacio, Mexico City, Nov. 24, 1846, MRPP 2205; *El Republicano*, Sept. 19 and 20, 1846; Zamacois, *Historia de México*, 12: 531-533. A list of men who were to contribute to the loan agreed on at the October 1 meeting can be found in AGNM/RG, box 303, leg. 210, exp. 3.

9. Bazant, *Antonio Haro y Tamariz*, 49-50; Dublán and Lozano, *Legislación*, 5: 172-175, 188-189; Ramírez, *Mexico During the War*, 90; Tenenbaum, *The Politics of Penury*, 78, 199, n. 109.

10. *Don Simplicio*, Jan. 6, 1847; *El Republicano*, Oct. 3, Nov. 6 and 15, 1846.

11. *Diario del Gobierno de la República Mexicana*, Sept. 23, 1846. The uproar created by the article led to Zerecero's removal from the *Diario del Gobierno*; he then went to work for *El Federalista Puro*. Bustamante, *El nuevo Bernal*, 237.

12. *Don Simplicio*, Sept. 26, 1846; *El Republicano*, Sept. 25, 26, and 28, 1846.

13. Santa Anna to the minister of war, San Luis Potosí, Nov. 9 and 16, 1846, AGNM/RG, box 303, leg. 210, exp. 2.

14 Bermúdez de Castro to Primer Secretario, Mexico City, Dec. 29, 1846, in *Relaciones diplomáticas*, 4: 27.

15. Michael P. Costeloe, "Church-State Financial Negotiations in Mexico During the American War, 1846-1847," *Revista de Historia de América*, 60 (Jul.-Dec. 1965), 92; Pletcher, *The Diplomacy*, 484; Robinson, *The View*, xxii. Details about the financial support that the Church furnished the rebels appear in Michael P. Costeloe, "The Mexican Church and the Rebellion of the Polkos," *Hispanic American Historical Review*, 46:2 (May 1966), 170-178, and Tenenbaum, *The Politics of Penury*, 80-83.

16. Bustamante, *El nuevo Bernal*, 73-74, n. 1.

17. Jan Bazant, *Alienation of Church Wealth in Mexico: Social and Economic Aspects of the Liberal Revolution, 1856-1875* (London: Cambridge University Press, 1971), 29-30; Bazant, *Antonio Haro y Tamariz*, 48-49; Lafragua, "Miscelánea," 44. The main contributors from the Federal District to the November 19 loan can be found in Tenenbaum, *The Politics of Penury*, 81.

18. Angel Binaghi to Gómez Farías, New Orleans, Sept. 14, 1846, VGFP 1803, f. 50.

19. Mora to Gómez Farías, Paris (France), Oct. 27, 1846, VGFP 2027, f. 51.

20. José de Arrillaga to Gómez Farías, Boca del Monte, Dec. 6, 1846, VGFP 1725, f. 50. Genaro García erroneously dated this letter September 6. It mentions Rejón's and Gómez Farías' inclusion in the constituent Congress that began its sessions in December 1846, and elections to that assembly had not been held as of early September.

21. Gómez Farías to Lemus, Mexico City, Nov. 10, 1846, VGFP 2077, f. 51.

22. *Diario del Gobierno de la República Mexicana*, Jan. 14 and 18, 1847; Dublán and Lozano, *Legislación*, 5: 240.

23. Santa Anna to Rejón, San Luis Potosí, Jan. 2, 1847, in the *Diario del Gobierno de la República Mexicana*, Jan. 14, 1847.

24. *Diario del Gobierno de la República Mexicana*, Jan. 22, 1847; *El Republicano*, Jan. 6, 1847; Zamacois, *Historia de México*, 12: 533.

25. *Memorias del diputado,* 21; *Diario del Gobierno de la República Mexicana,* Jan. 26, 184; *El Republicano,* Jan. 8, 1847; Costeloe, "Church-State Financial," 101; Sordo Cedeño, "El Soberano Congreso."

26. Bruce Colcleugh, "Damning the Barbarians: Mexican Intellectuals on the Mexican-American War, 1846-1853," paper delivered at the Rocky Mountain Council of Latin American Studies, Vancouver, British Columbia, April 1-4, 1993; Mariano Otero, *Obras,* 2 vols. (Mexico City: Editorial Porrúa, 1967), 1: 69; *El Republicano,* Jan. 8, 1847; Dublán and Lozano, *Legislación,* 5: 246-252.

27. Wilfrid Hardy Callcott, *Church and State in Mexico, 1822-1857* (New York: Octagon Books, 1971), 186; *Don Simplicio,* Jan. 16, 1847; *El Republicano,* Jan. 15, 1847; Alcaraz, *The Other Side,* 151; Bustamante, "Memorándum," Jan. 13 and 14, 1847; Costeloe, "Church-State Financial," 102-104.

28. Callcott, *Church and State,* 185; Costeloe, "Church-State Financial," 103-104, 104, n. 49.

29. Valadés, *Orígenes de la república,* 495.

30. *El Republicano,* Jan. 16, 1847; Alcaraz, *The Other Side,* 151.

31. Dublán and Lozano, *Legislación,* 5: 255-256.

32. Gómez Farías to Santa Anna, Mexico City, Jan. 9, 1847, VGFP 2304, f. 52.

33. Santa Anna to the minister of war, San Luis Potosí, Jan. 13, 1847, and Santa Anna to Rejón, San Luis Potosí, Jan. 14, in the *Diario del Gobierno de la República Mexicana,* Jan. 16, 1847.

34. Santa Anna to Crescencio Gordoa, San Luis Potosí, Jan. 14, 1847, in *El Republicano,* Jan. 19, 1847. 1847.

35. Ramírez, *Mexico During the War,* 100.

36. Ramírez to Gómez Farías, Mexico City, Jan. 19, 1847, VGFP 2404, f. 52.

37. *El Republicano,* Jan. 19 and 30, 1847.

38. Bustamante, "Memorándum," Jan. 20, 1847.

39. *Diccionario Porrúa,* 1: 868.

40. Jesús Ortiz to Gómez Farías, Guadalajara, Jan. 5, 1847, VGFP 2276, f. 52; Malo, *Diario de sucesos,* 1: 312.

41. Bustamante, "Memorándum," Jan. 27, 1847.

42. *Diccionario Porrúa,* 1: 868.

43. Valentín Canalizo to the Ministry of Foreign Relations, Mexico City, Jan. 13, 1847, and Ortiz Monasterio to Canalizo, Mexico City, Jan. 15, 1847, in the *Diario del Gobierno de la República Mexicana,* Jan. 15, 1847; *Diario del Gobierno de la República Mexicana,* Jan. 30, 1847.

44. Juan Rodríguez Puebla to Gómez Farías, Mexico City, Jan. 23, 1847, VGFP 2427, f. 52; Manuel Baranda to Gómez Farías, Mexico City, Jan. 24, 1847, VGFP 2433, f. 52; Francisco Suárez Iriarte to Gómez Farías, Mexico

City, Feb. 19, 1847, VGFP 2590, f. 53; *El Republicano*, Jan. 25, 1847; Bustamante, "Memorándum," Jan. 23, 1847; Malo, *Diario de sucesos*, 1: 312; Riva Palacio, *México a través*, 4: 604; Zamacois, *Historia de México*, 12: 566-570. It is questionable whether Rejón ever held his post, since the *Diccionario Porrúa* (1: 868) does not include him in its list of cabinet members.

45. *El Republicano*, Jan. 21, 1847.

46. Bustamante, "Memorándum," Jan. 20, 1847.

47. Santa Anna to Gómez Farías, San Luis Potosí, Jan. 7, 1847, VGFP 2285, f. 52. For letters of a similar tone that Santa Anna wrote to Gómez Farías between January 13 and January 28, 1847, see VGFP 2327, 2337, 2363a, 2390, 2391, 2447, 2459, f. 52.

48. Gómez Farías to Santa Anna, Mexico City, late Jan. 1847, VGFP 2486, f. 52.

49. Santa Anna to the secretaries of the sovereign national extraordinary Congress, San Luis Potosí, Jan. 26, 1847, in *El Republicano*, Jan. 29, 1847.

50. Callcott, *Santa Anna*, 250.

51. Anonymous to Gómez Farías, Mexico City, Jan. 4, 1847, VGFP 4655, f. 62.

52. *El Republicano*, Jan. 21, 1847.

53. Bustamante, "Memorándum," Jan. 22, 1847. For more details about these rumors, see Ignacia F. de Uhink to her mother, Veracruz, Jan. 28, 1847, VGFP 2458, f. 52; *Don Simplicio*, Jan. 27, 1847; *El Republicano*, Jan. 31, 1847.

54. Alcaraz, *The Other Side*, 91.

55. Santa Anna to Gómez Farías, San Luis Potosí, Dec. 30, 1846, VGFP 2184 and 2190, f. 51.

56. Bermúdez de Castro to Primer Secretario, Mexico City, Jan. 27, 1847, in *Relaciones diplomáticas*, 4: 39-40; *Diario del Gobierno de la República Mexicana*, Mar. 23 and Apr. 10, 1847; *El Republicano*, Jan. 29, 1847.

57. Bustamante, "Memorándum," Jan. 25, 1847; Rives, *The United States*, 2: 320.

58. Ramírez, *Mexico During the War*, 101-102, 104.

59. *El Republicano*, Feb. 13, 1847. For articles of a similar tone, see *El Republicano*, Feb. 23 and 25, 1847, and *Don Simplicio*, Feb. 13 and 24, 1847. Lesser publications such as *El Trueno* and *La Chicharra de a Cuartilla* also joined this campaign.

60. *El Federalista*, Feb. 13, 1847.

61. Alcaraz, *The Other Side*, 141, 152; Cuevas, *Historia de la nación*, 657; Lafragua, "Miscelánea," 45; Prieto, *Memorias*, 253.

62. Jacinto María de Olivares to Gómez Farías, Mexico City, Feb. 9,

1847, VGFP 2537, f. 53; Benito Juárez, Tiburcio Cañas, and Francisco Banuet to José Arteaga, Mexico City, Feb. 17, 1847, VGFP 2584, f. 54; Mº F. de Orihuela to Gómez Farías, Mexico City, Feb. 20, 1847, VGFP 2596, f. 53.

63. For additional details on the terms of these proposals, see A. Brooke Caruso, *The Mexican Spy Company: United States Covert Operations in Mexico, 1845-1848* (Jefferson: McFarland & Company, 1991), 140-144; Richard Griswold del Castillo, *The Treaty of Guadalupe Hidalgo: A Legacy of Conflict* (Norman: University of Oklahoma Press, 1990), 17-22; Pletcher, *The Diplomacy*, 476-480.

64. Carlos María Bustamante, *Campaña sin gloria y guerra de como la de los cacomixtles* (Mexico City: Imprenta de I. Cumplido, 1847), 8; Bermúdez de Castro to Primer Secretario, Mexico City, Feb. 28, 1847, in *Relaciones diplomáticas*, 4: 46; *El Monitor Republicano*, Feb. 25, 1847; Bustamante, "Memorándum," Feb. 24, 25, and 27, 1847.

65. *Don Simplicio*, Jan. 6, 1847; *El Monitor Republicano*, Jan. 24 and Feb. 1, 1847.

66. Malo, *Diario de sucesos*, 1: 314.

67. Juan José Baz to Fermín Gómez Farías, Mexico City, Feb. 25, 1847 (copying a Feb. 23, 1847, memorandum issued by the minister of war), VGFP 2622, f. 53.

68. *El Monitor Republicano*, Feb. 25, 1847; Alcaraz, *The Other Side*, 155.

69. Had Gómez Farías not moved the "Independencia" troops, the *moderados'* February 27 coup d'état may have exploded two days ahead of schedule and Gómez Farías would have been in greater danger at the National Palace, where he was close to the "Independencia's" National University headquarters. Riva Palacio, *México a través*, 4: 632.

70. *El Republicano*, Feb. 26, 1847; Dublán and Lozano, *Legislación*, 5: 254-255.

71. Alcaraz, *The Other Side*, 154; Bustamante, "Memorándum," Feb. 25, 1847; Malo, *Diario de sucesos*, 1: 314-315; Ramírez, *Mexico During the War*, 104. Mexico City's newspapers had warned their readers of this danger as early as February 24. See *El Republicano*, Feb. 24, 25, and 26, 1847, and the *Diario del Gobierno de la República Mexicana*, Feb. 25, 1847.

72. According to the Constitution of 1824, responsibility for Santa Anna's and Gómez Farías' election belonged to state legislatures. Actions taken by the deputies to the constitutional Congress gave the plotters a convenient pretext to argue against the election's validity. Tena Ramírez, *Leyes Fundamentales*, 179.

73. "Plan para la restauración de los verdaderos principios federativos, proclamado por la guarnición y guardia nacional de esta capital," Mexico

City, Feb. 27, 1847, in *El Republicano*, Feb. 27, 1847. The plan was altered twice. Lafragua, "Miscelánea," 45. One of the preliminary drafts appears in Bustamante, "Memorándum," Feb. 20, 1847. Authorship of the document is a matter of debate. It has been attributed to Gómez Pedraza—who denied it—to José Guadalupe Covarrubias and to members of Mexico City's Cathedral chapter. Alcaraz, *The Other Side*, 158; Ramírez, *Mexico During the War*, 106.

74. Bustamante, *Campaña sin gloria*, 14; Dublán and Lozano, *Legislación*, 5: 261.

75. Bermúdez de Castro to Primer Secretario, Mexico City, Mar. 31, 1847, in *Relaciones diplomáticas*, 4: 57.

76. Olaguíbel to the minister of foreign relations, Toluca, Mar. 1, 1847, Ministry of Foreign Relations to Luis Espino (Tlaxcala's *jefe político*), Mexico City, Mar. 2, 1847, and Ignacio Sierra y Rosso to the governor of Puebla, Mexico City, Mar. 5, 1847, Archivo General de la Nación, Mexico City, Ramo de Gobernación, Tranquilidad Pública (hereafter cited as AGNM/RG/TP), box 337, exps. 2, 3, and 19. Available documentation suggests that this appeal was not effective. Some militia commanders feared local agitation and refused to carry out the government's orders, while others simply could not muster their militiamen. Olaguíbel to the minister of foreign relations, Toluca, Mar. 8, 1847, and Antonio Sein to same, Tulancingo, Mar. 10, 1847, AGN/RG/TP, box 337, exp. 2; Joaquín Zarco to same, Texcoco, Mar. 3, 1847, AGN/RG/TP, box 338, exp. 13.

77. Ministry of Foreign Relations to its employees, Mexico City, Mar. 1, 1847, Antonio Horta to the minister of foreign relations, Mar. 7, 1847, and Ministry of Foreign Relations to the governor of the Federal District, Mexico City, Mar. 1, 1847, AGN/RG/TP, box 337, exp. 13, 15, and 20.

78. Almonte tried to take advantage of the uncertainty to satisfy his political appetite. He sought a new one-article plan that would have challenged Gómez Farías' authority and forced Congress to name him chief executive. The maneuver proved unsuccessful. Although Almonte's sister continued to champion his presidential aspirations among the contending factions by maintaining that only he could restrain Santa Anna, Almonte went into seclusion and remained inactive during the rest of the revolt. José Miguel Arroyo to his father, Mexico City, Feb. 28, 1847, VGFP 2642, f. 53; *Diario de la Guerra*, Mar. 1, 1847; Alcaraz, *The Other Side*, 154, 158, 160; Bustamante, *Campaña sin gloria*, 14.

79. Ramírez, *Mexico During the War*, 106.

80. Alcaraz, *The Other Side*, 159.

81. *Ibid.*, 162-163. See also Rangel to Gómez Farías, La Ciudadela, Mar. 10, 1847, VGFP 2726, f. 54.

82. Manuel Arteaga to Gómez Farías, Puebla, Mar. 12, 1847, VGFP 2735, f. 54; Alcaraz, *The Other Side*, 163; Costeloe, "Church-State Financial," 107.

83. Alcaraz, *The Other Side*, 157-158, 160-162.

84. Bustamante, "Memorándum," Mar. 3, 1847; Bustamante, *Campaña sin gloria*, 20-21.

85. *Boletín de la Democracia*, Mar. 8, 1847; *El Republicano*, Mar. 7, 10, 11, 12, 14, and 17, 1847.

86. Juan B. Ceballos to Gómez Farías, Mexico City, Mar. 5, 1847, VGFP 2693, f. 54; Bustamante, "Memorándum," Mar. 6 and 8, 1847; Bustamante, *Campaña sin gloria*, 32.

87. Alcaraz, *The Other Side*, 164-165.

88. *El Republicano*, Mar. 10, 1847; Ramírez, *Mexico During the War*, 106. Accounts differ on the date—either March 8 or 9—on which the plan was altered. See *El Católico*, Mar. 6, 1847; *El Republicano*, Mar. 10, 1847; Bustamante, "Memorándum," Mar. 10, 1847.

89. Costeloe, "The Mexican Church," 172; Prieto, *Memorias*, 254; Ramírez, *Mexico During the War*, 106-107.

90. Lafragua, "Miscelánea," 45-46; "Los diputados que suscriben, a sus comitentes," Mexico City, Mar. 10, 1847, in *El Republicano*, Mar. 11, 1847.

91. "A la nación, los diputados que suscriben," Mexico City, Mar. 11, 1847, in *El Republicano*, Mar. 19, 1847. Subscribers included Rejón, Vicente and Eligio Romero, José María del Río, Tiburcio Cañas, Agustín Buenrostro, Pedro Zubieta, and Juan Othón.

92. Ramírez, *Mexico During the War*, 105.

93. Zamacois, *Historia de México*, 12: 639.

94. Santa Anna to Gómez Farías, Matehuala, Mar. 6, 1847, VGFP 2707, f. 54.

95. Santa Anna to Gómez Farías, San Luis Potosí, Mar. 9, 1847, VGFP 2717, f. 54.

96. Santa Anna to Gómez Farías, San Luis Potosí, Mar. 9, 1847, VGFP 2722, f. 54.

97. Alcaraz, *The Other Side*, 165.

98. Bermúdez de Castro to Primer Secretario, Mexico City, Mar. 3, 1847, in *Relaciones diplómaticas*, 4: 53.

99. Bermúdez de Castro to Primer Secretario, Mexico City, Mar. 31, 1847, in *Ibid.*, 4: 57, 59.

100. Santa Anna to Gómez Farías, San Luis Potosí, Mar. 10, 1847, VGFP 2739a, f. 54; Santa Anna to Matías de la Peña y Barragán, San Luis Potosí, Mar. 10, 1847, in *El Republicano*, Mar. 14, 1847.

101. Bustamante, "Memorándum," Mar. 14, 1847.

102. Bermúdez de Castro to Primer Secretario, Mexico City, Mar. 31,

1847, in *Relaciones diplomáticas*, 4: 58. The letters that Rangel and Gómez Farías exchanged between February 27 and March 10 can be found in VGFP 2637, 2650, f. 53, and VGFP 2701, 2726, f. 54.

103. Gómez Farías to the secretaries of the constitutional Congress, Mexico City, Mar. 13, 1847, VGFP 2739, f. 54.

104. Gómez Farías to Santa Anna, Mexico City, mid-Mar. 1847, VGFP 2742a, f. 54.

105. Gómez Farías to the secretaries of the constitutional Congress, Mexico City, Mar. 13, 1847, VGFP 2739, f. 54.

106. Zamacois, *Historia de México*, 12: 641-643.

107. Bustamante, *El nuevo Bernal*, 259; Echanove Trujillo, *La vida pasional*, 404; Ramírez, *Mexico During the War*, 107; Valadés, *Orígenes de la república*, 497; Zamacois, *Historia de México*, 12: 643-644. The full text of Baz' discourse can be found in the *Diario del Gobierno de la República Mexicana*, Mar. 29, 1847.

108. *Diario del Gobierno de la República Mexicana*, Mar. 24, 1847; *El Republicano*, Mar. 24, 1847. Neither Otero or Rondero took the positions. Manuel Baranda replaced the former as minister of foreign relations while Francisco Suárez Iriarte became minister of finance, an appointment that displeased *El Republicano* because Suárez Iriarte had been a cabinet member under Gómez Farías. This daily published his name in italics to indicate its irritation and subsequently urged him to resign. *El Republicano*, Mar. 25 and Apr. 16, 1847; Riva Palacio, *México a través*, 4: 637.

109. *El Republicano*, Mar. 24, 1847.

110. Bermúdez de Castro to Primer Secretario, Mexico City, Mar. 31, 1847, in *Relaciones diplomáticas*, 4: 56, 59; Ramírez, *Mexico During the War*, 108.

111. *El Monitor Republicano*, Mar. 28, 1847; Ramírez, *Mexico During the War*, 109.

112. Alcaraz, *The Other Side*, 145.

113. Costeloe, "Church-State Financial," 107-108; Dublán and Lozano, *Legislación*, 5: 263; Ramírez, *Mexico During the War*, 112-114; Tenenbaum, *The Politics of Penury*, 80.

114. Alcaraz, *The Other Side*, 195-196; Echanove Trujillo, *La vida pasional*, 405; Ramírez, *Mexico During the War*, 109.

115. Bustamante, *Campaña sin gloria*, 33.

116. Lafragua, "Miscelánea," 46-47. The February 10, 1847, legislation appears in Dublán and Lozano, *Legislación*, 5: 256-257.

117. Ramírez, *Mexico During the War*, 110-111.

118. *Ibid.* United States confidential agent Beach had gained entry into Mexican political circles through his friendship with Almonte. Pletcher, *The Diplomacy*, 476. The relationship may have been the determining fac-

tor in leading Gómez Farías to oppose Almonte's candidacy at this crucial juncture.

119. Dublán and Lozano, *Legislación*, 5: 265-266. José Agustín de Escudero was one of three deputies who presented the decree before Congress. The section that abolished the vice-presidency was approved by a slim margin, thirty-eight votes to thirty-five. Available documentation, however, does not reveal the breakdown of the voting. The ballots for the presidential election were cast in a secret session of Congress. Chihuahua, Durango, Guanajuato, Mexico, Michoacán, Puebla, Querétaro, San Luis Potosí, Sinaloa, Sonora, Tabasco, Veracruz, Jalisco, Zacatecas, the Federal District, and the territories of Colima and Tlaxcala voted for Anaya, while only Chiapas, Oaxaca, and Tamaulipas supported Almonte. *Diario del Gobierno de la República Mexicana*, Apr. 12, 1847; *El Republicano*, Apr. 1, 1847.

120. Ramírez, *Mexico During the War*, 111.

VII—"An Unsuccessful Comeback"

1. Gómez Farías to the secretaries of the sovereign Congress, Mixcoac, June 30, 1847, VGFP 2776, f. 54; *El Republicano*, Apr. 14, 1847; Echanove Trujillo, *La vida pasional*, 416-419.

2. Velasco Márquez, *La guerra del 47*, 48-50.

3. González Cosío to Gómez Farías, Zacatecas, Feb. 11, 1848, VGFP 2901, f. 55.

4. Ramírez, *Mexico During the War*, 121.

5. *Diario del Gobierno de la República Mexicana*, Apr. 12 and 14, 1847.

6. *Ibid.*, Apr. 12, 14, and 15, 1847. The full text of the decree appears in Dublán and Lozano, *Legislación*, 5: 266-267.

7. Dublán and Lozano, *Legislación*, 5: 267-268; Zamacois, *Historia de México*, 12: 670-671, 685. A breakdown of the voting on the April 20 decree can be found in the *Diario del Gobierno de la República Mexicana*, Apr. 28, 1847.

8. José Cayetano de Montoya to Santa Anna, Querétaro, Apr. 6, 1847, and Manuel Baranda to Santa Anna, Mexico City, Apr. 8, 1847, in Antonio López de Santa Anna Papers, Library of Congress; *El Republicano*, Apr. 12 and 15, 1847; Alcaraz, *The Other Side*, 236; Ramírez, *Mexico During the War*, 119; Zamacois, *Historia de México*, 12: 510-511.

9. Bermúdez de Castro to Primer Secretario, Mexico City, Feb. 25, 1847, in *Relaciones diplómaticas*, 4: 38; Alcaraz, *The Other Side*, 234-235; Pletcher, *The Diplomacy*, 485; Ramírez, *Mexico During the War*, 122-123.

10. Bermúdez de Castro to Primer Secretario, Mexico City, Apr. 29, 1847, in *Relaciones diplomáticas*, 4: 90; Alcaraz, *The Other Side*, 224, 234-235;

Ramírez, *Mexico During the War*, 122, 126, 128, 140-141; Riva Palacio, *México a través*, 4: 658.

11. *El Boletín de la Democracia*, May 1, 1847; Echanove Trujillo, *La vida pasional*, 421; Ramírez, *Mexico During the War*, 129-130. The quote appears in Ramírez, *Mexico During the War*, 129.

12. "Acta de la expresión de la voluntad del pueblo oaxaqueño," Oaxaca, Feb. 15, 1847, Joaquín Guergué to Santa Anna, Oaxaca, Mar. 15, 1847, and Lorenzo Acosta to unknown (probably Santa Anna), Oaxaca, no day, Apr. 1847, AGNM/RG/TP, box 339, exp. 6; Brian Hamnett, *Juárez* (New York: Longman Publishing, 1994), 32-33; Ramírez, *Mexico During the War*, 126-127.

13. Bermúdez de Castro to Primer Secretario, Mexico City, June 28, 1847, in *Relaciones diplómaticas*, 4: 116-117; Ramírez, *Mexico During the War*, 126-127, 130-132.

14. Ramírez, *Mexico During the War*, 130-131.

15. Dublán and Lozano, *Legislación*, 5: 273-274.

16. *Ibid.*, 5: 275.

17 . Alcaraz, *The Other Side*, 231.

18. Pletcher, *The Diplomacy*, 506; Ramírez, *Mexico During the War*, 131, 133-137.

19. The results clearly illustrated Santa Anna's precarious political situation. Four state legislatures cast their ballots for General Juan Nepomuceno Almonte (Sonora, Sinaloa, Aguascalientes, and Tamaulipas), three for General José Joaquín Herrera (Querétaro, Oaxaca, and Michoacán), three for Angel Frías, (San Luis Potosí, Guanajuato, and Mexico), and one for Santa Anna (Chihuahua). Those of Puebla, Chiapas, Durango, and Zacatecas voted for other individuals. The remaining eight states—California, Coahuila, Jalisco, Nuevo León, New Mexico, Tabasco, Veracruz, and Yucatán—did not vote for different reasons. Bermúdez de Castro to Primer Secretario, Mexico City, June 28, 1847, in *Relaciones diplómaticas*, 4: 116-117.

20. Robert Ryal Miller, *Shamrock and Sword: The San Patricio Battalion During the Mexican War* (Norman: University of Oklahoma Press, 1989), 65-67.

21. Alcaraz, *The Other Side*, 236-237; Callcott, *Santa Anna*, 263-264; Ramírez, *Mexico During the War*, 145-146.

22. Alcaraz, *The Other Side*, 232; Callcott, *Santa Anna*, 264; García, *Documentos inéditos*, 59: 329; Ramírez, *Mexico During the War*, 127-128, 145-147; Roa Bárcena, *Recuerdos de la invasión*, 2: 170; Zamacois, *Historia de México*, 12: 695-697.

23. García, *Documentos inéditos*, 59: 329.

24. Bermúdez de Castro to Primer Secretario, Mexico City, May 29, 1847, in *Relaciones diplómaticas*, 4: 113-114; Alcaraz, *The Other Side*, 237; Bustamante, *El nuevo Bernal*, 301; Roa Bárcena, *Recuerdos de la invasión*, 2: 173.

25. *Diario del Gobierno de la República Mexicana*, June 2, 1847; *El Republicano*, May 24 and 30, 1847; Bermúdez de Castro to Primer Secretario, Mexico City, May 29, 1847, in *Relaciones diplómaticas*, 4: 113-114.

26. Bermúdez de Castro to Primer Secretario, Mexico City, May 29, 1847, in *Relaciones diplomáticas*, 4: 114. Santa Anna's letter can be found in *El Razonador*, June 1, 1847.

27. Trist to Buchanan, Puebla, June 13, 1847, in *Diplomatic Correspondence*, 8: 914; Bermúdez de Castro to Primer Secretario, Mexico City, June 28, 1847, in *Relaciones diplomáticas*, 4: 116. The commission's report and Santa Anna's letter appear in *El Razonador*, June 4 and 8, 1847.

28. Callcott, *Santa Anna*, 264.

29. *El Republicano*, June 8, 1847; Echanove Trujillo, *La vida pasional*, 421; Ramírez, *Mexico During the War*, 147-148.

30. *El Republicano*, June 8, 1847.

31. Ramírez, *Mexico During the War*, 147-148; Riva Palacio, *México a través*, 4: 667; Tenenbaum, *The Politics of Penury*, 82. The decrees can be found in Dublán and Lozano, *Legislación*, 5: 274, 283-284.

32. Lafragua, "Miscelánea," 47. Lafragua again refused to take the post when asked by Santa Anna two months later. José María Lafragua to Mariano Otero, Mexico City, Aug. 24, 1847, AHNM/MOC, microfilm reel 4, 162.

33. Zamacois, *Historia de México*, 12: 701.

34. Dublán and Lozano, *Legislación*, 5: 268.

35. Eugenio María Aguirre and Ignacio Muñoz Campuzano to the secretary of the ministry of [Foreign] Relations, Mexico City, June 18, 1847, in the *Diario del Gobierno de la República Mexicana*, June 23, 1847; Luis de la Rosa to José Bernardino Alcalde, José María del Río, Joaquín Ramírez de España, Fernando María de Ortega, J. Ambrosio Moreno, J. J. Cortina, Francisco Suárez Iriarte, José María Berriol, Manuel María de Villada, Joaquín Navarro, Agustín Buenrostro, and Eligio Romero, Mexico City, June 20, 1847, in *Ibid.*, June 26, 1847.

36. Manuel Iturribaría, Bernardino Carbajal, José B. Alcalde, Fernando María de Ortega, José María del Río, J. Ambrosio Moreno, Manuel María de Villada, Manuel Zetina Abad, Joaquín Ramírez de España, Lugardo Lechón, José María Espino, José Trinidad Gómez, José María Sánchez Espinosa, Francisco Suárez Iriarte, José María Benítez, Agustín Buenrostro, Juan Nepomuceno de la Parra, Eligio Romero, Joaquín Navarro, and

Ramón Gamboa to Luis de la Rosa, Mexico City, June 20, 1847, in *Ibid.*, June 26, 1847.

37. Domingo Ibarra to Aguirre and Campuzano, Mexico City, June 21, 1847, in *Ibid.*, June 23, 1847; Aguirre and Campuzano to Riva Palacio, Mexico City, June 21, 1847, MRPP 2296; de la Rosa to Riva Palacio, Mexico City, June 23 and 30, 1847, MRPP 2297, 2301, 2307.

38. Bermúdez de Castro to Primer Secretario, Mexico City, June 29, 1847, in *Relaciones diplomáticas*, 4: 116.

39. Ibarra to Buchanan, Mexico City, June 22, 1847, in *Diplomatic Correspondence*, 8: 914; Bermúdez de Castro to Primer Secretario, Mexico City, June 29, 1847, in *Relaciones diplomáticas*, 4: 122; Dublán and Lozano, *Legislación*, 5: 268; Pletcher, *The Diplomacy*, 508-509.

40. *Diario del Gobierno de la República Mexicana*, July 15, 1847.

41. The most renowned *puro* legislators who acted in this manner were José Bernardino Alcalde, Agustín Buenrostro, Ramón Gamboa, Juan Othón, José María del Río, Eligio or Vicente Romero (the document does not specify which one), and Pedro Zubieta. *Ibid.*, July 15, 1847.

42. José Ramón Pacheco to the minister of justice, Mexico City, July 7, 1847, in *ibid.*, July 7, 1847; Pacheco to the secretaries of Congress, Mexico City, July 16, 1847, in *ibid.*, July 18, 1847.

43. Pletcher, *The Diplomacy*, 512-514. For a discussion of the negotiations between Santa Anna and Scott, see Carlos Castañeda, "Relations of General Scott with Santa Anna," *Hispanic American Historical Review*, 29:4 (Nov. 1949), 455-473, and Griswold del Castillo, *The Treaty*, 27-29.

44. Pacheco to Antonio Salonio, Mexico City, Aug. 21, 1847, in the *Diario del Gobierno de la República Mexicana*, Aug. 21, 1847; Alcaraz, *The Other Side*, 302-303; Rives, *The United States*, 2: 509; Roa Bárcena, *Recuerdos de la invasión*, 2: 313-314.

45. Gómez Farías, José María de Lacunza, Luis de la Rosa, Pascual González Fuentes, Mariano Otero, Cosme Torres, Manuel Robredo, and J. Noriega to Salonio, Toluca, Aug. 22, 1847, in the *Diario del Gobierno de la República Mexicana*, Aug. 28, 1847.

46. Perdigón Garay to Otero, Mexico City, Aug. 28, 1847, AHNM/MOC, microfilm reel 3, 133-134.

47. Lafragua to Otero, Mexico City, Aug. 24, AHNM/MOC, microfilm reel 4, 162.

48. Otero to Perdigón Garay, Toluca, Aug. 30, 1847, AHNM/MOC, microfilm reel 4, 178.

49. Lafragua to Otero, Mexico City, Aug. 28, 1847, AHNM/MOC, microfilm reel 4, 170; Guillermo Prieto to Lafragua, Mexico City, Aug. 30, 1847, AHNM/MOC, microfilm reel 4, 174. The quote is from Lafragua to Otero, Mexico City, Sept. 2, 1847, AHNM/MOC, microfilm reel 3, 145.

50. Pletcher, *The Diplomacy*, 519, 530-531; Roa Bárcena, *Recuerdos de la invasión*, 3: 233-234.

51. Edward Thornton to Palmerston, Mexico City, Oct. 29, 1847, PRO/FO, 50/M, vol. 212, 75; Otero to Riva Palacio, Toluca, Sept. 21, 1847, MRPP 2412; Trist to Buchanan, Mexico City, Sept. 27 and Oct. 1, 1847, in *Diplomatic Correspondence*, 8: 955, 957; Alcaraz, *The Other Side*, 311-312; Pletcher, *The Diplomacy*, 532; Rives, *The United States*, 2: 586; Roa Bárcena, *Recuerdos de la invasión*, 3: 234-235, 237.

52. Only the peculiar circumstances brought about by the war permitted the constituent Congress to meet in Querétaro. According to the *Acta de Reformas*, legislative power fell on Congress until a new legislature met. A June 3, 1847, decree stated that elections for that assembly would be held between August 29 and October 1, 1847. The occupation of large portions of Mexican territory by United States' troops, however, prevented many elected boards from meeting and choosing the members of the new legislature. Thus, the constituent Congress maintained legislative powers. To correct the situation, Peña y Peña's government, through an October 19 decree, moved to stage new legislative elections in locations where they still had not been held. Dublán and Lozano, *Legislación*, 5: 278, 281, 297; Rives, *The United States*, 2: 586-587.

53. Salonio to Riva Palacio, Mexico City, Sept. 20, 1847, MRPP 2410; Trist to Buchanan, Mexico City, Sept. 27, 1847, in *Diplomatic Correspondence*, 8: 955; Pletcher, *The Diplomacy*, 533; Roa Bárcena, *Recuerdos de la invasión*, 3: 237.

54. Trist to Buchanan, Mexico City, Oct. 25, 1847, NTP/LC, microfilm reel 8; Bankhead to Palmerston, Mexico City, Sept. 28, 1847, PRO/FO, 50/M, vol. 211, 246-249; Thornton to Palmerston, Mexico City, Oct. 29, 1847, PRO/FO, 50/M, vol. 212, 75; *Colección de los documentos*, 52-67.

55. *México ante los ojos del ejército invasor de 1847 (Diario del coronel Ethan Allen Hitchcock)*, trans. George Baker (Mexico City: Universidad Nacional Autónoma de México, 1978), 108.

56. Trist to Buchanan, Mexico City, Oct. 25, 1847, NTP/LC, microfilm reel 8.

57. Fuentes Mares, *Santa Anna*, 232.

58. George Baker, "Una propuesta mexicana para la ayuda militar norteamericana, o sea, un recuerdo del liberalismo mexicano desconocido," in *Anuario de historia* (Mexico City: Universidad Nacional Autónoma de México, 1976), 254-257, 256, n. 6, 7, and 8; *México ante los ojos*, 104. "Prospectus," *La Razón*, Sept. 30, 1847, in *El Monitor Republicano*, Oct. 7, 1847.

59. F. C. to Trist, Mexico City, Nov. 14, 1847, NTP/LC, microfilm reel 9; George Baker, "Mexico City and the War with the United States: A Study

in the Politics of Military Occupation" (Ph.D. diss., Duke University, 1970), 194; Baker, "Una propuesta," 249-260.

60. Winfield Scott, *Memoirs of Lieutenant-General Scott*, 2 vols. (New York: Sheldon & Co., 1864), 2: 581-582; Bauer, *The Mexican War*, 381-382; Pletcher, *The Diplomacy*, 564-565.

61. Dennis E. Berge, "A Mexican Dilemma: The Mexico City Ayuntamiento and the Question of Loyalty, 1846-1848," *Hispanic American Historical Review*, 50:2 (May, 1970), 246, 246, n. 57.

62. "Instrucciones otorgadas por la junta general de Electores a los Representantes de la ciudad y Distrito de México," in *Defensa pronunciada ante el Gran Jurado el día 21 de marzo de 1850 por Francisco Suárez Iriarte, acusado en 8 de agosto por el secretario de Relaciones en aquella fecha, de los crímenes de sedición contra el gobierno de Querétaro e infidencia contra la patria, en sus actos como presidente de la asamblea municipal de la ciudad y distrito de México* (Mexico City: Tipografía de R. Rafael, 1850), 118-121.

63. Carmen Blázquez, *Miguel Lerdo de Tejada: Un liberal veracruzano en la política nacional* (Mexico City: El Colegio de México, 1978), 27-29; Baker, "Mexico City," 219-220; Roa Bárcena, *Recuerdos de la invasión*, 3: 213-219.

64. Berge, "A Mexican Dilemma," 246-247, 249-250. The Grand Jury of the Chamber of Deputies tried Suárez Iriarte for the crime of treason in 1850. Among the charges levied against him was that he had conspired to annex Mexico to the United States. Suárez Iriarte denied that accusation, saying that his sole objective had been to place the *ayuntamiento* between the local population and the United States army to protect the capital from military occupation and prevent a reign of terror. For more details about the trial, see Moisés González Navarro, *Anatomía del poder en México, 1848-1853* (Mexico City: El Colegio de México, 1983), 20-22; Berge, "A Mexican Dilemma," 252-255; *Defensa pronunciada*.

65. Riva Palacio to José María Godoy, Hacienda de la Asunción, Jan. 10, 1848, MRPP 2499.

66. Autobiographical statement of Gómez Farías, no place, no date, VGFP 4826, f. 63; Gómez Farías to González Cosío, Querétaro, Nov. 19, 1847, VGFP 2813, f. 54.

67. Juan N. Cumplido to Gómez Farías, Lagos, Sept. 22, 1847, VGFP 2814, f. 54; Gómez Farías to anonymous, Querétaro, Sept. 1847, VGFP 2819, f. 54; Gómez Farías to Isabel Gómez Farías and Ignacita de Uhink, Lagos, Oct. 8, 1847, VGFP 2824, f. 54; Bermúdez de Castro to Primer Secretario, Mexico City, June 29, 1847, in *Relaciones diplomáticas*, 4: 121.

68. "Los comisionados a la coalición por los estados de Jalisco, San Luis Potosí, Zacatecas, México, Querétaro y Aguascaliente, a la nación," Lagos, June 6, 1847, in *El Republicano*, June 16, 1847.

69. Bernardo Flores to Otero, Lagos, Oct. 24, 1847, AHNM/MOC, microfilm reel 4, 283.

70. Gómez Farías to Ignacita and Isabelita, Lagos, Oct. 4, 1847, VGFP 2821, f. 54.

71. *El Republicano*, June 16, 1847.

72. Trist to Buchanan, Mexico City, Oct. 1, 1847, NTP/LC, microfilm reel 8.

73. Dublán and Lozano, *Legislación*, 5: 305; Riva Palacio, *México a través*, 4: 701; Rives, *The United States*, 2: 586-587.

74. Francisco Berdusco to Gómez Farías, Querétaro, Oct. 22, 1847, VGFP 2844, f. 54; *El Monitor Republicano*, Nov. 2, 1847; Zamacois, *Historia de México*, 13: 36. With this end in sight, on November 6 Deputy Miguel García Vargas requested that the government state the reasons it had ordered Santa Anna prosecuted. The proposal failed. *El Correo Nacional*, Dec. 2, 1847; *El Razonador*, Nov. 17, 1847.

75. *El Razonador*, Nov. 13, 1847.

76. *Ibid.*, Nov. 17, 1847.

77. *Ibid.*, Nov. 13 and 17, 1847; Echanove Trujillo, *La vida pasional*, 430; Otero, *Obras*, 1: 87.

78. *Exposición o programa de los diputados pertenecientes al partido puro o progresista sobre la presente guerra con motivo de una proposición del sr. Otero, e imputaciones de ciertos periódicos que se publican en la capital bajo la influencia del conquistador, y que se dejan correr libremente por el actual gobierno de la Unión* (Querétaro: Imprenta de Francisco Frías, 1847).

79. *El Razonador*, Nov. 17, 1847.

80. Dublán and Lozano, *Legislación*, 5: 305. Anaya's victory margin was slim in two rounds of voting: seven states voted for Cumplido in the first round (Chiapas, Mexico, San Luis Potosí, Sonora, Jalisco, Zacatecas, and the Federal District), seven supported Anaya (Chihuahua, Coahuila, Durango, Guanajuato, Puebla, Tabasco, and Veracruz), two voted for Gómez Pedraza (Michoacán and Querétaro), and one cast its ballot for Domingo Ibarra (Oaxaca). The second round pitted Anaya against Cumplido, and the former prevailed, ten votes against seven. Chiapas, Chihuahua, Coahuila, Durango, Guanajuato, Oaxaca, Michoacán, Puebla, Tabasco, and Veracruz cast their ballots for Anaya, while Mexico, Querétaro, San Luis Potosí, Sonora, Jalisco, Zacatecas, and the Federal District favored Cumplido. *El Razonador*, Nov. 17, 1847.

81. Zamacois, *Historia de México*, 13: 66.

82. *El Correo Nacional*, Dec. 23 and 24, 1847.

83. Echanove Trujillo, *La vida pasional*, 436; Roa Bárcena, *Recuerdos de la invasión*, 3: 240.

84. *El Correo Nacional*, Oct. 21, 1847; Pletcher, *The Diplomacy*, 537;

Rives, *The United States,* 2: 592-593; Roa Bárcena, *Recuerdos de la invasión,* 3: 244-245.

85. Ramón Adame to the minister of foreign relations, Querétaro, Nov. 24, 1847, in *El Razonador,* Dec. 18, 1847.

86. P. de la Barrera to Gómez Farías, San Luis Potosí, Dec. 8, 1847, VGFP 2874, f. 54.

87. Godoy to Riva Palacio, Guanajuato, Jan. 24, 1848, MRPP 2523; Percy Doyle to Palmerston, Mexico City, Feb. 13, 1848, PRO/FO, 50/M, vol. 219, 167.

88. González Cosío to Gómez Farías, Zacatecas, Dec. 21, 1847, VGFP 2883, f. 54; Gómez Farías to Casimiro Gómez Farías, Querétaro, Jan. 4, 9, and 11, 1848, VGFP 2887, 2888, and 2889, f. 55. For further evidence of Zacatecas' participation in this plot, see J. M. Godoy to Riva Palacio, Guanuajuato, Jan. 17, 1848, MRPP 2517. Available documentation does not specify the whereabouts of Cuautitlán. Two communities bear the name, one in the state of Mexico and another in Jalisco. Although the Cuautitlán in Jalisco is closer to the state of Zacatecas, Gómez Farías' warning to his son suggests that the weapons were located in Cuatitlán, Mexico.

89. "Discurso que pronunció el Exmo. Sr. gobernador el día 1° del presente, en la solemne apertura de las sesiones ordinarias de la honorable legislatura del Estado," in *El Monitor Republicano,* Jan. 19, 1848.

90. P. G. to Riva Palacio, Querétaro, Jan. 2, 1848, MRPP 2224; *El Monitor Republicano,* Jan. 4, 1848.

91. The law stipulated that if Congress could not muster a quorum, the 1824 constitution would determine who would sit as president. The proviso allowed Peña y Peña, who had remained as president of the Supreme Court of Justice, to again take over as chief executive. Dublán and Lozano, *Legislación,* 5: 305.

92. "Pronunciamiento de los Estados del interior, desconociendo al gobierno de Querétaro," San Luis Potosí, Jan. 12, 1848, in *El Monitor Republicano,* Jan. 18, 1848; Mariano Avila to Anastasio Bustamante, San Luis Potosí, Jan. 16, 1848, in *El Razonador,* Jan. 29, 1848.

93. Doyle to Palmerston, Mexico City, Jan. 19, 1848, PRO/FO, 50/M, vol. 219, 96-97.

94. [General] Bustamante to Avila, Guanajuato, Jan. 18, 1848, in *El Razonador,* Jan. 29, 1848; Jesús Camarena to Gómez Farías, Guadalajara, Jan. 29, 1848, VGFP 2899, f. 55; Melchor Ocampo to the minister of foreign relations, Morelia, Jan. 19, 1848, in *El Monitor Republicano,* Jan. 26, 1848; Lorenzo Arellano to the minister of foreign relations, Guanajuato, Jan. 24, 1848, and Francisco P. de la Mesa to the minister of foreign relations, Querétaro, Jan. 24, 1848, in *El Monitor Republicano,* Feb. 4, 1848; Roa Bárcena, *Recuerdos de la invasión,* 3: 301, n. 10.

95. P. G. to Riva Palacio, Querétaro, Jan. 2, 1848, MRPP 2224; Godoy to Riva Palacio, Guanajuato, Jan. 17, 1848, MRPP 2517.

96. Griswold del Castillo, *The Treaty*, 49. Ocampo's ideas are analyzed by Colcleugh, "Damning the Barbarians."

97. Arellano to the minister of foreign relations, Guanajuato, Jan. 24, 1848, in *El Monitor Republicano*, Feb. 4, 1848; Ocampo to the minister of foreign relations, Morelia, Jan. 19, 1848, in *El Monitor Republicano*, Jan. 26, 1848.

98. Gómez Farías to Pomposo Verdugo, Querétaro, Apr. 10, 1848, VGFP 2954, f. 55; Gómez Farías to Casimiro, Benito, and Fermín Gómez Farías, Querétaro, Apr. 14, 1848, VGFP 2954, f. 55; Circular letter of the Ministry of Foreign Relations, Mexico City, Feb. 6, 1848, in *Algunos documentos*, 366-367; Echanove Trujillo, *La vida pasional*, 439; Griswold del Castillo, *The Treaty*, 43-46; Roa Bárcena, *Recuerdos de la invasión*, 3: 324, 327.

99. Prieto, *Memorias*, 293.

100. Gómez Farías to González Cosío, Querétaro, Feb. 18, 1848, VGFP 2903, f. 55; Isidoro Olvera to Gómez Farías, Toluca, Feb. 19, 1848, VGFP 2904, f. 55; González Cosío to Gómez Farías, Zacatecas, Feb. 22, 1848, VGFP 2906, f. 55; Casimiro Gómez Farías to Fermín Gómez Farías, Zacatecas, Mar. 2, 1848, VGFP 2913, f. 55; Rives, *The United States*, 2: 647.

101. Gómez Farías to Casimiro, Benito, and Fermín Gómez Farías, Querétaro, Mar. 13, 1848, VGFP 2923, f. 55. The British wanted Mexico to sign the peace treaty with the United States because the anticipated monetary indemnity would facilitate the payment of debts to British bondholders outstanding since 1827. Barbara Tenenbaum, "Neither a Borrower nor a Lender Be: Financial Constraints and the Treaty of Guadalupe Hidalgo," in *The Mexican and Mexican American Experience in the Nineteenth Century*, ed. Jaime E. Rodríguez O. (Tempe, Arizona: Bilingual Press, 1989), 80.

102. Gómez Farías to Casimiro, Benito, and Fermín Gómez Farías, Querétaro, Mar. 17 and Apr. 17, 1848, VGFP 2929, 2961, f. 55.

103. *El Correo Nacional*, May 19, 1848; Echanove Trujillo, *La vida pasional*, 439; Robinson, *The View*, 92.

104. *Observaciones del diputado saliente Manuel Crescencio Rejón, contra los tratados de paz, firmados en la ciudad de Guadalupe el 2 del próximo pasado febrero, precedidas de la parte histórica relativa a la cuestión originaria* (Querétaro: Imprenta de J. M. Lara, 1848), 1-62.

105. *Ibid.*, 62.

106. "El Sr. Peña y Peña, al abrir las sesiones del Congreso, en Querétaro, en 7 de mayo de 1848," in *Informes y manifiestos*, 1: 343-351; "Memoria del general Anaya, ministro de la Guerra, acerca de la situación del ejército," Querétaro, May 8, 1848, in *Algunos documentos*, 57; Alcaraz, *The Other Side*, 447; Rives, *The United States*, 2: 652-653; Roa Bárcena, *Recuerdos de la invasión*, 3: 327-328.

107. Godoy to Riva Palacio, Querétaro, May 11, 1848, MRPP 2641; Alcaraz, *The Other Side*, 448; Griswold del Castillo, *The Treaty*, 52-53; Prieto, *Memorias*, 294-295.

108. Griswold del Castillo, *The Treaty*, 52-53.

109. "Exposición dirigida por varios señores Diputados a la Corte Suprema de Justicia, intentando el recurso establecido por el Artículo 23 de la Acta de Reformas, para que se someta el Tratado de Paz al examen de las legislaturas de los Estados," Querétaro, June 1, 1848, and "Breve impugnación a las observaciones acerca del parecer fiscal y acuerdo de la Suprema Corte, sobre el ocurso que le dirigieron once señores diputados reclamando la inconstitucionalidad de los Tratados de Paz celebrados con el Gobierno Anglo-Americano," Mexico City, July 10, 1848, in *Algunos documentos*, 248-262, 268-272; Gómez Farías to Casimiro, Benito, and Fermín Gómez Farías, Querétaro, May 29, 1848, VGFP 2991, f. 55; Roa Bárcena, *Recuerdos de la invasión*, 3: 333-334.

110. J. M. Andrade, Rodríguez Puebla, Miguel Atristain, José Joaquín Castañares, and Gregorio (no last name) to Riva Palacio, Mexico City, May 18, 21, 23, and 28, 1848, MRPP 2647, 2648, 2651, 2653, 2656, 2664; *El Siglo XIX*, July 24, 1848; Miller, *Shamrock and Sword*, 137-138.

111. Gómez Farías to Casimiro, Benito, and Fermín Gómez Farías, Querétaro, June 13, 1848, VGFP 3001, f. 55.

VIII—"There Has Not Been…A National Spirit"

1. Brack, *Mexico Views*, 169.

2. Pletcher, *The Diplomacy*, 604.

3. The quotes can be found in Brack, *Mexico Views*, 138 and 136.

4. [Mariano Otero], *Consideraciones sobre la situación política y social de la república mexicana en el año de 1847* (Mexico City: Valdés y Redondas, 1848), 1-56. The quoted phrase appears in *ibid.*, 42.

5. Charles A. Hale, "The War with the United States and the Crisis in Mexican Thought," *The Americas*, 14:2 (Oct. 1957), 173-175; Bazant, "From Independence," 24-26, 29-31.

6. Sinkin, *The Mexican Reform*, 101-102; Bazant, "From Independence," 35; Olliff, *Reforma Mexico*, 5.

7. Ramírez, *Mexico During the War*, 95, 105, 108.

Bibliography

Manuscript Collections

The University of Texas at Austin, Benson Latin American Collection.
Justin Smith Papers.
Mariano Paredes y Arrillaga Papers.
Mariano Riva Palacio Papers.
Valentín Gómez Farías Papers.
Mejía, Francisco, "Epocas, hechos y acontecimientos de mi vida, y de los
que fuí actor y testigo, 1822-1878."

The University of California at Berkeley, Bancroft Library.
Bustamante, Carlos María, "Memorándum, o sea, apuntes para escribir la
historia de lo especialmente ocurrido en México." (Microfilm at El
Colegio de México, Mexico City).

Archivo Histórico Nacional, Madrid.
Mariano Otero Correspondence (Microfilm at the Benson Latin American
Collection, University of Texas at Austin).

Library of Congress, Washington, D.C.
Antonio López de Santa Anna Papers.
Nicholas P. Trist Papers.

Archival Material

Archivo del Ayuntamiento de la ciudad de México.
Actas de Cabildo.
Milicia Cívica.

Archivo General de la Nación, Mexico City.
Ramo Secretaría de Gobernación.

Biblioteca Nacional de México.
Colección Lafragua.

British Foreign Office:
Series 50, Mexico (Microfilm at the Benson Latin American Collection,
    University of Texas at Austin).

Printed Materials: Primary Sources

Alcaraz, Ramón, et. al. *The Other Side: or Notes for the History of the War
    Between Mexico and the United States.* Translated by Albert C. Ramsey.
    1850. Reprint. New York: Burt Franklin, 1970.
Bocanegra, José María. *Memorias para la historia de México independiente,
    1822-1846.* 2 vols. Mexico City: Imprenta del Gobierno Federal, 1892.
Bustamante, Carlos María. *Campaña sin gloria y guerra de como la de los
    cacomixtles.* Mexico City: Imprenta de I. Cumplido, 1847.
_____. *El nuevo Bernal Díaz del Castillo, o sea, historia de la
    invasión de los anglo-americanos en México.* Mexico City: Secretaría de
    Educación Pública, 1949.
*Colección de los documentos más importantes relativos a la instalación y
    reconocimiento del gobierno provisional del Exmo. Sr. presidente de la
    Suprema Corte de Justicia, don Manuel de la Peña y Peña.* Mexico City:
    Imprenta de Ignacio Cumplido, 1847.
*Comunicación circular que el Exmo. Sr. D. Manuel de la Peña y Peña
    extendió en el año de 1845 como ministro de Relaciones, para dirigirla a
    los gobiernos y asambleas departamentales, sobre la cuestión de paz o
    guerra, según el estado que guardaban en aquella época.* Querétaro:
    Imprenta de J. M. Lara, 1848.
Correspondencia inédita de Manuel Crescencio Rejón. Mexico City:
    Secretaría de Relaciones Exteriores, 1948.
Cuevas, Luis. *Porvenir de México.* Mexico City: Editorial Jus, 1954.

Bibliography

Davis, Thomas B., and Amado Ricon Virulegio, eds. *The Political Plans of Mexico*. Lanham: University Press of America, 1987

de la Peña, Antonio, ed. *Algunos documentos sobre el tratado de Guadalupe y la situación de México durante la invasión norteamericana*. Mexico City: Secretaría de Relaciones Exteriores (Archivo Histórico Diplomático num. 31), 1930.

——————————. *Lord Aberdeen, Texas y California*. Mexico City: Secretaría de Relaciones Exteriores, 1930.

Defensa pronunciada ante el Gran Jurado el día 21 de marzo de 1850 por Francisco Suárez Iriarte, acusado en 8 de agosto de 1848 por el secretario de Relaciones en aquella fecha, de los crímenes de sedición contra el gobierno de Querétaro e infidencia contra la patria, en sus actos como presidente de la asamblea municipal de la ciudad y distrito de México. Mexico City: Tipografía de R. Rafael, 1850.

Defensa que el Sr. General Don Tomás Requena hizo en favor del Sr. General Don Joaquín Rangel, en la causa que se le ha instruido por la revolución del día 7 de Junio de 1845. Mexico City: Imprenta de J. M. Lara, 1845.

Dublán, Manuel and José María Lozano, eds. *Legislación mexicana, o colección completa de las disposiciones legislativas expedidas desde la independencia de la república*, 42 vols. Mexico City: Imprenta del Comercio, 1876-1904.

Exposición o programa de los diputados pertenecientes al partido puro o progresista sobre la presente guerra con motivo de una proposición del sr. Otero, e imputaciones de ciertos periódicos que se publican en la capital bajo la influencia del conquistador, y que se dejan correr libremente por el actual gobierno de la Unión. Querétaro: Imprenta de Francisco Frías, 1847.

Humboldt, Alexander Freiherr von. *Ensayo político sobre el reino de la Nueva España*. Mexico City: Editorial Porrúa, 1966.

Informes y manifiestos de los poderes ejecutivo y legislativo de 1821 a 1904. 3 vols. Mexico City: Imprenta del Gobierno Federal, 1905.

La situación política, militar y económica en la república mexicana al iniciarse su guerra con los Estados Unidos, según el archivo del general Paredes. Edited by Genaro García. In *Documentos inéditos o muy raros para la historia de México*, 2d ed. Vol. 56. Mexico City: Editorial Porrúa, 521-639, 1974.

Lafragua, José María. "Miscelánea de política." In *Memorias de la Academia Mexicana de la Historia*: (1943-1944), 1-125.

Malo, José Ramón. *Diario de sucesos notables de José Ramón Malo (1832-1853)*. Edited by Mariano Cuevas. 2 vols. Mexico City: Editorial Patria, 1948.

Manning, William R., ed. *Diplomatic Correspondence of the United States: Inter-American Affairs, 1831-1860.* 12 vols. Washington: Carnegie Endowment for International Peace, 1932-1939.

Mateos, Juan A., ed. *Historia parlamentaria de los congresos mexicanos de 1821 a 1857.* 25 vols. Mexico City: Imprenta Madero, 1895.

Mayer, Brantz. *Mexico as It Was and as It Is.* 3rd revised ed. Philadelphia: G.B. Zideon & Co., 1847.

Memoranda and Official Correspondence Relating to the Republic of Texas, its History and Annexation. Chicago: The Rio Grande Press, 1966.

Memoria de la primera secretaría de estado y del despacho de Relaciones Interiores y Exteriores de los Estados Unidos Mexicanos, leida al soberano Congreso constituyente en los días 14, 15 y 16 de diciembre de 1846, por el ministro del ramo, José María Lafragua. Mexico City: Imprenta de Vicente García Torres, 1847.

Memoria del ministro de Relaciones Exteriores y Gobernación leída en el Senado el 11 y en la Cámara de Diputados el 12 de marzo de 1845. Mexico City: Imprenta de Ignacio Cumplido, 1845.

Memorias del coronel Manuel María Giménez. Edited by Genaro García. In *Documentos inéditos o muy raros para la historia de México.* 2d ed. Vol. 59. Mexico City: Editorial Porrúa, 283-408, 1974.

Memorias del diputado por el estado de Chihuhua, Lic. J. A. de Escudero, con documentos justificativos que pueden servir para la historia del Congreso constituyente mexicano del año de 1847. Mexico City: Tipografía de R. Rafael, 1848.

México ante los ojos del ejército invasor de 1847 (Diario del coronel Ethan Allen Hitchcock). Translated by George Baker. 1st Spanish ed. Mexico City: Universidad Nacional Autónoma de México, 1978.

Mora, José María Luis. *Obras sueltas.* 2d ed. Mexico City: Editorial Porrúa, 1963.

Observaciones del diputado saliente Manuel Crescencio Rejón, contra los tratados de paz, firmados en la ciudad de Guadalupe el 2 del próximo pasado febrero, precedidas de la parte histórica relativa a la cuestión originaria. Querétaro: Imprenta de J. M. Lara, 1848.

[Otero, Mariano]. *Consideraciones sobre la situación política y social de la república mexicana en el año de 1847.* Mexico City: Valdés y Redondas, 1848.

_____. *Obras.* 2 vols. Mexico City: Editorial Porrúa, 1967.

Papeles inéditos y obras sueltas del doctor Mora. Edited by Genaro García. In *Documentos inéditos o muy raros para la historia de México.* Vol. 6. Mexico City: Librería de la Vda. de Ch. Bouret, 1906.

Prieto, Guillermo. *Memorias de mis tiempos.* Mexico City: Editorial Porrúa, 1985.

Bibliography

Ramírez, José Fernando. *Mexico During the War With the United States.* Edited by Walter B. Scholes, translated by Elliot B. Scherr. Columbia: University of Missouri Press, 1950.

Relaciones diplomáticas hispano-mexicanas. Serie I. Despachos generales. 4 vols. Mexico City: El Colegio de México, 1949-1968.

Ruxton, George. *Adventures in Mexico.* New York: Outing Publishing, 1915.

Santa Anna, Antonio López de. *The Eagle: The Autobiography of Santa Anna.* Edited by Ann Fears Crawford. Austin: The Pemberton Press, 1967.

Scott, Winfield. *Memoirs of Lieutenant-General Scott.* 2 vols. New York: Sheldon & Co., 1864.

Sierra, Justo. *The Political Evolution of the Mexican People.* Translated by Charles Ramsdell. Austin: University of Texas Press, 1969.

Tena Ramírez, Felipe. *Leyes fundamentales de México, 1808-1982.* 11th ed. Mexico City: Editorial Porrúa, 1982.

Zavala, Lorenzo de. *Ensayo histórico de las revoluciones de México desde 1808 hasta 1830.* Mexico City: Editorial Porrúa, 1969.

Newspapers

El Aguila Mexicana, 1824.
Boletín de la Democracia, 1847.
Diario de la Guerra, 1847.
Diario del Gobierno de la República Mexicana, 1845, 1847.
Diario Oficial del Gobierno Mexicano, 1846.
Don Simplicio, 1846-1847.
El Aguila Mexicana, 1824.
El Amigo del Pueblo, 1845.
El Católico, 1847.
El Contratiempo, 1846.
El Correo Nacional, 1847-1848.
El Federalista, 1847.
El Estandarte Nacional, 1845.
El Monitor Constitucional, 1845.
El Monitor Constitucional Independiente, 1845.
El Monitor Republicano, 1846-1848.
El Razonador, 1847-1848.
El Republicano, 1846-1847.
El Siglo XIX, 1845.
El Sol, 1823.
El Tiempo, 1846.
La Reforma, 1846.

La Voz del Pueblo, 1845.
Memorial Histórico, 1846.
Niles' Weekly Register, 1833.

Dissertations

Baker, George Towne. "Mexico City and the War with the United States: A Study in the Politics of Military Occupation." Duke University, 1970.

Sanders, Frank. "Proposals for Monarchy in Mexico, 1823-1860." University of Arizona, 1967.

Urbina, Manuel. "The Impact of the Texas Revolution on the Government, Politics, and Society of Mexico, 1836-1846." University of Texas at Austin, 1976.

Warren, Richard Andrew. "Vagrants and Citizens: Politics and the Poor in Mexico City, 1808-1836." University of Chicago, 1994.

Books

Anna, Timothy E. *The Mexican Empire of Iturbide*. Lincoln: University of Nebraska Press, 1990.

Archer, Christon I. *The Army in Bourbon Mexico, 1760-1810*. Albuquerque: University of New Mexico Press, 1977.

Bancroft, Hubert Howe. *History of Mexico*. 6 vols. San Francisco: A.L. Bancroft & Co, 1883-1888.

Bauer, K. Jack. *The Mexican War, 1846-1848*. 1974. Reprint. Lincoln: University of Nebraska Press, 1992.

Bazant, Jan. *Alienation of Church Wealth in Mexico: Social and Economic Aspects of the Liberal Reform, 1856-1875*. London: Cambridge University Press, 1971.

————. *A Concise History of Mexico. From Hidalgo to Cárdenas, 1805-1940*. New York: Cambridge University Press, 1977.

————. *Antonio Haro y Tamariz y sus aventuras políticas, 1811-1869*. Mexico City: El Colegio de México, 1985.

Benson, Nettie Lee. *The Provincial Deputation in Mexico: Harbinger of Provincial Autonomy, Independence, and Federalism*. Austin: University of Texas Press, 1992.

Blázquez, Carmen. *Miguel Lerdo de Tejada: Un liberal veracruzano en la política nacional*. Mexico City: El Colegio de México, 1978.

Brack, Gene M. *Mexico Views Manifest Destiny, 1821-1846: An Essay on the Origins of the Mexican War*. Albuquerque: University of New Mexico Press, 1975.

Brading, David. *The Origins of Mexican Nationalism*. Cambridge, U.K.:

Centre of Latin American Studies, 1985.

——————. *The First America: The Spanish Monarchy, Creole Patriots, and the Liberal State 1492-1867.* New York: Cambridge University Press, 1991.

Bushnell, David, and Macaulay, Neill. *The Emergence of Latin America in the Nineteenth Century.* New York: Oxford University Press, 1988.

Callcott, Wilfrid Hardy. *Santa Anna: The Story of an Enigma Who Once Was Mexico.* Norman: University of Oklahoma Press, 1936.

——————. *Church and State in Mexico, 1822-1857.* 1926. 2d reprint ed. New York: Octagon Books, 1971

Caruso, A. Brooke. *The Mexican Spy Company: United States Covert Operations in Mexico, 1845-1848.* Jefferson: McFarland & Company, 1991.

Costeloe, Michael P. *La primera república federal de México (1824-1835).* Translated by Manuel Fernández Gasallo. Mexico City: Fondo de Cultura Económica, 1975.

——————. *The Central Republic in Mexico, 1835-1846: Hombres de Bien in the Age of Santa Anna.* New York: Cambridge University Press, 1993.

Cotner, Thomas Ewing. *The Military and Political Career of José Joaquín Herrera, 1792-1854.* Austin: University of Texas Press, 1949.

Cuevas, Mariano. *Historia de la nación mexicana.* 3rd ed. Mexico City, Editorial Porrúa, 1967.

Delgado, Jaime. *La monarquía en México (1845-1847).* Mexico City, Editorial Porrúa, 1990.

Díaz Díaz, Fernando. *Caudillos y caciques: Antonio López de Santa Anna y Juan Alvarez.* Mexico City: El Colegio de México, 1972.

Diccionario geográfico, histórico y biográfico de los Estados Unidos Mexicanos. 5 vols. Mexico City: Antigua Imprenta de Murguia, 1888.

Diccionario Porrúa de historia, biografía y geografía de México, 3rd revised ed. 2 vols. Mexico City: Editorial Porrúa, 1970-1971.

Echanove Trujillo, Carlos. *La vida pasional e inquieta de don Crescencio Rejón*: Mexico City, El Colegio de México, 1941.

Graham, Richard. *Independence in Latin America: A Comparative Approach.* 2d ed. New York: McGraw Hill, 1994.

Green, Stanley C. *The Mexican Republic: The First Decade, 1823-1832.* Pittsburgh: University of Pittsburgh Press, 1987.

Flores Caballero, Romeo. *La contrarevolución en la independencia: Los españoles en la vida política, social y económica de México (1804-1838).* Mexico City: El Colegio de México, 1969.

Fuentes Díaz, Vicente. *Valentín Gómez Farías, padre de la reforma.* 2d ed. Mexico City: Edición del Comité de Actos Conmemorativos del

Bicentenario del Natalicio del Dr. Valentín Gómez Farías, 1981.

Fuentes Mares, José. *Génesis del expansionismo norteamericano*. Mexico City: El Colegio de México, 1980.

——————. *Santa Anna, el hombre*, 4th ed. Mexico City: Editorial Grijalbo, 1982.

Gibson, Charles. *Spain in America*. New York: Harper & Row, 1966.

González Navarro, Moisés. *Anatomía del poder en México, 1848-1853*. 2d ed. Mexico City: El Colegio de México, 1983.

Griswold del Castillo, Richard. *The Treaty of Guadalupe Hidalgo: A Legacy of Conflict*. Norman: University of Oklahoma Press, 1990.

Hale, Charles A. *Mexican Liberalism in the Age of Mora, 1821-1853*. New Haven: Yale University Press, 1968.

Hamnett, Brian. *Juárez*. New York: Longman Publishing, 1994.

Haring, Clarence. *The Spanish Empire in America*. 1940. Reprint. Gloucester, Massachusetts: Peter Smith, 1973.

Helms, Mary W. *Middle America: A Cultural History of Heartland and Frontiers*. Englewood Cliffs, New Jersey: Prentice-Hall, 1977.

Hogan, William Ransom. *The Texas Republic. A Social and Economic History*. 2d paperback printing. Austin: University of Texas Press, 1975.

Hutchinson, Cecil Allan. *Valentín Gómez Farías: La vida de un republicano*. Translated by Marco Antonio Silva. Guadalajara: Unidad Editorial de la Secretaría General del Gobierno de Jalisco, 1983.

Ladd, Doris M. *The Mexican Nobility at Independence, 1780-1826*. Austin: University of Texas Press, 1976.

Langley, Lester D. *America and the Americas*. Athens: University of Georgia Press, 1991.

Lynch, John. *Spanish Colonial Administration, 1782-1810: The Intendant System in the Viceroyalty of the Río de la Plata*. London: Athlone Press, 1958.

——————. *The Spanish American Revolutions, 1808-1826*. 2d ed. New York: W. W. Norton, 1986.

——————. *Caudillos in Spanish America, 1800-1850*. New York: Oxford University Press, 1992.

McAlister, Lyle. *The "Fuero Militar" in New Spain, 1764-1800*. Gainesville: University of Florida Press, 1957.

McCaffrey, James M. *Army of Manifest Destiny: The American Soldier in the Mexican War, 1846-1848*. New York: New York University Press, 1992.

Miller, Robert Ryal. *Shamrock and Sword: The San Patricio Batallion During the Mexican War*. Norman: University of Oklahoma Press, 1989.

Meyer, Michael C. and Sherman, William E. *The Course of Mexican History*. 5th ed. New York: Oxford University Press, 1995.

O'Gorman, Edmundo. *Historia de las divisiones territoriales de México*. 3rd revised ed. Mexico City: Editorial Porrúa, 1966.

Ollif, Donathon. *Reforma Mexico and the United States: A Search for Alternatives to Annexation, 1854-1861.* University: University of Alabama Press, 1981.

Pletcher, David. *The Diplomacy of Annexation: Texas, Oregon, and the Mexican War.* Columbia: University of Missouri Press, 1973.

Quintana, José Miguel. *Lafragua, político y romántico.* Mexico City: Editorial Academia Literaria, 1958.

Raat, W. Dirk. *Mexico and the United States: Ambivalent Vistas.* Athens: University of Georgia Press, 1992.

Reyes Heroles, Jesús. *El liberalismo mexicano.* 3 vols. 1957. 2d reprint ed. Mexico City: Fondo de Cultura Económica, 1982.

Riva Palacio, Vicente, ed. *México a través de los siglos.* 5 vols. Mexico City: Editorial Cumbre, 1956.

Rives, George Lockhart. *The United States and Mexico, 1821-1848.* 2 vols. New York: Charles Scribner's & Sons, 1913.

Roa Bárcena, José María. *Recuerdos de la invasión norteamericana (1846-1848).* 3 vols. Mexico City: Editorial Porrúa, 1947.

Robertson, William Spence. *Iturbide of Mexico.* New York: Greenwood Press, 1968.

Robinson, Cecil, ed. *The View from Chapultepec: Mexican Writers on The Mexican-American War.* Tucson: University of Arizona Press, 1989.

Ruiz, Ramón Eduardo. *Triumphs and Tragedy: A History of the Mexican People.* New York: W.W. Norton, 1992.

Simpson, Lesley Bird. *Many Mexicos.* 3rd revised ed. Berkeley: University of California Press, 1960.

Sims, Harold D. *La expulsión de los españoles de México (1821-1828).* Translated by Roberto Gómez Ciriza. Mexico City: Fondo de Cultura de Económica, 1974.

Sinkin, Richard. *The Mexican Reform, 1855-1876: A Study in Liberal Nation Building.* Austin: University of Texas Press, 1979.

Smith, Justin. *The War with Mexico.* 2 vols. 1919. Reprint. Gloucester, Massachusetts: Peter Smith, 1977.

Sordo Cedeño, Reynaldo. *El congreso en la primera república centralista.* Mexico City: El Colegio de México and Instituto Tecnológico Autónomo de México, 1991.

Soto, Miguel. *La conspiración monárquica en México, 1845-1846.* Mexico City: EOSA, 1988.

Stevens, Donald F. *Origins of Instability in Early Republican Mexico.* Durham: Duke University Press, 1991.

Tenenbaum, Barbara. *The Politics of Penury: Debts and Taxes in Mexico, 1821-1856.* Albuquerque: University of New Mexico Press, 1986.

Valadés, José C. *Orígenes de la república mexicana. La aurora constitucional.* Mexico City: Editores Mexicanos Unidos, 1972.

Vázquez, Josefina Zoraida. *Don Antonio López de Santa Anna: Mito y enigma.* Mexico City: Centro de Estudios de Historia de México Condumex, 1987.

—————— and Lorenzo Meyer. *The United States and Mexico.* Chicago: University of Chicago Press, 1985.

Velasco Márquez, Jesús. *La guerra del 47 y la opinión pública (1845-1848).* Mexico City: Secretaría de Educación Pública, Sep Setentas 196, 1975.

Véliz, Claudio. *The Centralist Tradition of Latin America.* Princeton: Princeton University Press, 1980.

Zamacois, Niceto de. *Historia de México desde sus tiempos más remotos hasta nuestros días.* 22 vols. in 25. Barcelona: J. F. Parres y Cía., 1878-1902.

Articles and Papers

Anna, Timothy E. "The Rule of Agustín Iturbide: A Reappraisal." *Journal of Latin American Studies.* 17:1 (May 1985): 79-110.

——————. "Demystifying Early Nineteenth-Century Mexico." *Mexican Studies/Estudios Mexicanos.* 9:1 (Winter 1993): 119-137.

——————. "Inventing Mexico: Provincehood and Nationhood After Independence." *Bulletin of Latin American Research.* 15:1 (1996): 7-17.

Archer, Christon I. "Insurrection—Reaction—Revolution—Fragmentation: Reconstructing the Choreography of Meltdown in New Spain during the Independence Era." *Mexican Studies/Estudios Mexicanos.* 10:1 (Winter 1994): 63-98.

Arrom, Silvia M. "Popular Politics in Mexico City: The Parián Riot, 1828." *Hispanic American Historical Review.* 68:2 (May 1988): 245-268.

Bazant, Jan. "From Independence to the Liberal Republic, 1821-1867." In *Mexico Since Independence,* edited by Leslie Bethel, 1-48. New York: Cambridge University Press, 1991.

Baker, George Towne. "Una propuesta mexicana para la ayuda militar norteamericana, o sea, un recuerdo del liberalismo mexicano desconocido." In *Anuario de historia.* Mexico City: Universidad Nacional Autónoma de México, Year VII, 1976.

Benson, Nettie Lee. "The Plan of Casa Mata." *Hispanic American Historical Review.* 25:1 (Feb. 1945): 45-56.

——————. "Territorial Integrity in Mexican Politics, 1821-1833." In *The Independence of Mexico and the Creation of the New Nation,* edited by Jaime E. Rodríguez O., 275-307. Los Angeles: UCLA Latin American Center Publications, 1989.

Berge, Dennis E. "A Mexican Dilemma: The Mexico City Ayuntamiento and the Question of Loyalty, 1846-1848." *Hispanic American Historical Review*. 50:2 (May 1970): 229-256.

Castañeda, Carlos E. "Relations of General Scott with Santa Anna." *Hispanic American Historical Review*. 29:4 (Nov. 1949): 455-473.

Colcleugh, Bruce. "Damning the Barbarians: Mexican Intellectuals on the Mexican-American War, 1846-1853." Paper delivered at the annual meeting of the Rocky Mountain Council of Latin American Studies, Vancouver, April 1-4, 1993.

Costeloe, Michael P. "Church-State Financial Negotiations in Mexico During the American War, 1846-1847." *Revista de Historia de América*. 60 (July-Dec. 1965): 91-123.

_____. "The Mexican Church and the Rebellion of the Polkos." *Hispanic American Historical Review*. 46:2 (May 1966): 170-178.

_____. "A *Pronunciamiento* in Nineteenth Century Mexico: '15 de julio de 1840.'" *Mexican Studies/Estudios Mexicanos*. 4:2 (Summer 1988): 245-264.

_____. "Federalism to Centralism: The Conservative Case for Change, 1834-1835." *The Americas*. 45:2 (Oct. 1988): 173-185.

_____. "The Triangular Revolt in Mexico and the Fall of Anastasio Bustamante, August-October 1841." *Journal of Latin American Studies*. 20:2 (Nov. 1988): 337-360.

_____. "Los generales Santa Anna y Paredes y Arrillaga en México, 1841-1843: Rivales por el poder, o una copa más." *Historia Mexicana*. 39:2 (Oct.-Dec. 1989): 417-440.

_____. "Generals versus Politicians: Santa Anna and the 1842 Congressional Elections in Mexico." *Bulletin of Latin American Research*. 8:2 (1990): 257-274.

Fowler, Will. "Valentín Gómez Farías: Perceptions of Radicalism in Independent Mexico, 1821-1847." *Bulletin of Latin American Research*. 15:1 (1996): 39-62.

Guardino, Peter. "Barbarism or Republican Law? Guerrero's Peasants and National Politics, 1820-1846." *Hispanic American Historical Review*. 75:2 (May 1995): 187-213.

Haber, Stephen H. "Assessing the Obstacles to Industrialization: The Mexican Economy, 1830-1940." *Journal of Latin American Studies*. 24:1 (Feb. 1992): 1-32.

Hale, Charles A. "The War with the United States and the Crisis in Mexican Thought." *The Americas*. 14:2 (Oct. 1957): 153-175.

Hutchinson, Cecil Allan. "Valentín Gómez Farías and the 'Secret Pact of New Orleans,'" *Hispanic American Historical Review*. 36:4 (Nov. 1956): 471-489.

_____. "Valentín Gómez Farías and the Movement for the Return of General Santa Anna to Mexico in 1846." In *Essays in Mexican History*, edited by Carlos Castañeda and Thomas E. Cotner, 169-191. Austin: University of Texas Press, 1958.

Lamar, Curt. "A Diplomatic Disaster: The Mexican Mission of Anthony Butler, 1829-1834." *The Americas*. 45:1 (July 1988): 1-17.

Pletcher, David. "United States Relations with Latin America: Neighborliness and Exploitation." *The American Historical Review*. 82:1 (Feb. 1977): 39-59.

Rodríguez O., Jaime E. "The Struggle for the Nation: The First Centralist-Federalist Conflict in Mexico." *The Americas*. 49:1 (July 1992): 1-22.

Safford, Frank. "Politics, Ideology and Society in Post-Independence Spanish America." In *The Cambridge History of Latin America*, edited by Leslie Bethel, 3: 347-422. 9 vols. Cambridge, U.K.: Cambridge University Press, 1985.

Samponaro, Frank N. "La alianza de Santa Anna y los federalistas, 1832-1834. Su formación y desintegración." *Historia Mexicana*. 30:3 (Jan.-Mar. 1981): 358-390.

_____. "Mariano Paredes y el movimiento monarquista mexicano en 1846." *Historia Mexicana*. 32:1 (July-Sept. 1982): 39-54.

_____. "Santa Anna and the Abortive Federalist Revolt of 1833 in Mexico." *The Americas*. 40:1 (July 1983): 95-108.

Santoni, Pedro. "A Fear of the People: The Civic Militia of Mexico in 1845." *Hispanic American Historical Review*. 68:2 (May 1988): 269-288.

_____. "The Failure of Mobilization: The Civic Militia of Mexico in 1846." *Mexican Studies/Estudios Mexicanos*. 12: 2 (Summer 1996): 169-194.

Sordo Cedeño, Reynaldo. "El general Tornel y la guerra de Texas." *Historia Mexicana*. 42:4 (Apr.-Jun. 1993): 919-953.

_____. "El Soberano Congreso Constituyente y la Guerra con los Estados Unidos de América, 1846-1847." Paper delivered at the Academic Symposium "Reflections on the War Between the United States and Mexico," Matamoros, Mexico, May 9, 1996.

Tenenbaum, Barbara. "Neither a Borrower nor a Lender be: Financial Constraints and the Treaty of Guadalupe Hidalgo." In *The Mexican and Mexican American Experience in the 19th Century*, edited by Jaime E. Rodríguez O., 68-84. Tempe, Arizona: Bilingual Press, 1989.

_____. "The Emperor Goes to the Tailor." In *Mexico in the Age of Democratic Revolutions, 1750-1850*, edited by Jaime E. Rodríguez O., 281-301. Boulder: Lynne Rienner Publishers, 1994.

Vázquez, Josefina Zoraida. "El ejército: Un dilema del gobierno mexicano (1841-1846)." In *Problemas de la formación del estado y de la nación en*

Hispanoamérica, edited by Inge Buisson, Günter Kahle, Hans-Joachim Konig, and Horst Pietschmann, 319-338. Bonn: Bolhau Verlag, 1984.

——————. "The Texas Question in Mexican Politics, 1836-1845." *Southwestern Historical Quarterly.* 89:3 (Jan. 1986): 309-343.

——————. "La Supuesta República del Río Grande." *Historia Mexicana.* 36:1 (Jul.-Sept. 1986): 49-80.

——————. "Santa Anna y el reconocimiento de Texas." *Historia Mexicana.* 36:3 (Jan.-Mar. 1987): 553-562.

——————. "La crisis y los partidos políticos, 1833-1846." In *America Latina: Dallo stato coloniale allo stato nazione*, edited by Antonio Annino, 2: 557-572. 2 vols. Milan: Franco Angeli, 1987.

——————. "Los años olvidados." *Mexican Studies/Estudios Mexicanos.* 5:2 (Summer 1989): 313-326.

——————. "Political Plans and Collaboration Between Civilians and the Military, 1821-1846." *Bulletin of Latin American Research.* 15:1 (1996): 19-38.

Index

96-97; in "rebellion of the *polkos*," 163, 183-188, 191-192, 194-195; reduction of, 17-19, 26; reestablishment of (1845), 63-68; (1846), 140; public support for, 57-62
Coahuila. See Texas
coalition of states, 180, 202
Colonization, Law of, 25-26
Congress (Mexican): adopts belligerent measures (1847), 201-202; assembles in Querétaro (1847), 220; and centralism (1834-1835), 19-20; closure of (1841-1842), 21; and December 6, 1844, rebellion, 22-23; and federalism (1822-1823), 13-14; in Herrera's government, 34-35, 37, 48-49, 56, 59, 62-63, 66, 86; and nationalization of Church property (1846-1847), 169-174; in Paredes y Arrillaga's government, 102-105, 108-109; prerogatives during Salas' regime, 128, 134-135, 271 n. 12; and reforms (1833), 18-19; relations with Santa Anna (1847), 208-213; and Treaty of Guadalupe Hidalgo (1847-1848), 227-229; and trial of Santa Anna (1845), 74, 78; and U.S. peace proposals (1847), 203-213
conservatives: policies of, 3-4; see also Alamán, Lucas; Bustamante, Carlos María; *hombres de bien*; monarchists; Paredes y Arrillaga, Mariano
Constitution of 1812, 11-12
Constitution of 1824: provisions of, 14-15, 24, 26, 210; reestablishment of (1846), 134, 136, 271 n. 12; see also *Acta de Reformas*; federalism; press; *puros*
Constitution of 1836. See *Siete Leyes*

Constitution of 1843. See *Bases Orgánicas*
Constitution of 1857, 234
Contreras, Battle of, 211
Córdoba, Treaties of, 12
Cortez, Anselmo, 269 n. 101
Cortina, José Gómez de la, 149-155, 182
Council of State (Mexican): and civic militia (1845), 63-64, 97; to counter *puros* (1846), 143-146, 155; and Slidell mission, 40, 107
Covarrubias, José Guadalupe, 182, 194, 283-284 n. 73
Covarrubias, José María, 185, 194
Cuevas, José María, 228-229
Cuevas, Luis G., 37, 44-46, 63, 84, 88, 230, 250 n. 87
Cumplido, Ignacio, 110-111
Cumplido, Juan N., 219-220, 293 n. 80

de la Loza, Leopoldo Río, 61
de la Peña, Rafael, 57, 60-61
de la Rosa, Luis: 276 n. 93; appointed minister of justice, 136; and Council of State, 144-146; as minister of foreign relations (1847-1848), 214, 221, 225, 228; as president of Congress, 209; and transfer of Congress to Querétaro, 212; works for Santa Anna's return, 118
de la Vega, Joaquín González, 274 n. 60
de la Vega, Miguel Lazo, 201
December 6, 1844, rebellion of, 22-23, 33-34, 127; see also Herrera, José Joaquín; *moderados*
del Río, José María, 48, 60, 118, 209, 221, 248-249 n. 59, 252 n. 119, 285 n. 91, 290 n. 41
del Valle, Rómulo, 184
descamisados. See *léperos*
Desierto de los Leones, banquet at,

tions, 288, n. 19; personality of, 34; policy of, on army, 51-53, 74; policy of, on civic militia, 57-67, 96-97; policy of, on constitutional reform, 34-36; policy of, on Texas, 36-40; ponders resignation, 88; and revolt by Paredes y Arrillaga, 95-99; seeks reconciliation with Gómez Farías, V., 253, n. 4; tries to avert coup, 77-78; see also *moderados*

Hitchcock, Ethan Allen, 215-216, 218

hombres de bien, 6, 21, 42, 92, 101, 116, 126, 150, 178, 265 n. 54

Horta, Antonio, 176

Ibarra, Cayetano, 176
Ibarra, Domingo, 156-157, 188, 209-210, 293 n. 80
Inclán, Ignacio, 66
Independence, Mexican War of, 11-12, 15
intendancy system, 10
Irrizari, Bishop Juan Manuel, 173-174, 182, 190
Ituarte, Manuel María, 269 n. 101
Iturbide, Agustín de, 12-14

Jalisco, 22
Jarero, José María, 89-90
Jáuregui, Ignacio 84, 86
Jáuregui, José María, 70, 86, 177
Juárez, Benito, 183
Juárez Law, 234
July 15, 1840, revolt of, 20-21, 69
Junco, Bernardino, 269 n. 101
June 7, 1845, rebellion of, 54, 63, 74-87, 90
Junta Mercantil de Fomento, 97, 151-153

Lafragua, José María: 89, 122, 132, 136-138, 169, 210, 215, 247 n. 42; and *Acta de Reformas*, 210; advo-

cates return to federalism, 48-49; calls for unity, 147-148; and Constituent Congress (1846), analysis of, 159; and Council of State, 144-145; and decree of April 9, 1847, 201; elected to Congress, 260, n. 18; favors civic militia, 56-57, 60-62; and Manuel Othón's coup, 156-157; as minister of foreign relations, 155, 203; and ouster of Gómez Farías, V., 195-196; in "rebellion of the *polkos*," 182, 190, 194; reconquest of Texas, views on, 30-31, 48; rejoins *moderados*, 117-118; relations with Paredes y Arrillaga, 110-111, 118; role in June 7, 1845, rebellion, 76, 79-80, 84-85; and Santa Anna, 209; on transfer of Congress to Querétaro, 213

Lagos coalition, 219-220
Law of Colonization, 25-26
Lemus, Pedro, 84, 151, 154-156
léperos: 2-3; as a dangerous class, 16, 21, 57, 71, 88, 96-97, 130, 140, 163, 167, 191-192, 229-230
Lerdo Law, 169, 234
Lombardini, Manuel María, 75
Lombardo, Francisco, 46, 144, 215, 260-261 n. 111, 269 n. 101, 273-274 n. 58
López de Nava, Andrés, 176

MacKenzie, Alexander Slidell, 267-268 n. 82
Martínez, Ignacio, 87
Masons. See *escoceses*; *yorkinos*
Mazatlán: revolt against Gómez Farías, V., 180 revolt against Paredes y Arrillaga, 126
Mejía, Francisco, 81-82
Mejía, José Antonio, 27
Mier y Terán, Manuel, 24
Miñón, José Vicente, 74, 76-77, 79,